British Literature and the Life of Institutions

British Literature and the Life of Institutions

Speculative States

BENJAMIN KOHLMANN

OXFORD

UNIVERSITY PRESS

OXFORD
UNIVERSITY PRESS

Great Clarendon Street, Oxford, OX2 6DP,
United Kingdom

Oxford University Press is a department of the University of Oxford.
It furthers the University's objective of excellence in research, scholarship,
and education by publishing worldwide. Oxford is a registered trade mark of
Oxford University Press in the UK and in certain other countries

First Edition published in 2021

Impression: 1

Published in the United States of America by Oxford University Press
198 Madison Avenue, New York, NY 10016, United States of America

British Library Cataloguing in Publication Data

Data available

Library of Congress Control Number: 2021937354

ISBN 978-0-19-883617-9

DOI: 10.1093/oso/9780198836179.001.0001

Printed and bound in the UK by
TJ Books Limited

Acknowledgements

Much as I'm fond of the university as an institution, it takes people to transform this institution into a community. I was exceptionally fortunate to start work on this book as an Alexander von Humboldt Fellow at Columbia University's Department of English and Comparative Literature, thanks to the kind hospitality of Bruce Robbins. The Universities of Freiburg, Hamburg, and Regensburg offered inspiring academic homes, and I am grateful to my colleagues at these institutions for their intellectual companionship and encouragement as my initial ideas morphed into a monograph. Visiting fellowships at several other institutions—the University of East Anglia; Jesus College, Cambridge; and the University of California, Davis—helped to galvanize this project. I thank my sponsors—Monika Fludernik, Rod Mengham, Liz Miller, Matt Taunton—for their generous support.

I can't sufficiently express my gratitude to the many friends and colleagues who, over the years and in different places, gave so freely of their time and offered to share their ideas with me: Daniel Brückenhaus, Monika Class, Andrew Cole, Gero Guttzeit, Janice Ho, Nick Hubble, Marina MacKay, Doug Mao, Laura Marcus, Leo Mellor, Rod Mengham, Liz Miller, Alastair Morrison, Piers Pennington, Natalie Roxburgh, Glyn Salton-Cox, Peter Stansky, Matthew Stratton, and Matt Taunton. I thank them for making academic life synonymous with 'a real feeling of community' at a time when the marketisation of higher education at all levels erodes the very idea that universities *are* academic communities.

Several of the chapters in this book first took shape as guest lectures. For their critical insights and intellectual generosity, I am tremendously grateful to audiences and hosts at the University of Cambridge, CU Boulder, Durham University, the Max Planck Institute for Human Development (Berlin), Oxford University, UC Davis, the University of East Anglia, the University of Notre Dame, the University of Southern Denmark, Stanford University's Center for the Study of the Novel, and the University of Sussex.

Critique's proverbial 'ruthlessness' notwithstanding, many friends and colleagues offered advice and insight in ways that never felt other than helpful. For conversations and comments, I am immensely grateful to Richard Adelman, Timothy Alborn, Amanda Anderson, Isobel Armstrong, Ingo Berensmeyer, Mark Bevir, Beci Carver, Dani Caselli, Chris Chowrimootoo, Emily Coit, John Connor, Patrick Fessenbecker, Sabine Hake, Ben Harker, Marius Hentea, Emily Hogg, Simon J. James, Peter Kalliney, Ramesh Mallipeddi, John Marx, Steve Medema, Klaus Petersen, Caroline Pollentier, Rachel Potter, Joseph

Rosenberg, Peter Simonsen, James Smith, Benoît Tadié, David Trotter, Colin Tyler, and Rishona Zimring.

It is a pleasure to acknowledge the funding bodies that have supported this work along the way: the Alexander von Humboldt Foundation, the Fritz Thyssen Foundation, and the Landesstiftung Baden-Württemberg. I am particularly grateful to the German Research Foundation for funding me through its Heisenberg scheme at a time when it would have been difficult to continue otherwise.

Portions of Chapter 4 were previously published in 'Slow Politics: H. G. Wells, Reform, and the Idea of the Welfare State', *Modern Fiction Studies* 67.2 (2021): 342–65; excerpts from Chapter 5 in *Late Victorian into Modern, 1880–1920*, ed. Laura Marcus, Michèle Mendelssohn, and Kirsten Shepherd-Barr (Oxford University Press, 2016); and parts of the Coda in 'Proletarian modernism: Film, literature, theory' in *PMLA* 134.5 (2019): 1056–75. I am grateful to Johns Hopkins University Press, Oxford University Press, and the Modern Language Association for permission to reprint these passages here.

Materials from T. H. Green's unpublished manuscripts and lecture notebooks is reprinted by permission of the Master and Fellows of Balliol College, Oxford; passages from the unpublished letters of Mary Augusta Ward are reproduced by kind permission of the Claremont Colleges Library; the Sheffield Archives granted copyright to quote from Edward Carpenter's manuscripts; archival material pertaining to the Fabian Society is reprinted by permission of the British Library and the London School of Economics; unpublished material relating to Leo Chiozza Money and H. G. Wells is reproduced by permission of the Syndics of Cambridge University Library and the University of Illinois at Urbana-Champaign.

It has once again been a delight to work with Jacqueline Norton at Oxford University Press. I am grateful to her for taking an early interest in this project, and also for her patience as the book neared completion. Special thanks are due to Oxford University Press's readers for their incisive and exceptionally helpful comments on an earlier version of this book. Paula Clarke Baine's care and speed in compiling the index were once more unmatched.

Families, Hegel reminds us, are institutions in their own right. It's the beauty of families that they can offer encouragement even when other institutions don't. I am more grateful than I can say to my parents, Evi and Michael, for their love and support. Norbert and Monika's infectious enthusiasm for literature has been a source of inspiration for as long as I can remember. Uschi, Heiner, and Christian are all I could have wished for when I first met them some fifteen years ago. This book is for Katharina, with love and gratitude for our life together, and for Clara Marie, our new arrival, in happy anticipation of everything to come.

Contents

List of Illustrations

List of Archives and Collections

Introduction

Thinking the State (Again)

> Freedom consists in converting the state from an organ superimposed
> on society into one thoroughly subordinate to it.
>
> Karl Marx, 'Critique of the Gotha Programme' (1875)

Reforms rarely spur the collective imagination in the way revolutions do. But why is it so hard to get excited about reform? The different charisma of the two terms *revolution* and *reform* derives in part from the distinct modes of socio-political change associated with each. Karl Marx's pointed critique of the German Social Democratic Party's reformist Gotha Programme of 1875 suggests that revolutions respond to moments of social crisis by tearing down the institutions which sustain injustice: nothing short of a complete overhaul of existing social conditions and political structures will put an end to present inequities. Moreover, revolutions are frequently imagined as involving a fundamentally open temporality: they jolt us from the rut of custom and tradition by creating new horizons for human co-existence and new spaces for experiments in living. Finally, revolutions are typically taken to involve not just a remaking of social institutions but an emancipatory reinvention of subjectivity itself, 'the relearning of the sense of the most elementary actions: [...] seeing, listening, speaking, reading'.[1] By contrast, the slower, elongated rhythms of institutional reform are often described as the shoring-up of the political status quo, the strategic pacification of social tensions, and the imposition of hegemonic models of subjectivity. To the extent that revolutions are seen as creative, libidinal, and experimental, reforms can look like a rearguard defence of the state and its institutions.

This book offers a literary prehistory of the welfare state in Britain around 1900 by turning to a period that requires us to look beyond the connotations associated with the terms reform and revolution today. In doing so, I pursue two related

---

[1] Jacques Rancière, 'The Red of La Chinoise: Godard's Politics', in *Film Fables* (Oxford: Berg, 2006), pp. 143–55 (p. 144). Rancière's discussion looks back to the remaking of individuality envisioned in Marx's *Economic and Philosophical Manuscripts* (1844) and to Marx's description of radical democracy as the lived praxis of 'free and associated' individuals in 'The Civil War in France' (1871). See *The First International and After*, ed. David Fernbach (London: Verso, 2010), pp. 187–268 (p. 213). For an important discussion of the legacy of these Marxian ideas, see Isobel Armstrong, *The Radical Aesthetic* (Oxford: Blackwell, 2000).

British Literature and the Life of Institutions: Speculative States. Benjamin Kohlmann, Oxford University Press.
© Benjamin Kohlmann 2021. DOI: 10.1093/oso/9780198836179.003.0001

goals, one reconstructive and literary-historical, the other conceptual and theoretical. First, I reconstruct the emergence of a reformist literary mode around 1900 by exploring how literary texts responded and adapted to the elongated rhythms of institutional change that characterized the emergence of new state structures in this period. Focussing on specific moments of heightened reformist activity, *British Literature and the Life of Institutions: Speculative States* restores to view literature's engagement with the slow politics of reform by linking the development of the institutional forms of the state to the aesthetic forms of literary writing. But, secondly, I also aim to make visible a reformist idiom whose progressive and aspirational dimension has become nearly illegible to us. This idiom pervades literary, philosophical, political, and social writing of the period, and it insists that we need to think about the state as a speculative figure—as a form of life in its own right—rather than as a set of detached administrative procedures and bureaucratic processes.

In charting a genealogy of the reformist literary mode around 1900, this study shifts our attention away from the promises and threats of abrupt revolutionary change. Paying attention to the slow politics of reform, I argue, allows us to identify nodes of debate that brought together aesthetic, social, political, and economic questions, and that provoked deeply engaged responses from the authors under discussion here. I position the work of individual writers in relation to several moments and movements of reform: Chapter 2 turns to George Gissing's and Mary Augusta Ward's literary explorations of new institutional structures that began to emerge in the 1880s in the context of the settlement movement in London's East End; Chapter 3 identifies the speculative charge of Edward Carpenter's poetry and social criticism by placing his works in close dialogue with debates about land nationalization in the 1880s and 1890s; Chapter 4 shows how the aspirational language of taxation reform under Lloyd George's administration infuses the hybrid aesthetic of H. G. Wells's late Victorian and Edwardian writings; and Chapter 5 demonstrates that the creation of health and unemployment insurance under the National Insurance Act of 1911 helped to shape E. M. Forster's recalibrations of genre in *Howards End* and his novel fragment *Arctic Summer*. The writers whose works I examine here occupy different positions on the political and ideological spectrum, and they often take diverging views on the nature or desirability of state action. Despite these differences, however, all of these authors can be seen to operate within a reformist literary mode that entailed a distinctive understanding of the state and its institutions.

As my selection of writers and texts indicates, the reformist mode also straddles the periods conventionally called 'Victorian' and 'modernist'. While the present book does not undertake a systematic revision of these reified categories, my argument indicates that the aspirational literary mode I associate with the reformist moment around 1900 is positioned at a slant to both these period labels, and productively unsettles theoretical and literary-historical assumptions associated with each of them. For example, my readings of Ward and Wells indicate that their novels programmatically resist the politically quietist 'ontological commitment to the status quo' that some critics have associated with fictional realism as such.[2] I show that Wells's Edwardian novels infuse realism with a transformative impulse that works through the (social, political, aesthetic) forms of the present in order to transcend them. This narrative procedure, I suggest, dramatizes the gradual emergence of the utopian impulse from within a prior mimetic one, and it conveys a sense of the undeveloped possibilities inherent in established institutional arrangements. If the reformist literary mode can enrich our sense of the changes which realist fiction underwent around 1900, it also offers new political, artistic, and intellectual contexts for the emergence of modernism. As I show in more detail in an excursus at the end of Chapter 1, it was partly against the background of the reformist literary mode (with its artistic hopes for the resolution of social contradictions and the overcoming of fragmentation) that modernists could project their own ('revolutionary') valorization of radical particularity.

Central to the progressive literary-political imaginary outlined here is a form of speculative thinking that made it possible to envision the state not merely as an ensemble of institutional structures external to social life but as intimately connected to the sphere of the social itself. The book's Introduction and first chapter aim to make this reformist imaginary newly convincing to contemporary literary critics and cultural theorists. The term *speculation*, as I use it here, invokes the political theory of the German philosopher G. W. F. Hegel, who introduces it both as a name for dialectical thought as such but also, more specifically, as a technical term for the third step of the dialectic that appears to conclude the move through positivity (the historical givenness of institutional forms), negativity (the critique of those forms), and speculation (the simultaneous preservation and transcendence of institutional arrangements). The term *speculation* serves as a capacious heuristic for my exploration of the reformist literary mode, and it helps me explicate a configuration of literary engagements with the state that insisted on the need to critique and transform existing institutions instead of rejecting ('negating') those institutions altogether. But my use of the term—and its association with the Hegelian dialectic—also draws specific inspiration from British political theory's Hegelian moment around 1900. As I show, British Hegelianism—associated here with philosophical idealists and public intellectuals of the late Victorian and Edwardian periods such as Thomas Hill Green, William Wallace, D. G. Ritchie, Bernard Bosanquet, and Ernest Belfort Bax—made it possible to imagine state institutions in terms of shared forms of life, as an aspect of what Hegel's speculative philosophy dubs *Sittlichkeit*. In the literary texts discussed in subsequent chapters, the state functions as a speculative figure in

---

[2] Fredric Jameson, *Antinomies of Realism* (London: Verso, 2015), p. 145.

precisely this sense: these works imagine the state not as a set of administrative mechanisms and procedures that are imposed on the sphere of the social from without but as a concrete and lived social reality in its own right.

This understanding of the state differs markedly from another, more familiar late-nineteenth-century theorization of state institutions, namely Marx's. Marx's revolutionary vision—pointedly formulated in 'The Civil War in France' (1871) and 'Critique of the Gotha Programme'—begins to imagine the end of institutional mediation as such. In 'The Civil War in France', a tract incandescent with the excitement and political promise of the Commune, Marx observes that social revolution signifies 'the reabsorption of the State power by society as its own living forces instead of as forces controlling and subduing it.'[3] Marx describes a process in which the 'reabsorption' of the state into the sphere of the social takes the form of a revolutionary assault on, and total erasure of, its institutions. The reformist literary mode that I explore here does not reject Marxian critiques of the state so much as it stands in complex contrast to them: while Hegelianism's attention to the systemic deficiencies of existing institutions echoes central aspects of Marxian critique, the British idealists part ways with Marx's revolutionary agenda by insisting that reformed state institutions will be able to act as infrastructural guarantors of a richer social life. Whereas Marx wanted to see the abstract structures of the state collapsed into society, the British Hegelians insisted that the state, properly understood, never existed apart from society.

Following this thumbnail sketch of my argument, a historical and theoretical caveat is in order. While the Hegelian moment of British state theory is central to the book's Introduction and first chapter, my foregrounding of British Hegelianism serves an analytic and exploratory rather than narrowly historiographical purpose. In other words, this book does not delineate a literary prehistory of the welfare state from a narrowly Hegelian perspective (e.g. by revisiting Hegel's works in each chapter), nor does it focus exclusively on writers who took an overt and sustained interest in Hegel. Instead, I argue that recovering this neglected idiom of state theory provides an important point of entry into the reformist literary mode as well as into broader public conversations about state-centred institutional reform between roughly 1870 and 1920. The literary works explored in this study can be understood as complementing and concretizing the more abstract genre of theoretical exposition that we encounter in the philosophical works of Green, Wallace, Bosanquet, F. H. Bradley, and other British idealists.

To point out that literary works figure the concept of the state as a form of social life is to make a claim for literature as a mode of speculative thought in its own right. Literary texts, I suggest, present us with a mode of thought—with a type of conceptual poesis—that is 'concrete' not because it represents or describes what

---

[3] Marx, 'The Civil War in France', p. 250.

is empirically given but because it engages in acts of theoretical speculation that give abstract concepts a degree of experiential concreteness unattainable to philosophical thought alone. This theoretical work—the speculative concretization of abstract concepts—is best understood as the poetic figuration of a politics that works through existing social forms instead of rejecting them in favour of a revolutionary vision of total utopian difference: the reformist literary mode is Hegelian rather than Marxist insofar as it imagines the gradual transformation of existing social conditions. *British Literature and the Life of Institutions* considers several literary writers whose works figure state-centred institutional reform in terms of the modes of life which these reforms will enable. While these novelists, poets, and essayists are not usually known for their Hegelian sympathies, their literary projects share with British Hegelianism an aspirational understanding of institutional reform: they indicate that the ultimate end of a more democratic politics consists in nourishing a social sphere that relies on the infrastructural support of state institutions but that is not coercively subsumed under their logic. Later chapters suggest that literature took on the task of imagining the kinds of life that would be possible under the auspices of the emerging welfare state—this involved an anticipatory vision of new kinds of active citizenship and a shared orientation towards the common good.

Slow Politics: Writing in the Reformist Literary Mode

Before we move on to the speculative idea of the state that I associate with the decades around 1900, it will be worth pausing briefly to explain why we should be interested in recovering this particular idiom of institutional reform in the first place. If we find it hard to get excited about questions such as progressive taxation, land reform, or unemployment insurance as they relate to literary works, this is due partly to the way we talk about the state. As the historian Tony Judt observed in his book *Ill Fares the Land* (2010), several decades of neoliberal rhetoric have radically depleted our political vocabulary. Judt notably laments the left's uninspiring defences of the welfare state. It is hard to see, he points out, how a state that is imagined as an ensemble of administrative functions and redistributive mechanisms can become the object of affective investments:

> Our disability is *discursive*: we simply do not know how to talk about these things anymore. For the last thirty years, when asking ourselves whether we support a policy, a proposal or an initiative, we have restricted ourselves to issues of profit and loss—economic questions in the narrowest sense. But this is not an instinctive human condition: it is an acquired taste.[4]

---

[4] Judt, *Ill Fares the Land* (New York: Penguin, 2010), p. 34; orig. emph.

'Merely asserting that something is or is not in our material interest', Judt concludes, 'will not satisfy us most of the time': '[w]e need to learn to think the state again. [...] [W]e need a language of ends, not means.'[5] Judt draws attention to the fact that the narrow economism which so often dominates current debates about the welfare state signals an impoverishment that is at once intellectual, cultural, and political. The language that presents the state as an assemblage of governmental means runs the risk of assimilating defences of the state to the output-oriented metrics of the market—and by the same token it puts severe constraints on our ability to mount defences of the welfare state. What we lose in the process is an understanding of rationality that resists the brutal reduction to an economistic calculus of efficiency and profitability. As Bonnie Honig notes: under neoliberalism 'efficiency is no longer one value among others. It has become rationality itself, and it is the standard by which everything is assessed.'[6]

In his critique of our 'discursive disability', Judt implicitly advises a form of recuperative retrospection when he urges that 'we need to learn to think the state *again*'. Judt's comment is important because it can be read as a call to reactivate earlier understandings of the welfare state which are no longer readily available or legible to us. The present study proposes that we follow Judt's injunction by looking back to the period of intense reformist activity around 1900.[7] Revisiting this period makes visible an aspirational reformist idiom that usefully defamiliar-izes the economistic language prevalent today and that can also offer resources for alternative defences of the welfare state. The idea that the state should not be talked about merely as an assemblage of governmental means forms a baseline of many debates about emerging state institutions around 1900. According to the reformist literary mode that crystallizes in this period, the state is not an entity to which we adjust ourselves—or an institutional reality to which we gradually grow habituated—but an aspect of social life that is fundamental to the realization of individual and collective freedom.[8]

The literary prehistory of the welfare state outlined in this book focusses on particular historical moments of reform in order to explore what could be called the idea of the state. To imagine the state as an idea, as the reformist literary mode requires us to do, is not intended to erase the historical complexities of the welfare

---

[5] Judt, *Ill Fares the Land*, pp. 199, 180.

[6] Honig, *Public Things: Democracy in Disrepair* (New York: Fordham University Press, 2017), p. 14.

[7] The intellectual historian Tim Rogan has recently begun the work of recuperating the language and intellectual intensity of this reformist moment. While Rogan remains sceptical of Hegelian state theory, he criticizes our collective 'failure [...] to open up deeper questions of liberty and solidarity—questions which the narrower economism now prevailing systematically excludes. [...] We are the poorer intellectually, culturally, and even politically for the disappearance of that alternative approach'. See Rogan, *The Moral Economists: R. H. Tawney, Karl Polanyi, E. P. Thompson, and the Critique of Capitalism* (Princeton: Princeton University Press, 2018), p. 2.

[8] For pragmatist and sociological accounts of the state in terms of habitualized patterns of behaviour, see Lisi Schoenbach's important *Pragmatic Modernism* (New York: Oxford University Press, 2011) and Bourdieu's *On the State: Lectures at the Collège de France, 1989–1992* (Cambridge: Polity, 2014).

state's early institutional emergence, in which the practical demands of the moment frequently ran ahead of any coherent theorization of the state and its institutions. Rather, referring to the state as an idea signals that in the literary and non-literary texts under consideration here the state acts as a speculative figure in a broadly Hegelian sense: it signifies the concrete vision of a social sphere in which the contradiction between historically grown forms of social life and the abstract externality of institutions has been attenuated if not overcome. The recovery of the reformist mode undertaken here thus entails a different accentuation of Judt's sentence: the task is not only 'to learn to think the state *again*' by revisiting earlier moments of reformist activity, but to 'learn to *think* it again' by enriching our understanding of the intellectual forms which reformist thought has taken in the past.

It should be clear from these remarks that my project builds on a selective reading of Hegelian philosophy. The Hegel foregrounded in this book is not the much-feted theorist of the politics of recognition or the prophet of the end of art, but rather the neglected theorist of institutionality—not the author of the *Phenomenology of Spirit* or the *Lectures on Aesthetics* but of the *Philosophy of Right*. It might be objected that placing emphasis on the idea of the state in this way, as the speculative culmination of Hegel's dialectic, threatens to shut down the space available for social critique and the articulation of genuinely oppositional voices. Indeed, the case for an agonistic democratic sphere has been made by many scholars, ranging from political theorists to feminists and queer activists, and frequently these important interventions have entailed a rejection of positions explicitly associated with Hegel.[9] Jacques Rancière, to take an influential proponent of this anti-Hegelian line of argument, criticizes the state's attempts to silence dissensus and to impose order on an unruly social sphere composed of singular beings. Liberal states, Rancière argues with an eye on Hegel, control society by enforcing normative models of liberal subjecthood that eclipse dissident subjectivities and refuse them articulation in the political sphere.[10] Rancière describes the state's eclipse of radical social energies as 'the political suppression of politics', as the 'realist utopia' of a consolidated status quo 'which consists in making two separate spaces coincide, namely the social middle and the political centre.'[11]

---

[9] For influential proposals that explicitly resist or reinterpret positions identified as Hegelian, see Ernesto Laclau and Chantal Mouffe, *Hegemony and Socialist Strategy* (London: Verso, 1985); Judith Butler, *Subjects of Desire: Hegelian Reflections in Twentieth-Century France* (New York: Columbia University Press, 1987); Seyla Benhabib, 'On Hegel, women, and irony', in *Situating the Self: Gender, Community, and Postmodernism in Contemporary Ethics* (New York: Routledge, 1992), pp. 242–59; *Feminist Interpretations of G. W. F. Hegel*, ed. Patricia Jagentowicz Mills (University Park: Pennsylvania State University Press, 1996); Kimberley Hutchings, *Hegel and Feminist Philosophy* (Cambridge: Polity, 2002); and Rei Terada, 'Hegel's racism for radicals', *Radical Philosophy* 2.05 (2019): 11–25.

[10] Samuel A. Chambers offers an illuminating account of Rancière's opposition to the 'unifying' tendencies of the Hegelian dialectic (*The Lessons of Rancière* [Oxford: Oxford University Press, 2012], pp. 52–64). Rancière's position points to a foundational tension between Marxist and Hegelian views of the state that I touch on briefly in this chapter and revisit at greater length in Chapter 1.

[11] Rancière, *On the Shores of Politics* (London: Verso, 1991), pp. 19, 14.

Related types of centrism can be glimpsed in the reformist literary mode around 1900: they are present in Carpenter's vision of a new class of local-cum-cosmo-politan smallholders; in Wells's celebration of the 'great educated middle class' as the medium of a 'larger social synthesis'; and in Forster's vision of a stable social centre in which welfare measures support a social life so integrated that all we need to do is 'only connect'.[12] The reformist literary mode is thus vulnerable to Rancière's charge that political participation must not be restricted to those who already hold political rights: democracy, Rancière reminds us, 'still requires the force of the *demos*' which is more than 'a sum of social partners'.[13]

The reformist debates about institutionality which I recuperate here reckon with the irreducible force of social particularity, and they do not propagate a vision of the state as a quasi-authoritarian 'heroic actor' invested with nearly unlimited executive powers.[14] Indeed, my discussion of British Hegelianism in Chapter 1 indicates that the limitations of Hegel's theory of the state—so fully worked out by critics from Marx's *Critique of Hegel's 'Philosophy of Right'* (1843) onwards—were painfully obvious to most British Hegelians and that this recognition formed the starting point for their work. This observation even extends to literary texts such as George Gissing's *Thyrza* (1887) and Mary Ward's *Robert Elsmere* (1888), which engage most directly with late Victorian idealism, including the idealist thinking of the Oxford-based philosopher T. H. Green and his followers. Historians have long noted that Green's writings and lectures of the early 1880s had a formative influence on the settlement movement, the late Victorian reform movement that sought to bring material support and educational opportunities to London's economically depressed East End. However, it has been less well recognized that even a novel such as *Robert Elsmere*—a text which critics often describe as an unabashedly optimistic portrayal of the settlement experience, as a paradigmatic 'novel of purpose'—is alive to the limitations of Green's perfectionist model of liberal subjectivity.[15] Ward's text achieves this, I argue, by showing that the hegemonic cultural assumptions which underpinned

---

[12] Wells, *Anticipations [...]* (London: Chapman & Hall, 1902), p. 249.

[13] Rancière, *On the Shores of Politics*, p. 32.

[14] I borrow the phrase 'heroic actor' from Zarena Aslami's important recent intervention in the field. Aslami argues that in late Victorian Britain statism and state phobia came together in the contradictory structure of feeling she dubs 'state fantasy'. State fantasy occurs when individuals seek to make up for the loss in autonomy that results from the development of new state structures by making compensatory affective investments in the state. As Aslami explains, state fantasy signifies 'the painful condition of imagining oneself to be a liberal agent and thus independent from power-bearing institutions yet knowing—consciously or unconsciously—that one is not': 'pure agency is at once so dear and so threatened that, in order to hold on to it, subjects project it away from themselves and onto "the State".' State fantasy thus serves a compensatory function, an escape from the contradictions of the present rather than a dialectical or speculative attempt to resolve them. See Aslami, *The Dream Life of Citizens: Late Victorian Novels and the Fantasy of the State* (New York: Fordham University Press, 2012), pp. 8–9.

[15] For a theorization of the transatlantic genre of the novel of purpose, see Amanda Claybaugh, *The Novel of Purpose: Literature and Social Reform in the Anglo-American World* (Ithaca: Cornell University Press, 2007).

this model of subjecthood were thrown into sharp relief in the deprived working-class environment of the East End. *Thyrza* and *Robert Elsmere* respond to contemporary idealist arguments, and they can be read in light of the social conception of citizenship developed by Green in the lead-up to the Third Reform Act (1884) that edged Britain closer towards adult male democracy. At the same time, these works adopt a more ambivalent view of institutions, rearticulating Green's reformist *élan* through an unstable affective and generic mode which Gissing, in a contemporary essay, called 'the hope of pessimism'.[16] Like the other texts examined in this study, Gissing's and Ward's novels can be seen to respond to the specific socio-political pressures that found expression in the 1884 Reform Act: they register, in Isobel Armstrong's phrase, that 'the meaning of democracy is always in process', and that 'it is an open term' which remains receptive to the pressure of 'antihegemonic' voices.[17]

The intellectual complexion and political ambitions of the reformist (literary) mode were from the beginning complicated by an awareness of the potential failure of institutions to represent the particularity and sheer diversity of social experience. Moreover, British idealists, much like the literary writers explored in later chapters, frequently failed to reflect on the ways in which developing state institutions in Britain contributed to, profited from, or were modelled on the sprawling institutional networks that supported the growth of empire and that served to sustain colonial regimes of inequality abroad.[18] It is not my aim, then, to suggest that important critiques of Hegel's political theory, from Marx to Rancière, are simply mistaken. Indeed, I am deeply sympathetic to these critiques, and I do not wish to suggest that we should try to rehabilitate a fictitiously pure or immaculate form of Hegelian state theory. To the extent that British idealists such as Green, Bosanquet, and Ritchie sought to understand the state in exclusively philosophical terms, their work is open to Marx's charge, formulated in his 1857–58 *Grundrisse*, that this type of theoretical production is '*merely* speculative, *merely* theoretical' insofar as it fails to reckon with newly emerging social demands:

> The totality as it appears in the head, as a totality of thoughts, is a product of a thinking head, which appropriates the world in the only way it can, a way different from the artistic, religious, practical and mental appropriation of this world. The real subject retains its autonomous existence outside the head just as before; namely as long as the head's conduct is *merely* speculative, *merely*

---

[16] Gissing, 'The hope of pessimism', in *Essays and Fiction*, ed. Pierre Coustillas (Baltimore: Johns Hopkins University Press, 1970), pp. 76–97.

[17] Armstrong, *Novel Politics: Democratic Imaginations in Nineteenth-Century Fiction* (Oxford: Oxford University Press, 2017), p. 7.

[18] Hegel's *Philosophy of Right* had in fact discussed capital's hunger for colonial expansion. See Hegel, *Grundlinien der Philosophie des Rechts* (Frankfurt/Main: Suhrkamp, 1986), pp. 392–3 (§ 248).

theoretical. Hence, in the theoretical method, too, the subject, society, must always be kept in mind as the presupposition.[19]

Marx's Introduction to *Grundrisse* takes aim at Hegel's panlogistic 'illusion' according to which 'the real [is] the product of thought concentrating itself, probing its own depths, and unfolding itself out of itself, by itself'.[20] *British Literature and the Life of Institutions* qualifies this portrayal of idealism by rendering visible a historical configuration of statist thought that sought to meet such objections halfway. Green's practice-oriented philosophy, for example, called not just for new speculative ideas but for a new reformist praxis that would remain keenly attuned to the contradictions of its own historical conjuncture. Green's idealism inspired several of his students, including Arnold Toynbee, Sidney Ball, and Bosanquet, to engage in a number of reformist schemes, ranging from the settlement movement (in the case of Toynbee and Ball) to the Charity Organisation Society (in the case of Bosanquet). The history of these developments in turn gave rise to a distinctly British reprise of the division of mid-nineteenth-century Hegelianism into Left and Right Hegelians, with Right Greenians such as Bosanquet calling for less state intervention, and Left Greenians such as Ritchie highlighting the dramatic inadequacy of current state provisions in order to make the case for more intervention.[21] As these comments suggest, the aspirational vision that found articulation in the works of the British Hegelians appealed to reformers across a broad political spectrum. It also meant that writers who held diverging political convictions—from Ward and Wells to Carpenter and Forster—were able to inhabit a similar imaginary centred around the slow politics of reform rather than the irruptive temporality of the revolutionary event.

The reformist literary mode is marked by an awareness of the limitations of state-centred reform—an awareness that was fostered, as Green himself saw, by the epoch's revolutionary horizons and by the knowledge that state institutions can operate as instruments of veiled and overt class domination.[22] Similar to the

---

[19] Marx, *Grundrisse: Foundations of the Critique of Political Economy* (London: Penguin, 1993), pp. 101–2; emphasis added.

[20] Marx, *Grundrisse*, p. 101.

[21] For an excellent account of this polarization (and the reversal of left/right polarities concerning the desirability of state intervention), see Stefan Collini's 'Hobhouse, Bosanquet, and the state: Philosophical idealism and political argument in England, 1880–1918', *Past & Present* 72 (1976): 86–111 (pp. 107–8).

[22] Green formulated these points in a series of reflections penned in the wake of the 1871 Paris Commune. One set of manuscript notes elaborates on 'the modern idea' that state institutions are always partially an instrument for the exercise of 'sovereignty' and 'might'. The second set of notes, appended to a commentary on Aristotle's ethics, explores the economic reasons for the revolutionary events of 1871 and concludes by noting that the same structural conditions for revolution 'apply practically to London & Berlin'. THG, Ms Notes on Political Philosophy, 2a.19; and Ms Notes appended to Commentary on Aristotle's *Ethics*.

politico-aesthetic idiom of 'bleak liberalism' described by Amanda Anderson, works written in the reformist literary mode are never as naively or 'simply hopeful as [their] critics seem to suppose'.[23] Whereas liberalism is often 'associated with ideas of human perfectibility and assured progressivism', Anderson argues, bleak liberalism remains acutely aware of the challenges which such optimism faces when it is confronted with the pressures of social particularity.[24] To the extent that the literary works explored here imagine institutional responses that can accommodate such pressures, they illustrate how certain strands of liberalism avoided becoming bleak in the face of sustained and trenchant critique. Literary scholars, following the work of social historians, have sometimes labelled this formation of socially progressive argument 'New Liberalism'.[25] The present book largely refrains from using this label—not because of some principled opposition to the term, but because I seek to draw attention to underlying structures of argument and modes of literary thought that were not limited to this or that political grouping, however broadly conceived.

The specific historical content of these reformist debates, as well as the political latitude of British Hegelianism, will be the topic of subsequent chapters. However, it should already be clear that, across its different political manifestations, the reformist literary mode is rooted in an understanding of institutionality that is irreducible to some of the critical vocabularies available to literary scholars interested in the state today. This includes the Foucauldian language that has dominated so much recent debate in literary studies, most notably Foucault's influential theorization of governmentality in his 1978–79 Collège de France lectures. First published in English in 2008 under the title *The Birth of Biopolitics*, Foucault's lectures depart in crucial ways from the mode of total panoptic surveillance outlined in *Discipline and Punish* (1975). Abandoning his earlier analysis of the state as an omnipresent agent of objectifying domination, the 1978–79 lectures articulate a model of liberal governance by redescribing the state as a loose assemblage of administrative and managerial functions, what Foucault calls governmentality. The lectures present the state as an unfixed entity—as 'the mobile shape of a perpetual statification [*étatisation*] or statifications' that governs through indirect means such as economic incentivization. The state, so conceived, 'has no heart [. . .] not just in the sense that it has no feelings,

---

[23] See Anderson, *Bleak Liberalism* (Chicago: University of Chicago, 2016), p. 1.

[24] Anderson, *Bleak Liberalism*, p. 1. For a concise statement of this tension, see also Norberto Bobbio, *Liberalism and Democracy* (London: Verso, 2005).

[25] At a later stage in her argument, Anderson helpfully notes that the New Liberalism of the Edwardian years made liberalism's bleakness dialectical by emphasizing the 'interacting perspectives of critique and aspiration that are relevant to the broader economies of liberal thought as well as its aesthetic formations' (pp. 37–8). Lauren Goodlad, whose work I discuss elsewhere in this book, has also offered important literary-historical accounts of Britain's New Liberal moment. For classical surveys by intellectual and social historians, see Michael Freeden, *The New Liberalism: An Ideology of Social Reform* (Oxford: Clarendon Press, 1978), and *The New Liberalism: Reconciling Liberty and Community*, ed. Avital Simhony and D. Weinstein (Cambridge: Cambridge University Press, 2001).

either good or bad, but it has no heart in the sense that it has no interior. The state is nothing else but the mobile effect of a regime of multiple governmentalities.'[26] Much important critical discussion about the state has coagulated around Foucault's concept of governmentality.[27] And yet, the critical productivity of the Foucauldian paradigm notwithstanding, there can be little doubt that the reduction of the state to a 'mobile effect of a regime of multiple governmentalities' entails a 'theoretical and analytical antistatism' that has contributed to the impoverishment of reformist language diagnosed by Judt.[28] Most germane to the period explored here, Foucault's model does not adequately capture the reparative and forward-directed dialectic of critique and (speculative) transformation that forms the heart of the reformist literary mode. Whereas Foucault's model of governmentality gives us a vocabulary to describe site-specific historical trade-offs between the abstract externality of institutions and subjects who are imagined as essentially free and self-governing, British Hegelians imagine the state not merely as an ensemble of institutions (whether of centralized control or local incentivization) but as a socially grounded form of life, that is, as a moment of *Sittlichkeit*.[29]

This broadly Hegelian understanding of the state has led intellectual historians to claim that British idealists helped to lay the philosophical groundwork for new forms of politico-economic collectivism in Britain. The application of the term *collectivism* to late nineteenth-century debates is not, strictly speaking, anachronistic,[30] and it seems particularly apposite when the writings of idealists such as Green are contrasted with the extreme valorization of competition,

---

[26] Foucault, *The Birth of Biopolitics: Lectures at the Collège de France, 1978–1979* (New York: Picador, 2008), p. 77.

[27] For a particularly fruitful application of Foucault's ideas to the late Victorian and Edwardian context, see Lauren Goodlad, *Victorian Literature and the Victorian State: Character and Governance in a Liberal Society* (Baltimore: Johns Hopkins University Press, 2003), esp. pp. 1–31. See also John Marx, 'Literature and governmentality', *Literature Compass* 8.1 (2011): 66–79.

[28] Mitchell Dean and Kaspar Villadsen, *State Phobia and Civil Society: The Political Legacy of Michel Foucault* (Stanford: Stanford University Press, 2016), p. 4. Some recent scholarship has polemically insisted that Foucault's description of the liberal state as an assemblage of governmental mechanisms is ideologically complicit with the neoliberal turn of the 1970s and 1980s. See Brown, *Undoing the Demos: Neoliberalism's Stealth Revolution* (Cambridge, MA: MIT Press, 2015); and Behrent and Zamora (eds.), *Foucault and Neoliberalism* (Cambridge: Polity, 2015). For a more judicious assessment, see Ute Tellmann's, 'Foucault and the invisible economy' (*Foucault Studies* 6 [2009]: 5–24 [p. 9]) which notes that Foucault's failure to provide 'a critical visibility of the economy' is intimately linked to his theorization of governmentality.

[29] At one point in his lectures, Foucault himself countenances the possibility that the state can be imagined as a form of life rather than as an ensemble of governmental functions. He entertains this possibility in a tantalizing paragraph that raises the question of a fully 'socialist governmentality'. Foucault argues that governmentality has historically been 'connected up' to the external and negative freedoms of 'liberal governmentality' (Foucault, *Birth of Biopolitics*, p. 92). To the extent that socialist governmentality here constitutes the future horizon of governmentality as such, Foucault's last lectures—including his work on *parrhesia* and the care of self—can be read as speculative elaborations of an ethically more substantive form of active citizenship.

[30] The work commonly credited with introducing the term 'collectivism' into British political debate is the constitutional jurist A. V. Dicey's *Lectures on the Relation between Law and Public Opinion during the Nineteenth Century* (1905).

struggle, and self-interest in tracts such as Herbert Spencer's influential *The Man versus the State* (1884). However, the 'collectivism' label also runs the risk of obscuring some of the distinctive features of British Hegelianism by producing a thoroughly undialectical understanding of idealist political theory. Importantly, British idealists did not propagate an organicist view of society, and they also did not advocate a shutting down of dissensus and dissident subjectivities by a monolithic state.[31] The identification of British Hegelianism with collectivism is misleading insofar as it suggests that idealist thinkers desired a nostalgic return to some lost form of organic community, or that they postulated authoritarian political imperatives that blithely ignored (or even called for the eradication of) historically grown textures of social life. Such accounts associate British idealism much too neatly with the first term of the oppositional pair of 'positive' and 'negative' freedoms—a frozen dialectic that is recognizably rooted in the ideological antagonisms of the Cold War and that received its most momentous formulation in Isaiah Berlin's work of the 1950s.[32] Departing from such readings, it will be more productive to follow Lauren Goodlad's proposal that we understand 'Hegelian idealism' as a mode of progressive liberalism rather than authoritarian collectivism: as Goodlad remarks, Green's ambitiously dialectical understanding of negative and positive freedoms, along with John Stuart Mill's 'drift towards cooperative socialism', constitutes a 'defining moment in the transition to social democracy'.[33] In this context, what is meant by 'positive' liberty is a fully social understanding of individual freedom that encompasses citizens' rights as well as their obligations towards the state that enables their self-development. It was in this sense, as Ritchie pointed out in his *Principles of State Interference* (1891), that 'Green [was] willing to allow Hegel's term "freedom".'[34] Positive freedom so conceived offers a counter both to the classical liberal understanding of freedom in terms of property-based legal entitlements, and to Berlin's darkly dystopian vision of totalitarian coercion.

Instead of adhering to the stark bifurcation of freedom into negative and positive types, British Hegelians proposed a vision of institutional transformation

---

[31] For a more sceptical account of the hegemonic and consensus-generating functions of the liberal state, see Daniel Malachuk's *Perfection, the State, and Victorian Liberalism* (London: Palgrave, 2005).

[32] Isaiah Berlin's 1958 lecture 'Two Concepts of Liberty' gave the terms 'negative' and 'positive' freedom their current polemical edge. Comparing Berlin's lecture to Karl Popper's 'abusive and tendentious attack' on Hegel in *The Open Society and Its Enemies* (1945), Quentin Skinner has pointed out that these Cold War texts took aim specifically at Green and Bosanquet. See Skinner, 'A third concept of liberty', *Proceedings of the British Academy* 117 (2002): 237–68 (p. 241).

[33] Goodlad, 'Liberalism and literature', in: *The Oxford Handbook of Victorian Literary Culture*, ed. Juliet John (Oxford: Oxford University Press, 2016), pp. 103–23 (p. 107). It is only when we reinstate the properly dialectical nature of British Hegelian thought that it appears as something other than 'a late-Victorian offshoot of Mill's philosophy', as a volte face away from negative liberty towards positive liberty, from social atomism to collectivist organicism. See Goodlad, *Victorian Literature and the Victorian State*, p. 200.

[34] Ritchie, *The Principles of State Interference* (London: Swan Sonnenschein, 1891), pp. 145–6.

that combines the two related moments of critique and progressive institutional change. In developing this reformist vision, they adapted and repurposed precisely those elements of Hegelian state theory with which contemporary critics (not only on the left) tend to feel most uncomfortable—above all the belief in an ascending order of social forms presented in Hegel's *Philosophy of Right* (1820), and the special weight attributed to the speculative third step of the dialectic that appears to transcend critique's negativity by resolving it into a higher unity. As I discuss in more depth below and in Chapter 1, it was precisely these elements of Hegel's thought that provided a route towards a progressive reformist imaginary, and they can help us access the literary modes associated with this imaginary around 1900. Even if we find it difficult to give unqualified assent to the idealists' understanding of the state, engaging with these debates can have the salutary effect—to borrow a phrase from Anna Kornbluh—'to dialectically buck our reflexive anti-statism'.[35] Hegelians give us a sense of the transformability of the state in ways that even more moderate Marxists don't.

Crucially, the speculative elaboration of reformed institutional arrangements we encounter in the works of the British idealists did not seek to close down critique or to nip negation in the bud. Quite to the contrary, the writings of the British Hegelians popularized and, in some respects, even invented critique: the absence of an advanced Marxist theory of the state in Britain around 1900 meant that for a few decades Hegelian idealism, rather than dialectical materialism, became the language through which existing social arrangements could be explored and criticized. The Frankfurt School philosopher Rahel Jaeggi has recently observed that the considerable critical edge of Hegelianism is no longer easily visible to us, owing in large part to Marx's reading of Hegel's idealism as a form of political conservatism and social quietism. As Jaeggi points out, however, it is precisely Hegel's idealism that opens up a space for social interrogation and critique because it prompts us to inquire whether a particular form of social life, of *Sittlichkeit*, corresponds to its concept, i.e. to its systematic place in the ascending order of social forms. Thus, when Bosanquet notes that 'every institution, every life, works as a theory', he is suggesting that forms of life can be evaluated according to the degree of their correspondence to the fully realized concept or idea (*Begriff*).[36]

---

[35] Kornbluh, 'The state of contradiction', *Continental Thought & Theory* 2.4 (2019): 62–70 (p. 69). My project is also sympathetic to Kornbluh's larger enterprise of rehabilitating the essential ordering functions of form: 'My contention that form is simultaneously indispensable and reformable', she writes, 'countenances none of the denunciation of "institution as such," "law as such," "state as such," that has become so habitual after the [Foucauldian] genealogy of discipline.' Kornbluh, *The Order of Forms: Realism, Formalism, and Social Space* (Chicago: University of Chicago Press, 2019), p. 28.

[36] Bosanquet, *The Philosophical Theory of the State* (London: Macmillan, 1899), p. 265. For Jaeggi's reactivation of the critical potential of the Hegelian *Begriff*, see Jaeggi, *Critique of Forms of Life* (Boston, MA: Harvard University Press, 2018), esp. pp. 118–32.

In contrast to many later versions of *Ideologiekritik*, including the insistent negativity of Theodor W. Adorno's thought, the mode of critique developed by British Hegelians is characterized by a reparative forward momentum that derives its energy from the dialectical three-step presented in Hegel's *Philosophy of Right*. This is not to say that a fully speculative and forward-looking dialectic, as opposed to a mode of thought that lingers at the level of negativity and critique, must renounce critique in favour of a fixed telos or the vision of a stable social order. Such a view owes less to Hegel's writings than to Alexandre Kojève's Cold War misreading of Hegel as the liberal prophet of the end of history.[37] Indeed, even while British idealists advocate political positions that seek to resolve present antagonisms, they continue to reckon with the reversibility of any ideal in the face of the challenges of social particularity. The point is not to spirit away contradiction but to mitigate its most extreme forms.[38] As Diana Coole explains, the difference between the total eradication of social contradictions and their local alleviation is a matter of philosophical and political emphasis: 'if the "rational kernel" of the dialectic is recognized, does it not call for a politics that might avoid the traumas of contradiction by emulating processes of generativity whose fecundity lies in a play of differences which are not allowed to reach the stage of contradictory opposition?'[39] Coole is arguably too eager to downplay the importance of contradiction in Hegel, yet her observation usefully highlights a central feature of the reformist literary mode: like the thinkers and state theorists associated with Britain's Hegelian moment, the literary writers I discuss in subsequent chapters imagine the state's institutions not as homogenizing levellers of singularity and difference but as structures that might help to attenuate the potentially destructive or 'trauma[tic]' effects of social contradictions.

At this point, the theoretical stakes of this book can be stated in more programmatic fashion. *British Literature and the Life of Institutions* argues that the

---

[37] First published in French in 1947, Kojève's lectures have cast a long shadow on discussions of Hegel, but they crucially postdate the exploratory dialectical mode I explore here. Kojève associates the dialectic's speculative moment with the suppression of dialectical movement as such—a view that has been taken by some, most prominently Francis Fukuyama, as prophesying the inevitable global triumph of Western-style liberalism and free-market capitalism. For Kojève's account of the end of history, see his *Introduction to the Reading of Hegel* (Ithaca: Cornell University Press, 1969), pp. 157–62. For a competing interpretation of the end of history as revolutionary event and the reading of Absolute Spirit as collectivity, see Jameson's *The Hegel Variations* (London: Verso, 2010), pp. 75–115.

[38] Of course, as George Ciccariello-Maher notes, the effects of contradiction, even when they are psychologically traumatizing, can be politically liberatory. Ciccariello-Maher's brilliant study makes visible a revolutionary and anti-colonial counter-current of dialectical thought in the works of Georges Sorel, Frantz Fanon, and Enrique Dussel. While I am sympathetic to Ciccariello-Maher's project, the primary aim of my book is to describe a particular mode of reformist thought rather than home in on anarchist (or anarcho-syndicalist) attempts to reboot a stagnant political dialectic from positions outside the state. See Ciccariello-Maher, *Decolonizing Dialectics* (Durham, NC: Duke University Press, 2017).

[39] Coole, *Negativity and Politics: Dionysus and Dialectics from Kant to Nietzsche* (New York: Routledge, 2000), pp. 69–70.

reformist (literary) mode that crystallized around 1900 entailed a two-pronged approach to the sphere of the social. First, it involved an element of social critique. Unlike many contemporaneous Marxist forms of critique, this version of Hegelian social diagnosis did not call for a radical disassembling of society from the economic base up. Instead, the act of reimagining existing institutions involved working within them in order to effect a gradual transition from one stage of *Sittlichkeit* (the stage of capitalist society, Hegel's *bürgerliche Gesellschaft*) to the next (the modern reformed state).[40] British Hegelianism can help us foreground a reformist imaginary that identifies the damaged conditions of social life in the present, including its permeation by capitalist exchange relations and the tendency of institutional structures to appear as external impositions on the social sphere:

(1) In the closing decades of the nineteenth century Hegelianism offered the most advanced idiom of social critique. It lent support to a critical *symptomology of social life* that could be called (with a nod to current debates in literary theory) 'Hegelian symptomatic reading': this mode of social diagnosis is best described as Hegelian (idealist) because it pays special attention to the superstructural composition of a given social whole. As I indicate later in this chapter, the form of Hegelian symptomatic reading that emerged around 1900 anticipates types of immanent critique that we now associate with the later, twentieth-century tradition of Western Marxism.

Literary works written in the reformist mode envision a slow transformation of society rather than a complete revolutionary overhaul of existing forms of life. What results from this is a speculative understanding of institutional structures as a lived reality—as a moment of Hegelian *Sittlichkeit*—that could be described (with Elaine Hadley) as a 'lived political practice' or (with Amanda Anderson) as a 'lived relation to [...] political conditions'.[41] To put this another way:

---

[40] As Hegel explained in his *System der Sittlichkeit* (1802)—an early articulation of ideas subsequently expounded in more depth in the *Philosophy of Right*—this type of social diagnosis highlights pathologies that result from deficient institutional arrangements in which shared forms of life are 'injured rather than elevated to a higher plane'. The externality of institutions to the social also produces distinctive forms of life—but, Hegel submits, these will invariably be *injured* ones. See Hegel, *System der Sittlichkeit* (Hamburg: Meiner, 2002), p. 35. Hegel's German sentence reads: '*das Leben ist nur verletzt, nicht höher gehoben worden.*'

[41] Hadley, *Living Liberalism: Practical Citizenship in Mid-Victorian Britain* (Chicago: University of Chicago Press, 2010), p. 35; Anderson, *Bleak Liberalism*, p. 10. For related arguments about liberalism as a form of '*lived equality*', see Pierre Rosanvallon's *The Society of Equals* (Cambridge, MA: Harvard University Press, 2013), esp. pp. 55–9 (orig. emph.). Also: Axel Honneth, *Freedom's Right: The Social Foundations of Democratic Life* (London: Polity, 2014). The English translation of Honneth's title doesn't adequately capture the Hegelian overtones of the German: *Das Recht der Freiheit: Grundriss einer demokratischen Sittlichkeit.*

(2) Hegelian (idealist) social analysis crucially entailed a *speculative moment*. 'Speculation' here signifies the attempt to think through existing forms of life in order to show that a slow, reformist transition towards alternative social arrangements is possible. The forms of life that are imagined in this way constitute what Jürgen Habermas calls *entgegenkommende Lebensformen*, i.e. "anticipatory" or "emergent" forms of social life that make it possible to imagine new institutional arrangements not merely in the abstract—as detached assemblages of legal and administrative structures imposed on social life from without—but as a concrete lived reality.[42] These *entgegenkommende Lebensformen* do not mark a nostalgic return to an earlier, organicist model of community: rather, they signal the dialectical mediation of new institutional structures with existing forms of life.

I will spell out this double aspect of British idealism—its status as a critical symptomology of social life and as a mode of speculative thought about institutionality—at greater length in Chapter 1. For now, I only want to emphasize the centrality of the notion of *entgegenkommende Lebensform* to my site-specific exploration of particular moments of institutional reform around 1900: in the literary texts investigated in this book, reform is expected to give rise to new forms of life that will be more democratic and egalitarian; yet these texts also suggest that the success of these reforms will in turn be contingent on the prior emergence (*Entgegenkommen*) of a shared ethos of care and responsibility. Building on the understanding of institutionality outlined in the two opening chapters of this study, each of my literary-historical case studies could be subsumed under a broad concept that describes the contours of a set of *entgegenkommende Lebensformen* in this sense, such as 'hoping' (Chapter 2), 'owning' (Chapter 3), 'sharing' (Chapter 4), and 'caring' (Chapter 5). In the works of Ward, Gissing, Carpenter, Wells, and Forster, the forms of social life that are designated by these terms serve to figure particular moments in the uneven emergence of welfare state structures: the settlement movement in London's East End; late nineteenth-century debates about land nationalization; the introduction of new kinds of redistributive taxation under prime ministers William Harcourt and Lloyd George, culminating with the People's Budget of 1909–10; and finally the introduction of health and

---

[42] Habermas introduces the phrase *entgegenkommende Lebensformen* in his revision of Kantian deontological ethics. Building on Hegel's critique of Kant, Habermas indicates that deontologists are mistaken when they argue that moral questions can be considered in isolation from the thick social contexts which first lend meaning to the concept of the 'good life' (*'Moralität und Sittlichkeit: Treffen Hegels Einwände gegen Kant auch auf die Diskursethik zu?'*, *Revue internationale de philosophie* 42 (1988): 320–40 [p. 335]). Jaeggi has extended the idea, which she associates with Hegel rather than Habermas, to argue that institutions depend on *entgegenkommende Lebensformen* for their support and survival. 'Forms of life represent the background and the condition of possibility of certain institutions, or must accommodate them'. Jaeggi's German reads: '*Lebensformen stellen vielmehr den Hintergrund und die Möglichkeitsbedingung bestimmter Institutionen dar oder müssen ihnen "entgegenkommen"*.' See Jaeggi, *Kritik von Lebensformen* (Frankfurt: Suhrkamp, 2014), p. 75; and *Critique of Forms of Life*, p. 40.

unemployment insurance with the Insurance Act of 1911. In these texts, the vision of the state as a form of life is not imagined as something to be realized once and for all but as an anticipatory and forward-directed 'unfinished project', as a 'speculative account of some thinking of the future which has not yet been realized'.[43]

Reading Reform/Reformist Reading:
Description, Critique, Speculation

Britain's long Hegelian moment is a neglected episode in the history of the dialectical imagination. The speculative dimension of British Hegelianism help-fully reminds us that the dialectic is neither a purely descriptive procedure that is only interested in tracing the surface structures of a given social world, nor an exclusively aetiological method that fails to push beyond the critical diagnosis of (manifest or latent) social pathologies. In the hands of the British Hegelians, the dialectic is a fundamentally generative procedure: it produces concepts in light of which given social arrangements can be critiqued, yet it deploys such critique not in order to reject existing social arrangements out of hand but to imagine their simultaneous preservation *and* transcendence. In what follows, I want to spell out the implications of these observations by suggesting that Britain's Hegelian moment around 1900 provides us with a forgotten genealogy of current debates about critique: it prompts us to engage with the dialectic in ways that are unaccounted for in many versions of ideology critique (which tend to emphasize the moment of negativity at the expense of the dialectic's speculative thrust) and by a good deal of contemporary postcritical thought (which tends to prefer open metaphors such as 'collision' to the systematic overdetermination of Hegelian dialectics).[44] As my remarks in the previous sections indicate, British idealism invites fresh engagement with the speculative momentum of the

[43] I source Habermas's phrase 'unfinished project' via Fredric Jameson who observes that Hegel's dialectic 'is not a thing of the past, not some chapter in the history of philosophy, but rather a speculative account of some thinking of the future which has not yet been realized: an unfinished project, as Habermas might put it; a way of grasping situations and events that does not yet exist as a collective habit because the concrete form of social life to which it corresponds has not yet come into being.' Jameson, 'Persistencies of the dialectic', in *Valences of the Dialectic* (London: Verso, 2009), pp. 279–90 (p. 279).

[44] For a prominent statement of the interaction of forms in terms of a-teleological 'collisions', see Caroline Levine, *Forms: Whole, Rhythm, Hierarchy, Network* (Princeton: Princeton University Press, 2015), p. 18. We might also think of the spatial metaphors of surface—or of the Latourian heuristic of the decentred network—that are prominently deployed by Stephen Best and Sharon Marcus ('Surface reading: An introduction', *Representations* 108.1 [2009]: 1–21); Heather Love ('Close but not deep: Literary ethics and the descriptive turn', *New Literary History* 41 [2010]: 371–91); Rita Felski ('Latour and literary studies', *PMLA* 130 [2015]: 737–42); and others. A similar wariness of the dialectic's unfashionably teleological implications also pervades recent defences of critique: 'what is needed', argues Carolyn Lesjak in her perspicacious response to Best and Marcus's essay, 'is a better way of

Hegelian dialectic: to focus on speculation in this way is not to dispense with critical inquiry but to rearticulate a more expansive understanding of its scope and aims.

After nearly a century of ideology critique, from its Frankfurt School origins in the 1930s to more recent forms of 'suspicious' reading, it requires a leap of the imagination to free the concept of critique from its particular intellectual affiliation with Marxism. However, this is precisely what the history of British idealism requires us to do. Hegelianism—and not Marxism, which still lacked a developed theory of the state[45]—was a central intellectual motor for social critique in Britain around 1900. Importantly, though, the reformist literary mode entails a different understanding of critique than is assumed by recent scholars who stress the limitations of the hermeneutics of suspicion. Instead of circumscribing or even discarding the value of critical inquiry, British Hegelianism prompts us to rehabilitate a different modality of critique, one which insists on a normative understanding of historically evolving institutions and which stands in contrast to the more negative assessments of institutionality in the Foucauldian and Frankfurt School traditions. This mode of critique, which I have called Hegelian symptomatic reading, entails a fuller engagement with the dialectic as a mode of speculative thought. In the context of the reformist literary mode around 1900, *speculation* does not signify the cancellation of critique as such but an aspirational moment inherent in critique itself.[46] To adapt a phrase from Eve Kosofsky Sedgwick: speculative critique, as it is envisioned by British Hegelians, has 'explicit recourse to reparative motives' and is therefore 'frankly ameliorative ("merely reformist")'.[47] This kind of critique contributes to the project of social reparation instead of appearing as reform's incipiently revolutionary other: it is unabashedly ('frankly') ameliorative.

British Hegelians sometimes positioned their understanding of critique's reparative, reformist élan in opposition to the hermeneutic protocols of adjacent

---

reading surfaces as perverse rather than as obvious, as never identical to themselves in their "thereness", and always found within and constitutive of complex spatial relations' ('Reading dialectically', *Criticism* 55.2 [2013]: 233–77 [p. 251]).

[45]   Norberto Bobbio's essays are still among the most insightful accounts of this theoretical lacuna and its repercussions for liberal and socialist thought around 1900. See, e.g., 'Is there a Marxist doctrine of the state?', in Bobbio, *Which Socialism? Marxism, Socialism, and Democracy* (Cambridge: Polity Press, 1986), pp. 47–64.

[46]   As Simon Jarvis observes, critique's reparative impulse also sustains the work of thinkers who are most committed to the value of negativity. Properly understood, even Adorno's negative dialectics does not signify a thinking that 'stop[s] at stage two [i.e. at the moment of negativity], failing to count to three'. See Jarvis, 'What is speculative thinking?', *Revue internationale de la philosophie* 227 (2004): 69–83 (p. 71). We could also think of Jameson's call for a reparative 'positive hermeneutic' to supplement the 'Marxist negative hermeneutic': the former, Jameson argues, will contribute to 'a decipherment of the Utopian impulses of these same still ideological cultural texts'. See *The Political Unconscious: Narrative as a Socially Symbolic Act* (Ithaca, NY: Cornell University Press, 1981), p. 296.

[47]   Sedgwick, *Touching Feeling: Affect, Pedagogy, Performativity* (Durham, NC: Duke University Press, 2002), p. 144.

fields, most prominently sociology and Marxist theory. In doing so, they took their distance from (what they regarded as) the precritical positivism of the former and the totalized negativity of the latter. Departing from these two intellectual positions, British Hegelians look for a speculative resolution to the contradiction between description and critique: the right response to the perceived negativity of Marxist critique, they suggest, is not neo-sociological positivism but a mode of critical thinking that remembers how to tarry with the speculative aspect of the dialectic. In tracing these arguments, I am not suggesting that the British idealists' parsing of the Hegelian dialectic in terms of description ('sociological positivism'), critique ('Marxist negativity'), and speculation (the preservation and transcendence of the previous two moments) is correct or that it would seem tenable to contemporary intellectual historians. It would be more accurate to say that the British Hegelians' appropriation of the dialectic was partly strategic because it enabled them to position their thinking against protocols of 'mere' description as well as against forms of 'mere' critique. We can accordingly begin to grasp the specific contours of Hegelian symptomatic reading by turning briefly to British Hegelianism's engagements with forms of sociological description, on the one hand, and with Marxist practices of critique, on the other.

The decades around 1900 saw the emergence of sociology as a distinct academic discipline. As Stefan Collini points out in his study of the pioneering British sociologist and liberal politician L. T. Hobhouse, Britain was in some respects lagging behind the discipline's development in Continental Europe. Bucking this trend, late-nineteenth-century Hegelian idealism in Britain 'encouraged a more "organic" view' of society that made it possible to frame the social as an autonomous sphere capable of sustained empirical and theoretical exploration.[48] In the works of the British Hegelians 'the "social"' came to be 'conceptualized [...] in a way which revealed its pervasive role in the constitution of human action, and hence its central place in the explanation of that action.'[49] This new attention to the social sphere, Collini notes, produced a vision of the social totality as ontologically prior to the formation of individuality, but it also led British idealists to make a stronger claim, namely that human potentialities could be actualized only through the individual's participation in a grown community. While the emerging field of sociology demonstrated that individuality needed to be understood in relation to broader patterns of collective life, Collini's analysis indicates that

---

[48] Collini, *Liberalism and Sociology: L. T. Hobhouse and Political Argument in England, 1880–1914* (Cambridge: Cambridge University Press, 1979), p. 45. The opposing argument—that Britain, around 1900 lacked a fledgling discipline of sociology, and that Britons therefore had no way to theorize about their own society—has been influentially made by Perry Anderson. See, e.g., Anderson's 'Components of the national culture', *New Left Review* I.50 (1968): 3–58.

[49] Collini, *Liberalism and Sociology*, p. 3. See also Collini, 'Sociology and idealism in Britain, 1880–1920', *Archives européennes de sociologie* 19 (1978): 3–50.

sociology crucially lacked Hegelianism's critical edge vis-à-vis existing social arrangements.

In contrast to the nascent sociological understanding of the sphere of the social, British Hegelians insisted that positivist accounts which limited themselves to *describing* social relations were bound to miss the constitutive contradictions that characterize any given social whole. By contrast, British idealists advocated modes of social analysis that aimed at testing what we could call the conceptual coherence of social forms of life. This, I suggest, is how we should understand Bosanquet's insistence, levelled against the budding science of sociology, that '[w]e are dealing, in society and in the State, with an *ideal fact*': here, the observable 'facts' that constitute a given social reality are confronted with the speculative totalities of the Hegelian idea of society and the state.[50] If Bosanquet's phrase ('ideal fact') appears paradoxical to us today, this is because it belongs to a now-forgotten strand of early sociology—an ambitiously Hegelian alternative to the positivist social science that Bosanquet associated with the social evolutionism of Herbert Spencer. The 'prevailing spirit of Positivism', as the Hegelian John Muirhead noted in 1927, looking back to the decades around 1900, was as an incitement to lazy thinking, or, in fact, to not thinking at all.[51]

Bosanquet and other British idealists departed from types of description that seemed content to linger at the level of the empirically given, and they instead aimed to develop forms of social exploration that were capable of generating a critical understanding of society. This critical procedure is one of the animating impulses behind Bradley's *Ethical Studies* (1876), a book that starts out from empirical observation in order to ascend dialectically to 'philosophy which *thinks* what the vulgar *believe*', i.e. to philosophy which tests the conceptual coherence of given forms of life on the basis of a critical examination of the sphere of the social itself.[52] If Bradley's formulation—'to think what the vulgar believe'—displays an unabashed intellectual elitism, British idealists with a more explicit commitment to Hegel's thought took his attention to existing forms of social life as an inspiration to develop more capacious modes of social inquiry. By way of illustration, Chapter 1 will turn to the work of the journalist and socialist Ernest Belfort Bax to show that British Hegelianism supported a broad interest in the market-mediated forms of

---

[50] Bosanquet, *Philosophical Theory*, p. 255; orig. emph.

[51] Muirhead, 'How Hegel came to England', *Mind* 36 (1927): 423–47 (pp. 426–7). The critical and aspirational direction of Bosanquet's argument indicates that his concept of 'ideal facts' departs from the descriptive gist of Emile Durkheim's 'ideal' or 'moral facts'. See Durkheim, *The Rules of Sociological Method* (New York: The Free Press, 1982), and 'The determination of moral facts', in: Sociology and Philosophy (New York: The Free Press, 1974), pp. 35–62.

[52] Bradley, *Ethical Studies* (1876), 2nd ed. (Oxford: Clarendon Press, 1927), p. 41. Bradley's book advocates a mode of Hegelian argument not so much explicitly, at the level of philosophical content, but rather implicitly, through the organization of individual chapters. The ordering of the chapters implies a stadial ascent from the level of amoral hedonism to its negation in Kantian deontology, followed by a principled turn to the thick social contexts of Hegelian *Sittlichkeit*. I discuss Bradley's thinking in some more depth in Chapter 1.

social life. Bax's work illustrates a reformist imaginary that paid painstaking attention to the surface textures of social life while also remaining wedded to a reparative diagnosis of these social forms.

British Hegelians kept a wary distance from the perceived positivism of sociology, but they were also sceptical of more radical types of critique that rejected existing social forms outright and that seemed insufficiently attentive to the historical embeddedness of human values and norms. The mode of social critique I associate with British Hegelianism accordingly assumes that any properly speculative vision of social change will need to resist siren calls for the total revolutionary obliteration of existing forms of life and their displacement with a radically new social dispensation. Moreover, to the extent that the version of immanent social critique developed by British Hegelians largely predates the dialectic's calcification into a readily deployable ('dialectical-materialist') method, it is best understood as an exploratory procedure that combines a generous phenomenological attention to existing social forms with the reparative transformation of these forms. The reformist mode that crystallized around 1900—including its articulation in the narrower discursive field of British Hegelianism—does not aim to shut down critique in a rearguard attempt to conserve the status quo but rather seeks to direct it forward, generating new opportunities for critique instead of declaring its end.

Recent conversations in literary and cultural theory have tended to identify critique so comprehensively with a spirit of negativity and cynicism that it can be difficult to see how the hermeneutic protocols associated with critique might be developed in new directions. Rita Felski has offered a particularly incisive and provocative account of certain impasses of the project of ideology critique, and her book *The Limits of Critique* has helped to galvanize a set of projects sometimes collectively referred to as 'postcritical'. Felski has herself prominently used the term *postcritique*, yet unlike some academic fellow travellers she has remained wary of the moniker because it can be misread as suggesting too simple or straightforward a break with the hermeneutics of suspicion.[53] In referencing *The Limits of Critique*, then, I do not necessarily take issue with Felski's own account of disciplinary history, but with an understanding of critique which her book has, perhaps inadvertently, helped to foster. In a passage that dissects the alleged negativity of critique, Felski begins by ventriloquizing the voice of critique's most ardent defenders:

[53] See Felski, *The Limits of Critique* (Chicago: University of Chicago Press, 2015), pp. 172–82. Writing in a related context, Felski and Elizabeth Anker have qualified the idea of a complete break with ideology critique that seems to be implied by the term *postcritical*: 'the "post-" of postcritique denotes a complex temporality: an attempt to explore fresh ways of interpreting literary and cultural texts that acknowledges, nonetheless, its inevitable dependency on the very practices it is questioning'. See Anker and Felski, 'Introduction', in Anker and Felski (eds.), *Critique and Postcritique* (Durham, NC: Duke University Press, 2017), pp. 1–28 (p. 1). Felski professes only 'qualified sympathy' for scholarship which reduces critique to a matter of 'mood' and which advocates the cultivation of 'hope, optimism, and positive affect in intellectual life' (*Limits of Critique*, p. 12).

For many scholars in the humanities, [critique] is not one good thing but the only imaginable thing. Critique, as I've noted, just is the exercise of thoughtful intelligence and independence of mind. To refuse critique, by the same token, is to sink into the mire of complacency, credulity, and conservatism. Who would want to be associated with the bad smell of the uncritical? The negativity of critique is thus transmuted into a halo effect—an aura of rigor and probity that burnishes its dissident stance with a normative glow.[54]

These sentences shuttle seamlessly between an analysis of the negativity of critique (registered in Felski's own voice) and an interrogative ('Who would want to be associated with the bad smell of the uncritical?') that wryly mimics the critic's contempt for reading practices that fall short of critique's heroically 'dissident' acts of disclosure and demystification. What is problematic here is not the research programme that Felski proposes as an alternative to the procedures of symptomatic reading but the rhetorical identification of such acts of critique with a spirit of totalized negativity. While Felski's account has important therapeutic merits, it rather severely limits our understanding of critique by projecting an extreme (and historically quite late) intellectual position back onto a longer and significantly richer genealogy of critical practices. Recent conversations about the limits of critique accordingly run the risk of eclipsing alternative historical trajectories, some of which might help us articulate different versions of critique today. Hegelian symptomatic reading forms part of this vital prehistory of current forms of critique. As I have been suggesting, the British idealists' understanding of the labour of the negative never hardens into a hermeneutic of totalized suspicion—a fact that contradicts the currently prevalent assumption that wariness of critique must necessarily lead to its wholesale renunciation. Unlike the kinds of symptomatic reading scrutinized by recent postcritiquers and surface readers, the reformist mode around 1900 engaged in a type of social diagnosis that did not too quickly abandon the level of social forms in favour of a search for more rooted truths or hidden economic causes.

The idealist inflection of the debates I have been introducing here may not seem particularly appealing to contemporary Marxist critics to whose work I am in many ways indebted. For this reason, I want to close the Introduction by indicating why we should be in no rush to dismiss the reformist literary mode by pointing to its supposedly reactionary content or its quietist politics. The works of the British Hegelians, I suggest, offer an understanding of critique whose intellectual complexity would only be matched again decades later by the protocols of immanent critique that were developed in the traditions of Western (Hegelian) Marxism and early British cultural studies. British Hegelianism, as it appears from this vantage point, operates as a vanishing mediator in the history of critical

---

[54] Felski, *Limits of Critique*, p. 8.

theory: it opens up more capacious contexts for the analysis of critique's twenti-eth- and twenty-first-century development, and it invites us to recast the narrative of critical theory's historical emergence by suspending its reflexive association with the resolute negativity of revolution in favour of its neglected affiliation with projects of socio-political reform.

If, after another hundred-odd years of reception history, the Hegelian term *Sittlichkeit* seems philosophically overdetermined (or quite simply unattractively heavy-handed) to us, the writings of the British Hegelians offer alternative ren-derings of Hegel's terminology that resonate more closely with the vocabulary of cultural analysis we are familiar with today. Bosanquet, for example, whose *Philosophical Theory of the State* (1899) provided one of the most cogent explica-tions of Hegelian political theory in late Victorian Britain, often refers to the three spheres of *Sittlichkeit* as shared 'ways of living' characteristic of a given society.[55] Bosanquet's choice of words had been anticipated by Bradley whose writings implied that Hegel's philosophy made it possible to describe 'ways of life' as distinct social totalities: 'Our way of living', Bradley noted in *Ethical Studies*, 'is an end to our minds, and not a mere means'.[56] The language here anticipates types of social analysis that were championed by key figures of British cultural studies from the late 1950s onwards: while Bosanquet's and Bradley's vocabulary ('ways of life', 'ways of living') looks ahead to Raymond Williams's programmatic state-ments about the object domain of cultural studies, the specifically Hegelian inflection of the idealists' arguments is echoed in some of Stuart Hall's founda-tional theoretical writings of the 1970s.

Take, as an example, Stuart Hall's 1973 essay about Marx's 'Introduction' to *Grundrisse*. In this long piece, first delivered as a working paper at the Birmingham Centre for Contemporary Cultural Studies, Hall defends Hegel against the likes of Louis Althusser who would expel all traces of the Hegelian dialectic from Marxist thought. Hall reconstructs in impressive philosophical and philological depth the critical adoption of Hegelian thinking in *Grundrisse*. His essay points out that in spite of Marx's well-documented opposition to Hegelian idealism, 'there are many ways in which Marx may be said to have remained a Hegelian', and nowhere more so than in his desire to preserve 'the real scientific kernel' of Hegel's dialectic.[57] What Marx found in Hegel's *Logic* and the *Philosophy of Right*, Hall argues, was neither the blueprint for a teleology of history, nor a ready-made method that could be mechanically applied to existing

---

[55] Bosanquet, *Philosophical Theory*, p. 259 and *passim*.

[56] These historically grown 'ways of life', Bradley elaborates, can be subjected to a process of immanent critique, which holds them up to their 'concrete and real' concept without appealing to extraneous 'visions of superhuman morality, to ideal societies'. Bradley, *Ethical Studies*, p. 201.

[57] Hall, 'Marx's notes on method: A "Reading" of the "1857 Introduction"', in Ann Gray et al. (eds), *CCCS Selected Working Papers*, vol. 1 (Abingdon: Routledge, 2007), pp. 83–111 (pp. 89, 109). See also Hall, 'The hinterland of science: Ideology and the "Sociology of Knowledge"', *CCCS Selected Working Papers*, vol. 1 (Abingdon: Routledge, 2007)., pp. 127–47 (esp. pp. 134–9).

social conditions—instead, Hegel taught Marx to treat the dialectic as an exploratory and experimental procedure, as 'a mode of thought that was the very opposite of static' (85). On Hall's account, Hegelianism bequeathed to Marxism an attention to the forms of social life that was missed by more orthodox forms of economic reductionism, including the vulgar Marxism of the Second International (1889–1916). While Marxist economism aimed to 'reveal the "essential relations" behind the necessary but mystifying inversions assumed by their "surface forms"' (85), the type of Hegelian critique envisioned in Marx's Introduction to *Grundrisse* 'is a critique *of a certain distinctive kind*—one which *not only* lays bare the "real relations" behind their "phenomenal forms"' (105; orig. emph.). Like the British Hegelians around 1900, Hall does not simply reject forms of economic analysis (he in fact held that such analysis was of vital political importance), but rather insists that the economic should not be treated as the solely privileged level of Marxist critique. Instead of abandoning the surface level of social forms in favour of a set of hidden 'real relations', the mode of Hegelian symptomatic reading described by Hall insists on the need for painstaking engagement with the 'phenomenal forms' of our lifeworld. Critical concepts, in this view, do not descend—as they sometimes seem to do in the writings of Althusser—from the rarefied heights of Marxist science, ready to enter into a combative relationship with ideology and false consciousness.[58] To the intense negativity of this type of theoretical production Hall opposes a form of speculative social critique that works *through* existing social forms in order to effect their gradual transformation. Wary of the total revolutionary dismantling of society, this form of inquiry derives its intellectual and political energy from a double movement of preservation and gradual transcendence, what Hall calls 'the mutual articulation of historical movement and theoretical reflection' (102). Instead of setting itself up outside or above history, the mode of theoretical production, or conceptual poesis, envisioned by Hall is rooted in the limited resources of a given situation and operates by constructing concrete concepts from within existing forms of life.[59]

If Hall's thinking of the 1970s offers conceptually sophisticated engagements with the mode of Hegelian symptomatic reading described above, Williams's work

[58] Althusser's writings offer the most prominent exposition of this revolutionary mode of theoretical production. Arguing against the Hegelian emphasis on *Aufhebung* as simultaneous preservation and transcendence, Althusser's early philosophical texts insist that 'the Hegelian dialectic is the concept of negativity, that is, negativity's cognition of itself'. See Althusser, 'On content in the thought of G. W. F. Hegel', *The Spectre of Hegel: Early Writings* (London: Verso, 2014), pp. 17–172 (p. 119).

[59] Hall's procedure recalls Antonio Gramsci's insistence that critique is 'not a question of introducing from scratch a scientific form of thought into everyone's individual life, but of renovating and making "critical" an already existing activity.' Gramsci, Quentin Hoare and Geoffrey Nowell-Smith (eds.) *Selected Prison Notebooks* (London: Lawrence and Wishart, 1971), pp. 330–1. I touch on the connection between Gramsci's Hegelianism and Britain's Hegelian moment in the next chapter. On the social embeddedness of practices of critique, see also Robert Celikates, *Critique as Social Practice: Critical Theory and Social Self-Understanding* (London: Rowan & Littlefield, 2018).

evinces a related analytic practice that programmatically allies social description to forms of speculative (reparative rather than revolutionary) critique. Williams's hermeneutic praxis has been criticized by some for 'collaps[ing] the base forward, as it were, into the superstructure', and for being too 'idealist' and 'culturalist'.[60] Of course, such assessments should not be taken as indications that Williams's ('idealist') exploration of cultural artefacts came at the expense of an attention to material processes of social reproduction. Rather, they draw our attention to the specifically materialist dimension of his 'idealism'. For example, in *The Long Revolution* (1961), Williams proposes a '"social" definition of culture, in which culture is a description of a particular way of life, which expresses certain meanings and values not only in art and learning but also in institutions and ordinary behaviour'.[61] Williams's broad understanding of culture entails a revised understanding of institutional structures that presents them not as alien impositions on the sphere of the social but as profoundly interwoven with it. As Williams admits, this newly expansive concept of culture produces as its corollary 'a perhaps unusual revolutionary activity: open discussion, extending relationships, the practical shaping of institutions' (355). To the extent that this 'revolutionary activity' begins to imagine an emergent social order by working through the institutional forms of the present, it is at odds with the Marxist view of state institutions as 'organ[s] superimposed on society' which need to be razed in the name of a radically disruptive future 'freedom'. We could indeed say that Williams's belief in the gradual transformability of hegemonic socio-cultural forms—in *Culture and Society* (1958) and *The Long Revolution*, though not in his later writings—led him to envision a temporality of revolution so elongated and 'unusual' that it no longer looked revolutionary at all but instead began to resemble the slow politics of reform.[62] In *The Long Revolution*, this comparatively slow revolutionary movement from the superstructure, what Williams dubs 'cultural revolution', finds its most significant theoretical manifestation in the concept of 'structures of feeling', Williams's term for the lived experience of a particular historical moment as a whole. As Williams explains, there is a real sense in which social change—notably the overdue levelling of the flagrant economic inequalities that characterized 1960s Britain—will be dependent on 'structures of feeling' that are hospitable to such change:

---

[60] These remarks come from two of Williams's former students. See Terry Eagleton, 'Criticism and politics: Raymond Williams', *New Left Review* I/95 (1976): 2–23 (p. 22); and Anthony Barnett, 'Raymond Williams and Marxism: A rejoinder to Terry Eagleton', *New Left Review* I/99 (1976): 47–64 (p. 60).

[61] Williams, *The Long Revolution* (London: Chatto & Windus, 1961), p. 41. Subsequent references will be given parenthetically.

[62] Williams's early resistance to the total revolutionary dismantling of existing institutional structures is one of the topics addressed in the interview section dedicated to *The Long Revolution* in *Politics and Letters: Interviews with New Left Review* (London: Verso, 2015), pp. 406–37.

It is certainly my view that the [economic] differential will have to be revised, but the only possible basis for this is a real feeling of community—the true knowledge that we are working for ourselves and for each other, which though present now as an ideal, is continually confused and in some cases cancelled by the plain fact that most of us do not own or control the means and the product of our work.   (335)

What Williams begins to sketch out for us here is a specific interdependency of structural change ('the ownership or control of the means and the product of our work') and economies of feeling ('a real feeling of community'): on the one hand, the 'real feeling of community' operates as an *entgegenkommende Lebensform* that lends substance and direction to reformist efforts (what Williams, a few pages later, calls the 'human energy of the long revolution'; 347); on the other, it is this structure of feeling which makes it possible to imagine new institutional arrangements not merely in the abstract but as a concrete way of life.[63]

I have invoked Hall's and Williams's writings only briefly in order to note the suggestive analogies that exist between their work and that of the British idealists. As these cursory remarks indicate, paying renewed attention to the reformist debates in the decades around 1900 helps us extend backwards genealogies of critique by breaking with periodizing habits that point to the interwar years of the early twentieth century as critique's single most important originating context. As Simon During and Joseph North have noted in their important recent accounts of the origins of critical theory, the versions of ideology critique that have been most influential in the academy typically trace their intellectual roots back to the writings of the Frankfurt School of the 1930s. Developing the implications of this genealogy, During contends that Marxist critique is best understood as a 'mode of intellectual resistance' that developed as a compensatory response to the failure of left-wing political revolutions in the West in the 1920s and 1930s.[64] During's and North's accounts are important because they help to explain why, from the 1930s onwards, radical energies from the political realm were increasingly cathected to

---

[63] In addition to these links, we could also think of the reformist (literary) mode's attention to the sphere of *Sittlichkeit* as involving a Williamsian attention to 'hegemonic' socio-cultural forms that combine into a fully 'realized complex of experiences, relationships, and activities' rather than constituting a lifelessly abstract institutional 'system or structure' (Williams, *Marxism and Literature* (Oxford: Oxford University Press, 1977), p. 112). The very concept of 'structures of feeling' indicates the conceptual and practical impossibility of differentiating between the material givenness of a particular historical situation ('structure') and the subjective modes ('feeling') through which that situation is experienced. The reformist (literary) mode also anticipates Williams insofar as it prompts us to take seriously the material agency of social and cultural forms by exploring their ability to figure speculative '*solution[s]*' to social contradictions. See Williams, *Marxism and Literature*, p. 103. For Williams's own appreciation of 'Left Hegelianism', see 'Literature and sociology: In memory of Lucien Goldmann', *New Left Review* I.67 (1971): 3–18 (pp. 10–11).

[64] During, *Against Democracy: Literary Experience in the Era of Emancipations* (New York: Fordham University Press, 2012), p. 39.

particular styles of social inquiry. But what if the period of the interwar years constituted an anomaly in the intellectual history of critique rather than signalling the beginning of a completely new critical paradigm? By drawing our attention to critique's affiliation with projects of reformist transition, Britain's Hegelian moment asks us to suspend the habitual short-circuiting of revolutionary praxis and radical theory. During and North are certainly correct when they observe that scholarship which engages in Marxisant critique must appear politically inert when it is measured by the punishingly (or masochistically) high standard of a fully revolutionary praxis.[65] Departing from genealogies which trace the origins of critique to the dark and hostile political environment of the later interwar years, the experimental reperiodization I have proposed here makes it possible to reframe certain modes of theoretical production after 1945 not in terms of their failure to live up to a new revolutionary paradigm but as the resumption of an older reformist one—as the reinvigoration of a speculative *élan* that was temporarily eclipsed by the urgent and necessary revolutionary projects of the 1920s and 1930s.

Speculative States: Chapter Organization

British Literature and the Life of Institutions is a work of intellectual and political history but most of all it is a literary history that identifies literature as a crucial site for theorizations of the state. The attention which the Introduction and Chapter 1 bring to Britain's Hegelian moment also helps to delimit the book's chronological span: my study is framed, on the one hand, by the publication of key works of British idealist philosophy in the 1870s and 1880s and, on the other, by the outbreak of World War I, which was widely seen to confirm the association of Hegelianism with the violent excesses of (Prussian) nationalism and militarism. These developments had literary repercussions as well: while the emergence of British idealism in the 1870s and 1880s provoked immediate literary responses (sympathetic as well as critical) by authors such as Mary Ward and George Gissing, World War I put an end to the reformist literary mode I outline here, giving rise to a new artistic concern with the bureaucratic mechanisms that turn the state into a mechanism of control and oppression. Continuing on from the broader arguments advanced in the 'Introduction' and Chapter 1, subsequent chapters—particularly my readings of Carpenter, Wells, and Forster—will

---

[65] North's important revisionist account charts literary criticism's post-1945 shift away from 'an early period between the wars, in which the possibility of something like a break with liberalism, and a genuine move to radicalism, is mooted'. According to North, what came to replace these earlier radical critical practices after World War II was a 'historicist paradigm' that privileged contextualist description at the expense of activist intervention. See North, *Literary Criticism: A Concise Political History* (Cambridge, MA: Harvard University Press, 2017), p. 17.

sometimes delve quite deeply into the detail of the reformist debates explored here. If some of this detail seems overly technical, the level of attention is necessary because it reflects the reformist mode's intense attention to the situational pressures and possibilities of individual historical moments.

Chapter 1 turns to the Hegelian moment of British state theory between 1870–1914. This chapter can be read in part as a supplement to the Introduction: it spells out some points touched on only briefly here by showing that the distinctly British version of Hegelian state theory converges on an understanding of the state as an aspect of ethical and social life (*Sittlichkeit*). I argue that this innovative and ambitious concept of the state made it possible to think about the state's institutional structures as a distinct moment in the actualization of social life rather than a utilitarian assemblage of administrative means external to it. My reconstruction of British state theory's Hegelian moment identifies a reformist idiom in which the idea of the state appears as an aspirational figure that makes it possible to imagine the transition from capitalist society (Hegel's *bürgerliche Gesellschaft*) towards a new and more egalitarian socio-political order. This transformation is imagined through close engagement with existing social forms rather than through a complete break with (or total revolutionary overhaul of) existing social arrangements. Crucially, instead of subordinating individual needs and desires to the absolute logic of the state, British Hegelians incorporate central insights of Victorian liberalism when they insist that a continued critique of socio-political forms is necessary so that non-hegemonic subjectivities can find expression in the social sphere. In the works of these Hegelian thinkers, the state does not exert an iron control but rather helps to create spaces in which the articulation of new forms of life becomes possible in the first place. The chapter acts as an exploratory preamble to later chapters, and it ends by homing in on the fraught afterlives of Britain's Hegelian moment after 1914, including the emergence of a self-consciously 'revolutionary' literary modernism.

The second chapter begins my exploration of the reformist literary mode by offering readings of two novels—George Gissing's *Thyrza* (1887) and Mary (Mrs Humphry) Ward's *Robert Elsmere* (1888)—in the context of the settlement movement of the 1880s. The chapter turns to the idealism of Green, which provided one of the most philosophically advanced articulations of statist and welfarist thinking in this period. The interventionist state, Green insisted, could serve the common good by creating institutions that were not merely mechanical supplements to social life but that enabled citizens to conduct lives which were otherwise impossible under the market-mediated conditions of civil society. Gissing's and Ward's texts both feature characters who are demonstrably modelled on Green (or who echo modes of Greenian thinking), even as they respond differently to Green's optimistic account of institutionality. Gissing's novels of the 1880s, I argue, can be read as attempts to work through the central impasse of idealist thought—the seemingly insurmountable dualism between reality and ideal—to which the

British Hegelians, too, were trying to offer new responses. In doing so, Gissing's *Thyrza* casts radical doubt on the idea that institutions can create social harmony from above, and this scepticism continues to haunt later engagements with state action in works by Carpenter, Wells, and Forster. By contrast, Ward tries to meet such scepticism halfway, by suggesting that the success of Robert Elsmere's ambitious reformist schemes—the establishment of new educational institutions in London's East End—will depend on their ability to incorporate dissenting social voices into new and non-hegemonic forms of life. To put this another way: in *Robert Elsmere*, critique—especially when it is voiced by members of the working class who are the intended beneficiaries of Robert's settlement—energizes a more capacious understanding of institutionality.

The third chapter focusses on the work of Edward Carpenter, the socialist poet, cultural critic, and early queer activist. Carpenter is often described as an anarchist who resisted all forms of state interference. However, as I show, Carpenter's form of ethical socialism tried to keep open a middle ground for people who could accept some role for the state while regarding full centralization askance. In the 1880s and 1890s Carpenter's thinking about the scope of state-action crystallized around questions of land reform. Key to Carpenter's social and aesthetic reformist vision, I argue, is the attempt to re-signify the language of capitalist society by advocating an ethos of proprietary care and concern (what Carpenter calls 'true ownership')—this form of custodial attention is supported by the state, but it cannot be reduced to purely legal entitlements. The chapter explores Carpenter's literary oeuvre of the period, ranging from his first collection *Narcissus, and Other Poems* (1873) to his poetic magnum opus, *Towards Democracy* (1883–1902), and it places this poetry in dialogue with Carpenter's social criticism, tracing his engagement with the works of land reformers such as Henry George and Alfred Russel Wallace. Building on George's and Wallace's ideas and influenced by his own experience of rural living in Derbyshire, Carpenter developed a reformist vision that fused his interest in the institutional means of land reform (the nationalization of land and subsequent creation of small-scale tenancies) with a concern for its ethical ends (the emergence of new ways of life). Carpenter's version of the reformist literary mode, I suggest, marks his aspiration to turn poetry into the very ground where a shared social ambition for thoroughgoing, albeit non-revolutionary, change can take root.

The deep embedding of reformist politics in the medium of poetic form, which Chapter 3 describes with a view to Carpenter, is a central feature of the reformist literary mode. Chapter 4 considers how this imbrication of literary and political forms—and the speculative association of the state with a new form of social life (or *Sittlichkeit*)—plays out in the writings of another turn-of-the-century socialist, H. G. Wells. The chapter begins by reconstructing the fractious political environment in which the then-Fabian Wells began to articulate his version of the reformist mode. I counterpoint the vision of class strife that haunts Wells's scientific romances from the 1890s with the gradualist reformist impulse that came to the fore in tax debates in the early 1900s. The development of more nuanced forms of graduated taxation in the Edwardian period turned the tax system into a means of social integration, leading to the emergence of a new institutional idiom that can help us understand the puzzling generic hybridity of Wells's works of this period. For example, *The Food of the Gods* occupies a transitional position in Wells's oeuvre insofar as it can be read as his first extended literary response to ongoing debates about the role of redistributive taxation: 'our whole story is one of dissemination', the novel announces with a view to the slow diffusion and trickle-down spread of the miraculous growth substance Herakleophorbia IV. The bulk of the chapter, however, focusses on Wells's Edwardian trilogy (*Anticipations*, 1901; *Mankind in the Making*, 1903; *A Modern Utopia*, 1905): these books, I suggest, responded to a new understanding of national wealth in terms of kinetic, redistributable 'incomes' rather than in terms of fixed forms of private 'wealth'. The Edwardian shift in the language of tax reform reflected a new understanding of the common good—and of individual economic entitlements—by defining individual property in terms of dynamic and composite incomes: while wealth was generally taken to signify a fixed amount of capital that was embodied in stable values such as land and that could be handed down from generation to generation, thinking about capital in terms of income suggested the essential fluidity of *all* property. The chapter turns to Wells's friend, the economist Leo Chiozza Money, as a key proponent of this revised view of property. As I show, the new ethos of public ownership and wealth-sharing that animates this recasting of the idea of private wealth becomes central to the formal organization of Wells's professedly utopian texts (such as *A Modern Utopia*) as well as of his ostensibly realist ones (such as *Kipps*, 1905; and *The New Machiavelli*, 1911).

The case of E. M. Forster demonstrates that the reformist literary mode was capacious enough to accommodate liberal authors who kept their distance from more emphatically statist arguments. Chapter 5 shows that several of Forster's Edwardian works—including 'The Machine Stops' (1909), *Howards End* (1910), and the novel fragment *Arctic Summer* (c. 1911–12)—respond to the heated reformist debates that surrounded the passing of the National Insurance Act in 1911. 'The Machine Stops', I argue, presents the growth of institutional structures as a rigid imposition on (and negation of) the organic spontaneity of human life, and the various rules to which the citizens of Forster's dystopian society are expected to conform appear to double as a parody of Prussian-style welfare policies. The dystopian and satirical edge that characterizes 'The Machine Stops' is significantly softened in Forster's slightly later fiction. A central portion of the chapter explores Forster's most complex, and most troublingly ambivalent, treatment of insurance in *Howards End*. What Forster calls 'preparedness'—the attempt to protect the most vulnerable members of society against the risk of unemployment—is central to the generic instabilities of *Howards End* as Forster confronts the economically secure life of the Schlegels with that of Leonard Bast, the insurance clerk who is teetering on the brink of unemployment. *Howards End* invokes two distinct genre categories—tragedy and romance—in order to think about the possibility and desirability of insurance reform. As I show, both of these categories undergo a process of conceptual revision that coalesces around Leonard's story: this process can be described as reformist insofar as it begins to imagine a democratization of access to the self-determined *Lebensformen* signified by the term 'romance'. These reformist hopes are echoed in Forster's novel fragment *Arctic Summer*. This text tries to formulate a satiric response to the emerging welfare state, yet, like any successful parody, it also involves a committed and sustained effort to enter into the progressive idiom it wants to satirize.

The Coda offers a necessarily abbreviated account of the afterlife of the reformist literary mode around the mid-twentieth century. Starting out from an examination of the (seemingly democratic) aesthetic we encounter in the high modernist works of Virginia Woolf and the critique of this aesthetic by proletarian modernists of the 1930s, the Coda highlights one last moment of speculative reformism, namely the establishment of the Arts Council of Great Britain in 1946. As Raymond Williams recognized, the reformist vision associated with the Arts Council involved a self-reflexive artistic turn that presented literary writing itself as the embodiment of a democratic *Lebensform* and as the image of a more egalitarian future. This reformist vision involved attempts to democratize the experimental ('modernist') artistic vision that had originated in part among the members of the Bloomsbury group—the clique Williams famously criticized as 'a fraction of the upper class'.[66] The debates which surrounded the issue of state sponsorship of the arts from the mid-1940s onwards touch on some of the constitutive features of the reformist literary mode described in this book: the democratization of opportunities for individual flourishing; the lingering risk of statal authoritarianism; and the speculative elaboration—in the medium of art—of a shared orientation towards the common good (what Green had called 'active citizenship' and what John Maynard Keynes, the Arts Council's first Chairman, described as the intertwined roles of public servant and autonomous artistic creator).

As I indicated earlier, each of the literary-historical chapters of this study could be read in relation to a broadly defined term that designates a set of social *Lebensformen*. However, I wish to offer these terms—'hoping' (Chapter 2), 'owning' (Chapter 3), 'sharing' (Chapter 4), and 'caring' (Chapter 5)—as purely provisional labels which can help us articulate the ethico-aesthetic imaginary that lent experiential concreteness to the technical and economic abstractions of

---

[66] Williams, 'The Bloomsbury Fraction', in *Culture and Materialism: Selected Essays* (London: Verso, 2005), pp. 148–69 (p. 150).

state-centred reform in the decades around 1900. Ranging from the East End reformers of the 1880s to debates about land nationalization, redistributive taxation, and national insurance in subsequent decades, the literary works explored here offer up intellectually and artistically rich engagements with the ethical texture and substance of 'the state'. In doing so, these texts do not seek to legitimize the social status quo but rather aim to defend a belief in society's fundamental democratic reformability: in doing so, the works by Ward, Gissing, Carpenter, Wells, and Forster equip us with a fresh political language of reform, and they also go some way towards providing us with the expanded political imagination we so desperately need today.

1

Literature as Speculative Thought

Britain's Long Hegelian Moment, *c.*1900

The works of the British idealists, much like the literary texts explored in subsequent chapters, present us with an understanding of institutions that is not reducible to the administrative logic of governmental rationality. As I have begun to indicate, the vocabulary that is currently available to literary scholars and cultural historians makes it difficult to formulate more ambitious concepts of institutionality, and the present chapter continues the work of the Introduction by developing in greater conceptual and intellectual-historical detail the idea of the state that I associate with reformist debates around 1900. The question of institutionality, as it takes shape in the works of the British idealists, is centred around the intertwined themes of active citizenship, positive freedom, and a broadened understanding of the social. The first two sections of this chapter approach these questions by reconstructing relevant debates in late Victorian political theory and by homing in on the understanding of the state as a form of life that emerged in the context of these debates. Central to these conversations is the fresh attention which some British idealists brought to the sphere of the social (to Hegel's *Sittlichkeit*). By presenting state institutions as an aspect of—rather than an alien imposition on—society, the British Hegelians illustrate the kinds of philosophical argument that energized the reformist imagination in the decades around 1900. The work of the philosopher T. H. Green can serve as a useful entry point into these discussions: it sheds light on the momentous conjunction of philosophical argument and practical reform proposals in this period, but it can also help us understand how philosophical thought informed literary production.

While some of my reconstructive work in the first two sections is necessarily technical, the rest of the chapter will begin to connect these philosophical debates more programmatically to the literature and journalism of the period. It is here that I will revisit the two modes of exploratory social analysis identified in the Introduction: these are, first, a form of critical social symptomology, and second, a speculative impulse that made it possible to imagine new institutional arrangements, not merely in the abstract, as detached assemblages of legal and administrative structures, but as a concrete and lived social reality. Britain's long Hegelian moment, I argue, prompts us to understand literary engagements with the state, not in terms of realist mimesis—not, that is, in terms of the true-to-life or satirically inflected representation of actually existing institutions—or in terms

British Literature and the Life of Institutions: Speculative States. Benjamin Kohlmann, Oxford University Press.
© Benjamin Kohlmann 2021. DOI: 10.1093/oso/9780198836179.003.0002

of a radically future-directed utopianism: instead, it requires us to grasp literature as a mode of speculative thought that imagines the advent of new institutions as a distinct moment in the actualization of the social.[1] The chapter concludes by briefly considering the afterlives of Britain's long Hegelian moment—its position as a vanishing mediator in the emergence of Western Marxism and its place in the rise of a self-consciously revolutionary brand of artistic modernism.

Reimagining Hegel's Political Theory in Late Victorian Britain

My turn to Hegel takes its cue from a simple historical observation. In the decades around 1900 Britain saw a spike in publications—philosophical studies as well as popular journalism—that drew on Hegelian political thought in order to develop a new and distinctive version of British state theory. Taken together, these works— and the advocacy of institutional reform which they helped to foster—constitute Britain's Hegelian moment, whose core period lasted from roughly 1870 to the beginning of World War I. During these decades, Hegelian thinking about institutions fuelled debates about state-centred reform in Britain, but it also helped to clarify the desirable scope of such reform. Working through some of these philosophical positions can help us conceptualize literature's role vis-à-vis the new welfarist structures that emerged around 1900.[2] Late nineteenth-century Hegelianism offers a vantage point from which literature's speculative idiom, what I call the period's reformist literary mode, becomes visible again.

If Hegel's influence on reformist thinking around 1900 has become nearly invisible to literary and cultural scholars, this has much to do with the fact that Hegel's work—from the absolute idealism of *The Phenomenology of Spirit* (1807) to the political theory of the *Philosophy of Right* (1820)—has since fallen under the shadow of an ideologically driven misreading of Hegelian Marxism, deployed by liberal Cold War anti-communists, 'in which a direct line' is held to run 'from Absolute Spirit to Stalin's Gulag'.[3] Whereas this reductive reading of Hegel insists

---

[1] As I discuss later in this chapter, my rendering of *Sittlichkeit* as 'the social', rather than as 'ethical order', or 'ethical substance' reflects the use of the word by many British Hegelians. I largely avoid the term 'ethical' because it suggests a particular intellectual indebtedness to Greek (especially Aristotelian) traditions that were being upheld by the Oxbridge 'Greats' (*literae humaniores*). On this point, see also Collini, 'Sociology and idealism in Britain, 1880–1920', *Archives Européennes de sociologie* 19 (1978): 3–50: 9–10; and Charles Taylor, *Hegel and Modern Society* (Cambridge: Cambridge University Press, 2015), pp. 82–92.

[2] The main focus of this chapter is the broader question of institutionality, but my discussion also looks ahead to the more specific state-welfarist measures discussed in later chapters. As Shlomo Avineri has pointed out, in what is arguably still the best book-length exposition of Hegel's state theory, 'Hegel [was] one of the first to propose something which has, despite all the differences in terminology, many of the characteristics of the modern welfare state.' See *Hegel's Theory of the Modern State* (Cambridge: Cambridge University Press, 1972), p. 101.

[3] This is Fredric Jameson's memorable paraphrase of the anti-Hegelian position. See *The Political Unconscious: Narrative as a Socially Symbolic Act* (Ithaca, NY: Cornell University Press, 1981), p. 51.

on the inherent totalitarianism of his thought, the Hegelianism that found expression in British state theory around 1900 does not advocate an absolute state which controls the lives of individuals. The particular circumstances of Hegel's reception in Britain in the 1880s and 1890s meant that the ideas of the *Philosophy of Right* could be adapted quite freely and pragmatically by writers who occupied different positions on the political spectrum. Socialists, for example, were able to draw on Hegel's philosophy to plug the gap that was created by the relative dearth of translations of Karl Marx's own writings and by the concomitant lack of an advanced Marxist theory of the state.[4] Analogously, for liberals, Hegelian political theory made it possible to introduce arguments for state intervention into a theoretical framework that remained firmly centred on the premise of individual freedom.

Moving British Hegelianism centre-stage usefully defamiliarizes the reified categories of intellectual history (such as 'Hegelian Marxism') that force Hegelianism into the role of a supporting actor, granting it mere cameo appearances in the onward march of the twentieth century's ideological grand narratives. Such accounts ignore the fact that Hegelianism attracted a wide range of ideological positions to itself, and that it managed to transform these positions in its turn. It is tempting to reverse the customary emphasis by introducing competing labels such as 'Marxist Hegelianism' or 'liberal Hegelianism'. Yet, while these alternative labels highlight the various political inflections which Hegelianism underwent around 1900, I doubt that they would succeed in identifying the specifically Hegelian content of the debates investigated here. In what follows, then, I seek to demonstrate the relevance of Hegelianism to late Victorian and Edwardian arguments about the state by emphasizing its status as a mode of politico-philosophical argument in its own right. British Hegelianism, I suggest, was less a fixed body of ideas about individual freedom, society, and the state, than a speculative way of connecting these three terms.

The mid-Victorian reception of Hegel had failed to spread beyond a small circle of cognoscenti that included professional philosophers and enthusiastic amateurs (such as the formidable Glaswegian physician-turned-idealist James Hutchison Stirling). This early reception history had centred in large part on Hegel's forbidding *Science of Logic* (1812–16), and it is perhaps unsurprising that the study of Hegel at this time remained limited to one or two university towns. While notable efforts were made to introduce Hegel's thought to a slightly larger anglophone audience (e.g. Stirling's two-volume *Secret of Hegel*, from 1865), and to elucidate his metaphysics (e.g. William Wallace's 1873 translation of the opening sections of Hegel's *Encyclopaedia*), these isolated attempts had failed to

---

[4] Mark Bevir, *The Making of British Socialism* (Princeton: Princeton University Press, 2011), p. 64; and Norberto Bobbio, 'Is there a Marxist doctrine of the state?', in Bobbio, *Which Socialism? Marxism, Socialism, and Democracy* (Cambridge: Polity Press, 1986), pp. 47–64.

capture the imagination of writers and intellectuals ('Conversancy with Hegel tends to deprave one's intellect', John Stuart Mill concluded apropos of Stirling's book[5]). It was only from the 1880s onwards that Hegel's thinking began to receive more attention. This time, however, it was not the arcana of Hegel's logic but his political philosophy which attracted the curiosity of a growing readership. Attention to Hegel's as-yet untranslated *Philosophy of Right* was raised in part through the teachings and writings of the Oxford philosopher Thomas Hill Green. Green did not publish much during his brief lifetime (he died in 1882 at the age of forty-six), and many of his most important philosophical works—including *Prolegomena to Ethics* (1883) and 'Lectures on the Principles of Political Obligation' (1883)—were only printed posthumously. However, Green's influence had begun to spread widely from the 1870s onwards, during his tenure as Fellow and Whyte's Professor of Moral Philosophy at Balliol College, Oxford. Green had acted as mentor to numerous students and colleagues, and his teachings had reached a wider public audience through his popular lay sermons and his vast network of personal contacts. Among the individuals who would later claim that Green's work had exerted a significant influence on them were prominent politicians, civil servants, and government officials, including the prime ministers Herbert Asquith and Henry Campbell Bannerman as well as William Beveridge (one of the founding figures of the British welfare state after 1945).

By the early 1870s, Green had translated much of Hegel's *Philosophische Propädeutik* (1808–11), an extensive compilation of lecture notes that prefigured Hegel's mature theory of the state. 'There can be little doubt,' the political theorist Ben Wempe concludes, 'that Green, who had been so taken with Hegel in his earlier years, was also acquainted with Hegel's main works.'[6] Green's unpublished manuscript formed part of a continued translation effort that had been started by his colleague Benjamin Jowett and that would be continued by William Wallace, Green's successor in the Whyte's Chair of Moral Philosophy. Green also used the *Propädeutik* as a textbook in his teaching at Balliol in the 1860s, and it seems that the process of translating and lecturing on Hegel's text served as a sort of preparatory exercise that assisted him in formulating the central questions—about the status of individual freedom in relation to the state and about the possibilities for self-realization afforded by institutional reform—that would guide his subsequent thinking.

---

[5] Mill, Letter to Alexander Bain, 4 November 1867, in *The Later Letters of John Stuart Mill, 1849–1873*, ed. Francis Mineka and Dwight Lindley (Toronto: University of Toronto Press, 1972), p. 1324.

[6] Wempe, *T. H. Green's Theory of Positive Freedom: From Metaphysics to Political Theory* (British Idealist Studies, vol. 3) (Exeter: Imprint Academic, 2004), p. 24. Wempe's analysis suggests that these translations date from the second half of the 1860s. For Green's early interest in Hegel, see also Muirhead, 'How Hegel came to England', *Mind* 36 (1927): 423–47.

Literary scholars may feel some instinctive discomfort when faced with the British idealists' strong arguments in favour of state-centred reform. This unease derives in part from Hegel's more programmatic proclamations about the nature of the state in the *Philosophy of Right*. Hegel's assertions can appear in equal degrees perplexing and provocative: 'The state, which is the realized substantive will, having its reality in the particular self-consciousness raised to the plane of the universal, is absolutely rational.'[7] Importantly, the universal aspect of the state's 'rationality' (*das an und für sich Vernünftige*) does not imply that the state has an 'absolute', or coercively absolut*ist*, claim over its citizens. Instead, Hegel's reference to the state's rationality announces something like an immanent criterion that makes it possible to evaluate the degree to which given institutional structures correspond to the philosophical concept (*Begriff*) of the state. Approaching the state as the realization of an idea, Hegel indicates, lays it open to rational inquest and progressive transformation. Accordingly, 'the state is absolutely rational' is not a propositional statement but a critical and speculative one. As Gillian Rose explains in her defence of Hegel's most infamous pronouncement in the Preface to the *Philosophy of Right*, the claim that 'the rational is the real' must not be understood as the statement of an actually existing state of affairs. Instead, she points out, we need to learn to 'read this proposition "speculatively"' again—as the affirmation of 'a lack of identity between subject and predicate', as 'a result to be achieved'.[8] It is important to remember, then, that far from decreeing an unchangeable standard, British Hegelianism lent support to an aspirational political momentum that was deeply invested in the critique of existing institutional arrangements. Indeed, Rose's remarks suggest that the progressivist impulse that flows from Hegel's appeal to the state's 'rationality' might also perform an important function in today's political environment because it counters the obsession with economic and output-oriented metrics, what we could call neoliberalism's fetish of rationality-as-efficiency.

To the extent that speculation carries a critical charge, it also resists the reification of one particular set of (social, racial, sexual) identities into a universal standard to be imposed on all citizens. Even thinkers who are otherwise critical of Hegel's theory of the state, such as Herbert Marcuse and Domenico Losurdo, have observed that the central criterion for the state's rationality is its ability to protect personal freedoms and to create spaces for citizens' (individual or collective) self-actualization. 'The tendencies in Green to reify the universal as against the individual', Marcuse observes, 'are counteracted by his adherence to the progressive tendencies of Western rationalism': Green 'insists throughout his work that

---

[7] Hegel, *Grundlinien der Philosophie des Rechts* (Frankfurt/Main: Suhrkamp, 1986), p. 399 (§ 258). Henceforth abbreviated *PhdR*. English translations are adapted with some local changes from H. B. Nisbet's translation *Elements of the Philosophy of Right*, ed. Allen Wood (Cambridge: Cambridge University Press, 2003).

[8] Rose, *Hegel Contra Sociology* (London: Verso, 2009), p. 52.

the state be submitted to rational standards, such as imply that the common good is best served through advancing the interest of free individuals'.[9] While the use of the term 'interest' here suggests a narrowly utilitarian understanding of what Green called 'self-realization', Marcuse is certainly right when he notes that the thinkers associated with Britain's Hegelian moment are particularly concerned with institutional conditions that safeguard freedom and enable individuals and communities to flourish. The literary works that I consider in later chapters reflect this central concern with freedom from state coercion by figuring institutional reform in terms of a shared ethos of mutual responsibility and care for the common good.

Green's writings, including his translations of Hegel, shed helpful light on the British idealists' rich view of personal freedom and the individual's position in relation to the state. Green's translation of the *Propädeutik*'s section on the 'Philosophy of Right' begins with a description of freedom in terms of purely legal protections: 'Right consists in the fact, that every individual is respected and treated by every other as a free Essence.'[10] Hegel notes that while legal rights enshrine the inviolability of individual life, this understanding of rights remains essentially negative (because it only emphasizes freedom from interference) as well as purely abstract and external (insofar as it fails to reflect the fact that formal rights are in their turn socially grounded). In the context of Green's own thinking about the nature of citizenship, Hegel's double movement—the simultaneous description and critique of legal rights—proved significant for two reasons. On the one hand, it helped to convince Green of the importance of individual freedom vis-à-vis a potentially overweening sovereign state ('The modern idea of "sovereign"', Green had warned elsewhere, 'is that of supreme might, recognized as having right').[11] On the other, it helped him to see the conceptual and practical reduction of freedom to legal rights as a problem that needed to be explored: the notion of negative rights, as Green came to see it, offered an impoverished understanding of the relationship between citizen and state.

Hegel's *Propädeutik* spoke to Green in part because it took aim at a distinctly British tradition of classical liberalism. Hegel's targets in the *Propädeutik* include John Locke's canonical defence of individual freedom in *Treatises of Government* (1689), which had proposed a property-based understanding of individual autonomy. Against Locke, Hegel points out that the attempt to pass off property as the quasi-metaphysical basis of legal rights is skewed because it misses the

---

[9] Marcuse, *Reason and Revolution: Hegel and the Rise of Social Theory* (London: Routledge, 1942), pp. 391–2. Domenico Losurdo defends Hegel against the charges of absolutism and quietism that were brought against the *Philosophy of Right* from Rudolf Haym's *Hegel* (1857) onwards: see Losurdo, *Hegel and the Freedom of Moderns* (Durham, NC: Duke University Press, 2004), esp. pp. 23–31.

[10] THG, Ms Analysis of Hegel and translation of §§ 1–163 of Hegel's *Philosophische Propädeutik*, 2b.06 (here: § 3).

[11] THG, Ms *Notes on Political Philosophy*, 2a.19.

fundamentally social nature of property as well as the acts of originary violence (*Besitznahme*) that ground it. Like the later *Philosophy of Right*, the *Propädeutik* introduces a conceptual distinction in order to flag the moment of social convention that turns *Besitz* (the private appropriation of goods formerly held in common) into *Eigentum* (the codification of *Besitz* through law): 'Possession [*Besitz*] becomes property [*Eigentum*], in other words rightful, in so far as it is acknowledged by everyone else that the thing which I have appropriated is mine, in the same way as I acknowledge the possession of others to be theirs.'[12] Property, this suggests, is not the natural basis of personal rights but a historical feature particular to modern societies.[13] Green's own ideas about state-centred reform were shaped in part by the recognition that private property was a social phenomenon grounded in prior acts of dispossession (such as the enclosure of common lands). It followed, in Green's mind, that the reformist restructuring of current patterns of property ownership was necessary because expanding opportunities for property ownership was a way of giving more people a stake in the common good. In pursuing this aim, Green did not demand the abolition of private property as such: on the contrary, he believed that a more democratic distribution of property would help to nourish new forms of active and engaged citizenship.[14]

There are good reasons to be sceptical of Green's defence of private property, but it is also important to recognize that his reformist vision did not involve a simple affirmation of existing patterns of private ownership and wealth distribution. Indeed, Green's advocacy of active citizenship—what he called 'freedom in the positive sense'[15]—was rooted in a deep-seated abhorrence of the social fragmentation wrought by capitalist property relations.[16] It was this aspect of Green's progressive liberalism that made it so appealing to reformers who were leaning towards socialism. One of these thinkers, Green's former student David George Ritchie, concluded that Green and Hegel had 'begun to free political theory and

---

[12] THG, Ms [...] Translation of [...] Hegel's *Philosophische Propädeutik*, 2b.06 [here: § 11].

[13] This, broadly, is also the gist of Rose's reading of the relevant sections in the *Philosophy of Right*: 'Hegel is stressing, in opposition to liberal natural law, that the institutions which appear most "natural" and "immediate" in any society, such as the family or the sphere of needs, presupposed an overall economic and political organization which may not be immediately intelligible.' See *Hegel Contra Sociology*, p. 50.

[14] For discussion of these points, see David Brink, *Perfectionism and the Common Good: Themes in the Philosophy of T. H. Green* (Oxford: Clarendon Press, 2007), pp. 61–3.

[15] Studies of Green's notion of positive liberty are legion. For important interventions that double as helpful historical surveys, see Avital Simhony, 'Beyond negative and positive Freedom: T. H. Green's view of freedom', *Political Theory* 21.1 (1993): 28–54: 29); Wempe, *Green's Theory of Positive Freedom*; and Colin Tyler, *The Metaphysics of Self-Realisation and Freedom* (Exeter: Imprint, 2010).

[16] Green's thinking thus entailed a critique of what Ellen Meiskins Wood has called the 'historical priority of negative liberty' in the Anglo-American democratic tradition, i.e. the damaging 'detachment of the individual (not to mention individual property) from customary [...] identities and obligations'. Meiksins Wood, *Democracy Against Capitalism: Renewing Historical Materialism* (Cambridge: Cambridge University Press, 1995), p. 208.

practice from the narrowness and false abstractions of the individualist philosophers of the seventeenth and eighteenth centuries.'[17] Hegel's and Green's speculative statements about the nature of the state mattered to radical reformers like Ritchie because they cast into sharp relief the limitations of a purely negative understanding of freedom: the 'content and aim' of the state, Hegel had observed in the *Propädeutik*, 'is the realization of the natural i.e. absolute rights of the citizens, which they do not renounce (by their position) in the state, but rather by it alone attain the full enjoyment and perfection of them.'[18] This argument does not return us to the nostalgic vision of an unfractured organic community. On the contrary, as the Hegel scholar Todd McGowan has recently remarked, it is only

> through the encounter with the state [that] the subject recognizes the logical priority of its public being. The state provides the form through which the subject sees that it is a public being before it is a private one. Hegel doesn't value the state for the mutual protection that it offers subjects—to his mind, this is an impoverished view of the state—but for the constitutive role that it plays in subjectivity. Without the state, the subject cannot recognize its freedom because it cannot recognize its dependence on the public.[19]

Green's arguments in favour of the democratically expandable stakes in the common good—along with his expectation that such an expansion would support an ethos of active citizenship—lent fresh intellectual force to progressive reformist thinking around 1900. Reformist endeavours that were invigorated by this mode of argument included several of the causes explored in this book, such as the nationalization of land (Chapter 3), the redistribution of wealth (Chapter 4), and the collectivization of risk (Chapter 5).

It is difficult to overestimate the impact which Green's lectures and published works had on the generation of young reform-minded intellectuals who came under his influence as either students or readers. Recent work in the history of political economy and the history of political ideas has charted the pervasive influence which Green's advocacy of active citizenship and progressive social reform exerted on a younger generation of reformers.[20] Around 1900, the crop of publications—by Green's students and others—that addressed Hegelian political theory included books by Edward Caird (*Hegel*, 1883), Ritchie (*The Principles*

---

[17] Ritchie, *The Principles of State Interference* (London: Swan Sonnenschein, 1891), p. 156.

[18] THG, Ms [...] Translation of [...] Hegel's *Philosophische Propädeutik*, 2b.06 (here: § 29).

[19] Todd McGowan, *Emancipation After Hegel: Achieving a Contradictory Revolution* (New York: Columbia University Press, 2019), p. 5.

[20] See Roger Backhouse and Tamotsu Nishizawa, 'Introduction: Towards a reinterpretation of welfare economics', in *No Wealth but Life: Welfare Economics and the Welfare State in Britain, 1880-1945*, eds. Backhouse/Nishizawa (Cambridge: Cambridge University Press, 2010), pp. 1–24. Also: W. J. Mander, *British Idealism: A History* (Oxford: Oxford University Press, 2011), esp. pp. 268–74.

of State Interference, 1891), Wallace (*Hegel's Philosophy of Mind*, 1894; *Lectures and Essays on Natural Theology and Ethics*, 1898), and Bernard Bosanquet (*The Philosophical Theory of the State*, 1899), as well as the journalistic popularization of idealist philosophy by the socialist Ernest Belfort Bax. Since knowledge of Hegel's *Science of Logic* had failed to enter wider circulation in the mid-Victorian period, the version of his political theory that found a broader reader-ship in the last three decades of the nineteenth century was generally unencum-bered by the technical vocabulary of Hegel's metaphysics.[21] This meant that Hegel's theory of the state could speak more immediately to present concerns, and many contemporary commentators pointed out that Hegel's thinking made it possible to synthesize seemingly contradictory views of the state. For example, William Wallace, the Scottish philosopher who did much to promote Hegel's philosophy in Britain during his tenure at Oxford, observed that Hegelian think-ing resisted 'partisan' appropriations precisely because it managed to articulate extreme positions into a single speculative theory of the state: on the one hand, Wallace recalled, Hegel was 'the true parent of Marx' and of the Left Hegelians, so that *fin-de-siècle* socialists could with some justification claim him as a forbear in their attack on liberal state institutions; on the other, Wallace reminded his readers that the *Philosophy of Right* had been successfully invoked around the mid-century by Right Hegelians who sought to defend Prussia's constitutional order.[22]

For the British idealists, updating Hegel for their own reformist moment involved the attempt to heal the ideological rift that had characterized Hegel's nineteenth-century reception history in Continental Europe. In doing so, British Hegelians anticipate the central concerns of the most important continental study of Hegel written around 1900, Franz Rosenzweig's *Hegel und der Staat* (1920). Like Wallace several decades before him, Rosenzweig traced the division of Hegelianism to the political struggle between Prussian Liberals and the radical 'friends of the people' (*Bürgerfreunde*) in the 1820s and 1830s: while the former had appealed to Hegel's description of civil servants as the 'universal estate' in order to bolster demands for stronger state institutions, the *Bürgerfreunde* had

---

[21] Even so, as I will point out, British Hegelians clearly recognized the central significance of the dialectical method and its bearing on Hegel's analysis of the state as a sphere of social (*sittlich*) life. For example, Bax's beginner's compendium *Handbook to the History of Philosophy* from 1886 affirmed the central place which the dialectical method occupied in modern philosophy: 'In the word Dialectic we have the key to the whole Hegelian system. The method of Hegel is the dialectical method, and to have discovered the full significance of this method, to have struck upon the innermost dynamic principle of the world, gives to Hegel a pre-eminence in a sense above all other thinkers. See *Handbook to the History of Philosophy* (London: George Bell, 1886), p. 313. Bax specifically emphasized that Hegel's use of the dialectic in the *Philosophy of Right* had allowed him to overcome the one-sided abstractions of Fichtean natural law and Kantian moral law.

[22] Wallace, 'Relations of Fichte and Hegel to socialism', in *Lectures and Essays on Natural Theology and Ethics* (Oxford: Clarendon Press, 1898), pp. 427–47 (p. 427).

called for the revolutionary overthrow of the (Prussian) state.[23] In Rosenzweig's account, this bifurcated view of Hegel subsequently fed into the positions of the Hegelian Right (represented by historians, legal scholars, and theologians such as Heinrich Leo, Johann Philipp Gabler, and Leopold von Henning), and the Hegelian Left (comprising a motley cast of figures, including Bruno Bauer, Ludwig Feuerbach, Arnold Ruge, and Marx). Rosenzweig's *Hegel und der Staat* has been celebrated for rescuing Hegel's political philosophy from such reductively polarized readings,[24] but it has not been recognized that Rosenzweig's efforts were prefigured in the writings of British idealists such as Green, F. H. Bradley, Wallace, Bosanquet, Caird, and John Muirhead, who were influenced to varying degrees by Hegelianism, and who likewise sought to position their readings of Hegel outside of, or as a 'solution' to, partisan divides. Green's interlinked concepts of self-realization and active citizenship—as outlined in texts such as 'On the different senses of "freedom"' (1879) and 'Lectures on political obligation' (1879–80)—were key to this endeavour, because they suggested that while individual freedom lay at the heart of idealist political thought, individuals could not hope to realize this freedom outside the reformed redistributive structures of the state. Green's political thought appealed to socialist reformers because it indicated that individuals were unable to realize their freedom fully without support by the state, but Liberals such as L. T. Hobhouse could likewise draw on Green to argue that 'the right of the individual' to pursue her own ends was the highest good that had to be defended against undue state intrusion.[25]

Ritchie's writings illustrate the intense interest which Green's understanding of the state held for some late Victorian socialists. In an essay on 'Locke's theory of property', Ritchie gave the Greenian critique of property-based rights a distinctly socialist spin:

> The soldiers that guard a country from invasion, so that harvests can be reaped in peace; [...] all those who increase the knowledge, quicken the intelligence, and raise the character of the community, and so make complicated industrial

---

[23] Rosenzweig, *Hegel und der Staat* (Frankfurt: Suhrkamp, 2010), esp. pp. 330–5.

[24] For a now-canonical account Rosenzweig's reading of Hegel, see Michael Theunissen's *Die Verwirklichung der Vernunft: Zur Theorie-Praxis-Diskussion im Anschluss an Hegel* (Tübingen: Mohr/Siebeck, 1970), pp. 2–28.

[25] Hobhouse, *The Metaphysical Theory of the State: A Criticism* (London: George Allen, 1918), p. 122. As the case of Ritchie illustrates, 'logic' alone 'encouraged a move toward socialism beyond the mild interventionism Green and Toynbee preached' (cp. Meacham, *Toynbee Hall and Social Reform 1880–1914: The Search for Community* [New Haven: Yale University Press, 1987], p. 20). The idea that liberals and socialists were able to inhabit common ground was also captured in 1899 by the German social democrat and Marxist Eduard Bernstein: 'There is actually no really liberal thought which does not also belong to the elements of the ideas of socialism. [...] Without responsibility there is no freedom.' See Bernstein, *Evolutionary Socialism: A Criticism and an Affirmation* (New York: Schocken, 1961), p. 151. For Green's appeal to socialists, see Colin Tyler's *The Liberal Socialism of Thomas Hill Green*, 2 vols (Exeter: Imprint, 2010/2012).

relations more possible between human beings;—all these might claim a part in the making even of a loaf of bread. That is to say, the loaf is not merely the product of Nature *plus* Labour, but of Nature *plus* Social Labour; and this social labour is not merely an aggregate of the various individuals, but it is the labour of individuals working in an organised society. It is not, therefore, the individuals *as individuals* that have mixed their labour with Nature, but the individuals as members of a society.[26]

Ritchie's criticism of Locke doubles as a broader critique of individualist theories of desert in philosophy and political economy. While Ritchie does not argue for total economic collectivization or the abolition of private property as such, he does call for substantial state-centred regulative interventions in the capitalist economy. Ritchie's recognition of the social character of productive labour notably leads him to call for new redistributive mechanisms and for the democratic extension of property rights across society: 'Property is not merely [to be] preserved, but *regulated*.'[27] Ritchie's socio-economic analyses dovetail seamlessly with Green's critique of negative liberty as mere freedom from external constraint, and he expends much energy in spelling out the economic dimension of Green's interest in the social ties—the rights and obligations—that bind modern societies together. What is largely missing from Ritchie's writings, however, is a sustained account of the ethos—the shared forms of life, or *entgegenkommende Lebensformen*—that Green had begun to discuss under the headings of active citizenship and the 'positive realisation' of rights.[28] In his 'Lecture on liberal legislation and freedom of contract' (1881), Green had outlined the contours of active citizenship by contrasting it with negative liberty:

We do not mean merely freedom from restraint or compulsion. We do not mean merely freedom to do as we like irrespectively of what it is that we like. We do not mean a freedom that can be enjoyed by one man or one set of men at the cost of a loss of freedom to others. When we speak of freedom as something to be so

---

[26] Ritchie, 'Locke's theory of property', in *Darwin and Hegel, with Other Philosophical Studies* (London: Swan Sonnenschein, 1893), p. 191. For discussion of Ritchie, see Colin Tyler's 'Contesting the common good: T. H. Green and contemporary republicanism', in *T.H. Green: Ethics, Metaphysics and Political Philosophy*, ed. Maria Dimova-Cookson and W. J. Mander (Oxford: Clarendon Press, 2006), pp. 262–91.

[27] Ritchie, 'Locke's theory of property', p. 193; orig. emph. John Muirhead's *The Service of the State*, arguably the best contemporaneous book on Green's political theory, agrees that 'the aim of the reformer must always be the twofold one of the extension to each and all of the opportunity of self-development and self-expression that the ownership of "means" affords, and the penetration of property in all its forms by a sense of responsibility to the social end which is served by the self-development of individuals.' See *The Service of the State* (London: John Murray, 1908), pp. 79–80.

[28] Green, 'Lecture on liberal legislation and freedom of contract', in *Lectures on the Principles of Political Obligation and Other Writings*, ed. Paul Harris and John Morrow (Cambridge: Cambridge University Press, 1986), p. 200; Green, 'Lectures on the principles of political obligation', in *Lectures*, p. 26.

highly prized, we mean a positive power or capacity [...] something that we do or enjoy in common with others. We mean by it a power which each man exercises through the help or security given him by his fellow-men, and which he in turn helps to secure for them.[29]

Green's descriptions of active citizenship typically proceed by way of a detour that contrasts positive liberty with the negative freedoms that are mandated by 'liberal legislation' and 'freedom of contract'. The result is that Green's explications of the concept, including the above passage, often remain strangely abstract. As I have suggested, it fell to literary works to imagine the forms of life that would lend substance to these abstractions. Taken together, the literary texts explored in this study begin to answer the questions Green raised in his own lectures: how should we imagine 'the institutions' that are 'giving reality to [human] capacities, as enabling them to be really exercised'?[30] How can we imagine the state with 'increasing concreteness'? How do we picture, in its totality, the state's 'gradual development [...] into a conception of a complex organisation of life, with laws and institutions, with relationships, courtesies, and charities, with arts and graces'?[31] The next section continues my recuperation of British political theory's Hegelian moment around 1900 by considering how British Hegelians sought to answer these questions. In so doing, I will home in on the conceptual work that led British idealists to think about the state as a form of life.

Theorizing the Social: *Sittlichkeit* and/as Forms of Life

Hegel's idea of the state, only embryonic in the *Propädeutik*, received its fullest expression in the *Philosophy of Right*. The book is subdivided into three main sections—on 'abstract right', 'morality', and *Sittlichkeit*—with the last, the sphere of social life (*Sittlichkeit*), again split into three distinct aspects (family, civil society, and the state). As elsewhere in his work, Hegel contends that the specific arrangement of these sections conforms to a logical or hierarchical ordering that mirrors the inner dynamic of the dialectic, rather than reflecting a merely historical sequence. This is true of the transitions from abstract law and morality to *Sittlichkeit*, but it applies equally to the three spheres of *Sittlichkeit* which (according to Hegel) constitute an ascending series of increasingly rational social and institutional arrangements.[32] The British reception of Hegel revolved centrally

---

[29] Green, 'Lecture on liberal legislation', p. 199.

[30] Green, 'Lectures on the principles of political obligation', p. 16.

[31] Green, 'On the different senses of "freedom" as applied to will and to the moral progress of man', in *Lectures*, p. 246.

[32] Hegel, *PhdR*, pp. 399–400 (§ 258); Bernard Bosanquet, *The Philosophical Theory of the State* (London: Macmillan, 1899), p. 265.

around his ambitious reframing of the state as an aspect of social life, and a brief recapitulation of the relevant arguments from the *Philosophy of Right* can help us clarify British idealism's particular investment in this aspect of Hegelian political theory.

Hegel argues that while abstract law and morality do not belong to *Sittlichkeit* proper, both shed light on the constitution of the sphere of social life. As for abstract law, Hegel closely aligns it with the Enlightenment idea of innate natural rights and their legal codification in the institutions of property (*Eigentum*) and freedom of contract (*Vertrag*). The sanctity of property and contract, Hegel contends, has been central to the historical development of modern societies, because it enshrines the concept of individual freedom. Importantly, however, abstract law fails to give the realization of freedom any particular ethical content— instead, it posits freedom as a purely formal, or merely legal, quality. In contrast to the external guarantees provided by law, morality refers to the inner, personal feeling of duty that is associated with the modern conception of freedom as an individual's capacity for moral self-determination. In Hegel's forward-directed dialectical schema, morality's inwardness negates the abstract externality of natural right by setting up an intimate conjunction of particularity (i.e. the individual will) and universality (i.e. the imperatives of duty). As Wallace concluded in 1888: while abstract law was 'but the protecting shell, the restricting framework of peculiarly human life to be carried on by individual agents for their several interests', morality 'ignored the value of such mere organization' and instead 'laid down that the good will is everything, that the conviction and persuasion of being in the right is what defines the moral nature of an action.'[33] Given their close, albeit negative relationship, how do abstract law and morality relate to the final moment of Hegel's dialectical three-step, the sphere of *Sittlichkeit*? Axel Honneth has observed that external law and the imperatives of moral duty remain equally abstract and 'indeterminate'.[34] This is the case because both disregard the concrete social contexts in which individuals develop into moral agents in the first place: they neglect richer, socially grounded conceptions of freedom either in favour of the legal protections of negative liberty (abstract law) or in favour of the equally abstract judgments arrived at by isolated moral agents (as in the case of the universal precepts generated by Kant's categorical imperative). Hegel does not deny that abstract law, and even moral sense, may evolve historically, but he stresses that they are fundamentally indifferent to the contexts in which individuals are socialized and to the formative pressures of social custom that shape them.

---

[33] Wallace, 'Fichte and Hegel', p. 437.

[34] My argument here builds on a set of related observations by Axel Honneth, in *The Pathologies of Individual Freedom: Hegel's Social Theory* (Princeton: Princeton University Press, 2010), pp. 28–42.

While Hegel's comments on abstract right and morality were widely understood to be critical in intent, British idealists believed that the *Philosophy of Right*'s sections on *Sittlichkeit* constituted the truly innovative and constructive parts of his political theory. British Hegelians accordingly emphasized the importance of paying attention to the concrete social and cultural forms that made up the three spheres of *Sittlichkeit*: the family, civil society, and the state. In his 1899 study *The Philosophical Theory of the State*, Bosanquet noted apropos of the *Philosophy of Right* that Hegel's *Sittlichkeit* acted as 'the third term' which 'expresses the "truth" of the extremes' of abstract law and morality.[35] What Bosanquet suggests here is that, like abstract law, *Sittlichkeit* denotes a set of conventional norms, rules, and expectations, according to which social life is organized; at the same time, these norms recall central characteristics of morality inasmuch as they are not simply external to the individual, but rather inform their choices and sense of selfhood at an intimately personal level. Building on these insights, most British Hegelians—ranging from Green, Wallace, and Bosanquet, to Caird, Ritchie, and Muirhead—agreed that Hegel's discussion of *Sittlichkeit* in the *Philosophy of Right* was fundamentally aspirational. For example, Bosanquet's striking description of '*Sittlichkeit* as a theory of life' captures the Hegelians' hope that the dialectic would make it possible to articulate the ideal internal logic—as well as the specific social pathologies—pertaining to each of the spheres of *Sittlichkeit*.[36] To put this another way: describing family, civil society, and state as so many ascending moments in the actualization of spirit offered a powerful tool of social critique as well as a way of measuring the success with which each form of life overcame the internal contradictions of the previous sphere(s).

For Hegel, family and civil society (*bürgerliche Gesellschaft*) constitute two antagonistic configurations of the relationship between individual and community. In the family, the individual's needs and desires are entirely subordinate to the needs of the kinship-collective; by contrast, the more expansive social structures of civil society explode (or 'negate') the closed circle of the nuclear family. Hegel famously conceives of civil society in economic terms: whereas in the family, the interests of the kinship-collective are valued at the expense of the individual, political economy—the science most closely associated with *bürgerliche Gesellschaft*—prioritizes attention to the desires of atomized economic agents and to the (supposedly natural) tendency of those desires to redound to the (financial) interest of society as a whole. Hegel notes that both family and civil society offer lopsided versions of the relationship between individual and community, and he presents the state as the medium in which particular and universal are finally reconciled. In Hegel's account, the state figures as the speculative idea of an uncoerced unity of self and social whole that is made possible by

[35] Bosanquet, *Philosophical Theory*, p. 264.   [36] Bosanquet, *Philosophical Theory*, p. 265.

the emergence of new institutional (state) structures. Crucially, these institutional structures are not detached from social life—or externally imposed on it, as in the case of abstract law—but instead appear as actualizations of the social, of *Sittlichkeit*, itself.

The attempt to develop an autonomous notion of the social on the basis of Hegel's discussion of *Sittlichkeit* was key to the reception of Hegel in Britain around 1900. It also helps to explain the verbal gymnastics performed by many Hegelian thinkers in Britain, including Bax, Wallace, and Bosanquet, as they struggled to disentangle the concept of the social as such, of Hegelian *Sittlichkeit*, from the notion of 'civil society', which was merely one of *Sittlichkeit*'s aspects. Many British Hegelians tried to clear up this confusion by renouncing the more restricted term 'civil society' altogether and opting instead for alternative renderings such as '"tradesmen" society, the society of industry and commerce' (Wallace[37]) or 'bourgeois society' (Bosanquet[38]). They hoped that these alternative labels would be more successful at conveying the predominantly economic, capitalist character of *bürgerliche Gesellschaft*. From today's perspective, it can be difficult to grasp the significance of these seemingly obscure conceptual manoeuvres. However, it is important to recognize that, for the British Hegelians, these were not just verbal quibbles. Instead, this terminological reshuffling created a space in which the three stages of Hegelian *Sittlichkeit* could be described as a comprehensive cataloguing of existing social forms, customs, and ways of life.[39]

The focus on the social—on shared ways of life—became one of the central preoccupations of Britain's Hegelian moment. This tendency is already observable in one of the first publications of British idealism, F. H. Bradley's *Ethical Studies* (1876). Bradley is perhaps best-known among literary historians today as the subject of T. S. Eliot's doctoral dissertation. However, Eliot's thesis was mainly concerned with Bradley's metaphysical treatise *Appearance and Reality* (1893), and it gives little indication of the profound influence which Bradley's earlier work had had on the formation of British idealist thought. While *Ethical Studies* does not offer a straightforward adaptation of Hegel, Bradley shares many concerns with his idealist contemporaries, as well as with Green, who was Bradley's colleague at Oxford.[40] At one point in his brilliant study, the thirty-year-old

---

[37] Wallace, 'Fichte and Hegel', p. 438.   [38] Bosanquet, *Philosophical Theory*, p. 269.

[39] The difficulty of differentiating *bürgerliche Gesellschaft* from *Sittlichkeit* arose not only because of a slip in translation—it also resulted from the assumptions of bourgeois society itself, namely from the implicit equation of bourgeois social arrangements with the social as such.

[40] William Mander's authoritative history of British idealism notes that what made *Ethical Studies* 'truly radical when it was first published was its use of Hegel. [...] *Ethical Studies* was in fact the most Hegelian of Bradley's writings.' See Mander, *British Idealism: A History* (Oxford: Oxford University Press, 2011), p. 182. Robert Haldane similarly asserted in the 1920s that 'Mr Bradley had himself, as he has told us, inherited his doctrine of logical stages from the idealism which culminated in Hegel early in the last century'. See Haldane, *The Reign of Relativity* (London: Macmillan, 1921), p. 252.

Bradley begins to develop a theory of how individuals come to inhabit larger social forms. Discussing philosophical accounts of volition, Bradley positions his account as an alternative to two contradictory claims: first, the belief that individual agency is radically unconditioned and belongs to the sphere of absolute freedom; and second, the conviction that human volition is fully determined by extraneous factors. Bradley argues that the first position—the liberal belief in autonomous, self-generating selfhood—is as reductive and one-sided as the attempt to negate the autonomy of the self completely by pointing to external determinants. Bradley tries to resolve the contradiction between absolute freedom and total social determination by way of a dialectical manoeuvre that edges his argument closer to the sphere of Hegelian *Sittlichkeit*.

Bradley elaborates on his speculative resolution by proposing a revision of the concept of character. Approaching the problem of character, Bradley points out two common but mutually contradictory assumptions: on the one hand, he reminds us, it is often said that characters are absolutely unique; on the other, most people would admit upon reflection that individual character is co-formed by various social, economic, and cultural factors. Bradley objects to both propositions on the grounds that the very distinction between autonomy and heteronomy is misleading:

> [I]f, turning from suppositions, which we can not here discuss, but which we believe to be at the mercy of criticism, we hold, as the only conclusion possible, that the character of the man is not what is made, but what makes itself, out of and from the disposition and environment; and if, again, we suppose that everything, which exists outside the self, must, to make that definite self which we know, be fused together in the self, in such manner as to be one thing or another thing; if every part is in the whole, and determines that whole—if the whole is in every part, and informs each part with the nature of the whole—then it does seem mere thoughtlessness to imagine that by 'compounding' and 'deducing' we are likely to do much.[41]

Rooted firmly in the sphere of the social (or *Sittlichkeit*), Bradley's concept of character is the terrain where the contesting claims of individual autonomy and social determination are played out. While it is impossible, as more vulgar versions of social determinism might claim, to predict or 'deduce' character from social conditions, it is also true that character takes its particular flavour from the social relations that enable its realization:

> Character is fixed, but only relatively fixed. When we see how the first comes about, we see that the latter is true. The material of the character is disposition in

---

[41] Bradley, *Ethical Studies* [1876], 2nd ed. (Oxford: Clarendon Press, 1927), pp. 22–3.

relation to circumstances. The character is what I have made myself into from these elements, and the reason it remains fixed is that the conditions have so to speak been used up and realized into the individuality. What I am I have made myself, out of, in relation to, and against my raw material with its external conditions. The external conditions are more or less permanent, and the raw material is more or less systematized.[42]

The conflicting poles of absolute freedom and determination are both too abstract: while the former posits the liberal fiction of a completely un-relational self ('the "individual" apart from the community is an abstraction', Bradley notes[43]), the latter dissolves the very thing that it hopes to explain (because 'to explain the origin of a man is utterly to annihilate him'[44]).

Bradley shows that social relations contribute to the making of character in all its experiential concreteness. Yet, instead of being merely mechanically determining, these relations become the enabling precondition of the individual's richer and socially embedded self-realization:

> If we suppose the world of relations in which [a person] was born and bred, never to have been, then we suppose the very essence of him not to be; if we take that away, we have taken him away; and hence he now is not an individual, in the sense of owing nothing to the sphere of relations in which he finds himself, but does contain those relations within himself as belonging to his very being.[45]

Bradley's account of character can be read as a response to two positions that became prominent in social-reformist discourses around 1900. As Lauren Goodlad points out in her important study of Victorian and Edwardian governance, reformist debates tended to polarize between groups (such as the Charity Organisation Society) which stressed the self-reliance of character, and others (including the Fabian Society) which claimed that environmental circumstances were determining of character. 'Liberal mythologies of self-generating character', Goodlad writes, had come under pressure at various points in the nineteenth century, yet these tensions had 'long been simmering beneath the placid surface of mid-Victorian equipoise' and only came to the fore around 1900.[46] Goodlad highlights two influential associations, 'both of which sought to meet this demand':

> The Charity Organization Society and the Fabian Society offered two contrasting strategies through which to impose order and authority on what had long been

---

[42] Bradley, *Ethical Studies*, p. 52.   [43] Bradley, *Ethical Studies*, p. 173.
[44] Bradley, *Ethical Studies*, p. 22.   [45] Bradley, *Ethical Studies*, pp. 166–7.
[46] Goodlad, *Victorian Literature and the Victorian State: Character and Governance in a Liberal Society* (Baltimore: The Johns Hopkins University Press, 2003), p. 193.

celebrated as a nation of self-reliant individuals and communities. In actuality the COS's voluntary casework had a great deal in common with the bureaucratic expertise urged by the Fabians. Nevertheless, the COS drew on Idealist philosophical foundations and sought to enlarge organized voluntary initiative, while the Fabians drew on materialist philosophy and aimed to justify state intervention along socialist lines. Hence, COS and Fabian proposals emerged from within two disparate worldviews.[47]

Goodlad demonstrates that various trade-offs were achieved between these two positions, and she traces in rich detail how these compromises were given expression in literary works by H. G. Wells, E. M. Forster, and other writers. By contrast, Bradley's argument suggests that he is not just another seeker of the middle ground. What he gives us is not compromise, but a double negation that initiates a dialectical movement: on the one hand, his assertion that human nature is relational in its very being undercuts the liberal belief in character as free self-determination; on the other, his contention that the telos of the individual is self-realization—as social relationality is 'realized into individuality'—negates crude forms of socio-economic determinism. In contrast to the debates explored by Goodlad, *Ethical Studies* reflects the specifically Hegelian atmosphere of statist debates around 1900: the arguments in favour of autonomous selfhood and of social determinism, Bradley indicates, rely on equally reductive understandings of the social as external to the individual, and they accordingly miss the crucial mediating role which *Sittlichkeit* plays in the individual's self-realization.[48]

Bradley's thinking illustrates the intertwining of idealist arguments and late Victorian debates about institutional reform that characterizes Britain's Hegelian moment. Goodlad's identification of the COS as an 'Idealist' undertaking takes its cue from Bosanquet's involvement in the organization, but it arguably underplays the extent to which forms of (Hegelian) idealist thought—for example in the work of Ritchie and to a more limited extent in Green's later writings—supported specifically socialist arguments about state intervention. Indeed, as Stefan Collini has observed, Bosanquet's tone in the 1890s was essentially defensive: while Bosanquet's mantra—'Only give scope to character, and it will unfailingly pull us through'—rehearsed a commonplace of 'the mid-Victorian ethos', he clearly recognized 'that from the early 1880s onwards a rival "paradigm" was being increasingly canvassed, in which social and economic forces beyond the

---

[47] Goodlad, *Victorian Literature and the Victorian State*, p. 193.

[48] The Hegelian philosopher Henry Jones often commented on related problems in his writing. In an essay from 1905, he argued that the antagonistic ideas of self-generating character and determining environment were merely 'metaphorical hypotheses'—so extreme and reductive that they lacked real explanatory value. In truth, 'what we call character from one point of view, we call environment from another. Character and environment are not even separate elements, far less are they independent, isolated, externally interacting objects.' See Jones, 'Working faith of the social reformer', in *Working Faith of the Social Reformer* (London: Macmillan, 1910), p. 48.

individual's control largely determined his fate.'[49] Bosanquet's vision of reform as a Smilesian character-building exercise is unlikely to win him many fans on the left today, and it is certainly true that Green's practice-oriented brand of idealism responded more successfully to the period's new social and political pressures. After all, it was Green who viewed 'the modern state as the reconciling ground of the autonomous person with social institutions' and who encouraged new arguments about institutional reform and state-centred welfare provision that were profoundly alien to Bosanquet.[50]

In his ground-breaking writings and lectures of the 1870s and 1880s, Green had begun to theorize the non-externality of reformed institutions to the sphere of the social under the labels of *positive liberty* and *active citizenship*. Yet, while Green provided a subtle conceptual analysis of these categories, there remained the difficulty of imagining the concrete lived forms which such positive freedom might take. Subsequent chapters of this book will argue that the task of imagining these forms of positive freedom fell, in part, to literature. The literary works examined in this study incorporate the two intertwined approaches to the sphere of the social that my Introduction associated with British Hegelianism: first, they deploy a form of social symptomology that makes it possible to identify and criticize pathologies of individual and collective life; and second, they entail a speculative momentum that involves the reimagining of existing forms of life and their gradual reshaping into what Jürgen Habermas calls *entgegenkommende Lebensformen*—a piecemeal transition from one stage of *Sittlichkeit* (the stage of capitalist society, or *bürgerliche Gesellschaft*) to the next (the modern state). The subsequent two sections begin to illustrate these twinned forms of literary-social analysis in some more detail.

Hegelian Symptomatic Reading: The Case of Ernest Belfort Bax

The work of the late Victorian journalist and socialist Ernest Belfort Bax can serve as an entry point into the literary-political imaginary I describe here. It illustrates the mode of Hegelian critique I have been sketching out, but it also indicates how Hegelian social symptomology differed from its contemporary Marxist counterpart. Bax played an important role in popularizing Hegelian ideas in the 1880s and 1890s, and he also holds an important place in the annals of the British socialist movement. He was a leading member of Henry Hyndman's Social Democratic Federation (SDF), having joined in 1882 (just one year after its foundation) before

[49] Stefan Collini, 'Hobhouse, Bosanquet, and the state: Philosophical idealism and political argument in England, 1880–1918', *Past & Present* 72 (1976): 86–111: 93.

[50] Avital Simhony, 'The political thought of the British idealists', in W. J. Mander (ed.), *The Oxford Handbook of British Philosophy in the Nineteenth Century* (Oxford: Oxford University Press, 2014), p. 441.

moving on to cofound the breakaway Socialist League with his friend William Morris and other leading lights of the SDF in 1885. Despite the Socialist League's later reputation as a hotbed of anarchist activity, Bax and Morris had originally conceived of the organization as a broad church for the British socialist movement, and Bax contributed regularly to the League's newspaper *Commonweal*, which was set up under Morris's editorship in 1885. As the Socialist League started to tilt ever more decisively towards anarchism, Bax left the organization and re-joined the SDF in the late 1880s, soon becoming its main theoretician. Owing in part to Hyndman's enthusiasm for Marx's ideas, the SDF has acquired a reputation as the main disseminator of Marxism in late Victorian Britain. This claim is somewhat misleading, since Marx's inner circle of followers, including Friedrich Engels, fell out with Hyndman over his perceived misrepresentation of Marxian ideas.[51] The label of orthodox Marxist also fails to capture the intellectual eclecticism of Bax, who had returned to Britain in 1882 after a three-year stay in Germany, during which he had lived on a motley intellectual diet of German idealism and continental socialism. The idealists whose works Bax had studied closely during his time in Germany included Kant, Fichte, and Hegel, and Bax's books and journalism of the 1880s and 1890s are pervaded by the ideas of these philosophers.[52] Thanks to Bax's prominent position in Britain's flourishing socialist milieu, his writings helped to grow a wider audience for the idealism previously associated with the comparatively narrow academic circle of professional philosophers flocking to Green in Oxford. Kant's and Hegel's writings left a particular mark on the young Bax's thinking, and even as late as 1920, in his last book-length philosophical study, he revisited at some length (albeit more critically than before) the 'Hegelian positions which dominated English speculative thought during the last quarter of the nineteenth century, and [which] were still powerful in the opening years of the present.'[53] Bax's works, in particular the bulk of his journalism, illustrate that, for some thinkers and activists affiliated with the left, Hegel's political theory filled the gap in progressive socialist thought that was created by the comparative dearth of translations of Marx's works.

Bax's journalism of the 1880s develops procedures of social analysis that could be called superstructural symptomology—a form of Hegelian diagnosis that does

---

[51] Most famously, Henry Hyndman's popular digest of Marxian ideas, *England for All* (1880), had failed to mention Marx by name, a fact that drew the ire of the exiled German thinker and his cabal.

[52] See, e.g. Bax's memoirs *Reminiscences and Reflections of a Mid- and Late Victorian* (1918) for approving comments about the 'Young Hegelian' movement of the 1880s and 1890s and its opposition to Spencerian positivism. Robert Arch's early biography *E. B. Bax: Thinker and Pioneer* (1927) likewise provides a record of Bax's early interest in German idealism.

[53] Bax, *The Real, the Rational, and the Alogical: Being Suggestions for a Philosophical Reconstruction* (London: Grant Richards, 1920), p. 9. Hegel was not the only classical German thinker who had a significant influence on Bax's socialism or indeed on fin-de-siècle socialism more generally. For example, Eduard Bernstein's *Evolutionary Socialism* (1899) praised Kant's transcendental critique of cognitive 'prejudices' for its (vaguely) democratic implications. See Bernstein, 'Kant against Cant', in *Evolutionary Socialism*, pp. 200–24.

not restrict itself to describing economic modes of production but instead generates critical accounts of the contradictory experiences and collective pathologies that characterize contemporary social life. Consider, for example, the opening of Bax's essay 'Conscience and commerce', first published in the Socialist League's periodical *The Commonweal* in November 1885:

> We often come across a species of virtuous indignation which is apt to be aroused by some tale of the woes of a railway company whom the wicked passenger 'defrauds' by travelling without having previously paid his fare. 'Strange,' it is said (and we find the sentiment commonly repeated whenever the subject comes up in the Press) 'that a man who would scorn to rob his neighbour in his individual capacity, yet will not hesitate to "defraud" a company;' for it is acknowledged to be by such persons that the bulk of these 'frauds' (so-called) are perpetrated. The inconsistency of such a proceeding is then enlarged upon with all due emphasis. This, in itself, comparatively unimportant incident of modern life opens up a curious ethico-economical problem. Two things are quite clear. One is that a considerable section of persons instinctively feel a difference between their moral relations to individual men and women and their relations to a joint-stock company. The other is that the ordinary middle-class intellect cannot see any reason for this distinction, and having possibly a sense of the instability to commercial relations which would ensue from its recognition, adopts the high moral tone.[54]

The passage heeds Bax's own advice, in a contemporary essay, that the 'speculative intellect' ought to begin not with 'the exceptions of life: battles, murder and pestilence' but 'with ordinary phenomena', with the recurrent patterns of feeling and behaviour that have become second nature through 'everyday routine'.[55] The article 'Conscience and commerce' opens by describing the phenomenal structure of a situation whose regular recurrence ('we often come across' this kind of dilemma) involves a habituated emotional response ('a sentiment commonly repeated'). Moreover, individual affective states are also shown to be embedded in—and to derive their peculiar social force and authority from—collectively shared structures of feeling. Bax notably demonstrates that the instinctive and seemingly subjective response portrayed in the article is overdetermined by a set of social expectations that lend it the appearance of a more general symptom. Indeed, as the title of his article ('Conscience and commerce') indicates, the affective response that is expected of us—'virtuous indignation' at the passenger who has

---

[54] Bax, 'Conscience and commerce', reprinted in Bax, *The Religion of Socialism* (London: Swan Sonnenschein, 1890), pp. 83–91 (p. 83).

[55] Bax, 'The curse of civilisation' [1887], reprinted in *The Ethics of Socialism* (London: Swan Sonnenschein, 1890), pp. 106–19 (p. 106).

neglected to pay his railway fare—is itself mediated by legal relations and economic structures: because, under the hegemonic 'commercial' dispensation, companies are treated as legal persons and moral agents in their own right, we habitually display the same ethical responses towards them that we would ordinarily reserve for other human beings.

Bax's patient uncovering of the structures that shape individual responses might seem to involve a social hermeneutic that traces symptomatic expressions from the level of socio-cultural life back to their hidden (economic) causes. In truth, however, Bax's Hegelianism enables a nuanced type of symptomology that is more closely attuned to the surface structures of given social situations and that also requires us to pay similarly close attention to the language of Bax's passage. Already in the article's opening sentences, Bax's prose is shot through with evaluative comments that foreground the expected, socially sanctioned response either by mimicking or by exaggerating it ('*virtuous* indignation'; 'the *wicked* passenger'; and note the scare quotes around 'defraud'). Significantly, Bax also hints that the subtly ironical tone of the passage—and the moment of internal distanciation which it inserts into the scene—is not merely a function of his own knowing position as a social critic, but that it arises from *within* the represented situation. The key observation here—that 'a considerable section of persons instinctively feel a difference between their moral relations to individual men and women and their relations to a joint-stock company'—indicates that a spontaneous recognition of the incongruousness of the expected response is produced by the structure of the situation itself. Bax's phrasing specifically suggests that the incident in itself performs the critical task of 'open[ing] up' for us 'a curious ethico-economical problem'.[56] The narrative perspective adopted in Bax's passage recalls what Andrew Cole, in a discussion of *The Phenomenology of the Spirit*, has called Hegel's 'phenomenological style', in which 'exposition takes *the point of view of the concept*, just short of personifying concepts.'[57] Bax, too, shows that dialectical critique needs to go beyond the mechanical task of assigning (economic) causes to (socio-cultural) effects: the task of a properly Hegelian symptomology is not to display the critic's ingenuity by unearthing previously hidden structures, but to trace how substantive contradictions unfold from within—how they are 'opened up' for us by—a given situation.[58]

When Bax's copious journalistic output of the 1880s and 1890s is read as a single body of work, it becomes clear that he was working towards a broad

---

[56] Axel Honneth, in a related discussion of the tension between abstract legal rights and the fully social perspective of Hegelian *Sittlichkeit*, describes this experience of incongruousness as a feeling of 'dis-ease' that gives rise to 'a certain diagnostic suspicion' (*Pathologies*, p. 44).

[57] Cole, *The Birth of Theory* (Chicago: University of Chicago Press, 2014), p. 156; orig. emph.

[58] See my related comments in the Introduction on Stuart Hall's reading of Hegel: like Hall, Bax does not deny that hegemonic forms arise from economic determinants, but he insists that the economic should not be treated as the solely privileged level of Marxist critique.

panorama of the market-mediated forms of social life that were characteristic of Britain's civil society. Bax's writings map out complex patterns of affective response similar to those outlined in 'Conscience and commerce', but they also offer brilliant characterological sketches, such as the snapshot of the staid 'middle-class intellect' in the passage above. Bax's interest in Hegelian political theory clearly deepened his attention to shared forms of social life, and his writings also provide a window onto more general trends in the development of what is today called 'critique'. As I noted in the Introduction, Hegelian political theory contributed to the development of analytical procedures that we are more likely to associate with the work of Raymond Williams or Antonio Gramsci. For example, it would be relatively easy to reformulate Bax's comments about conflicting structures of feeling in 'Conscience and commerce' by introducing terminology from Williams's work, such as his triad of residual, dominant, and emergent value systems; and it would also be possible to describe the chafing of emerging social forms against dominant ones—with Gramsci—in terms of the brittle hegemony of bourgeois society which unwittingly creates footholds for socialist critique.

In his philosophical works, Bax frequently invokes Hegel's thinking in order to suggest that the contradictions of social life can be shown to be *'momenta'* in a progressive dialectical movement.[59] Bax's numerous contributions to *The Commonweal* indicate that he has in mind a mode of social change that will start its work at the level of the superstructure by transforming dominant forms of life.[60] Noting in one essay that 'some men are lumps of class-feeling' in whom a 'hypocritical vulgarity has absorbed humanity', Bax goes on to ask: 'How, then, it may be said, if we admit class-feeling to be that element in the modern character in which its worst and anti-social features are embodied, can we make the accentuation and exacerbation of class-feeling the starting point for a social reconstruction in which classes shall be abolished?'[61] Bax's striking proposal is that 'social reconstruction' must begin with a critique of dominant structures of feeling and the cultivation of emerging (*entgegenkommende*) ones—a proposition that looks ahead to Williams's observation that 'it is primarily to emergent formations [...] that the structure of feeling, *as solution*, relates'.[62] Like Williams, Bax attempts to imagine the conditions under which new forms of life might emerge—a 'real feeling of community' (Williams) that will help to generate structural 'solutions' to

---

[59] Bax, *Handbook [...] of Philosophy*, p. 312 and *passim*.

[60] It is indicative of the tensions that run through Bax's writings—a result, in some part, of his intellectual eclecticism—that this undercurrent of Hegelian social symptomology sometimes works against Bax's noisier revolutionary proclamations: 'Our function', Bax wrote in 1886, 'is to educate the people by criticizing all attempts at so-called reform.' Quoted in Elizabeth Carolyn Miller, *Slow Print: Literary Radicalism and Late Victorian Print Culture* (Stanford: Stanford University Press, 2013), p. 42.

[61] Bax, 'Men versus classes', in *The Ethics of Socialism*, pp. 101, 103; my emph.

[62] Williams, *Marxism and Literature* (Oxford: Oxford University Press, 1977), p. 103; orig. emph.

present social contradictions and antagonisms.[63] Some accounts of fin-de-siècle socialism present Bax as an ethical idealist who believed that all that was required for a transition to socialism was a change of heart, a new ethos of sharing, trust, and mutual care to replace the rapacious greed of capitalist society.[64] Contrary to this view, however, Bax's writings frequently address questions of institutional change, and they demonstrate that he never lost sight of the material and structural aspects of social transformation. Bax's aim in engaging with hegemonic forms of life was accordingly a more modest one, namely, to position social and cultural critique at the heart of a more capacious reformist project. In Bax's estimation, the critical examination of ways of life was not just a meaningless superstructural exercise, as more orthodox Marxists of the Second International might argue. Much like the literary writers discussed in British Literature and the Life of Institutions, British Hegelians were convinced that such critique was vital to the project of institutional reform: to them, transforming hegemonic ways of life was a first step towards achieving the larger project of socio-political reconstruction.

Speculative Fictions about the State

The mode of social symptomology I associate with Britain's Hegelian moment started out from the assumption that existing forms of life could be criticized in light of their immanent rationality. The case of Bax suggests that this symptomology was put to use by reform-minded writers who wanted to explain why the work of institutional change could legitimately start at the level of hegemonic forms of life rather than with the revolutionary root-and-branch eradication of existing social relations. But my comments on Bax and Bradley have also begun to indicate that the writings of British Hegelians engaged in speculations about an emergent form of Sittlichkeit in which individual self-realization and external institutional structures, personal freedom and the common good, were reconciled. Bax's programmatic focus on socio-cultural forms was designed to counter a danger that he found to be implicit in Hegel's own writings—namely, that the democratically expanded liberties guaranteed by a reformed state might once more devolve into empty forms of abstract law and negative freedom.[65] The literary works

---

[63] Williams, The Long Revolution (London: Chatto & Windus, 1961), p. 335. I offer further discussion of this passage in the Introduction. Like Bax, Williams warns that premature dreams of a new social ethos must not be allowed to take the place of structural reform: 'While we still talk of a labour market, as despite long protest many of us continue to do, we must expect the behaviour appropriate to it, and not try to smuggle in, when it becomes convenient, the quite different conception of common interest and responsibility' (Long Revolution, p. 301).

[64] For an opposing account, see Bevir, The Making of British Socialism, pp. 45–64.

[65] In an extended commentary on Hegel's discussion of Sittlichkeit, Bax emphasized that Hegel's description of the state as a form of the social had paradoxically not given enough attention to questions of ethics. Hegel's theory of the state had 'virtually surrendered the standpoint of the "ethics of

explored in this book engage in related acts of speculation that aim to imagine the reformed state as a concrete form of *Sittlichkeit* rather than an abstract set of institutional structures. The *entgegenkommende Lebensformen* that are imagined in these works can occasionally take the shape of future projections, as in some of Wells's writings, but they typically steer clear of more aggressive brands of utopianism which pit the spectacular vision of a radically revamped social order against the inequities of an imperfect present.

British idealists recognized that Hegel's state theory was in some ways ill equipped to respond to the political changes around 1900, as Britain began to enter the age of mass democracy. For example, Hegel's exploration of the structures of civil society had heralded skilled workers' corporations as the embodiment of a new ethos of solidarity and cooperation between clearly defined social estates (*Stände*): these corporations, Hegel claimed, institutionalized *entgegenkommende Lebensformen* which facilitated the growth of new state structures.[66] The elitism of Hegel's model of skilled labour—much like his focus on quasi-medieval *Stände* rather than the social classes of industrial society—looked increasingly anachronistic following the Representation of the People Act of 1884 (which addressed imbalances in parliamentary representation between the countryside and Britain's new industrial conurbations) and the Act of 1918 (which lifted property restrictions for voting and gave the vote to nearly half of British women). These developments ran well ahead of Hegel's belief that citizens should be represented in the state, not through universal suffrage, but as members of distinct and self-contained estates, with the only truly 'universal estate' being composed of a caste of state administrators that resembled the Samurai of Wells's *A Modern Utopia* (1905).[67]

Some British Hegelians were quicker than others to recognize the difficulty of reimagining Hegelian state theory for the changed political environment of the late nineteenth and early twentieth centuries. There were those, like Bosanquet, who reaffirmed the validity of Hegel's argument about *Stände*: if the citizen 'is to have a fuller sense of the social good', Bosanquet claimed, 'he must either take part in the work of the State, or at least be familiar with such work, through interest in his fellows' share of it, and in the organizations which connect his class interests

inwardness," as such, [...] although professing to have placed them on an inexpugnable footing' (*Handbook*, pp. 329–30). The state here appears as a negation of existing forms of life—a dilemma which Bax sought to remedy by reinserting ethics into the debate about state-centred reform.

[66] Hegel, *PhdR*, pp. 393–8, 411–12 (§§ 250–6, 264–5).

[67] Hegel, *PhdR*, p. 357 (§ 205). Notwithstanding such criticism, it has been argued that in his last published work, on the English Reform Bill of 1832, Hegel recognized that the concept of 'estates' could no longer account for the deep structural contradictions of more fully industrialized societies. See Hegel, 'The English Reform Bill', in *Hegel's Political Writings*, ed. Z. A. Pelczynski (Oxford: Clarendon Press, 1964), pp. 295–330. Habermas explores the possibility that Hegel's later writings anticipate Marx's critique of the estates: see Habermas, 'On Hegel's political writings', in *Theory and Practice* (Boston: Beacon Press, 1974), esp. pp. 188–93.

with the public good.'[68] Others were more attuned to the new pressures which the period's radical energies exerted on reformist visions of the state. One of these Hegelians was Bax, whose political consciousness had first been galvanized by the events of the Paris Commune and who went on to author two accounts of the Commune in the 1880s and 1890s.[69] Reform, Bax noted, had to reckon with the real possibility of social revolution that characterized the period—reformers would not be able to move in a straight line towards the full integration of all social groups into an unfractured political consensus but had to remain open to the conjunctural articulation of new social demands. In his writings, Bax used the category of the 'alogical' to refer to the irreducible particularity of social experience: the uniqueness of such experiences, he argued, could not be captured by thought alone and thus offered a crucial counterweight to the Hegelian 'panlogism' that gave in to the philosophical temptation to synthesize particularity into purely rational categories.[70]

The speculative literary mode which I illustrate in subsequent chapters is characterized by an amalgamation of political and aesthetic concerns, as writers sought to develop literary styles that were capable of articulating the relationship between state and society in new ways. In contrast to many contemporaneous philosophical texts, the exploration of active citizenship and positive freedom in literary works remained more open to non-hegemonic subject positions, including queer, female, and working-class identities. The literary texts discussed in this study show that the speculative figure of the state registered the pressures which democratization brought to bear on Britain's political system, and these texts also raise the related question of how this process of democratization influenced the ability of aesthetic forms to integrate the particularity of social experience, especially the experiences of politically under- and unrepresented groups. At the same time, however, most of these texts—including the writings of the socialist and queer activist Edward Carpenter—also display a deep commitment to Britain's established liberal system. For example, despite significant differences in political

[68] Bosanquet, *Philosophical Theory*, p. 293. Bradley, though not a political theorist like Bosanquet, also favoured this model of social integration, contrasting it with Charles Fourier's more radically disruptive socialist utopianism (*Ethical Studies*, pp. 105, 201).

[69] Bax, Victor Dave, and William Morris, *A Short Account of the Commune of Paris of 1871* (1886); and Bax, *A Short History of the Paris Commune* (1894).

[70] Bax, *The Real, the Rational, and the Alogical: Being Suggestions for a Philosophical Reconstruction* (London: Grant Richards, 1920). Bax does not here advocate a renunciation of Hegelian speculative thought as such. Instead, he seeks to introduce into Hegel's thought what Etienne Balibar has called a social 'dialectic' that 'does not remain *purely* speculative'—a dialectic of 'insurrection and institutionalization' that constitutes the dynamic essence of citizenship (Balibar, *Equaliberty: Political Essays* [Durham, NC: Duke University Press, 2014], p. 9; orig. emph.). Balibar explains elsewhere that because '*existence in the form of resistance* is not always possible' it is necessary to identify 'the movement that, by regrouping the insurrectional origins of citizenship [...] can give them institutional form' (*Citizenship* [Cambridge: Polity, 2015], pp. 66, 119; orig. emph.). Bax's own willingness to recognize previously unmapped social demands only extended to a certain point, as is evidenced by his vocal opposition to women's suffrage.

outlook, the texts by Ward, Gissing, Carpenter, Wells, and Forster all participate in a reformist moment that hoped to defuse social antagonisms through the vision of a stable and inclusive social centre. As I indicated in the Introduction, Carpenter's vision of a new class of local-cum-cosmopolitan smallholders is a case in point here, as is Wells's political hope for the 'great educated middle class' as the medium of a 'larger social synthesis'.[71] These texts often mark for our attention the narrative erasure of more vulnerable subject positions: this is true in particular of the narrator of *Howards End* whose declaration that 'the very poor are unthinkable' recalls Bax's attention to the 'alogical' (i.e. 'un-thinkable') status of marginalized social experiences.[72] In spite of these ideological limitations, the works I examine here contribute to a reformist literary mode that succeeds in mapping out a range of non- and counter-hegemonic *Lebensformen*. For example, Carpenter's writings—including his poetic magnum opus *Towards Democracy* (1883–1905)—envision new forms of life that are centred around ideas of collective ownership and communal belonging: these experimental social practices, Carpenter hopes, will nourish a popular desire for the state-organized nationalization and redistribution of Britain's enclosed land. In a related vein, Wells's works of the early 1900s attempt to defuse the threat of class warfare by projecting a new ethos of cross-class sharing that Wells associates with the development of new taxation schemes under William Harcourt and Lloyd George. The texts I have just mentioned project their visions of *entgegenkommende Lebensformen* in terms of their mimetic content (e.g. through the representation of new practices of land ownership) as well as in terms of their specific generic and formal choices (e.g. through the unstable combination of realist and utopian generic modes that characterizes some of Wells's best-known Edwardian fictions).

The observation that Carpenter, Wells, Forster, and the other writers discussed in this book responded to certain historical moments of institutional reform—to debates about worker welfare, land nationalization, graduated taxation, and national insurance—might seem to suggest that the best way to explore the reformist literary mode is by adopting a broadly New Historicist method, whereby a particular set of literary forms is shown to resemble or mirror the internal discursive logic of some other extra-literary—legal, political, social—formation. The theoretically thin concept of historical resemblance suggests that one discourse bears the homological imprint of another, and (as Andrew Cole writes) it therefore comes to 'look like a Hegelianism without Hegel, a figurative method of reading without the hard concept of history but only "social energy" [...] that gives literature both the capacity to be an anecdote—representative but not caused—and the power to be a monad, within which is expressed a total state of

---

[71] Wells, *Anticipations [...]* (London: Chapman & Hall, 1902), p. 249.
[72] Forster, *Howards End*, ed. Paul B. Armstrong (New York: Norton, 1998), pp. 35–6.

affairs.'[73] While I pay a good deal of attention to the historical and political specificity of individual reformist moments, my suggestion that we view literature as a mode of speculative thought in its own right is also meant to indicate the limitations of certain types of historicist work. The New Historicist attempt to map literary and social forms onto one another most notably fails to capture the richer varieties of dialectical thinking embodied in the literary texts explored here. *British Literature and the Life of Institutions* indicates that literary texts themselves evolved dialectical procedures that were capable of figuring the concept of the state as a shared form of life: these literary texts, I argue, espouse modes of speculative thought by experimenting with various configurations of genre, tone, and forms of address that make it possible to imagine reformed state institutions with increasing degrees of experiential concreteness.

Foregrounding literature's capacity for speculative thought does not relieve literary criticism of its duty to attend to socio-historical context, but it productively defamiliarizes the reflexive assumption that the deciphering of literary works in terms of their socio-historical content should be literary critics' main—or indeed their only—task. As Fredric Jameson has observed of the historicizing impulse:

> as far as Marxist literary criticism is concerned, I think it can generally be agreed that its most embarrassing move tends to be this (unavoidable) shifting of gears in which we pass from literary analysis to Marxian interpretation and find ourselves obliged to evoke the social and political meaning of the text in terms of the classes, historical contradictions, political and economic background, the conjunctures of forces and ideologies, capitalist alienation, commodification, and ideological occultation and repression, all of which lurk behind the aesthetic curtain and are suddenly unveiled in all their impoverished extraliterary nakedness like the wizard of Oz.[74]

The apparent conflict between the aesthetic and the political—the 'embarrass-[ment]' of having to shuttle back and forth between literary text and historical context— has been the point of departure for much of Jameson's most incisive critical

---

[73] Cole, *Birth of Theory*, p. 155. In response to this immobile opposition of figure and concept, Cole identifies a buried Hegelian strand of late Victorian literary criticism that was roughly coterminous with the Hegelian moment in state theory I identify here, and that included now-forgotten intellectuals such as William John Courthope and Vida Dutton Scudder as well as some more familiar names such as Leslie Stephen. According to Cole, these critics developed a dialectical criticism which sought to reintegrate the torn halves of concept and figure. In a passage that anticipates Cole's argument, F. H. Bradley rejects the theoretically unambitious idea of 'resemblance'. According to Bradley, 'resemblance' is the methodological 'catchword of "advanced thinkers"' who pretend to resolve the tension between 'identity and diversity' by collapsing difference into sameness. Bradley argues this point at length in *Appearance and Reality: A Metaphysical Essay*, 2nd ed. (London: George Allen, 1897), pp. 348–58; for a related discussion of 'likeness', see *Ethical Studies*, pp. 166–8.
[74] Fredric Jameson, 'Marxist criticism and Hegel', *PMLA* 131.2 (2016): 430–8 (p. 432).

thinking. Indeed, to the extent that Jameson's own work attempts to overcome this opposition by demonstrating the politicalness of narrative form itself—that is, by imagining politics and history as something other than literature's hidden content or inert backdrop—his mode of Marxist criticism is speculative (Hegelian) in its own right. My book makes a related claim, though it locates the source of speculative energy in literary works themselves rather than in the activity of the critic: texts written in the reformist literary mode, I suggest, engage in a form of speculative thought that works towards resolving the tension between philosophical concept (the notion of the state) and artistic figure (the concrete forms which this concept takes in literary works).[75]

The attempt to understand literature as a mode of speculative thought is likely to raise a series of political objections. As I noted in the Introduction, literary and cultural theorists have long been sceptical of Hegel's speculative enterprise, and they often contend that Hegel neglected the labour of the negative in favour of a misguided ('speculative') attempt to think the absolute.[76] The line of critics who are wary of Hegel's supposedly anti-democratic tendencies is long, and it also includes readers who are sympathetic towards certain other aspects of Hegel's thought. Isobel Armstrong, for example, in her important recent reassessment of the nineteenth-century novel's 'democratic imagination', has commended the *Philosophy of Right*'s exploration of the production of 'deficit subjects' under capitalism: 'Whatever the reactionary elements elsewhere in his work [...], Hegel makes a devastating analysis of civil society, and its structural propensity to create poverty, with the corollary of dehumanization.'[77] Yet, even as Armstrong praises Hegel's analysis of the pathologies of capitalist civil society, she criticizes the 'reactionary' thrust of Hegel's speculative idea of the state. In the *Philosophy of Right*, Armstrong concludes, 'it is never clear how exactly the state can create the political conditions of freedom-to-be-human'.[78] Distancing herself from Hegel's political theory, Armstrong instead invokes the work of Jacques Rancière which insists—against Hegel, as it were—that politics 'is not vested in institutions' and that it can be 'affirmed only when it is enacted.'[79] Building on Rancière's anti-institutionalism, Armstrong argues that the nineteenth-century novel mirrored the historical drift towards greater democratic participation by loosening the 'tyranny' (Rancière's word) of class-bound macro-forms such as genre—that

---

[75] The difficulty of reconciling concept and figure, which arises in aesthetic theory and critical practice alike, is brilliantly explored in Gillian Rose's account of Hegel's 1802 *System der Sittlichkeit*. Discussing nineteenth-century conceptions of 'the aesthetic', Rose notes that 'in bourgeois society intuition [associated with literary figuration] is displaced and distorted': as a result, '[a]rt in such a society is unable to unify concept and intuition, or meaning and form (*Gestaltung*), but emphasises one or the other. [Art] falls into a contradiction' (*Hegel Contra Sociology*, p. 81; orig. emph.).

[76] A notable recent exception to this tendency is Todd McGowan's *Emancipation After Hegel*.

[77] Armstrong, *Novel Politics: Democratic Imaginations in Nineteenth-Century Fiction* (Oxford: Oxford University Press, 2016), p. 67.

[78] Armstrong, *Novel Politics*, pp. 74–5.   [79] Armstrong, *Novel Politics*, p. 78.

is, by unfastening the purely conventional authority of aesthetic categories that determine in advance whose actions will get represented.[80] Truly 'democratic' novels, Rancière argues, depart from these conventions either by drawing attention to lives that were hitherto deemed unworthy of literary scrutiny (e.g. in Gustave Flaubert's *Madame Bovary*), or by presenting us with a dehierarchized perceptual field that conveys 'the irreconcilable singularity' of individual sensations (e.g. in the fiction of Virginia Woolf).[81]

The differences between this important new work in aesthetic theory and the speculative literary engagements with the state that I trace in this book reflect disagreements between Marxist and Hegelian traditions of thought, including diverging understandings of the value of institutional reform. These differences are marked out with great clarity in Marx's 1843 *Critique of Hegel's 'Philosophy of Right'*, which undertakes a systematic, paragraph-by-paragraph refutation of Hegel's speculative theory of the state. Marx agrees with Hegel that humans are by nature social—that, in Bradley's phrase, individuals 'contain relations within [themselves] as belonging to [their] very being'. However, Marx attacks Hegel's political theory on the grounds that state institutions bar individuals from participating in the concrete life of a community:

> To stop at the abstraction of 'being a member of the state' and to conceive of individuals in terms of this abstraction does not therefore seem to be just superficial thinking which clings to abstractions. That the abstraction of 'being a member of the state' is really an abstraction is not, however, the fault of this thinking but of Hegel's line of argument and actual modern conditions, which presuppose the separation of actual life from political life and make the political quality an abstraction of actual participation in the state.[82]

As Marx points out, the process of abstraction that takes place between the two spheres of state and society is mediated by a complex system of legal rights. In the liberal-capitalist state, Marx notes, freedom is codified in purely negative terms as freedom-from-interference. This narrowly legalistic understanding of liberty is enshrined in the freedom of contract and the right to personal property: 'liberty as a right of man is not based on the association of man with man but rather on the separation of man from man.'[83] The classical liberal notion of rights reinforces the atomization of society (*bürgerliche Gesellschaft*) by conceiving of individuals as

---

[80] Rancière, *The Lost Thread: The Democracy of Modern Fiction* (London: Bloomsbury, 2017), p. 54.

[81] Rancière, *The Lost Thread*, p. 61. *The Lost Thread* contains exemplary discussions both of *Madame Bovary* and *To the Lighthouse*.

[82] Marx, *Critique of Hegel's 'Philosophy of Right'*, ed. Joseph O'Malley (Cambridge: Cambridge University Press, 1977), p. 116.

[83] The quotation is from Marx's *Zur Judenfrage* (*Selected Writings* [Indianapolis: Hackett, 1994], p. 16), the 1844 text that continues Marx's discussion of some of the central issues of the *Critique of Hegel's 'Philosophy of Right'*.

independent economic agents, and it also renders invisible the lives of those who are not granted such rights. Creating a truly democratic (communist) society, Marx submits, will necessarily involve a revolutionary tearing-down of the liberal-capitalist state and the system of rights and legal entitlements which it upholds.

The vision of reform that is embraced by the literary authors discussed in this book contrasts markedly with Marx's advocacy of revolutionary change. These writers are closer to a Hegelian model of political transformation—a fact that is reflected in their speculative investment in an expanding middle class (rather than the urban proletariat), in the political centre (rather than the anarchistic fringe), and in the state (rather than civil society) as key sites of change. As the political essayist John Rae acknowledged in an 1881 article on 'Marx and the Young Hegelians': 'Hegel sought the principle of organic development in the State, but Marx sought it rather in civil society, and believed he had discovered it in that most mighty, though unconscious product of the large system of industry, the modern *proletariat*, which was born to revolution as the sparks fly upward'.[84] Even so, most British Hegelians—whether their works make allusion to Marx's writings or not—recognized the limitations of Hegel's *Philosophy of Right* identified by Marx, Rancière, Armstrong, and many other critics. It would indeed be naïve to pretend that Hegel's political theory is innocent of the charges that have been brought against it from so many different disciplinary perspectives. My aim here is accordingly not to whitewash Hegel by denying the potentially authoritarian implications of his theory of the state. Instead, I suggest that the works by Ward, Gissing, Carpenter, Wells, and Forster are speculative in a more limited sense. The idea of the state which we find in their texts is not—as Marx or Rancière would have it—that of an alien institutional structure which needs to be broken down before the social sphere can re-emerge; rather, these authors believe that the state can be made more democratic through structural reform and that it will be capable of healing class antagonisms, instead of being simply an instrument of class domination.

Marxist Hegelianism, Prussophilia, Modernism

So far, this chapter has described the contours of British state theory's Hegelian moment, and for practical reasons I have focussed on those aspects of British Hegelianism that can help us shed light on the reformist literary mode discussed in this book. Before moving on to my more site-specific literary-historical case studies, however, I want to conclude by reflecting on some of the endpoints of Britain's Hegelian moment in the 1910s and 1920s. This will also include some

---

[84] See Rae, 'The socialism of Karl Marx and the young Hegelians', *The Contemporary Review* (October 1881): 585–607: 597.

comments, speculative in their own way, about British Hegelianism's missed encounter with turn-of-the-century Marxism.

The antagonism between Hegelianism and Marxism in the decades around 1900 is a well-established part of intellectual-historical lore. There is some obvious truth in this version of the story: the Second International—the organization of socialist parties that existed between 1889 and 1916 until it was succeeded by the Communist International—was unwavering in its hostility to Hegelianism. As Stathis Kouvelakis reminds us, it was 'the devalorization or rather repression of Hegel that was the distinctive sign of Second International Marxism in general.'[85] Fuelled by Friedrich Engels's late writings, which were being canonized into orthodoxy by the Second International's leaders, this opposition to Hegel involved attempts to draw a cordon sanitaire around the dialectical *method* by artificially differentiating it from Hegel's *system*: while the latter supposedly suffered from Hegel's political conservatism and philosophical idealism, the former had been recast ('stood on its feet') by Marx and successfully repurposed in the interest of revolutionary critique. According to this account of the history of Marxism, it was only in subsequent decades—with the work of Georg Lukács and Antonio Gramsci, and with the emergence of Western Marxism from the 1920s onwards—that Marxists turned once more to Hegel in order to explain the workings of hegemony and the material efficacy of socio-cultural forms.

It is tempting to imagine what might have been the outcome of a more sustained intellectual encounter between British Hegelianism and Marxism in Britain around 1900. There is some textual evidence that points to these moments of missed connection. For example, Bax's work indicates that Hegel's thinking— not just Hegel's dialectical 'method', but also his 'system' (the stadial progression of objective spirit and the *Philosophy of Right*'s theory of *Sittlichkeit*)—managed to speak to figures on the socialist left.[86] As I have suggested, Hegelianism lent support to Bax's interest in exploring a broad range of social forms: instead of etherealizing the (cultural, social, artistic, legal) superstructure into a mere epiphenomenon of deeper structural contradictions, Hegelian thought presented these forms as a key site of socio-political contestation and transformation. Bax's concurrent interest in Hegel and Marx is well documented by numerous essays he wrote for socialist journals in Britain and Germany, including one of the first sympathetic articles on Marx to be published in Britain.[87] At the same time that Bax was promoting Hegel, his translation of several chapters from Marx's

---

[85] Kouvelakis, 'Lenin as reader of Hegel: Hypotheses for a reading of Lenin's notebooks on Hegel's *The Science of Logic*', in *Lenin Reloaded: Toward a Politics of Truth*, ed. Sebastian Budgen, Stathis Kouvelakis, and Slavoj Žižek (Durham, NC: Duke University Press, 2007), pp. 164–94 (p. 170).

[86] Hegel had used the term 'objective spirit' in his *Encyclopedia* (1817) to denote the degrees of rationality specific to a given society's social practices and institutions. Like the concept of *Sittlichkeit* itself, 'objective spirit' is a recurrent term in the works of British Hegelians.

[87] Bax, 'Karl Marx' (Leaders of Modern Thought 23), *Modern Thought* 3.12 (1881): 349–54.

Capital (book 1) had begun to be published in the journal *To-Day: A Monthly Gathering of Bold Thoughts*. These overlapping theoretical interests indicate that—instead of framing British Hegelianism as an antiquarian relic or as a frivolous by-product of intellectual history—we should try to reimagine it as a vanishing mediator in the emergence of critical theory. In this view, Hegelianism helped to set in motion modes of cultural inquiry that would only become fashionable again around the mid-twentieth century, following the theoretical interventions of Hegelian Marxism. Unfortunately, in spite of his role as a trailblazer for British Marxism, Bax never elaborated at a theoretical level how the gulf between Hegelianism and Marxism might be bridged. If he had done so, the results of this theoretical synthesis would have to be discussed under the label of 'Marxist Hegelianism' rather than 'Hegelian Marxism', given the relative historical predominance of Hegelianism over Marxism in late-nineteenth-century Britain.

It seems that some Hegelian Marxists of the 1920s and 1930s recognized the significance of British state theory's Hegelian moment as well as its ability to speak to contemporary impasses in Marxist thought. This is true in particular of figures such as Karl Korsch who were concerned about the paucity of advanced Marxist theories of the state. Just before the outbreak of World War I—and some time before he rose to fame as one of the towering figures of early Western Marxism— the young Korsch had spent two years in England during which he joined the socialist Fabian Society and participated in its debating circles. Recalling these experiences one decade later in his best-known work *Marxism and Philosophy* (1923), Korsch remarked that 'the crisis of Marxist theory' around 1900 had 'show[n] itself most clearly in the problem of the attitude of social revolution towards the State'. Korsch lamented that the theory of the state had 'hardly concerned the major theoreticians and publicists of the Second International'.[88] As a result of this neglect, he observed, Marxists lacked a cogent explanation of how the transition from the bourgeois state to communism was to be imagined. It was also unclear how this transition was to be achieved in practice: would it entail a complete revolutionary break with bourgeois institutions, or would it involve something more like a dialectical *Aufhebung* of the bourgeois state into the communist one? Korsch believed that a properly dialectical communist theory of this transformation had only started to come into view in 1917, with Lenin's elaboration of Marx's and Engels's concept of the proletarian dictatorship in *The State and Revolution* (1917).

While Korsch lamented the absence of a communist theory of the state, his slim-line *Marxism and Philosophy* made no attempt to supply such a theory. Even so, his book included a few pointers that served to highlight neglected traditions

---

[88] Korsch, *Marxism and Philosophy* (London: Verso, 2012), pp. 52–3.

of Hegelian thought on which communists of the 1920s might be able to build. It is in these sections of his book that Korsch evokes the years he had spent in England. German progressives, he points out, 'with a few exceptions quite failed to see that the Hegelian system, although pronounced dead in Germany for decades, had continued to flourish in several foreign countries, not only in its content but also as a system and a method.'[89] Korsch's nod to British Hegelianism, so tantalizing for its brevity, forms part of his broader attempt to re-establish Marxism as the successor to Hegel's philosophy. It is especially significant that Korsch advocates—*contra* Engels—an attention to Hegel's philosophy 'as a system *and* a method': any serious attempt to develop a fully communist theory of the state, Korsch suggests, must work through those systematic aspects of Hegel's political theory that seemed most unpalatable to Marxists. Korsch's recommendation renounces Engelsian orthodoxy, but it also sheds light on a forgotten philosophical schism within 1920s Western Marxism: after all, it was Lukács's Engelsian defence of the dialectical 'method' in *History and Class Consciousness* (1923)—rather than Korsch's more contentious suggestion that communists engage with the whole 'system' of Hegelian state theory—that would enter the mainstream of Western Marxism.[90]

Korsch's writings offer a glimpse of the kind of political thinking that might have been produced by a more sustained exchange between Marxists and British Hegelians around 1900. It was a consequence of this missed intellectual encounter that British Marxism in the first half of the twentieth century failed to evolve a body of critical theory that resembled—either in ambition or theoretical sophistication—the mode of Hegelianism represented in Italy by Antonio Labriola, Benedetto Croce, and Antonio Gramsci. As numerous scholars have pointed out, Gramsci's attention to hegemonic (superstructural) forms— grounded in a principled resistance to Second International orthodoxy—was mediated through Croce's non-revolutionary brand of Hegelian idealism,[91] and much the same could be said of Gramsci's influential attempts to formulate a Marxist theory of the state. Gramsci's writings often recall central motifs of British Hegelianism. This includes Gramsci's vision of a speculative overcoming of the opposition between individuals and institutions: 'Structure', Gramsci observes in the *Prison Notebooks*, 'ceases to be an external force which crushes man,

---

[89] Korsch, *Marxism and Philosophy*, p. 39.

[90] Lukács's earliest statement of his position came in 'What is Orthodox Marxism?' (1919): 'whether someone is or is not a Marxist is not determined by his conviction of the truth of individual theses, but by something quite different: *the method.*' See Lukács, *Tactics and Ethics, 1919-1929* (London: Verso, 2014), p. 19. Lukács's return to a form of Hegelian stadial ontology in his later writings, notably in *Die Eigenart des Ästhetischen* (1963) and the unfinished *Zur Ontologie des Sozialen Seins*, was a response to very different conjunctural pressures and don't need to concern us here.

[91] Edmund E. Jacobitti, 'Hegemony before Gramsci: The case of Benedetto Croce', *The Journal of Modern History* 52.1 (1980): 66–84; Perry Anderson, *The Antinomies of Antonio Gramsci* (London: Verso, 2017), pp. 98–100.

assimilates him to himself and makes him passive and is transformed into a means of freedom, an instrument to create a new ethico-political form and a source of new initiatives.'[92] In a related vein, Gramsci's anticipation of the post-bourgeois (communist) state describes it as a form of life in its own right: the vision of the state that emerges from Gramsci's work does not involve a complete demolition of existing institutions, but rather their piecemeal transformation into an 'ethical state', what Gramsci calls 'the "image" of a State without a State'.[93]

As I indicated in the Introduction, it was only with the publication of Raymond Williams's works of the 1950s and 1960s that British Marxists began to develop an understanding of institutional change able to match Gramsci's. To be fair, the course of Hegelianism in the 1910s had not helped to encourage the interest of political radicals. Detractors on both sides of the Channel gloated that World War I had demonstrated once and for all the link between Hegel's theory of the state and the violent excesses of Prussian militarism. In his book-length attack on Bosanquet's *The Philosophical Theory of the State*, L. T. Hobhouse noted, with an eye to Hegel, that 'when the state is set up as an entity superior and indifferent to component individuals, it becomes a false god, and its worship the abomination of desolation, as seen at Ypres or on the Somme'.[94] The most important Continental Hegelian of the period, Franz Rosenzweig, seconded Hobhouse's assessment, and in his 1920 Preface to *Hegel und der Staat* he lamented that his book came too late to rekindle progressive interest in the 'free and cosmopolitan' (*freie Weltluft atmend*) state Hegel had envisioned in the early nineteenth century. Hegel's philosophy, Rosenzweig pointed out, had been used to legitimize a nationalist war that had turned Germany into a 'field of rubble'.[95]

In Britain no one did more to cement Hegel's image as a proponent of Prussian militarism than the redoubtable politician-cum-philosopher Richard Haldane. In the mid-1870s, Haldane's parents had briefly considered sending their teenage son to Balliol College, Oxford, where Green was a Fellow. Fearing the influence of Anglicanism on their son, Haldane's father decided to send his son to Göttingen instead—Göttingen being at the time one of Prussia's centres of learning. Green's works had made a great impression on the young Haldane, and Göttingen continued to fuel his budding love affair with German idealism. Upon his return to Britain in the late 1870s, Haldane began to mingle with progressive Liberal politicians such as Hobhouse and Herbert Asquith, and his Greenian and Hegelian leanings quickly led him to sympathize with the social reform movements associated with the period's New Liberalism. Haldane's Hegelianism—and

---

[92] Gramsci, *Selected Prison Notebooks*, ed. Quentin Hoare and Geoffrey Nowell-Smith (London: Lawrence and Wishart, 1971), pp. 366-7.

[93] Gramsci, *Selected Prison Notebooks*, p. 263.

[94] Hobhouse, *The Metaphysical Theory of the State: A Criticism* (London: George Allen, 1918), p. 136.

[95] Rosenzweig, *Hegel und der Staat*, p. 18.

his admiration of all things Prussian—came to the fore when he joined the
Liberal Government of Henry Campbell-Bannerman as Secretary of War in
1905, an appointment he held for seven years. It was in this post that Haldane
implemented a set of modernizing reforms (popularly known as the Haldane
Reforms) that would make him famous. The reforms, Haldane recalled in his
Autobiography (1929), were intended to transform Britain's troops into a
'Hegelian Army' whose efficiency and unconditional sense of duty would put
them on a par with Prussia's.[96] Haldane's presentation of the state as the
enforcer of iron discipline and authoritarian control so completely tarnished
Hegel's popular image in Britain that one critic dismissed it as an acute case of
'Hegelitis'.[97] A conspicuous symptom of Haldane's Hegelitis was his tendency to
flatten the dialectical progression of the forms of *Sittlichkeit* into a linear historical
teleology: ignoring the function attributed to critique and speculation in the works
of the British idealists, Haldane reimagined Hegel's political theory as a blueprint
for authoritarian experiments in social engineering. Needless to say, Haldane's
reading of Hegel as a champion of Prussian-style militarism bore about as little
resemblance to the exploratory and speculative spirit of British Hegelianism as
Stalin's Diamat of the 1930s did to Marx's revolutionary dialectic. And yet,
Haldane's prominent status as a political figure meant that his reductive and
biased misreading of Hegel's political theory was able to acquire significant
cultural cachet in the 1910s and 1920s, thereby eclipsing the more intellectually
nuanced versions of Hegelianism I have traced in this chapter.[98]

The hostility towards Hegelian rationalism kept intensifying throughout the
1910s, but it also yielded some unexpected literary results. Most importantly
perhaps, anti-Hegelianism came to support the emergence of a distinctly modernist aesthetic. While late Victorian and Edwardian authors writing in the
reformist literary mode had characteristically imagined political change in terms
of a painstaking engagement with the limited cultural, social, and aesthetic forms
of the present, many modernist writers began to flirt with irrationalist philosophies that lent intellectual substance to their revolutionary assault on the old and
to their desire to 'make it new'. A key site for this artistic transition was *The New*

---

[96] Haldane's brutalist version of Hegel's thought found articulation in a string of publications that
included his autobiography as well as the philosophical study *The Reign of Reality* (1921).

[97] Oscar Levy, 'A reply to Lord Haldane's lecture on German literature', *The New Age* (Supplement)
9.23 (1911): 1–7 (p. 4).

[98] The heated resistance that was generated by these developments foreclosed interest in new
engagements with Hegel's thought. A notable side effect was the failure of Benedetto Croce's work to
spark progressive (or Marxist) enthusiasm for Hegel. Croce had had an important influence on
Gramsci and his writings were beginning to be translated by Douglas Ainslie in the mid-1910s—see,
e.g., Croce's *What Is Living and What Is Dead of the Philosophy of Hegel* (London: Macmillan, 1915). As
early as 1893, Croce had drawn attention to Hegel's thought as an antidote to the prevailing spirit of
'positivism' which, Croce claimed, had effectively flattened the dialectical concept of 'becoming' into a
question of teleological 'evolution'. See Croce, *La storia ridotta sotto il concetto generale dell' arte*
(Milan: Adelphi, 2017).

Age, the little magazine that became one of the principal outlets for modernist work in the 1910s. Under the editorship of A. R. Orage, the magazine regularly featured articles—by Hubert Bland, T. E. Hulme, and others—that reflected on the complex legacies of Hegelian thought and that sought to spell out their implications for the formulation of a self-consciously modernist aesthetic.

A central figure in this particular genealogy of anglophone modernism is Hulme, whose theoretical writings had a formative influence on the Imagism of the 1910s and on the high modernism of the 1920s. In several of his essays for *The New Age*, Hulme expresses his opposition to Hegelian speculation which he (even more so than Bax) finds at risk of sliding into hyperrational panlogism. For example, writing in 1909, Hulme praises Bax for updating Hegel for the late nineteenth century: commending Bax's 'lucidity and directness' as a thinker, Hulme notes approvingly that Bax 'has made a brilliant and powerful attack from a new point of view on Hegelian panlogism.'[99] Hulme insists that Bax's attention to the 'alogical' is not an isolated critique of Hegel, but that it points to a much larger (modernist) vogue for irrationalist thought. Hulme explains this new fashion by noting that it is a reaction against the work of the British Hegelians, modernism's philosophical *Übervater*: 'You must have been sophisticated and have sinned before you can experience the relief of repentance. You must first have been a Hegelian before you can get enthusiastic over the general anti-intellectualist movement in philosophy.' (265) According to Hulme, however, Bax had not gone far enough in his criticism of Hegelian rationalism. It was therefore necessary to look abroad, to Continental Europe: whereas, for Bax, rational concepts 'do ultimately contain and control the alogical as the hexagons in the comb contain the honey', the French philosopher Henri Bergson had taken the more radical step of proclaiming the absolute ontological priority of the (experiential) particular over the (philosophical) concept.

> There are two ways in which a man may be led to the denial of the possibility of including the alogical under the logical. If one emphasises the character of the flux as motion one sees that the static concepts can never represent it. So Bergson. If one emphasises the infinity of detail in the immediately given, its grittiness, its muddiness, and hence the impossibility of pulling it in the smooth, tidy, geometrical concepts, one arrives at Bax. This difference affects their view of the function of concepts in the flux.   (265)

Scholars of modernism are familiar with the aesthetic and political dimensions of Hulme's Bergsonism: on the one hand, his propagation of Imagism (the poetic movement that proclaimed the importance of experiential instants), and on the

---

[99]   Hulme, 'Searchers after reality', *The New Age* 5.13 (1909): 265–6 (p. 265).

other his advocacy of Georges Sorel's brand of anti-institutional anarcho-syndicalism.[100] However, literary historians have generally failed to recognize the extent to which Hulme's modernist irrationalism was a reaction against British idealism.[101] Hulme's dialogue with Bax's thought suggests that his aesthetics and his politics—both of which exerted such a profound influence on the complexion of Anglo-American literary modernism—were intimately connected to his rejection of Hegelian speculation. It was only against the backdrop of a reformist literary mode that aimed at the overcoming of social fragmentation that Hulme's own modernist valorization of singularity could take on a fully revolutionary aspect.[102]

Literary modernism's revolutionary imperative to 'make it new' was only one (albeit a particularly prominent) domain in which the anti-Hegelian impulse of the 1910s and 1920s began to manifest itself. Given the prestige of modernism in literary studies today, it is easy to understand why a reflexive opposition to Hegelian idealism should (with a few exceptions) continue to be the order of the day in this field. The next couple of chapters will backtrack a little in order to explore in more literary-historical detail the progressive reformist imaginary that crystallized around 1900.[103] The specifically Hegelian inflection of the debates I have reconstructed in this chapter will slowly fade into the background although the contours of these debates will continue to inform my discussion of the reformist literary mode's critical and aspirational dimensions—at the centre of the literary texts explored in subsequent chapters, I suggest, lies the attempt to imagine the state in terms of emerging forms of life.

---

[100] Hulme was the translator of the first English edition of Sorel's syndicalist classic *Reflections on Violence* (1915).

[101] An exception to this trend is Henry Mead's *T. E. Hulme and the Ideological Politics of Early Modernism* (London: Bloomsbury, 2015).

[102] In contrast to my observations here, C. D. Blanton has recently offered a rich alternative account of (late) modernism's Hegelian dimensions, notably of modernist epic's ability to incorporate history. Blanton, *Epic Negation: The Dialectical Poetics of Late Modernism* (New York: Oxford University Press, 2015).

[103] I will return to the afterlives of the reformist literary mode, and to its complex relationship to interwar modernism, in the Coda.

2

'The Hope of Pessimism'

George Gissing, Mary Ward, and the Idea of an Institution

The 1880s and 1890s saw the growth of the settlement movement—the late Victorian reform movement that aimed to offer material support and education to London's poor, notably in the severely depressed working-class neighbour-hoods of the East End. The first wave of settlements included Toynbee Hall (set up by Henrietta and Samuel Barnett in 1884), Oxford House (also established in 1884), and the Bloomsbury-based University Hall (founded by Mary Augusta Ward in 1890 and consolidated in 1898 with another institution to form the larger Passmore Edwards Settlement). These institutions broke with the mid-Victorian practice of home visits to the poor in favour of a more centralized provision of care, and they were united in their attempt to mitigate the worst forms of socio-economic deprivation. The settlements offered some alimentation, but they were mainly intended to foster a range of activities that focussed on a combination of recreational activities, clubs, classes, and university extension lectures, while also sometimes comprising sick benefit societies and penny banks.

The Barnetts had first moved to the East End in the early 1870s when Samuel took up work as a vicar in Whitechapel. However, they soon found that their initial uncoordinated attempts to alleviate the plight of the poor had little effect, and Toynbee Hall—arguably the most famous of the settlements—was set up partly in response to this keen sense of failure. Toynbee Hall was to be a new kind of institution which would bring university students to London to work as volunteers for a few years. These young (male) students would help the poor, but they would also witness East End poverty at first hand and possibly help to devise solutions for it.[1] The university graduates would live together in the settlement houses, using their time to establish educational and cultural pro-grammes for their poorer neighbours, while also volunteering as members of workingmen's associations and local governing bodies. The Barnetts hoped that these innovations would help to mitigate what they saw as the main problems

---

[1] While settlers were predominantly male, settlements—owing not least to the examples of Henrietta Barnett and Mary Ward herself—also held an 'enormous appeal [...] for a generation of women reformers'. See Emily K. Abel, 'Toynbee Hall, 1884–1914', *Social Service Review* 53.4 (1979): 606–32 (p. 609).

British Literature and the Life of Institutions: Speculative States. Benjamin Kohlmann, Oxford University Press.
© Benjamin Kohlmann 2021. DOI: 10.1093/oso/9780198836179.003.0003

of contemporary British society—the segregation of social classes and the immiseration of the urban proletariat. The East End settlements, Samuel Barnett noted, were intended as a reformist alternative both to 'revolutionary schemes' which threatened to 'turn the world upside down', and to merely personal 'philanthropic schemes which touch but the edge of the question'.[2]

As Daniel Siegel explains, the central innovation of the settlements was their break with older philanthropic practices of 'visiting' and a new shift towards institutionalized practices of 'hospitality' (which turned the tables on the reformers by 'showcas[ing] the life of the cultured classes' to members of the working class).[3] While the Barnetts' settlement continued to place special emphasis on charity and tutelary relationships, university graduates were also asked to see their role as that of neighbours. Toynbee Hall, Samuel Barnett hoped, would nourish more egalitarian forms of coexistence: he 'wanted not only "settlement", but sharing of experience, not only contact, but community.'[4] Toynbee Hall was designed to offer numerous formal and informal opportunities for exchange: 'those who live in settlements do ask to their rooms whom they learn to know in clubs, in committees, or at meetings, and are in turn asked again.'[5] The new practices of hospitality entailed an 'interrogation' of the idea of education itself: 'in most accounts of Toynbee Hall, the settlers, not their working-class neighbors, are the ones who seem to be the objects of an experiment'.[6] This suggests that for reformers, discovering the meaning of active citizenship and positive freedom was not simply a matter of conforming to a preestablished social 'station and its duties': more often than not, this process involved unsettling encounters across class boundaries and a defamiliarization of social and cultural preconceptions.[7] Literary writers understood that the London settlements were intended to foster the growth of active citizenship—the sense of social responsibility and service, theorized by T. H. Green and others, that I began to describe in Chapter 1—but they also recognized that this process would be at best an exploratory and halting one.

The university graduates who flocked to the settlements in the closing decades of the nineteenth century may have been animated by a feeling of social duty to help those who were less fortunate than themselves, yet, as many critics have

---

[2] Samuel Barnett, 'University settlements' [1884], in *Practicable Socialism* (London: Longmans, 1888), pp. 165–74 (p. 167).

[3] Siegel, *Charity and Condescension: Victorian Literature and the Dilemmas of Philanthropy* (Athens: Ohio University Press, 2012), pp. 111–12.

[4] Asa Briggs and Anne Macartney, *Toynbee Hall: The First Hundred Years* (London: Routledge, 1984), p. 5.

[5] Barnett, 'Hospitalities' [1895], quoted in Siegel, *Charity and Condescension*, p. 111.

[6] Siegel, *Charity and Condescension*, p. 112.

[7] 'My station and its duties' is the title of the fifth chapter of F. H. Bradley's *Ethical Studies* (1876). The distorted view of Bradley as an advocate of social organicism and political quietism is the result of a selective reading of 'My station and its duties', a much-anthologized text that is often misleadingly reprinted as though it were a stand-alone essay. See Chapter 1 of the present book for discussion of Bradley's dialectical thought.

pointed out, this shared sense of vocation should not blind us either to the fundamental religious and political divisions that fissured the settlement movement or to the propagation of class-specific concepts of culture which these institutional projects entailed. The present chapter pays attention to these important qualifications. However, I also contend that criticism of the settlement project—especially when it was being voiced by members of the working class who were the settlements' intended beneficiaries—in its turn energized a more capacious understanding of institutionality. This more expansive vision of institutionality presented settlements as sites of social coexistence and cross-class solidarity that were hospitable to counter-hegemonic critique. I focus on two novels which can be situated in the historical ambit of the settlement movement, George Gissing's *Thyrza* (1887) and Mary Augusta Ward's *Robert Elsmere* (1888). Published within a year of each other, the two books are connected by a web of intellectual, political, and biographical links, and they offer us an entry point into the period's tangled debates about institutional reform. Gissing's and Ward's novels give strikingly different assessments of the socio-political promise of the settlement movement, yet as I suggest, they can both be read as contributing to debates about the social and political dimensions of philosophical idealism around 1900. More specifically, both texts respond to the reimagining of institutionality, which the previous two chapters associated with Britain's Hegelian moment.

Many contemporary scholars describe the late Victorian settlement movement as an early step in the implementation of proto-welfare state structures in Britain, and they also note the galvanizing influence which Green's writings and teaching had on the movement. Seth Koven comments that 'Green's call for a more expansive role for the state in rectifying social inequalities (even as he continued to exalt the efficacy of voluntary associations and individual moral action and growth) powerfully influenced the first generations of male settlers.'[8] In a related vein, the historian Derek Fraser notes that 'the two men most closely associated with the creation of the Welfare State'—William Beveridge (the author of the 1942 Report that paved the way for the founding of the National Health Service in 1948) and Clement Attlee (the prime minister who oversaw the creation of the welfare state in Britain after 1945)—'both spent formative years in the East End settlements.' 'These experiences', Fraser observes, 'exposed many young men and women to the practical shortcomings of the individualist ideology, now being theoretically challenged by the idealist philosopher T. H. Green.'[9] Green

[8] Koven, *Slumming: Sexual and Social Politics in Victorian London* (Princeton: Princeton University Press, 2006), p. 239. Gertrude Himmelfarb writes that the settlements were 'the existential realization of Green's philosophy' (*Poverty and Compassion* [New York: Knopf, 1991], p. 243).

[9] Fraser, *The Evolution of the British Welfare State: A History of Social Policy since the Industrial Revolution*, 4th ed. (London: Palgrave, 2009), p. 162. Mark Bevir explores Green's contribution to 'social-welfare liberalism' from the perspective of intellectual history: see *The Making of British Socialism* (Princeton: Princeton University Press, 2011), Chapter 11.

encouraged a more positive approach to state intervention, and he also argued that the state needed to intervene to protect individuals from the demeaning effects of poverty. Britain's poor, Green noted, were 'left to sink or swim in the stream of unrelenting competition, in which we admit that the weaker has not a chance'.[10] What was required was a form of state intervention that curbed 'competition' and that helped to protect individuals from the worst effects of freewheeling laissez-faire.[11]

The specifically aesthetic repercussions of this line of reformist thought—its particular contribution to what I have called the period's reformist literary mode—have not been spelled out. As I argue, Gissing's and Ward's novels offer complementary artistic explorations of the new institutional structures that began to emerge in the context of the settlement movement of the 1880s. Unlike most other literary works discussed in this book, these two novels also intervene directly in idealist debates about institutionality: while *Thyrza* (a book which had carried the working title *The Idealist*) critiques forms of idealist dualism which contrast the world of appearances with an impossibly distant sphere of moral and political ideals, *Robert Elsmere* (a book dedicated to the recently deceased Green) presents us with an understanding of institutional innovation that responds more closely to the speculative form of the state I sketched out in the preceding two chapters.[12] Whereas Gissing treats the stark antagonism of ideal and reality as the source of intense pessimism, Ward's novel tries to imagine institutions as a fully realized form of life capable of mediating between the two spheres. Ward's characterization of Robert Elsmere, the fictional parson who abandons his parish in order to create a settlement in London, could, with some justice be applied to Ward's book itself: instead of 'resting in negation or opposition', her novel instantiates an aspirational mode of idealist thought that 'presse[s] forward to a new synthesis', namely towards a mediation of the real with the ideal that Green had described as 'the fulness of the idea'.[13]

Before we move on to Gissing's and Ward's novels, however, a caveat is in order. To talk about the aesthetic work of *Robert Elsmere* in terms of a quasi-Hegelian 'new synthesis' could be taken to suggest that Ward imagines the settlement movement as the imposition of socio-cultural hegemony on an inert working class—as the consolidation of a homogeneous consensus that shuts down

---

[10] Green, *Prolegomena to Ethics* (Oxford: Clarendon Press, 2004), p. 288 (§ 245).

[11] Among the forms of state support advocated by Green was the introduction of compulsory basic education, although he also left the door ajar for the provision of additional services (e.g. free health care) as and when circumstances called for them. See Tyler, *Common Good Politics: British Idealism and Social Justice in the Contemporary World* (London: Palgrave-Macmillan, 2017), pp. 83–5.

[12] For Gissing's initial thoughts about *Thyrza*'s title, see Pierre Coustillas, *The Heroic Life of George Gissing, Part I: 1857–1888* (London: Pickering & Chatto, 2011), p. 279.

[13] Mary Augusta Ward [Mrs Humphry Ward], *Robert Elsmere*, ed. Miriam Elizabeth Burstein (Brighton: Victorian Secrets, 2013), p. 413; Green, 'An estimate of the value and influence of works of fiction in modern times' [1862], in *Works of Thomas Hill Green*, vol. 3: *Miscellanies and Memoir* (London: Longmans, 1906), pp. 20–45 (p. 31).

the space for further conversation. Importantly, however, *Robert Elsmere* echoes the internal dynamic of the reformist literary mode that I described in previous chapters: the novel does not discard the criticisms brought against the settlement movement by Gissing and others, but rather aims to install the principle of reparative critique at the heart of its understanding of institutional reform. It is in this sense that we should understand the retrospective assessment of Green's reform-minded idealism by his fellow Hegelian John Muirhead: 'To [Green] reform did not mean the triumph of one class or political party over another, but the development of the idea of what the social union could be made to mean for all. [. . .] In origins and idea institutions are the repository of man's ideas of the social good, and even at their worst much more frequently ossifications than forcible intrusions from without.'[14]

As I spell out in more detail in my reading of *Robert Elsmere*, Green's emphasis on 'social union' and the 'social good' does not signify a unitary vision of unfractured social consensus. On the contrary, Green calls for institutional guarantees that support a way of life built around individual freedom and the possibility of articulating dissent. In his 'Lectures on the Principles of Political Obligation' (1879–80), Green had acknowledged that to the economically deprived, state institutions can seem 'an external necessity, which he no more lays on himself than he does the weight of the atmosphere or the pressure of summer heat and winter frosts'—an imposition that is felt all the more keenly by a member of 'the "proletariat"' who is expected 'to keep his hands off the superfluous wealth of his neighbour, when he has none of his own to lose'.[15] Similarly, Ward's account of Elsmere's attempt to set up a settlement in London shows that contradiction and disagreement—including the especially acute challenges of working-class atheism and socialism—are the settlement's vital life force. Ward's essentially aspirational account of settlement life, published two years before the founding of University Hall in 1890, does not imagine the growth of citizenship as a character-building exercise that inculcates in workers the middle-class entrepreneurial ideal of hardy self-reliance. Instead, Ward presents settlements as necessary supports for new forms of social life (*entgegenkommende Lebensformen*) that will foster the desire for further reform. Gissing's *Thyrza* offers an important preamble to the speculative work of Ward's novel because it homes in on constitutive tensions of the reformist literary mode: on the one hand, the

---

[14] Muirhead, *The Service of the State: Four Lectures on the Political Teaching of T. H. Green* (London: John Murray, 1908), pp. 74, 56. Muirhead adds that 'the Settlement, which owes its original inspiration, if not its actual inception, to Green, had he lived to see its spread, would have been an institution after his own heart' (83).

[15] Green, 'Lectures on the principles of political obligation', in *Lectures on the Principles of Political Obligation and Other Writings*, ed. Paul Harris and John Morrow (Cambridge: Cambridge University Press, 1986), p. 94.

tension between literature and ideas, and on the other, between philanthropic idealism and the harsh reality of London's East End.

Impasses of Idealism: Gissing and the 'Philanthropic Motif'

Gissing's artistic development in the 1880s is often understood either in relation to his embrace of a philosophically grounded pessimism (following his study of Arthur Schopenhauer in the first half of the decade), or in terms of his dread of the possibility of proletarian revolution. Critics sometimes resort to biographical explanations in order to make sense of Gissing's dual *ressentiment* towards middle-class respectability and collective proletarian agency: following an auspicious academic start, Gissing had been forced to leave university over a scandal involving petty theft, and after serving a month of jailtime in 1876, he found his social ambitions stalled and most conventional routes towards social upward mobility closed off. These experiences, Fredric Jameson explains, meant that the young Gissing sustained a social '"wound"—his particular way of living the Hegelian Unhappy Consciousness—[which] condemned him to wander forever between two classes in neither of which he was able to feel at home, or to know the stability of some definitive class identification'.[16] While there is truth in this version of the story, we should be careful not to dismiss the artistic corollary of this social dilemma—the fact that in Gissing's early novels 'virtually all subject positions and philosophies are undercut by competing positions and philosophies'—as a sign of mere 'narrative confusion'.[17] Instead, the sustained inconclusiveness of Gissing's novels—their profound ambivalence towards both reform and (proletarian) revolution—needs to be understood partly as a response to the crisis of idealist thought which Gissing encountered around 1880 through his study of post-Kantian philosophy. Gissing's philosophically sophisticated novels, I argue, can be read as attempts to resolve the stark opposition of reality and ideal that characterized this body of thought. Far from espousing Schopenhauerian pessimism completely, Gissing began to formulate an incipiently dialectical solution—what Gissing in an essay from 1882 calls 'the hope of pessimism'—that sought to mediate the sphere of the real with the ideal.[18] The case of *Thyrza* indicates that Gissing's difficulty in overcoming this dualism is connected to his analogous inability to think of the educational institutes in the East End as anything other than the foisting of

---

[16] Jameson, 'Authentic ressentiment: The "Experimental" novels of Gissing', *Nineteenth-Century Fiction* 31.2 (1976): 127–49 (p. 147).

[17] Constance D. Harsh, 'Gissing's the unclassed and the perils of naturalism', *ELH* 59.4 (1992): 911–38 (p. 913).

[18] The essay, entitled 'The hope of pessimism', remained unpublished during Gissing's lifetime. See Gissing, *Essays and Fiction*, ed. Pierre Coustillas (Baltimore: Johns Hopkins University Press, 1970), pp. 76–97.

middle-class ideals on an intellectually paralyzed working class. Gissing does not seem to have been aware of the new form of social-reformist idealism represented by Green and other British Hegelians, and it would be unfair to criticize Gissing for failing to develop a properly Greenian understanding of institutions.[19] What I want to propose here, then, is that Gissing's novels of the 1880s can be read as attempts to work through the central impasse of idealist thought—the seemingly insurmountable dualism between reality and ideal—to which the British Hegelians, too, were trying to offer new responses.

Gissing's first published novel *Workers in the Dawn* (1880) offers a succinct and explicit statement of the broader philosophical themes that govern Gissing's writings of the 1880s, including the particular institutional problematic that lies at the heart of *Thyrza*. The plot of *Workers in the Dawn* revolves around Arthur Golding, a young man living in London's slumlands, and the central storyline concerns Arthur's erotic involvement with two women: Helen Norman, an idealistic social reformer, and Carrie Mitchell, a working-class girl and prostitute. The various romantic complications and adulterous entanglements that ensue and that ultimately lead to Arthur's suicide don't need to concern us here. More relevant to the present discussion is Helen Norman's intellectual formation as an aspiring social reformer, parts of which take place during an extended sojourn in the German university town of Tübingen. The novel records Helen's intellectual interests in some detail, and parts of her reading mirror Gissing's own philosophical commitments and his declared ambition to 'preach [...] just and high *ideals* in this age of unmitigated egotism and "shop"'.[20] The texts that Helen studies with particular attention range from David Friedrich Strauss's *Life of Jesus Critically Examined* to Auguste Comte's philosophy of Positivism and Schopenhauer's *Parerga and Paralipomena*. Helen's reading of Strauss's historico-critical examination of the Bible helps to set the stage for her subsequent study of Comte: Comte's progressivist optimism appeals to Helen mainly because his account of humankind's transition from religious illusion to scientific enlightenment seems so neatly to fill the vacuum left by Strauss's demystification of Christian religion. The linking of Strauss and the secularist Comte was not unusual in the British context, given the towering status attained by the two thinkers thanks to translations by George Eliot (whose rendering of Strauss's *Life of Jesus* had been published in 1846) and Harriet Martineau (whose reader's digest *The Positive Philosophy of*

---

[19] In 1880's *Workers in the Dawn*, the Reverend Edward Norman, who adopts the novel's male protagonist Arthur Golding, is said to have been part of the 'set at Balliol', Green's Oxford college. Gissing, *Workers in the Dawn* (Brighton: Victorian Secrets, 2010), p. 25. It is impossible to ascertain, however, to what extent Gissing was aware of the precise philosophical content of Greenian idealism.

[20] Gissing's remarks about his aims in writing *Workers in the Dawn* are quoted in P. J. Keating, *The Working Classes in Victorian Fiction* (London: Routledge, 1971), pp. 53–4 (orig. emph.).

Auguste Comte was first printed in 1853). It is Gissing's mention of the as-yet untranslated Schopenhauer that calls for our attention.[21]

Gissing had read some texts by Schopenhauer in the original German, and it appears from his journals, essays, and fictional writings that he quickly assimilated key aspects of Schopenhauer's thinking. The reference to Schopenhauer's *Parerga and Paralipomena* in *Workers in the Dawn* is particularly instructive because it hints at the nature of Gissing's view of post-Kantian idealism. *Parerga and Paralipomena*, first published in German in the 1850s, comprised a series of shorter essays and reflections that elaborated on ideas Schopenhauer had presented in his earlier *The World as Will and Representation* (1819). The book's opening essay, entitled 'Sketch of a History of the Doctrine of the Ideal and the Real', offers a programmatic statement of Schopenhauer's position in post-Kantian German philosophy. The 'Sketch' is organized around the claim that the history of philosophy centres on 'the problem of the ideal and the real, i.e. the question what in our cognition is objective and what subjective, thus what is to be ascribed to any things distinct from ourselves and what to ourselves.'[22] Schopenhauer notes that while the relationship of the real and the ideal had concerned Western philosophers since Plato (who posited a realm of ideas entirely distinct from reality and therefore unattainable to humans), this problematic received its most acute modern formulation in the work of Kant. By demonstrating that the world is only ever accessible to us in the form of mental representations, Kant bequeathed to subsequent thinkers, including Hegel and Schopenhauer himself, a stark dualism—a 'chasm' between the noumenal sphere of things in themselves and the world as it appears to us (8–9). The unknowability of the world outside the categories of our understanding, Schopenhauer observes, even extends to the realm of moral ideals which, according to Kant, are unknowable and can only be posited as regulative guidelines for practical action.

Workers in the Dawn suggests that Schopenhauer's philosophical pessimism offers a solution to the Kantian dualism that had left individuals stranded in a world emptied of human meaning and value. After 'reading through the two volumes of Schopenhauer [the *Parerga and Paralipomena*] twice, very carefully,' Helen admits that 'I am sure they will exercise a lasting influence upon my mind.' Having initially responded to Schopenhauer's writings with revulsion and 'expect[ing] to find him a misanthrope', she is surprised to find that Schopenhauer teaches the value of compassion:

---

[21] The first English edition of any of Schopenhauer's writings—a collaborative translation of *Die Welt als Wille und Vorstellung* (1819) by Robert Haldane and John Kemp—was published between 1883–86 as *The World as Will and Idea*.

[22] Schopenhauer, 'Sketch of a history of the doctrine of the ideal and the real', in *Parerga and Paralipomena: Volume 1*, ed. Sabine Roehr and Christopher Janaway (Cambridge: Cambridge University Press, 2014), p. 7.

Am I then a convert to the doctrine of pessimism? Not by any means, for, after all it appears to me that his pessimism is the least valuable part of Schopenhauer's teaching. The really excellent part of him is his wonderfully strong sympathy with the sufferings of mankind. Again and again he tells us that we should lose the consciousness of self in care for others, in fact identify ourselves with all our fellows, see only one great self in the whole world. For this doctrine alone I thank him heartily; it chimes exactly with the principle which has long been yearning for expression in my own mind.   (160)

As Helen discovers, Schopenhauer's philosophy is constructed around a foundational dualism of its own. She records a confession by her mentor in Tübingen, Dr Gmelin: 'with Gmelin, [Schopenhauer's philosophy of pessimism] is nothing more than a theory, it does not in the least influence his practical life, as indeed I know from experience. Yet it is strange to be pessimistic in theory and optimistic in practice; such a contradiction would be impossible in my own nature' (159). Helen is initially puzzled by Gmelin's views, but she finally comes around to his reading of Schopenhauer. Studying Schopenhauer teaches Helen to practice pessimism of the intellect and optimism of the will—a strategic division of labour that overcomes political paralysis by altogether ignoring the Kantian dualism between being and morality.

Helen focusses on Schopenhauer's defence of empathetic 'fellow-feeling' (*Mitleid*) because it resonates most immediately with her desire to engage in philanthropic work in London's East End.[23] Her reading of Schopenhauer leads Helen seamlessly on to Comte's positivism: 'It seems to me it is Comte's principle that the true destination of philosophy must be social, practical, and herein I heartily agree with him. He, too, insists strongly upon the development of sympathetic instincts for the human race at large. The latter principle I have thoroughly imbibed from Schopenhauer' (160). Comte's secular philosophy of social improvement is presented as a direct continuation of Schopenhauer's thought, although Comte's thinking comes with the added benefit of being more explicitly oriented towards practice: 'What encouragement he gives to ardent work!', Helen enthuses in her diary, anticipating a 'speedy rectification of all the errors of our social system': 'How grand to feel that one is actually helping on the progress of humanity' (161).

As several critics have pointed out, Helen's intellectual interests closely mirror Gissing's own immersion in Comtean ideas in the late 1870s. It was indeed only a few years later, in the early 1880s, that Gissing made 'the transition from Comtean Positivism to Schopenhauerian Pessimism'—a development that also led him to

---

[23] For the place of Schopenhauerian *Mitleid* in the conceptual system of British idealism, and for its difference from philanthropic 'condescension', see W. J. Mander, *Idealist Ethics* (Oxford: Oxford University Press, 2016), esp. pp. 201–5.

revise the centrality attributed to Comtean optimism in *Workers in the Dawn*.[24] Schopenhauerian pessimism, as Gissing came to view it in the 1880s, recognized the irremediable dualism of idealistic thinking that Comte's thinking had so blithely ignored. This new appreciation of Schopenhauer was useful to Gissing because it helped him to articulate, with greater cogency, the dilemmas that faced social reform movements in the closing decades of the nineteenth century. This impasse, as Gissing presented it in *Thyrza*, consisted in the tendency of reformers to confront a sordid reality with abstract moral imperatives for social improvement—a tendency that resulted in a sterile and socially inefficacious form of idealism. While the working title of Gissing 1887 novel (*The Idealist*) clearly signals his desire to explore the impasses of idealism as a reformist doctrine, *Thyrza* was not the only text in which Gissing satirized projects for social amelioration. For example, in *Demos* (1886), the young proletarian Mutimer comes into an inheritance that enables him to set up as a socialist employer. Before long, however, the disillusioned Mutimer abandons his idealism and begins to reinvent himself as a capitalist entrepreneur—in due course, his scheme for social reform implodes and the cooperative factory is forced to shut down. In a related vein, Gissing's slightly later novel *The Nether World* (1889) echoes the pessimism that runs through *Demos* and *Thyrza*: the novel offers a remorseless account of the corruption of philanthropic benevolence through economic interest—and once more an unexpected inheritance creates opportunities for charitable action that lead on to disastrous consequences and moral corruption.

Thyrza is particularly noteworthy in this context because it displays a topical interest in the settlement movement. The novel takes place over the course of four years in the early 1880s, and its core cast is formed by a group of three characters. First, there is Walter Egremont, an educated and wealthy young man who decides to set up an educational institution in Lambeth for the uplift of working men. During his work in Lambeth, he meets the thirty-five-year-old proletarian Gilbert Grail, who turns out to be the only worker receptive to Walter's high-minded educational aims. Thyrza, Gilbert's youthful and ethereally beautiful fiancée, completes the ill-fated trio. Soon enough, Walter and Thyrza fall in love with each other, and the resulting complications will in due course lead to Walter's self-imposed exile, the breakdown of his reformist schemes, and Thyrza's tragic death.

At several points in the novel, Gissing links Walter's idealist hopes for reform to the optimistic Comtean programme which Gissing himself had begun to reject after completing *Workers in the Dawn*. Walter repeatedly reminds Gilbert that in the future the 'religious spirit' will be of value only insofar as it lends affective support to the ethical imperatives of altruism—by contrast, theological 'Dogma

---

[24] Gissing, *Workers in the Dawn*, p. 609 (fn. 89).

will no longer help us. Pure love of moral and intellectual beauty must take its place.'[25] Gilbert, always eager to prove himself a good disciple, echoes these sentiments on various occasions. Broadcasting Walter's message to his fellow workers, he informs his friends that 'I think pretty much as you do about Christianity—about the dogmas that is, but we've no need to fear it in this way. Let's take what good there is in it and have nothing to do with the foolish parts' (193). Gissing's novel ruthlessly exposes the naivety of such attempts to wipe Christianity clean of its dogmatic 'parts' while preserving its 'spirit'. For example, Walter soon tries to convince himself that true reform is the result of a change of heart rather than of substantial institutional change:

> Well, now, we know there's no lack of schemes for reforming society. Most of them seek to change its spirit by change of institutions. But surely it is plain enough that reform of institutions can only come as the natural result of a change in men's minds. Those who preach revolution to the disinherited masses give no thought to this. It's a hard and a bad thing to live under an oppressive system; don't think that I speak lightly of the miseries which must drive many a man to frenzy. [...] I know perfectly well that for thousands of the poorest there is no possibility of a life guided by thought and feeling of a higher kind until they are lifted out of the mire. But if one faces the question with a grave purpose of doing good that will endure, practical considerations must outweigh one's anger. There is no way of lifting those poor people out of the mire; if their children's children tread on firm ground it will be the most we can hope for. But there is a class of working people that can and should aim at a state of mind far above that which now contents them. It is my view that our only hope of social progress lies in the possibility of this class being stirred to effort.   (114)

Walter's unconvincing 'hope of social progress' combines a resigned acceptance of the fate of the most deprived citizens of London ('There is no way of lifting those poor people out of the mire') with a wish to infiltrate working-class life with a distinctly middle-class ethos of self-help, self-reliance, and 'effort'. Walter's view of reform as an exercise in character-building links his project to the work of the Charity Organisation Society (COS), which had propagated similar views since its founding in 1869. As I indicated in Chapter 1, members of the COS sought to organize and enlarge voluntary initiative as a way of curbing the growth of new interventionist institutional mechanisms: interventionist policies, they claimed, threatened to sap the individual's independent moral energies. 'The duties of citizenship', Bernard Bosanquet affirmed with a view to the COS's work, had to be learnt first of all through the individual's participation in local collectives such

---

[25] Gissing, *Thyrza* (Brighton: Victorian Secrets, 2013), p. 115. Further citations will be given parenthetically in the main text.

as families, village communities, and personal relationships: while 'a healthy political interest is one mark of a good citizen, [...] we do not rightly indicate the duties of citizenship by demanding that politics—that some separate concern to be called citizenship—should play a great part in our lives.'[26] Walter's rationale for social reform, outlined in the previous passage, likewise privileges the improvement of character over the promises of large-scale institutional change. In Walter's case, his opposition to the 'change of institutions' grows in part from his anxious fixation on the threat of social 'revolution': fearful of a cataclysm that would level existing political structures and set England 'aflame in hideous warfare between luxury and hunger' (276), he fails to picture institutional change in non-revolutionary terms.

Thyrza locates the source of Walter's ineffectual reformist endeavours—including his failure to reckon with the promises of piecemeal institutional change—in the otherworldly quality of his idealism. In a characteristic moment of intense introspection and self-reflection, Walter muses over his abiding 'mental malaise': 'Had he not been growing conscious for some time of the artificiality of the link between himself and that so-called Society? Nay, conscious of it he had always been; therein consisted much of his idealism. [...] Now he was fast passing from that negative frame of mind to one of active opposition. He assured himself that a true and worthy impulse had gradually isolated him' (235). Walter's longing for solitude ('I mean to see less of people in general'; 103), which he repeatedly professes in his conversations with Thyrza and Gilbert, is the existential or experiential dimension of an idealism that tries to protect the purity of the ideal from the absorbing viscosity of the world. *Thyrza* dramatizes what Schopenhauer had identified as the impasses of idealist thought, and the novel specifically mirrors the stark antagonism between self and world—between inward morality and external law—that I described as the foundational problem addressed by the British Hegelians. Yet, while the British idealists (Green, Bradley, and others) had explored how reform might push beyond this debilitating impasse, Gissing's portrayal of Walter gives us a claustrophobic glimpse of an idealism that fails to translate its aspirations into the real world. *Thyrza* diagnoses the intellectual and political inefficacy of an overly abstract idealism: it exposes Walter's inability to imagine institutions as the very medium through which reformist hopes must be realized.

Thyrza shows how the problem of an otherworldly idealism metastasizes into the lives of other characters. Gissing's account of Gilbert's early life, for example,

---

[26] Bosanquet, 'The duties of citizenship', in Bosanquet (ed.), *Aspects of the Social Problem* (London: Macmillan, 1895), p. 9. As Stefan Collini observes, it is one of the internal contradictions of Bosanquet's Hegelianism that he vehemently opposed state intervention in his practical work for the COS, even as his writings often pushed for a stronger state by presenting it as the metaphysical embodiment of the common good. Collini, 'Hobhouse, Bosanquet, and the State: Philosophical idealism and political argument in England, 1880–1918', *Past & Present* 72 (1976): 86–111 (p. 93).

likewise exhibits the psychopathologies of a socially inert idealism: 'Gilbert', we are told, 'would stray alone in the quietest streets until he tired himself, then go home and brood over fruitless longings. In love, as afterwards in study, he had his ideal' (92). The same could be said of Thyrza who suffers from a tendency to regard her 'ideals' as 'too good, of course, to be realized' (357). Indeed, as the novel progresses, Thyrza becomes the symbolic embodiment of the tensions that plague Walter's idealism: 'Thyrza was [...] always dreaming of something beyond and above the life which was her lot,' the narrator informs us: '[she] was so deficient in the practical qualities which that life demanded' (72). By the end of the novel, Thyrza herself seems to transcend the confines of material existence. Contemplating the dying Thyrza's serenely quiet face, one character (Mrs Ormonde) marvels 'how spiritual was its beauty': 'sacred and inextinguishable', this vision of Thyrza's face directs Mrs Ormonde's 'thoughts to the purest ideals' (500). And Walter's description of Thyrza's deathbed portrait similarly finds in the painting 'the secret of the girl's soul, [...] something for which she yearned, passionately, yet with knowledge that it was for ever forbidden to her. A face of infinite pathos, which drew tears to the eyes, yet was unutterably sweet to gaze upon' (531).

Gissing's decision to change the title of his novel from *The Idealist* to *Thyrza* has diverted critical attention away from the political dimensions of Walter's idealism and towards the pathos-laden figure of Thyrza, whom the book's closing pages transfigure into a sentimental allegory of suffering 'womanhood' (500). However, we can bring the novel's philosophically sophisticated engagement with the question of social reform back into focus by recalling Fredric Jameson's comments on the peculiar status of 'philanthropy' in Gissing's early novels. The occurrence of 'the philanthropic motif' in these texts, Jameson argues, carries with it specific 'aesthetic dangers' because it introduces into the literary work an abstract language of moral demand—'an obligation or a *Sollen* rather than an already given state of being in the world'—that seems unassimilable into fictional discourse.[27] Jameson explains these tensions by invoking Tzvetan Todorov's 'modal poetics' according to which 'the "facts" or events—the fable or raw material—of a given fictive discourse undergo as it were transpositions from one register of potentiality or realization to another, in much the same way as the verb or a sentence may be reformulated in, say, the subjunctive or the imperative or the optative moods.' 'In such a perspective,' Jameson notes, 'the fundamental register of realistic narrative would constitute something like an indicative mood of full narrative realization.' By contrast, 'the philanthropic narrative register' resembles

---

[27] Jameson, 'Authentic *Ressentiment*', p. 136. The bulk of Jameson's article was reprinted in *The Political Unconscious* (1981), which omits central points of Jameson's earlier discussion of the 'modal poetics' of deontological *Sollen*.

a more complex modal auxiliary, of the type of the "ought to" or the verbal
obligation. At this point the structural account intersects with one of the great
themes of German idealistic philosophy, namely that of the relationship of the
ethical—always unrealized, always an obligation or a *Sollen* rather than an
already given state of being in the world—to being, history, and in the present
instance the aesthetics of narrative.   (Jameson 1976: 136)

On Jameson's account, the idealist novel is a chimera because any attempt to
incorporate ideas into a literary work is bound to expose fictional discourse to a
series of dualisms—between the novel and philosophy, between figure and
thought, between philosophical abstraction and experiential particularity. In
Chapter 1, I illustrated the abstract character of *Sollen* ('ought to') by way of
Hegel's critique of the universalist imperatives of Kantian morality: whereas
Kant had positioned the purity of moral intentions in total opposition to the
sphere of the social, Hegel sought to bridge the chasm between being and duty by
shifting attention to the sphere of *Sittlichkeit*, i.e. to a fully social understanding of
ethical responsibilities and obligations. Gissing's novel faces these problems head-
on. The stories of Walter, Thyrza, and Gilbert illustrate the unattainability and
unrealizability of the ideal, and they indicate that by 1887 Gissing had come to
agree with Schopenhauer's (and Hegel's) critique of the intransigent dualisms of
Kantian thought. Walter's inability to translate his idealism into action specifically
stems from his failure to entertain a more dialectical model of institutional
change—an understanding of institutions that is Hegelian in the sense that it
seeks to mediate the sterile imperatives of practical reason with the material
givenness of institutional structures. *Thyrza*, we could say, remains stuck at the
level of critique: the novel diagnoses the political, practical, and narrative impasse
of a certain form of idealism, but it does not present us with institutional
arrangements that would help to mitigate the harshness of this problem.

Thyrza fails to imagine how abstract (Kantian) *Sollen* can be given institutional
form. However, there are moments in the novel which begin to register
the unavailability of such a (Hegelian) speculative solution. For instance, despite
Jameson's assertion that *Thyrza* is governed by a 'philanthropic motif', the novel
is in fact highly critical of established practices of philanthropy. Frequently,
personalized charity is shown to be animated by self-centred motives: 'If ever
personal troubles began to worry her', we are told of Thyrza's sister Lydia, 'she
diligently bent her thoughts upon someone for whose welfare she was anxious,
and whom she might possibly aid. The rule had to submit to an emphatic
exception; the person to be thought of must be any one *save* that particular one
whose welfare she especially desired' (224; orig. emph.). In Gissing's novel,
practices of philanthropy magnify such comparatively inconspicuous psychological tics and finally reveal their ideological character. Walter's self-imposed
exile in America drives home to him philanthropy's complicity with the forces of

capitalism. 'American equality is a mere phrase,' he writes in a letter to his friend Mrs Ormonde,

> there is as much brutal injustice here as elsewhere. [...] I will submit to your reverent consideration the name of a great American philanthropist. Personally he was a disgusting brute; ignorant, base, a boor in his manners, a blackguard in his language [...]. Yet the man was a great philanthropist, and became so by the piling up of millions of dollars. Of course he did that for his own vulgar satisfaction. (466)

Gissing's novel shows up philanthropy's haphazardness—a charge that extends to attempts, by the COS and others, to make charity more rational by organizing it more efficiently. 'The approach by the Charity Organisation Society', Stefan Collini points out, was 'by the 1900s increasingly recognized as representing the anti-interventionist prejudices of a previous generation'.[28] *Thyrza* reflects this growing recognition of philanthropy's anachronism by painting personalized philanthropy as a psychological pathology.[29] The novel's opening chapters indicate that Walter's desire to engage in philanthropic work borders on obsession: as the novel's original title suggests, idealism is Walter's single defining character trait, so much so that he appears as a type ('The Idealist') rather than a fully rounded character. Finally, Gissing shows us how quickly Walter's philanthropic desire devolves into erotic attraction: as soon as Walter meets Thyrza, his ostensibly disinterested care for the poor hardens into an all-consuming romantic 'passion' (270).[30]

Gissing's antagonistic treatment of philanthropy in *Thyrza* also helps to explain his intensely hostile response to a contemporary review by the young writer Edith Sichel which categorized him as a 'philanthropic novelist'. Published in April 1888, Sichel's article contrasted the outlook of Gissing's books with the novels of Walter Besant. Besant's books, including his popular *All Sorts and Conditions of Men* (1882), had tried to raise awareness for hardship among the deprived population of England's urban centres. While Gissing's fiction homed in on the spectacular failures of socialist politics (in *Demos*) and of liberal philanthropic endeavours (in *Thyrza*), Besant's novels took a significantly brighter view of the

---

[28] Collini, 'Hobhouse, Bosanquet, and the State', p. 87.

[29] Gissing's biographer Pierre Coustillas observes that Gissing 'was aware of the inefficiency of charity, whether it came from the clergy or from rich private donors'. See Pierre Coustillas, *The Heroic Life of George Gissing*, vol. 1 (London: Pickering & Chatto, 2011), p. 291.

[30] The slippage between disinterested care and eroticized desire is explored in Bruce Robbins's discussion of 'erotic patronage' in *Upward Mobility and the Common Good: Toward a Literary History of the Welfare State* (Princeton: Princeton University Press, 2007), pp. 22–54. In a related vein, Jennifer Conary has observed that for Walter 'love, or at least true personal sympathy,' is the precondition of 'his social endeavours'. See Conary, '"Things of the heart and mind": Gender and philanthropy in George Gissing's *Thyrza*', *Victorians Institute Journal* 39 (2011): 293–315 (p. 306).

possibilities of social reform. *All Sorts and Conditions of Men*, for example, had imagined the founding of a 'Palace of Delight' that would deliver sweetness and light to the doorsteps of London's impoverished East Enders. For Sichel, the distinction between Gissing and Besant boiled down to contrary temperamental dispositions: 'the pessimism of Mr Gissing [. . .] allows him to believe in none but the blackest of futures; [i]t causes him at the same time and from sheer hopelessness to accept the present with much more resignation than the optimistic Mr Besant'.[31] While Gissing agreed that Sichel had correctly identified his resistance to abstract idealism (Gissing, Sichel had noted, 'writes to prove the failure of Idealism'[32]), the review stirred his anger because it misrepresented him as an advocate of the localized and personalized practices of cross-class philanthropy that Gissing regarded as outdated and inefficient.[33]

Sichel's review concluded that Gissing was writing according to a recognizable ('pessimistic') artistic formula, what Sichel memorably calls 'resolute wailing': while 'Mr. Besant [. . .] continually gallops away from truth' in his pursuit of the ideal, she asserted, Gissing's writing stuck to unembellished reality. In response to these apparently disparate artistic outlooks, Sichel proposed that a 'Via Media' was possible: Besant was 'the best in ideal, though Gissing be the best in fact; and if we could join [Besant's] aims, his buoyancy, [. . .] to the latter's love of truth, of facing the worst without flinching and of describing what he sees, we might perhaps find at least the alpha of the Sphinx's enigma.'[34] The unbridled idealism of Besant's novels and the disillusioned bent of Gissing's naturalism, Sichel claims, can be combined into a single reformist literary mode. Sichel is often chastised by Gissing scholars for being tone-deaf to the subtle modulations of his prose, with some critics unfairly dismissing her article as a form of attention-grabbing on the part of a young female author.[35] While I think that critics have been too quick to reject Sichel's argument out of hand, I would agree that it is problematic to locate the possibility of a speculative reformist literary mode in some spectral third space outside Gissing's and Besant's texts, where social critique ('pessimism', in Sichel's shorthand) is happily sublated into hopeful reformist aspiration ('optimism'). In fact, *Thyrza* itself registers the factors that stand in the way of a speculative resolution and that block the translation of abstract philanthropic imperatives (Kantian *Sollen*) into institutions that support

---

[31] Sichel, 'Two philanthropic novelists', *Edith Murray's Magazine* (April 1888): 506–18 (p. 515). The review has also been reprinted in Gissing, *The Critical Heritage*, ed. Pierre Coustillas (London: Routledge, 1972), pp. 114–26.

[32] Sichel, 'Two philanthropic novelists', p. 512.

[33] For Gissing's reaction to Sichel's review, see Coustillas, *The Heroic Life of George Gissing*, vol. 2 (London: Pickering & Chatto, 2012), pp. 60–1.

[34] Sichel, 'Two philanthropic novelists', p. 518.

[35] A combination of these views is at play in Coustillas's description of Sichel as a 'newcomer to the literary arena [. . .] quite prepared to solicit opinions [from Gissing] when they were not forthcoming'. Coustillas explains Gissing's apparent reluctance to engage in correspondence with Sichel by pointing to 'her own shallow optimism'. See Coustillas, *Heroic Life*, vol. 2, p. 61.

the growth of new forms of collectivity and social life. *Thyrza* presents us with the tentative outline of an institution (Walter's settlement) that might perform such a role, but the book depicts this institution exclusively as a receptacle for Walter's own philanthropic ambition. Most strikingly, perhaps, Walter's educational mission is cast in terms that pointedly recall older forms of personalized philanthropy—apart from a very limited number of classroom scenes, in which the workers appear as a deindividuated mass, the only interactions we see taking place in the school are those between Walter and Gilbert (and Walter and Thyrza). Gissing's well-documented opposition to older forms of philanthropy notwithstanding, his novel does not attempt to reimagine philanthropy as anything other than a type of personal charity and middle-class condescension.[36]

Gissing's novel mirrors the tensions that Chapter 1 identified as central to the philosophical projects of the British idealists of the 1870s and 1880s. *Thyrza* notably figures the 'philanthropy motif' as an abstract moral imperative, as a form of unrealizable Kantian *Sollen*, and it fails to reimagine this *Sollen* as a realized form of life, as a type of Hegelian *Sittlichkeit* that would lend such imperatives a degree of experiential and existential concreteness. Accordingly, the novel's constitutive strains—what one critic has called the text's 'narrative confusion'—derive not from Gissing's inability 'to identify wholeheartedly with an urban proletariat' or from some primal envy for proletarian 'class solidarity', but from the unavailability of an aspirational understanding of institutions. To put this another way: these formal strains do not stem from an inability to be fully revolutionary but from a failure to be sufficiently reformist.[37]

The narrative and philosophical problems that animate *Thyrza*—and the unrealized resolution towards which the novel gravitates—come into additional focus in Gissing's 1882 essay 'The Hope of Pessimism'. As I noted previously, this essay marks Gissing's break with Comte, who comes in for severe criticism because he tries to install a new 'Religion of Humanity' in place of older theological systems. Comte's post-theological 'Religion of Humanity', Gissing writes, is 'a creed essentially optimistic [. . .], founding itself, as it does, on the solid-seeming accretions of human knowledge, seeking its guarantee in the most obvious tendencies of what we call progress'.[38] By identifying Comte's smug anthropocentric 'religion' as a symptom of Europe's current stage of over-confident civilizational 'progress', Gissing shows that Comte introduces us to a particularly acute version of the problem of idealism: after all, 'it is not Humanity which the new religion makes the object of its worship, but an ideal embodiment of man's noblest faculties and attainments, a terrene divinity such as will never

---

[36] For discussion of philanthropy in terms of middle- and upper-class condescension, see Siegel, *Charity and Condescension*.
[37] Harsh, 'Gissing's *The Unclassed*', p. 913; Jameson, 'Authentic *Ressentiment*', pp. 148, 146.
[38] Gissing, 'Hope of Pessimism', p. 77.

find its avatar in human flesh' (88). Arguing against this extreme version of idealism, Gissing proposes a form of pessimism which he claims to derive from Schopenhauer. This pessimism is not a collective mood or *Stimmung*—on the order, say, of fin-de-siècle *ennui*—but a principled, 'conscious and consistent pessimism' (79): resisting the period's self-congratulatory celebrations of social and civilizational 'progress', it recognizes the 'material difficulties' (80) of human existence as well as the specific socio-economic inequities that characterize contemporary British society. As examples of the latter, Gissing mentions the immense 'wealth accumulated in the hands of yet fewer capitalists, and the immense majority toiling desperately for mere subsistence' (89), as well as the 'scheme of commercial competition tempered by the police-code, to which we are pleased to give the name of social order' (90). Our recognition of the debilitating injustices that characterize our collective life, Gissing warns, should not tempt us to give in to total resignation and defeatism. Instead of wholly 'subordinat[ing]' our 'metaphysical instinct' to the sobering dictates of 'realist philosophy', 'we should do our utmost to cherish and strengthen the metaphysical tendencies of the human mind, seeing that in such tendencies alone [. . .] is at present discernible a hope of the better order of the common life of men' (82). Hope, here, appears to emerge from within pessimism itself. What Gissing calls 'conscious and consistent' pessimism is accordingly best described as a critical tool that works to clear the ground for a future reparative engagement with given social conditions. Recalling the language of previous chapters, we could say that 'the hope of pessimism' describes an incipiently *dialectical* figure: it marks the precise point at which the aspirational dialectic in Gissing's work begins to stall, freezing it in place just as it should be moving from critique to reparative speculation.[39]

Gissing's intense antipathy to forms of personalized philanthropy—including the type of organized philanthropy practiced by the COS—led him to regard the Oxbridge graduates settling in the working-class neighbourhoods of London with less hostility than we might expect. Indeed, while Gissing never subscribed to state socialism, his views of charity seem to have evolved in step with the development of the settlement movement. Toynbee Hall had been set up by two supporters of the COS, Samuel and Henrietta Barnett, and their settlement grew from a related set of principles, notably from the belief that the poor would benefit most from paternalistic guidance exercised through personal relations. As I have suggested, Gissing had this model of charitable care in mind when he wrote *Thyrza*—a novel

---

[39] Upon finishing the 'Hope of pessimism' essay, Gissing commented in a letter to his brother that 'I think there is little doubt that my work will ultimately follow the line which has been hinted at all along, I mean that of philosophico-social speculation.' See *Collected Letters of George Gissing*, ed. Paul F. Mattheisen et al. (Athens: Ohio University Press, 1991), p. 103. Scholars have tended to emphasize the critical edge of Gissing's pessimism over its speculative momentum. 'No directly affirmative and collective movement could count on Gissing's allegiance for long', writes David Grylls: 'All of them, he felt, were too optimistic. [. . .] As usual, his positive impulses were eventually corroded by pessimism.' See Grylls, *The Paradox of Gissing* (London: Routledge, 1986), p. 25.

in which the educational enterprise of the workers' school never seems to extend beyond Walter's interactions with one or two students. By the late 1880s, however, the complexion of the settlement movement started to change as 'the Barnetts began distancing themselves from the narrowly charitable orientation of the COS. They demonstrated this difference [...] in their developing support in the 1890s and 1900s for state provisions such as old age pensions and school lunches for children.' It was these new attitudes—notably the settlers' ambitious view of what institutionalized care might accomplish—which pointed ahead 'to the establishment of the welfare state'.[40] Gissing seems to have become aware of these shifts in 1888 when he read William Gladstone's review of *Robert Elsmere*, which emphasized that the emerging conditions of popular democracy necessitated adjustments in the scale of reformist endeavours. Only a few years later, Gissing ended his novella *Sleeping Fires* (1895) with a tentative recommendation of the settlement idea.[41] The difference between the COS's programme of social reform and the settlements of the 1880s, Gissing realized, involved not only a new emphasis on the conditioning influence of material environments, but a wholly different understanding of institutionality as such. As the case of *Robert Elsmere* indicates more clearly, the settlement movement invited a new way of thinking about institutions that associated them with an emerging ethos or shared way of life, what I have called *entgegenkommende Lebensformen*.

Robert Elsmere, Idealism, and Institutionality

Gladstone's review singled out Gissing's 1884 novel *The Unclassed* (with a further appreciative nod to *Thyrza*) and Ward's *Robert Elsmere* as the most remarkable contemporary novels of 'the didactic and speculative class'.[42] Gladstone's linking of Gissing and Ward productively unsettles assessments which find Ward's and Gissing's artistic outlooks irreconcilable: the naturalist Gissing had no use, so the conventional literary-historical story goes, for the sort of idealist fiction represented by Ward's novel. The philosophical sophistication of Gissing's books, especially his substantive interest in post-Kantian philosophy, should suffice to dispel this reductive myth. Indeed, *Thyrza* features several episodes which reflect

---

[40] Diana Maltz, 'Blatherwicks and busybodies: Gissing on the culture of philanthropic slumming', in *George Gissing: Voices of the Unclassed*, ed. Martin Ryle and Jenny Bourne Taylor (London: Routledge, 2017), p. 22. Maltz also considers the possibility that Gissing 'reject[ed] the COS's model of discriminate philanthropy and opt[ed] for slum settlement instead' (25).

[41] Gladstone observed that any new reformist endeavour would have to address the concerns of 'the broad mass': see William S. Peterson, 'Gladstone's review of Robert Elsmere', *Review of English Studies* 21 (1970): 442–61 (p. 452). Gissing's diaries indicate that he saw Gladstone's review in 1888 but did not read *Robert Elsmere* until 1891. See *London and the Life of Literature in Late Victorian England: The Diary of George Gissing*, ed. Pierre Coustillas (Brighton: Harvester Press, 1978), pp. 28, 252.

[42] William Ewart Gladstone, 'Review of *Robert Elsmere*', *The Nineteenth Century* (May 1888): 766–88 (p. 787).

explicitly on the artistic pressures that burden novels of the 'didactic and speculative' class, and these episodes can help us shed light on the particular artistic tensions shared by *Thyrza* and *Robert Elsmere*.[43]

In a plotline which Gissing decided to cut for the second edition of his novel, Thyrza finds temporary refuge with Mrs Ormonde's friends Harold and Clara Emerson before returning to London to be reunited with the novel's other protagonists. In the central chapter of this narrative interlude, entitled 'A Minor Prophet', Harold confesses that he considers himself a poet and that he has been working on a long poem which he expects will do more to transform society than the French Revolution. As Constance Harsh has pointed out, Harold is in some ways Walter's *Doppelgänger*: both men are single-mindedly devoted to the cause of social reform ('What do you think of our present state of society', the earnestly probing Harold asks Thyrza: 'I mean, do you think the world is arranged well? Do you think things are all that they should be?'; 423); moreover, the social and artistic projects pursued by Walter and Harold turn out to be equally ineffectual; and finally, both men develop a passionate obsession with Thyrza, whom Harold briefly considers his 'Muse'.[44] Harold declares to Thyrza that he has 'found a new poetical form' that will be capable of conveying his 'interest in these large subjects' of 'social progress' (425). His radically new literary work, Harold enthuses, belongs to the burgeoning age of mass democracy: its appeal is not 'to a small class of cultured people, but to *all* people, to *all* ranks' (427). Gissing presents Harold as a ridiculous figure who manifestly lacks the talent to distil his tremendous ambitions into verse. When he finally recites parts of his 'epico-dramatico-dithyrambic poem' to a patiently suffering Thyrza, he 'work[s] himself to such a pitch of excitement that he could not keep his seat':

> What he read was strange and sad stuff, crude to the point of ghastliness, abounding in bathos, so impotently earnest that no burlesque ever written could surpass it in side-splitting effects. Thyrza had at first tried to go on with her sewing at the same time that she listened, but she soon found it impossible. The utter incomprehensibility of everything she heard had a painfully depressing effect upon her; her head began to ache; Harold's occasional pause to ask her how she liked it threw her into a state of painful nervousness, for she dreaded to seem inappreciative, yet could not find words which sounded at all natural. (426–7)

Gissing spares us the gruelling and 'bathetic' experience of having to read portions of Harold's poem. However, the lack of specificity that surrounds Harold's

---

[43] Ward herself admitted in a letter that Gissing's work 'has interested me very much', finding much in *Demos* that was 'excellent'. MAW, Letter to George Smith, 17 August 1892.

[44] Constance Harsh, 'George Gissing's *Thyrza*: Romantic love and ideological co-conspiracy', *Gissing Journal* 30.1 (1994): 1–12.

magnum opus also serves another purpose. Gissing's satire is not limited to Harold's brand of 'earnestly' reformist writing, but rather offers a picture of the artistic risks that are endemic to 'didactic and speculative' fiction as such: the embarrassment felt by Thyrza, we are led to suspect, exemplifies most people's default response to this type of writing.

Gissing's novel reflects quite explicitly on these risks. 'It would be disagreeable to me', notes one minor character when it transpires that Walter harbours artistic ambitions of his own, 'if I heard that Mr. Egremont was writing a novel' (523)—presumably because the result would be as grotesque as anything dreamed up by Harold Emerson. As the novel approaches its end, however, Gissing indicates that during a visit to the United States, Walter has finally found a writer on whom he can model himself. 'I am sending you Whitman's "Leaves of Grass"', he writes to Mrs Ormonde:

> I have studied Whitman, enjoyed him, felt his force and his value. And, speaking with all seriousness, I believe that he has helped me, and will help me, inestimably, in my endeavour to become a sound and mature man. [...] Such an ideal of course is not a new-created thing for me, but I never felt it as in Whitman's work.
>
> (467–8)

Walter's blustering enthusiasm is intended as a satirical swipe at Whitman, whose voluble optimism recalls the Comtean Religion of Humanity that Gissing had recently condemned in 'The Hope of Pessimism'. In a related vein, the generic hybridity of Whitman's writings serves as an inspiration for Harold's grandiose and overambitious plans for a work that will be 'neither dramatic, nor epic, nor lyric' (425). But the reference to Whitman is also significant because it highlights the artistic portability of Whitman's literary idiom in the reformist debates of the 1880s and 1890s—an aspect of Whitman's influence that I will return to at more length in my discussion of Edward Carpenter in Chapter 3. Gissing's invocation of Whitman is not merely satirical but also gestures towards the aspirational tone and generic openness of the period's reformist literary mode.[45]

The broader artistic questions that are raised by the Harold Emerson episode and by Walter's enthusiasm for Whitman are analogous to the problem of (moral) idealism that is addressed by Gissing's novel as a whole: are ideals necessarily alien to the literary work, or is it possible for them to be completely assimilated into the medium of literary form? Can ideals become aesthetically productive, or does their inclusion in literary texts necessarily result in artistic embarrassment? Questions of this sort are all too familiar to readers of Robert Elsmere, a novel brilliantly

---

[45] Harold's last name nods to another American writer, Ralph Waldo Emerson—an author Gissing found equally culpable of the sort of abstract idealism Thyrza condemns in Walter Egremont and Walt Whitman.

described by Oscar Wilde as 'simply Arnold's *Literature and Dogma* with the literature left out'.[46] 'Dogma' is Wilde's term for ideas that remain unassimilated into the medium of the literary text, and his quip astutely captures the central artistic problem of Ward's novel. *Robert Elsmere*, I suggest in what follows, tries to overcome the dualistic tendencies of idealism on several fronts. As Green had shown, these dualistic tendencies emerged in the sphere of institutional reform where they produced a view of institutions as alien impositions on the sphere of the social. But the threat of dualism also extended into the sphere of the aesthetic itself where it gave rise to the assumption that abstract moral imperatives—what Jameson dubs 'the philanthropic motif' and what Wilde calls 'dogma'—cannot be successfully integrated into the literary work. Of course, few people who have read *Robert Elsmere* and who have chafed at Robert's lengthy and ponderous reflections about religion and social reform will think that *Robert Elsmere* successfully resolves the tension between literature and dogma. My aim here is accordingly more limited: I want to show that the series of dualisms mentioned previously—between institutions and the sphere of the social; between literature and dogma—are not embarrassments that Ward happened to meet with while writing her book. Instead, these dualisms constitute the artistic fabric of the novel itself—they are the foundational dilemmas which Ward hoped to resolve in her text.

Ward began to work on *Robert Elsmere* as early as 1885, around five years before the establishment of the University Settlement over which Ward presided, and it is important to remember that the novel's representation of the settlement experience is therefore in key respects aspirational rather than descriptive. In this sense, the novel followed the trend set by Walter Besant's *All Sorts and Conditions of Men*—the book that had inspired the building of the People's Palace, an educational and recreational institution in the East End neighbourhood of Beaumont Square. In addition to offering a hopeful vision of the settlement movement, however, Ward's book also reflects the period's intense social strains, to which the settlement movement tendered a tentative and deeply ambivalent response: 'This social progress of ours we are so proud of,' Robert Elsmere notes at one point, 'is a clumsy limping jade at best.'[47] It did not take Gissing's pessimism to remind Ward of these social pressures, or to drive home to her the countless ways in which settlements were prone to fail. Late Victorian London, Scott McCracken reminds us, 'was haunted by the ever-present threat of popular

---

[46] Wilde adds that '[T. H.] Green's philosophy very pleasantly sugars the somewhat bitter pill of the author's fiction'. See 'The decay of lying', in *De Profundis and Other Writings* (London: Penguin, 1986), p. 64. Of course, Green's philosophy had sugared a good deal of Wilde's own work. For the early influence of Oxford Hegelianism on Wilde's thinking, see *Oscar Wilde's Oxford Notebooks: A Portrait of a Mind in the Making*, ed. Philip E. Smith and Michael S. Helfand (Oxford: Oxford University Press, 1989). Echoes of Green's political philosophy can also be found in Wilde's *The Soul of Man under Socialism* (1891).

[47] Ward, *Robert Elsmere*, p. 218.

insurrection'; and, as Green had observed in a set of reflections penned in the wake of the Paris Commune of 1871, the same conditions of socio-economic distress that had sparked the events in Paris 'apply practically to London & Berlin'.[48] As recently as 1886–87, London's West End had been shaken by violent riots as angry mobs of unemployed Londoners rampaged through some of the city's most affluent neighbourhoods.[49] These riots received literary attention in works by W. H. Mallock (The Old Order Changes, 1886), Margaret Harkness (Out of Work, 1888), and George Gissing (In the Year of the Jubilee, 1894), and they also provided a good deal of the energy that fuelled the settlement movement around 1890. These events form Robert Elsmere's vital historical context, and, I shall argue, they are registered as such in the novel. It would accordingly be a mistake to describe the insurrectionary events of the 1880s as Robert Elsmere's political unconscious or as its repressed historical subtext—as so much social raw material which Ward tries to push out of sight by hiding it behind a smokescreen of religion and ethics.

The plot of Ward's novel revolves around the character of Robert Elsmere, a young Oxford-trained clergyman. The book narrates Robert's courtship, marriage, and life as a country rector in Surrey, his profound spiritual crisis, and finally his decision to resign his clerical living and engage in social work in London. Robert first suffers religious doubts when he takes up his duties in a parish that borders on the estate of Squire Wendover. The rationalist and religious sceptic Wendover bristles at Robert's unexamined orthodoxy, and he prompts Robert to study works of historical Bible criticism that have come to Britain from the Continent, most notably Strauss' Leben Jesu.[50] As a result of the profound doubts about the truth of revealed religion which his research stirs in him, Robert begins to neglect his duty to his family and parishioners, and before long he renounces holy orders. Robert never manages to return to his old beliefs, but he finds a new form of faith by freeing himself from Anglican orthodoxy and taking up educational work in London's East End. Robert's ultimate espousal of a new sense of social duty is made possible through the mentorship of his old Oxford tutor, the agnostic Henry Grey (a character modelled on Green, the dedicatee of the novel), whom Ward describes as 'ardently idealist and Hegelian'.[51] The closing chapters, leading up to Robert's premature death, depict his new educational work in London's East End,

---

[48] McCracken, 'The commune in exile: Urban insurrection and the production of international space', in Nineteenth-Century Radical Traditions, ed. Joseph Bristow and Josephine McDonagh (London: Palgrave-Macmillan, 2016) p. 115; THG, Ms Notes appended to Commentary on Aristotle's Ethics, 2a.20.

[49] A recent account of these events and their literary repercussions is Matthew Beaumont's Utopia Ltd: Ideologies of Social Dreaming, 1870–1900 (Leiden: Brill, 2005).

[50] The philosophical criticism of Ernest Renan, author of Vie de Jésus (1863), is also part of Robert's motley intellectual diet.

[51] Ward, Robert Elsmere, p. 78. All further references will be given in the text.

where his pedagogical methods (including his use of story-telling) win him many admirers.

The novel's account of religious crisis places the book in a long tradition of religious literature: John Bunyan's seventeenth-century spiritual autobiography *Grace Abounding to the Chief of Sinners* is repeatedly invoked by Ward as a reference point for Robert's spiritual torment, but the book's intertexts also extend to J. A. Froude's novel *The Nemesis of Faith* (1849) and Elizabeth Gaskell's *North and South* (1855). *Robert Elsmere*'s affinity with these earlier texts notwithstanding, the novel's insistence on the particular urgency of Robert's social mission—and Ward's attempts to picture his settlement as fostering new forms of social life and active citizenship—go beyond anything imagined by the book's Victorian precursors. It is also significant that the specific religious issues on which the novel focusses—the Tractarian Movement of the 1830s and the shockwaves set off by Strauss's *Life of Jesus* in the 1840s—belong to the mid-Victorian years, and therefore no longer appeared quite as topical by the time the novel was published. Ward sets up these historical references as a historical foil against which more contemporary issues are allowed to unfold without imposing their urgency on the text, much in the same way that George Eliot's novels utilize the conceit of historical distance to enable an engagement with more topical and pressing social issues. Ward's programmatic re-envisioning of the social mission of Christianity revolves around the same set of questions that Green had identified as central to the new reform movements in London's impoverished eastern districts: how can idealism become an active force in the world? How can abstract ideals be translated into institutional structures?

Ward's account of idealism's dualistic tendencies closely echoes Gissing's Schopenhauerian critique of the sterile 'chasm' between the ideal and the real. Ward's initial diagnosis of idealism's impasses and pathologies is centred around the character of Edward Langham, Robert's first tutor at the fictional St Anselm's College in Oxford. Seven years older than Robert and possessing 'exceptional personal beauty', Langham is a fabled presence at Oxford, 'a man about whom, on entering the college, Robert had heard more than the usual crop of stories' (67–8). During Robert's conversations with Langham, it emerges that the haunted air of languorous resignation that surrounds his tutor has a very specific source: his mind is oppressed by '[t]he uselessness of utterance, the futility of enthusiasm, the inaccessibility of the ideal, the practical absurdity of trying to realize any of the mind's inward dreams: these were the kind of considerations which descended upon him, slowly and fatally, crushing down the newly springing growths of action or passion' (69). Langham's pessimism grows from his conviction that reality must inevitably fail to live up to the ideal—a recognition that the inexperienced mind of the 'ardent, impulsive' and 'boy[ish]' Robert fails to grasp. '*I can*, the soul said to itself, and *I will*; I will do all that is right,' Langham explains to Robert: 'But soon resistance, difficulty, unforeseen, coming we know not whence, arrest us, undeceive us, and the human yoke grows heavy around our necks' (72). The drama of Langham's mind recognizably mirrors the Kantian tragedy of the pure will—a form of pure intentionality and unsullied future-directed hope that is thrown into traumatic contradiction with the debasing materiality of the world. Langham's vignette dramatizes the experience of the idealist who suffers the contradictions and setbacks of an uncompromisingly aspirational orientation towards the world.

Ward's novel repeatedly presents Langham as a case study in the psycho-pathologies of idealism.[52] After Langham has been rejected as a suitor by Robert's sister-in-law Rose, he writes to his former student to ask 'whether their friendship was to be considered as still existing or at an end': 'The calm and even proud melancholy of the letter,' the narrator records, 'showed a considerable subsidence of that state of half-frenzied irritation and discomfort in which Elsmere had last seen him. The writer, indeed, was clearly settling down into another period of pessimistic quietism' (462). Langham's 'half-frenzied irritation and discomfort' give affective expression to what the novel identifies as his 'cynicism' (211, 360, 533, *passim*). Similar to *Thyrza*, where pessimism was tasked with an important clarificatory function, Ward ascribes to Langham's cynicism an intensely negative force that very nearly stymies the 'metaphysical instinct' Gissing sought to rescue in 'The Hope of Pessimism'. Unlike Gissing, however, Ward also attributes to Langham's cynicism a richly dialectical function: it acts not just as a strategic 'anti-idealism' that provides temporary 'relief from the exacting standards of idealism' but rather helps to prepare us for the more fully articulated idealism of Robert's erstwhile tutor Henry Grey.[53] Langham's cynicism is thus not only 'a reality check on prescriptive idealism'—that is, it serves not just to whittle down Langham's idealist ambition to 'an appropriately manageable level'.[54] Instead, it is a necessary opening move that sets the stage for Grey's dialectical understanding of institutional structures: Grey's (Greenian) vision of

---

[52] John Sutherland observes that Langham appears to be modelled on Walter Pater: he is 'a spectator of life, unable to act on his love for Rose Leyburn [Robert's sister-in-law], or even leave an Oxford which he has come to despise'. See Sutherland, *Mrs Humphry Ward: Eminent Victorian, Pre-eminent Edwardian* (Oxford: Clarendon Press, 1990), p. 121.

[53] Helen Small, 'George Eliot and the cosmopolitan cynic', *Victorian Studies* 55.1 (2012): 85–105 (pp. 94, 92). On the dialectical pattern of Ward's novel, see also William S. Peterson, *Victorian Heretic: Mrs Humphry Ward's Robert Elsmere* (Leicester: Leicester University Press, 1976), pp. 136–7.

[54] Small, 'George Eliot and the Cosmopolitan Cynic', p. 102. A more schematic rendering of this process is also possible: Elsmere's youthful 'ardent, impulsive' self, which has never experienced resistance to its wishes, is negated by Langham's cynicism before the two are sublated into a higher idealism. This movement is broadly Hegelian in the sense sketched out in Chapter 1, and it provides the blueprint for the bildungsroman narrative of *Robert Elsmere*. However, as should have become clear by now, my argument in this book emphasizes the progressive aspects of this movement instead of presenting it as the painful adjustment to a social reality that takes on the appearance of an unalterable 'second nature'. For a reading of the bildungsroman as an essentially conservative (and ostensibly 'Hegelian') literary genre, see Franco Moretti, *The Way of the World: The Bildungsroman in European Culture* (London: Verso, 1987).

institutionality proposes that institutions act not as a restraint on reformist hopes but that they are the very medium through which these hopes find fulfilment. As we shall see, this revised idealism is reflected in the novel's closing vision of new welfarist structures.

Grey, who is introduced to Robert by Langham and who becomes Robert's good angel, embodies this more mature understanding of idealism. When the Mephistophelean Squire Wendover tries to convince Robert that '[Grey] is like all idealists, he has a foolish contempt for the compromise of institutions,' Robert is quick to set the record straight: 'Not at all, [. . .] you are mistaken: he has the most sacred respect for institutions' (387). This 'respect for institutions'—the belief that institutions can be subjected to transformative processes of immanent critique rather than having to be razed in the name of some radiant revolutionary ideal—is indebted to Green. In his 'Lectures on the Principles of Political Obligation', Green had observed that '[t]he phaenomena of life are not "ideal", in the sense in which the ideal is opposed to that which is sensibly verifiable': ideals, he argued, were best understood as an immanent principle 'related to the processes of material change which are their conditions, as ideas or ideal ends which those processes contribute to realize'.[55] To think of ideals in terms of the material processes of their realization is to insist that these processes can be evaluated according to internal criteria—there is no transcendentally external principle or otherworldly moral *Sollen* that dictates the forms which social change must take.

When *Robert Elsmere* first addresses the institutional innovations that emerged in the context of the settlement movement, the novel does so obliquely, by turning to the sphere of religion. Central to the narrative of religious crisis that dominates two thirds of Ward's novel is Robert's encounter with mid-nineteenth-century German Biblical criticism. Wendover tempts the intellectually curious Robert with the use of his well-stocked library to apply the problem of historical testimony to Biblical accounts of miracles. Robert, who has already discovered the historico-cultural contingency of testimony through his private research on early modern Spain, is immediately drawn to the topic. In due course, further exploration leads Robert to share one of Green's central theological insights: he becomes convinced that '[m]iracles call for an unacceptable dualism' because they allow only for local and limited intersections of the ideal (the divine) with the real, thus tearing asunder the deep interpenetration of reality and the divine which Robert holds to be the indispensable bedrock of Christian faith.[56] Wendover and Langham

---

[55] Green, 'Lectures on the principles of political obligation', p. 98.

[56] Robert's study of miracles thus undermines the essential religious conviction he expresses early on in the novel: 'To the Christian, facts have been the medium by which ideas the world could not otherwise have come at have been communicated to man. Christian theology is a system of ideas indeed, but of *ideas realized, made manifest in facts*' (82; my emph.). Green's remarks regarding the 'unacceptable dualism' of the doctrine of miracles are discussed in W. J. Mander, *British Idealism: A History* (Oxford: Oxford University Press, 2011), pp. 139–42.

represent what the novel calls 'the growth of the critical pessimist sense' (232), and Ward foregrounds the significant critiques which these two figures bring against Robert's faith. Led into devastating experiences of total 'intellectual dislocation' (286), Robert comes to feel that 'Christianity' itself is only 'something small and local' (371). Spurred on by a kind of inner 'critic, [who has] no interests to serve, no *parti pris* to defend' (330), critique takes on a momentum of its own, independent of Robert's conscious volition: '[it] fill[s] my mind more and more', a powerless Robert admits to his wife Catherine, 'I feel more and more impelled to search [it] out' (407). Contrary to many previous nineteenth-century accounts of religious crisis, the insatiable inner 'critic' that Robert faces is not a figure whose eventual defeat would clear the path for a return to Robert's old Anglican faith. A renewal of his faith, Robert realizes, will only be possible once he has found a way to overcome the dualism of the real and ideal—and, since a return to the unexamined naivety of his earlier Anglican faith is impossible, it becomes increasingly clear that this revitalization will need to take place on completely different ground.

The language of religious crisis is of central importance if we want to understand the novel's contribution to idealist debates in Britain around 1900. The specific function which Ward attributes to Langham's cynicism indicates that the entire novel is energized by the dialectical attempt to direct critique forward. Cynicism's bleakness, Ward suggests, is a key moment in the development of idealism, and its function is essentially reparative: it occasions a recasting of the status of the ideal vis-à-vis reality rather than necessitating a rejection of idealism as such. The resolution which Ward imagines for Robert's religious crisis illustrates this process. When Robert's alienation from his faith reaches its climax, and his marriage with the orthodox Anglican Catherine is on the verge of breakdown, he escapes Surrey for a few days to return to Oxford for a meeting with his former tutor. 'As to religious belief, everything was a chaos', the narrator informs us, as Strauss's historico-criticism continues to gnaw away at Robert's '*habit* of faith': 'What might be to him the ultimate forms and condition of thought, the tired mind was quite incapable of divining. To every state in the process of destruction it was feverishly alive' (354; orig. emph.). Grey, to whom Robert reveals his mind, admits the force of these arguments. Modern critiques of religion, he tells Robert, are 'all a question of literary and historical evidence': 'You have come to see how miracle is manufactured, to recognize in it merely a natural inevitable outgrowth of human testimony' (360). Grey recognizes that human testimony has traditionally played a key role in the 'manufactur[ing]' of religious consent. In fact, this very insight has put Grey irreconcilably at odds with orthodox belief, although it has not pulled him away from Christian faith as such: 'after having prepared himself for the Christian ministry', we are told early in the book, Grey 'had remained a layman because it had become impossible for him to accept miracles' (78–9). Crucially, Robert's visit to Oxford and his final conversation with Grey also confirm an aspect of Grey's character that Robert had first glimpsed years earlier while attending his tutor's philosophical lectures: while Grey acknowledges the necessity of enlightened critical inquiry, 'the negative and critical side of him was what in reality told least upon his pupils' (79). Grey's 'reserved' argumentative style—the fact that he 'talk[s] with difficulty' as he pauses over every possible critical objection—does not negate his 'ideal fervour' but paradoxically heightens the conviction which his ideas carry in the minds of his listeners (79). The peculiar way in which Green's thinking is reflected in his lecturing performance recalls what Elaine Hadley has described as the physical embodiment of abstract ideas and styles of argument in mid-Victorian novels.[57] Grey's manner of lecturing, we might say, conveys the dialectical nature of his thought—the speculative preservation and transcendence of 'negativ[ity] and criti[que]' in the medium of a more richly realized 'ideal fervour'.

The advice which Robert receives from Grey reflects this pattern of dialectical thought. Instead of completely rejecting religious belief in a transcendent (divine) principle, Grey insists that the status of the ideal can be recast as the immanent principle of reality itself: 'The thought of man,' he explains, 'as it has shaped itself in institutions, in philosophies, in science, in patient critical work, or in the life of charity, is the one continuous revelation of God!' (362). Under Grey's influence, the dualism that had plagued Robert is dislodged in favour of the ideal's worldly 'immanence'.[58] Robert duly echoes these ideas towards the end of the novel, in a climactic final speech at his newly established East End school. Although he grants that '*Miracles do not happen*', he concludes that '*There,* [...] in the unbroken sequences of nature, in the physical history of the world, in the long history of man, physical, intellectual, moral—*there* lies the revelation of God' (494).[59]

Education and Dissent: *Robert Elsmere* and the Settlement Movement

Ward's literary engagement with late Victorian idealist debates is inflected by her own theological agenda. This is most obviously true of the depiction of Robert's momentous crisis of faith, but it applies equally to the novel's final two books

[57] Hadley, *Living Liberalism: Practical Citizenship in Mid-Victorian Britain* (Chicago: University of Chicago Press, 2010).

[58] The idea of an 'immanent God' is central to the two lay sermons by Green ('The Witness of God' and 'Faith') on which Ward drew in composing Grey's and Robert's speeches. See Green, *The Witness of God* and '*Faith': Two Lay Sermons*, ed. Arnold Toynbee (London: Longmans, 1886), pp. 29, 32.

[59] Douglas Mao observes that Robert's new social commitment can also be understood as fulfilling a specific psychological need. Following his meeting with Grey, Robert is finally able to give his mental distress (his profound sense of being 'troubled') a particular direction: he learns to be 'troubled by' the plight of the poor. I am grateful to Douglas Mao for sharing with me the text of his keynote address at the conference *Troublesome Modernisms*.

('New Beginnings' and 'Gain and Loss'), which concern Robert's attempt to set up a settlement house (modelled on Toynbee Hall) in London. In these chapters, Ward seeks to formulate a response to the widely perceived decline of orthodox religious faith among England's urban working classes.[60] However, the substratum of Green's social and political philosophy—his ambitious reimagining of the nature of institutions—remains clearly discernible through the multiple discursive layers of Ward's text. The novel's representation of Robert's settlement works towards an understanding of institutions that resembles the one I have associated with Britain's Hegelian moment, as it emphasizes the necessity to think of institutions not as detached administrative structures but as the embodiment of new and shared *Lebensformen*. Ward hoped that the institutional structures of the settlement movement would become the material 'shelter of human aspiration', but she also believed that the experimental forms of collective life which the settlements would foster needed to be capable of accommodating the kinds of fundamental critique of 'negation and opposition' (413) that her novel had described as a feature of the age. Ward was accordingly sceptical of institutions such as Oxford House—the Bethnal Green settlement founded by High Church Anglicans in 1884—because she deemed them too theologically conservative and insufficiently open to critique to fulfil their educational function.[61] In what is partly a nod to Oxford House, *Robert Elsmere* contrasts Robert's settlement with the fictional church of 'St. Wilfrid's' which sends out 'cassocked monk-like clergy' who 'preach and "process" in the open air' (470).[62] Whereas the aim of St. Wilfrid's is the affirmation of an outdated form of high church faith, Robert's settlement house does not promote medieval ideals of monastic fraternity.[63] The attachments that are fostered at Robert's settlement house instead meet Hegel's prerequisite for distinctly modern forms of citizenship: they are open to critical examination, and thus break with the premodern 'bonds of brotherhood that have their roots in a prereflective attachment citizens feel to one another by virtue of all their belonging, through birth, to a single people'.[64]

---

[60] See, e.g., Gerald Parsons, 'A question of meaning: Religion and working-class life', in Gerald Parsons (ed.), *Religion in Victorian Britain*, vol. 2: *Controversies* (Manchester: Manchester University Press, 1988), pp. 63–87.

[61] Thomas Dixon, *The Invention of Altruism: Making Moral Meanings in Victorian Britain* (Oxford: Oxford University Press, 2008), p. 256.

[62] The origins of Oxford House and other 'Oxford Colleges in the East End'—as well as working-class resistance to the religious mission of these institutions—are mapped out in illuminating detail in Nigel Scotland's *Squires in the Slums: Settlements and Missions in Late-Victorian London* (London: I. B. Tauris, 2007), pp. 55–78.

[63] Chapter 4 turns very briefly to Hilaire Belloc to illustrate a related species of unreconstructed retro-Catholicism. Such forms of collective fraternal identity need to be distinguished from the kind of community—sometimes referred to in the novel as the 'New Brotherhood of Christ' (574 *passim*)—which begins to form at Robert's settlement.

[64] Frederick Neuhouser, *Foundations of Hegel's Social Theory: Actualizing Freedom* (Cambridge, MA: Harvard University Press, 2000), p. 138.

The form of active citizenship that Ward associates with Robert's institution is illustrated by a series of incidents surrounding Robert's last two settlement lectures, delivered shortly before his death at the end of the novel. At the first of these two meetings, Robert hopes to speak about the theological significance of Holy Week and Good Friday, but he meets with strident opposition from several audience members. One of 'a knot of workmen sitting together at the back of the room'—an 'elderly workman', 'Genevese by birth, Calvinist by blood, revolutionist by development'—gets up to '[make] a dry and cynical little speech': 'a good many of those present', he points out, 'understood the remarks [Robert] had just made as an attack' (477). 'Scratch him and you find the parson', a gasfitter weighs in: 'Them upper-class folk, when they come among us poor ones, always seem to me just hunting for souls, as those Injuns he was talking about last week hunt for scalps. They can't go to heaven without a certain number of 'em slung about 'em.' As the room breaks into 'applau[se]', the workers challenge Robert 'to a more thorough discussion of the matter, in a place where he could be both heard and answered'. Although Robert is at first unsure how to respond to this protest, he agrees to take on the objections at a specially arranged meeting that will be dedicated to 'The Claim of Jesus upon Modern Life' and that will consist of a lecture 'to be followed, as usual, by general discussion' (477–8).

Robert's final lecture reprises central portions of his last conversation with Grey, and many of these passages look back to ideas which Green himself had expressed in two lay sermons from the 1870s.[65] Robert begins by addressing the untenability of the doctrine of miracles and he also 'grant[s] that the true story of Jesus of Nazareth was from the beginning obscured by error and mistake' (495). Robert's lecture articulates several significant disagreements with Anglican ortho-doxy, and it concludes by holding out a version of Christian faith that has been wiped clean of the ossified elements of church dogma: 'The fact is merely a call to you and me, who recognize it, to go back to the roots of things, to reconceive the Christ, to bring him afresh into our lives, to make the life so freely given for man minister again in new ways to man's new needs' (495–6). As soon as Robert's speech has ended—with a call for 'new forms of social help' (498–9)—the audi-ence breaks into 'a sudden burst of talk and movement' (499). The gasfitter, who had challenged Robert during the previous lecture, stomps out of the room 'with an impatient shrug' that seems to signal an angry and embarrassed admission of defeat. However, Robert's oratorical triumph is only temporary. Shortly after the gasfitter's exit, his companion Andrews mounts the platform and delivers—'slowly and deliberately'—a response in which he vents his dissatisfaction with Robert's speech. Invoking Thomas ('Tom') Paine—'a Socialist, as most of us are'—Andrews falls into a condemnation of 'the rich loafers, and the sweaters, and the

[65] See fn. 58.

middlemen' that culminates 'with a fierce denunciation of priests, not without a harsh savour and eloquence' (499). Andrews' vitriolic speech is followed by a response from another 'Socialist' who warns his fellow workers that 'Mr Elsmere's new church, if he ever got it, would only be a fresh instrument in the hands of the bourgeoisie' (499–500).

The vociferous opposition by the workers in the audience is not merely rhetorical, and while the exchange between Robert and the workers is officially billed as a 'discussion', the radicals' persistent defiance goes well beyond the consensus-generating dialogue implied by that label.[66] The socialists' protest notably doubles as a veiled threat to Ward's middle-class readership ('people should not be too smooth-spoken', one of the workers notes: 'what the working class want beyond everything just now [is] grit'; 500), and their dissent points us to the novel's most immediate political contexts—the West End riots of 1886–87 and concomitant middle-class fears that the East End settlements might be breeding grounds for socialism.[67] The scenes involving the socialist radicals clearly respond to contemporaneous debates about the London settlements. Toynbee Hall, for example,—the institution that served as the real-life model for Ward's fictionalized account of a settlement house—had been set up as an alternative to the religious mission settlements that had for some decades been features of middle-class philanthropic interventions in London's poorer districts. Rejecting heavy-handed theological moralizing, Samuel and Henrietta Barnett departed from the religious brief of these older East End missions and opened their institution to new ideas and new experiments in living. As a recent social historian has noted, it was partly thanks to the radical ideas percolating at Toynbee Hall that the Barnetts came to revise their own 'orthodox views of poverty as caused by the individual' by placing greater weight on impersonal socioeconomic forces and the need for government intervention.[68]

Robert Elsmere does not simply silence radical political voices or repress all traces of class conflict. It would be more accurate to say that Robert's settlement gives us an aspirational vision of what Jürgen Habermas, in a discussion of

[66] As recent scholars have pointed out, the dissipation of political dissent can be one of the functions of 'discussion'. On this view, the 'dominant voices' in a discussion *'require'* their minor counterparts to participate so that the status quo that sustains their position remains unaltered.' Discussion, so conceived, is 'an aggressive disenfranchising instrument because it transforms inclusion into a form of obligatory participation.' See Juan Meneses, *Resisting Dialogue: Modern Fiction and the Future of Dissent* (Minneapolis: University of Minnesota Press, 2019), p. 19; orig emph. Robert's lecture, which anticipates some of the routine criticisms levelled against religion by contemporary socialists, might seem to effect just such an act of silencing 'inclusion'. It is important to recall, therefore, that Robert himself occupies a profoundly marginalized (and 'dissenting') theologico-political position in relation to religious orthodoxy.

[67] 'Toynbee [Hall]', the philosopher Benjamin Jowett, T. H. Green's Oxford colleague, jotted down in a notebook from 1890, 'seems to be gradually becoming a house of extreme socialists which it is very difficult to keep in order'; quoted in Scotland, *Squires in the Slums*, p. 36.

[68] Gutzke, 'Britain's "social housekeepers"', in ed. Gutzke, *Britain and Transnational Progressivism* (London: Palgrave Macmillan, 2008), p. 176 (fn. 7).

democratic political systems, has called the institutional 'context of discovery' where 'unregulated' dissenting voices can emerge, a sphere 'in which equal rights of citizenship become socially effective'.[69] Written in the tumultuous wake of the Third Reform Act of 1884 that threatened to upset any semblance of liberal political consensus, *Robert Elsmere* does not (and indeed could not possibly) 'project a vision of social harmony' or affirm a 'liberal and reforming view of the social order'.[70] Instead, Ward's text attributes special significance to dissenting voices by figuring them as necessary counterpoints to middle-class 'idealist blindness' (509). The closing scenes of the novel recall Green's recognition—energized by the 'imaginative proximity of social revolution' in the 1870s and 1880s—that Britain's socio-economic system was producing a proletariat that was exceptionally vulnerable to exploitation and immiseration.[71] As one character notes towards the end of Ward's novel, 'political dissent or social reform' are inevitable because 'since the [French] Revolution, every generous child of the century has been open to the fascination of political or social Utopias' (568). Negativity and critique, whose most extreme form Ward dubbed *cynicism*, occupy a central place in *Robert Elsmere*, and they remind us that for Ward there exists no such thing as a preestablished social harmony or political consensus. A persistent element of critique is woven into the forms of social life—the shared *Lebensformen*—that Ward's novel identifies with the settlement movement. The presence of political and theological doctrines in Ward's text should accordingly not be understood as an unresolved non-artistic remainder (what Wilde had called 'dogma'); instead, the dialogic confrontation between different kinds of 'dogma' constitutes the very social fabric of the institution that *Robert Elsmere* begins to imagine.

[69] Habermas adds that the social substance of 'democratic institutions' resides in a 'public of citizens that has emerged from the confines of class and thrown off the millennia-old shackles of social stratification and exploitation'. See Habermas, *Between Facts and Norms: Contributions to a Discourse Theory of Law and Democracy* (Cambridge, MA: The MIT Press, 1996), pp. 307–8.

[70] Jameson, 'Authentic *Ressentiment*', p. 147. While *Robert Elsmere* holds out the hope of a future consensus, it makes little sense to say that the novel—or, for that matter, any of the other texts discussed in the present study—succeeds in repressing 'all traces of class conflict' (Jameson, 'Authentic *Ressentiment*', p. 147). Ward's next novel, *The History of David Grieve* (1892), turned to two urban centres (Manchester and Paris) and to a different period (the post-Commune 1870s) as a way of foregrounding her political concerns. Ward's personal study of works by radical autodidacts such as Samuel Bamford (*Passages in the Life of a Radical*, 1844) and Alexander Somerville (*The Autobiography of a Working Man*, 1848) is discussed in Norman Vance's *Bible and Novel: Narrative Authority and the Death of God* (Oxford: Oxford University Press, 2013), p. 137.

[71] On the 'imaginative proximity' of revolution, see Perry Anderson, 'Modernity and revolution', *New Left Review* I.144 (1984), p. 104. *Robert Elsmere* echoes Green's analysis, but it also forms part of much broader discussion among British idealists about those who were excluded—as a result of property qualifications, economic injustice, or social prejudice—from Britain's political life. Bernard Bosanquet's work features a few pages on the proletarian '*declassés*' who live in a state of 'absolute economic dependence' (*Philosophical Theory of the State*, pp. 316–20). Many British Hegelians made mention of Hegel's comments of the 'rabble' (*Pöbel*), the exploited and disenfranchised segments of society that Marx referred to as the proletariat. See Hegel, *Grundlinien der Philosophie des Rechts* (Frankfurt/Main: Suhrkamp, 1986), pp. 389–90 (§ 244). Marx's recasting of Hegel's *Pöbel* in the figure of the proletariat is discussed in Frank Ruda's *Hegel's Rabble: An Investigation into Hegel's Philosophy of Right* (London: Bloomsbury, 2013), pp. 169–80.

The novel's openness to non-hegemonic and counter-hegemonic social voices is reflected in the pedagogical technique which Robert brings to his teaching at the settlement. This technique involves a deliberate relinquishment of the teacher's mastery: 'As you know,' Robert tells his proletarian students when classes at the settlement begin to convene, 'I am endeavouring to make what is practically a settlement among you, asking you working-men to teach me, if you will, what you have to teach as to the wants and prospects of your order, and offering you in return whatever there is in me which may be worth your taking' (492). Robert's approach to teaching recalls the unassertive and 'reserved' lecturing style which the novel associates with Grey, but it also resonates with what Jacques Rancière—in a reconstruction of the democratic pedagogy of the early nineteenth-century educational philosopher Joseph Jacotot—called 'universal teaching'. Jacotot's emancipatory pedagogy was designed to resist the stultifying effects of traditional teaching methods as practiced in religious and state schools. Universal teaching, as Rancière describes it, experimentally suspends institutional hierarchies by insisting that intelligence is a shared property which belongs in equal parts to teacher and pupil: universal teaching, Rancière writes, 'was not a method for instructing the people; it was a benefit to be announced to the poor: they could do everything any man could.'[72] Teaching, so conceived, consists not in the inculcation of a pre-existing body of knowledge but in the coproduction of knowledge by teacher and student.[73]

Similar motifs appear in many other (literary and non-literary) accounts of late Victorian settlement teaching. Will Reason, who acted as warden and congregational minister at the nonconformist East End settlement Mansfield House, observed in his account of 'Settlements and Education' from 1898 that 'it is pretty certain that a little experience will considerably modify the teacher's estimate of his own educational superiority': 'He will find that even a University curriculum, with all its apparatus of tutors, lectures, classes, and libraries, leaves large provinces of knowledge untouched, and is in many ways not so successful in training the powers of observation and judgment as is the rough schooling of a knockabout practical life.'[74] On Reason's view, the expanded sense of the settlements'

---

[72] Rancière, *The Ignorant Schoolmaster: Five Lessons in Intellectual Emancipation* (Stanford: Stanford University Press, 1991), p. 18.

[73] We should not overemphasize these Rancièrean echoes, and I certainly do not mean to suggest that Robert Elsmere is a radical pedagogue on the order of Jacotot. Ward repeatedly reminds us that old pedagogical habits die hard even at Robert's settlement: 'Week by week the lecture became more absorbing to him, the men more pliant, his hold on them firmer' (504). Even so, Rancière's observations usefully highlight an aspect of *Robert Elsmere* that has not received sufficient attention. For a related point on the shared production of knowledge in *Robert Elsmere*, see Patrick Fessenbecker, 'Autonomy, divinity, and the common good: Selflessness as a source of freedom in Thomas Hill Green and Mary Augusta Ward', in Sandrine Berges and Alberto L. Siani (eds.), *Women Philosophers on Autonomy: Historical and Contemporary Perspectives* (London: Routledge, 2018), pp. 149–63.

[74] Reason, 'Settlements and education', in Reason (ed.) *University and Social Settlements* (London: Methuen, 1898), p. 47.

pedagogical aims meant that these institutions could 'be likened to a People's University'. Toynbee Hall, Reason added, was 'far ahead of all other Settlements' in this respect.[75]

The temporary suspension of the teacher's 'educational superiority', for which the institutional environment of the settlements seems to have provided especially fertile ground, can help us explain the broader significance of the dissent and critique that are registered in Ward's and Gissing's texts. As David Lloyd and Paul Thomas have observed, the closing decades of the nineteenth century saw 'the crystallization of the Victorian state and its transition from a predominantly coercive to a hegemonic form'. During these decades—following the Elementary Education Act of 1870 which set the framework for schooling of all five- to twelve-year-olds—Britain witnessed

> the consolidation of what Gramsci termed the 'ethical state', a state represented not merely in its legal and police apparatuses, but in the extension of its paradigms into the organs of civil society itself: schools, trade unions, even religious bodies. What characterizes the ethical state is, beyond the antagonisms of particular classes, groups, or sects to the actual practice of a given government, the saturation of discourse on society with an 'idea of the state' or, more evidently, with the subordinate conception of the proper relation of the subject as citizen to the state.[76]

Lloyd and Thomas point out that it was precisely the settlements' relative structural autonomy from the state that enabled these institutions to take on important hegemonic functions in the attempt to co-opt radical working-class cultures into the liberal status quo. By contrast, what we are given in *Robert Elsmere* and in *Thyrza* is nothing quite as monolithic or hegemonically solidified as the fully evolved 'ethical state' described by Gramsci. Ward and Gissing indicate that instead of simply extending or reproducing the hegemonic authority of the state, the ideologically diverse social environment of the settlements lent support to modes of argument that made such hegemonizing tendencies visible and, at times, rendered them ripe for ridicule: 'Academic sweetness and light was a feeble antidote to offer' (193), notes *Thyrza*'s narrator apropos of Walter's ineffective Arnoldian educational schemes—a comment that must have piqued Mary Ward,

---

[75] Reason, 'Settlements and Education', p. 52.

[76] Lloyd and Thomas, *Culture and the State* (New York: Routledge, 1998), p. 115. For Antonio Gramsci's discussion of 'the ethical State, the cultural State, [...] in which the school has a positive educative function', see *Selections from the Prison Notebooks*, ed. Quintin Hoare and Geoffrey Nowell-Smith (London: Lawrence and Wishart, 1991), pp. 257–64. Relevant to the argument of the present book, Peter Thomas has recently noted that the two seemingly antithetical terms of Gramsci's neologism ('ethical state') are connected by way of a unified (and explicitly Hegelian) understanding of the state as a form of social life. See Thomas, *The Gramscian Moment: Philosophy, Hegemony, and Marxism* (Leiden: Brill, 2009).

whose novel is peppered with quotations from her uncle Matthew Arnold.[77] *Thyrza* and *Robert Elsmere* present us with types of counter-hegemonic critique that undermine organicist visions of British society as a closed and unified ethical community (what Gramsci calls the 'ethical state'). It is certainly true that Green's social philosophy is sometimes associated with the propagation of social organicism—yet while Green occasionally asserts such an understanding of society in his metaphysics and ethics (especially in his best-known work, the *Prolegomena to Ethics*), it appears much less frequently in his writings on politics and the state, which formulate a participatory concept of citizenship that invites the possibility of effective dissent.[78] In a related vein, *Robert Elsmere* indicates that the form of aspirational *Sittlichkeit* that characterizes the settlements—what Green had described as active citizenship and what Ward calls 'the culture of democracy' (491)—tends to trip up hegemonization.[79] On Ward's account as much as on Green's, not 'all mankind will be bourgeois'.[80]

In concluding, I want to turn to another aspect of Robert's teaching that illustrates how Ward's vision of new educational institutions moves beyond the overwhelmingly negative portrayal of such institutions in *Thyrza*. Central to Robert's pedagogical method is the aforementioned technique of 'story-telling' that Richard first tries out on workmen in Surrey before reprising it to great effect in London. 'My story-telling', Robert informs Langham, 'is the simplest thing in the world': 'I told my stories all the winter—Shakespeare, Don Quixote, Dumas—

---

[77] To be sure, Gissing's swipe at Arnold is mild compared to the barbs we find in some other reform and settlement novels. Declaring his desire to educate the worker Dick Coppin ('the reddest of red-hot Rads'), Walter Besant's hopeful young reformer Harry le Breton absurdly proclaims: 'He shall learn to waltz. This will convert him from a fierce Republican to a merely enthusiastic Radical. Then he shall learn to sing in parts: this will drop him down into advanced Liberalism.' See *All Sorts and Conditions of Men* (Brighton: Victorian Secrets, 2012), p. 193.

[78] The conflation of citizenship and 'ethical' belonging is a problematic which Green revisits repeatedly in his writings, typically in connection with ancient Greek theorizations of the polis: 'What Aristotle has before him', Green observes in a set of manuscript notes on Aristotle's understanding of pedagogy, 'is properly whether virtue can be taught and how: & whether a way of teaching it is the state [. . .], wh[ich] acc[ording]: to A[ristotle]: is the only true way: so that with him πολιτική [politics] is the only true ἠθική [ethics]' (THG, Ms Notes on Aristotle's *Ethics*, 2a.20). Elsewhere, Green objects to this view: 'To an Athenian slave who might be used to gratify a master's lust, it would have been a mockery to speak of the State as a realization of freedom.' See Green, 'On the Different Senses of "Freedom" as Applied to Will and to the Moral Progress of Man', p. 233. On this point, see also Sarah den Otter, *British Idealism and Social Explanation* (Oxford: Clarendon Press, 1996), pp. 48–50.

[79] *Robert Elsmere* depicts another institution that manages to integrate dissent into a shared form of life: this (exclusively male) institution is the university, where disagreements between Robert (the 'ardent' youth), Langham (the 'cynic'), and Grey (the theorist of social reform) can play out without inflicting any lasting harm on their friendship.

[80] Gramsci, *Prison Notebooks*, p. 259. In contrast to Gramsci, then, Ward and Green offer more expansive understandings of the term *Bürger* as *citoyen* rather than *bourgeois*. Of course, for the writers discussed in this book, the concept of *citoyen* was rarely universally expandable: for the anti-suffragist Ward, for example, it notably excluded (female) *citoyennes*. On this point, see Emily Coit, 'Mary Augusta Ward's "Perfect Economist" and the logic of anti-suffragism', *ELH* 82.4 (2015): 1213–38. I discuss the concept of *bürgerliche Gesellschaft* in Chapter 1; for Hegel's discussion of the content of the conceptual *bourgeois*/*citoyen* distinction, see *Philosophie des Rechts*, pp. 343–5 (§ 187).

Heaven knows what. And on the whole it answers best.' As Robert explains, his aim as a priest in Surrey had been to 'get at the *imagination*' of his parishioners, by inducing 'them for only half an hour to live someone else's life' (193; orig. emph.). Langham, albeit sceptical, is curious enough to follow Robert to the Workmen's Institute where the next 'story-telling' session—the reading of an episode about Richard Lionheart—is about to take place:

> Langham not only endured, but enjoyed the first part of the hour that followed. Robert was an admirable reader, as most enthusiastic, imaginative people are. As he read on, his arms resting on the high desk in front of him, and his eyes, full of infectious enjoyment, travelling from the book to his audience, surrounded by human beings whose confidence he had won, and whose lives he was brightening from day to day, he seemed to Langham the very type and model of a man who had found his *métier*, found his niche in the world, and the best means of filling it.   (194)

Ward's novel describes Robert's storytelling as a purposefully unassertive mode of teaching. In the scene described above, Robert does not occupy a position of educational authority—any sense of pedagogical mastery is immediately undercut by the multiple lines of imaginative projection that run between Langham, Robert, the audience, and the recited text. Robert's own 'imaginative' immersion in the episode he is reading out indicates that he experiences the same leap of the sympathetic '*imagination*' that his storytelling is intended to elicit in his students. But the suspension of the role of schoolmaster also subverts Langham's impression that Robert has finally settled into his proper '*métier*'. Soon enough we will discover that Robert's *métier* as priest—what F. H. Bradley might have called Robert's 'station and its duties'—is not nearly as fixed as this word suggests: once Robert has relinquished his priesthood, he will begin to reorient his professional vocation around a non-denominational commitment to the lives of others for which his own storytelling has begun to prepare him.

At the London settlement, Robert's pedagogical methods 'strike the neighbourhood as a great novelty' (472). By 'rang[ing] the whole world for stories'—from newspaper items about colliery explosions or 'some feature of London life itself' to Greek myth and the novels of Walter Scott—Robert hopes to achieve 'the rousing of moral sympathy and the awakening of the imaginative power pure and simple' (472). As Robert's diverse list of literary and non-literary texts suggests, he utilizes storytelling to different ends, employing it as a helpful supplement to religious instruction but also sometimes as its replacement. Crucially, Robert's storytelling is not designed to instruct his students in the doctrines of a particular faith. Instead, as Langham admiringly notes, Robert's storytelling teaches an active attention to the world we inhabit in common with others: his reading performances provide 'the very type and model' for the kinds of social coexistence that

Ward expected the settlement movement to nourish. This pedagogical method is of course not innocent—after all, the forms of our attention to the world are fully as ideological as this or that religious dogma—but it helps to explain why Ward could view Robert's settlement as the 'shelter' (413) of a new and shared ethos of social responsibility.

Ward's association of Robert's storytelling with an emerging social *Lebensform* dramatizes ideas that Green had developed in his writings of the early 1880s. In February 1881, for example, Green had delivered his 'Lecture on Liberal Legislation and Freedom of Contract' to an audience of working men in Leicester. A much more conventionally academic performance than Robert's undogmatic storytelling, Green's lecture began by noting the moral and political significance of negative freedom: 'We shall probably all agree that [such] freedom, rightly understood, is the greatest of blessings; that its attainment is the true end of all our effort as citizens.'[81] However, as he goes on to note, this negative concept must be complemented by other modalities of freedom: 'When we speak of freedom as something to be so highly prized,' Green writes,

> we mean a positive power or capacity of doing or enjoying something worth doing or enjoying, and that, too, something that we do or enjoy in common with others. [. . .] That end is what I call freedom in the positive sense: in other words, the liberation of the powers of all men equally for contributions to the common good.[82]

Green's technically philosophical talk was never likely to meet with the kind of vocal working-class dissent that greets Robert's settlement lecture in Ward's novel. And yet, Green clearly tried to anticipate possible objections to his argument about positive freedom, and to meet these objections halfway. The category of citizenship, he insists in his lecture, must remain open and contestable: the content of positive freedom cannot be fixed, and the multiplicity of its realizations will reflect the pluralism of democratic societies.[83] Robert's emphasis on the ethical openness of storytelling—its appeal to the imaginative capacities 'of all men equally'—echoes Green's reluctance to prescribe a particular content for his notion of the common good. Instead of inculcating a specific dogma or set of ethical values, storytelling offers a 'model' of engaged citizenship by inviting imaginative attempts 'to live someone else's life' and to reflectively examine

---

[81] Green, 'Lecture on liberal legislation and freedom of contract', in *Lectures on the Principles of Political Obligation and Other Writings*, ed. Paul Harris and John Morrow (Cambridge: Cambridge University Press, 1986), p. 199.

[82] Green, 'Lecture on liberal legislation', p. 200.

[83] In a gloss on Green's lecture, the political theorist Colin Tyler notes that Green's concept of the common good is capacious enough to acknowledge that 'value pluralism' is 'an endemic and permanent feature' of modern societies. See Tyler, *Common Good Politics*, pp. 78–9.

one's own. Finally, *Robert Elsmere*'s central narrative shift—from the monologic imperiousness of church dogma towards the dispersed opportunities for sympathetic identification offered by fictional discourse—also entails a transformation in what Jameson calls the reformist novel's 'modal poetics': this shift signals a move away from the abstract demands of *Sollen* (which tend to enter the text only locally and in ways that disrupt narrative cohesion) and towards an 'optative' mode that pervades the narrative and that teaches us 'not through obedience to [. . .] codes, but through openness to example—through responsive, unpredictable engagements with other people'.[84] The problematic dualism of literature and dogma is here revised in favour of (what the novel calls) 'an ideal, poetical truth' (406). This 'poetical truth' does not exist independently of the narrative—like some remote or external ideal—but has been fully actualized into the novel's complex interplay of embodied intellectual and political positions.

In an early essay that strikingly anticipates Ward's artistic choices in *Robert Elsmere*, Green had explored the status of fiction as the exemplary artform of the dawning democratic age. The genre of the novel, Green explained in 1862, could claim a 'place as the great reformer and leveller of our time' because it 'acts on more extensive material and reaches more men' than any other literary genre.[85] However, Green warns, the reformist novel must not merely reproduce the world by offering us a superficial 'texture of incident' or naturalist 'levelness with life'.[86] Instead, Green tasks the novel with realizing the 'fulness of the idea': much like Ward's 'poetical truth', this fully realized idea can be achieved by 'the unifying action of speculative philosophy, but [also] by the combining force of art'.[87] Green here describes what I have called literature's capacity for speculative thought: novels, Green insists, must insert into their aesthetic procedures an aspirational sense of the emerging forms of life that make it possible to imagine new institutional arrangements not merely in the abstract but as an experientially concrete reality. As I have suggested, Ward takes up this idea at the level of content by showing us that Robert's teaching in Surrey and London encourages the type of sympathetic identification and mutual care that forms the settlement's lifeblood. But Ward also gives this idea a self-reflexive artistic turn by inviting her readers to view Robert himself as a character whose self-questioning can provide a 'type and model' for the kinds of undogmatic critique that will ground new forms of citizenship. By suggesting that her readers learn to identify with Robert, Ward prompts us to rehearse a lived orientation towards the common good and a hospitable meeting of the needs of others.

---

[84] On the 'optative' as an imaginative orientation towards (real or fictional) others, see Andrew H. Miller, *The Burdens of Perfection: On Ethics and Reading in Nineteenth-Century British Literature* (Ithaca: Cornell University Press, 2008), here: pp. 3–5.

[85] Green, 'Value and influence of works of fiction', p. 41.

[86] Green, 'Value and influence of works of fiction', pp. 33, 28.

[87] Green, 'Value and influence of works of fiction', pp. 31, 23.

The idealist debates of Britain's Hegelian moment form the immediate intellectual and cultural context of Gissing's and Ward's novels. By contrast, the literary works which I explore in subsequent chapters do not involve a similarly sustained awareness of these philosophical conversations. And yet, these texts—by Edward Carpenter, H. G. Wells, and E. M. Forster—can be seen to continue the work of developing the period's reformist literary mode as well as the understanding of literature as a form of speculative thought. In charting these developments, the next three chapters will track the fortunes of the reformist literary mode across a range of different political positions. The differences in political orientation that exist between some of the writers explored here are considerable (and nowhere more so than in the case of Ward and Carpenter), yet these texts are useful objects of study precisely because they illustrate the characteristic political latitude of the period's reformist literary imaginary. The authors I discuss in the remaining three chapters envision institutional reforms that begin to make good on Green's larger ambitions: these reforms go well beyond the local innovations of the East End settlements and they involve plans for a large-scale restructuring of the nation's economy.

3

'True Ownership'

Edward Carpenter and the Nationalization of Land

In 1896 the philosopher and socialist activist Sidney Ball published a Fabian Tract entitled 'The Moral Aspects of Socialism'.[1] Inspired by the work of his former academic mentor T. H. Green, Ball had played an important role in initiating the founding of Toynbee Hall in the 1880s, and as a fellow of St John's College, Oxford, he was teaching just down the road from Green's former college Balliol.[2] Ball's Tract proposes an understanding of state action that owes much to Green's teachings. He argues that the institutions of the modern state can play a positive role in promoting the welfare of its citizens, and like Green, he is careful not to present the interventionist state as an external imposition on citizens' lives. The state, as it emerges from Ball's analysis, is a complex aggregate of institutions, yet this institutional 'machinery' is always 'a means to an end' (3): the 'State', Ball notes, is 'not some mysterious entity outside individuals, but simply represents the individuals organized for a common purpose' (13). Like Green, Ball insists that this language of means and ends, and of a shared common purpose, does not cancel out the central value that Hegel and other thinkers in the liberal tradition had attributed to individual freedom. At the same time, Ball points out that this emphasis on individual freedom must not be misconstrued as a defence of merely economic freedoms and 'form[s] of competition [...] in which the gain of one man is the loss of another': society consists in the 'cooperation' of free individuals, and 'it implies the recognition of a common good and a common interest which gives to our "individual" work its meaning, its quality, and its value' (4–5). While the organization of modern states must reflect the central value of individual liberty, Ball concludes, it would be a mistake to view them solely as the guarantors of negative rights or legal entitlements. States also crucially rely on a lived ethos of social solidarity and 'cooperation'—what Green had described as a positive and active orientation towards the common good.

---

[1] Ball, 'Moral Aspects of Socialism' [Fabian Tract No.72] (London: Fabian Society, 1896). Ball had joined the Fabian Society in 1886.

[2] F. S. Lee observes that '[i]t was in a meeting at Ball's college rooms, on 17 November 1883, that Samuel Barnett outlined detailed plans for establishing a university settlement [Toynbee Hall] in the East End of London' (Lee, 'Ball, Sidney', *Oxford Dictionary of National Biography*, www.oxforddnb. com>, accessed 10 July 2018).

British Literature and the Life of Institutions: Speculative States. Benjamin Kohlmann, Oxford University Press.

In the 1880s and 1890s, Ball and Edward Carpenter—the socialist poet, cultural critic, and early queer activist—moved in similar intellectual circles, including the Fellowship of the New Life and the Fabian Society (which had split from the Fellowship in 1884). In what follows, however, I do not map specific lines of influence or intellectual affiliation that connect Ball's writing and activism to Carpenter's. Instead, I want to suggest that the speculative account of the state as a shared form of life that I outlined in previous chapters and that also informs Ball's Fabian Tract can shed light on the reformist literary mode Carpenter developed in his poetry and essays. Carpenter's works of the 1880s and 1890s, I suggest, project a vision of the state that experimentally elides the state's institutional structures with an emerging ethos of collective ownership. Carpenter's engagement with the idea of private property in the context of late Victorian land reform debates specifically entailed the attempt to re-signify the capitalist notion of 'ownership' from within: his writings critically explore the social pathologies to which private proprietorship gives rise, but they also (speculatively) associate the development of new institutional structures with an emerging proprietorial ethos that is irreducible to impoverished negative conceptions of freedom. In the 1880s, Carpenter came to advocate reformist schemes that proposed a version of temporary proprietorship under which individuals would rent land from the state rather than becoming its sole owners. While Carpenter hoped that this democratization of landholding patterns would encourage a new proprietorial stance of care, responsibility, and tact, his poetry also proleptically imagines this stance as an enabling condition—or *entgegenkommende Lebensform*—that points the way for further efforts at large-scale structural reform.

The nationalization of land was a topic that attracted significant reformist attention from the 1870s onwards. While the cause of land redistribution had a long and fraught history in Britain, the key event that galvanized reformist energies in the later nineteenth century was the publication of *Return of Owners of Land*, the 1873 parliamentary report that offered the first comprehensive record of land distribution patterns in Britain since the Domesday Book. The House of Lords had intended *Return of Owners of Land* to assuage popular distrust towards the landed elites, yet when the report was published it caused public outrage because it revealed the full extent of the monopolization of land ownership in the hands of a wealthy few.[3] As José Harris has observed, the report was deemed so scandalous and revelatory that its findings 'defined the terms of both sociological

---

[3] The report revealed that 'approximately 75 per cent of the acreage of Britain belonged to about 5,000 people, 710 of whom owned one-quarter of the land of England and Wales'. See Matthew Cragoe and Paul Readman, 'Introduction', in *The Land Question in Britain, 1750–1950*, ed. Cragoe/Readman (London: Palgrave Macmillan, 2010), pp. 1–18 (p. 2).

and political debate over the next half-century.'[4] Carpenter's reputation as a mystic poet and utopian dreamer has given rise to the assumption that he did not 'show much enthusiasm for isolated reforms, limited in scope'.[5] Such assessments project Carpenter's later mysticism of the 1900s back onto his early work and consequently underestimate his keen political and poetic interest in more technical questions of reform.[6] In what follows, I explore Carpenter's social criticism as well as his literary works, ranging from his early poetry of the 1870s to his magnum opus, *Towards Democracy* (1883–1902), in order to demonstrate his deep engagement with questions of institutional reform in the 1880s and 1890s. As activists and politicians were polarizing over the difficult question of land reform, Carpenter tried to keep open a middle ground for those who could accept some role for the state while regarding full centralization askance.[7] For Carpenter, debates about land reform—and its radical sibling, land nationalization—brought together two closely related issues: first, the question of who should be allowed to own land and how existing landholding patterns were to be changed; and second, the fundamental ethical issue of what it meant to 'own' land—to live on it and tend to it—in the first place. Carpenter's writings negotiate these tensions by formulating a distinction between *land* (the term Carpenter uses to describe the status of habitable ground as a form of private property) and *Earth* (a term referring to ground as a collectively owned and cared-for good).

'That Earthborn Song': Carpenter's Early Poetry of the 1870s

Born in 1844 as the scion of a prosperous middle-class family in Brighton, Carpenter seemed destined for a clerical or academic career, and he became a

---

[4] José Harris, *Private Lives, Public Spirit: A Social History of Britain, 1870–1914* (Oxford: Oxford University Press, 1993), p. 101. Equally scandalous, as Brett Christophers observes in his recent critique of landholding patterns in Britain, was 'financial landownership'—a term coined in the 1880s to describe the way banks had begun to acquire land as a capital asset that could be bought and sold speculatively. See Christophers, *The Appropriation of Public Land in Neoliberal Britain* (London: Verso, 2019).

[5] Marie-Françoise Cachin, '"Non-governmental society": Edward Carpenter's position in the British Socialist Movement', in *Edward Carpenter and Late Victorian Radicalism*, ed. Tony Brown (London: Frank Cass, 1990), pp. 58–73 (p. 69).

[6] This interest also briefly led Carpenter into the conventicles of the materialist, reform-minded Fabian Society. Carpenter gave lectures to the Fabian Society in the 1880s and kept up a steady correspondence with the Society's secretary, Edward Pease, even after leaving the organization. See the correspondence in the Fabian Society Archives, London School of Economics (FSLSE, A/6/3). The image of Carpenter's work as the expression of a 'luxuriant' mysticism originated partly in the 1890s, and it was further cemented by *Edward Carpenter, in Appreciation* (1931), the memorial volume—published shortly after Carpenter's death—that included contributions by E. M. Forster, Raymond Unwin, and others. On Carpenter's 'luxuriant socialism', see Thomas Linehan, *Modernism and British Socialism* (London: Palgrave Macmillan, 2012), p. 3.

[7] For an exploration of these debates, including Carpenter's position, see Matthew Taunton, 'Cottage economy or collective farm? English socialism and agriculture between Merrie England and the Five-Year Plan', *Critical Quarterly* 53.3 (2011): 1–23.

curate in the Anglican Church shortly after graduating from Cambridge in 1868. However, Carpenter held this position only for a few years before experiencing—as he recorded in his autobiography *Days and Dreams* (1916)—a 'profound change' while reading the poetry of Walt Whitman.[8] Inspired by Whitman's ecstatic celebration of freedom and equality, Carpenter abandoned his career in the church and in 1874 took up teaching for the University Extension Movement in Leeds and Sheffield. He also began to write free verse that echoed Whitman's ethical and political ideals by imagining a radical simplification of modern life and by advocating a non-exploitative relationship to nature. Thanks to a large inheritance from his father, Carpenter was finally able to put these ideals into practice from 1882: he used the money to buy a smallholding in Millthorpe, outside Sheffield, and it was here that he came to occupy the complexly intertwined roles—homosexual icon, spiritualist mystic, simple-lifer, poet—for which he is mostly remembered today. The move to Millthorpe is usually described as marking Carpenter's definitive break with social convention, yet as I suggest here, it is better understood as a culmination of the ethical, political, and aesthetic concerns that had occupied Carpenter during the previous decade. The decision to buy the cottage in Millthorpe was important because it signalled a pivotal moment in his thinking about land reform: for Carpenter, the smallholding came to act as a 'public thing' in Bonnie Honig's sense—as an affectively charged figure of the common good[9]—but it also brought to the fore the deep tensions which beset land nationalization debates and contemporary thinking about common ground as a form of the common good.

In later years, Carpenter chose to downplay the significance of his early verse of the 1870s, insisting that these texts 'were only, so to speak, exercises in literature and efforts to vie with then-accepted models.'[10] Stressing the unoriginal quality of his early verse was partly a strategic move that allowed Carpenter to throw into relief the radical renunciation of Western civilization that coincided with his later immersion in Hindu mysticism. Indeed, Carpenter's remarks have obscured the degree to which his early poetry, in particular his first collection *Narcissus and Other Poems* (1873), prefigures the reformist literary mode of *Towards Democracy* and the latter text's complex engagement with the urgent political question of land reform. However, a closer look reveals that the poems in *Narcissus* develop a poetic vocabulary—as well as a set of observations about the social and individual pathologies to which privatized land ownership gave rise—that enabled Carpenter to key into the debates about land nationalization after 1880.

As the title of Carpenter's first poetry collection suggests, many of the texts in *Narcissus* indulge in relatively conventional forms of classical poetic erudition.

---

[8] Carpenter, *My Days and Dreams, Being Autobiographical Notes* [1916] (London: Allen & Unwin, 1921), p. 64.

[9] Honig, *Public Things: Democracy in Disrepair* (New York: Fordham University Press, 2017), pp. 3–5.

[10] Carpenter, *My Days and Dreams*, p. 190.

The two long poems which open the volume, 'Narcissus' and 'Persephone', centre on mythological figures, and both contain extended descriptions of arcadian scenes and pastoral idylls. 'Narcissus' begins:

> The valley there
> Lays out its sunny slopes to light and air
> Crowned with eternal forest: fir and pine
> With silver birch and maple intertwine.
> But all about, as if the earth in sport
> Ran riot of her riches, every sort
> Of flowering shrub and dainty flower is seen
> To deck those lawny dells and coverts green.[11]

The description of nature's plenty in these lines remains strangely formulaic and abstract as if to mirror the self-absorption that makes the figure of Narcissus oblivious to the bountifulness of his natural surroundings. Other poems in *Narcissus* foreground the beauty of nature in order to trouble the serene detachment Carpenter associated with classical mythology. 'Persephone', for example, opens with an Edenic scene set on Mount Olympus:

> No rude intrusions rouse
> This quiet that the Gods hold for their own,
> But they can hear like a far distant tone
> The murmurs and the music of the Earth—
> Its lamentations and high tones of mirth,
> Loud sylvan choruses and lovely song[.]
>
> (24–5)

The capitalized spelling of 'Earth' in this passage looks forward to the anthropomorphized Earth of the first book (1883) of *Towards Democracy*, and the 'earth-born song' (25) of the 'sylvan choruses' anticipates the keen sense of belonging and rootedness that characterizes *Towards Democracy*'s reparative vision of the relationship between humans and the ground they inhabit. The myth of Persephone—daughter of the harvest goddess Demeter, whose abduction by Hades caused winter on Earth—creates an important ambiguity at the heart of the poem: on the one hand, it enables Carpenter to celebrate Earth's abundance in a way that anticipates the iconography of later land-reformist tracts such as Charles Wicksteed's proto-environmentalist *Our Mother Earth* (Figure 1); on the

---

[11] Carpenter, *Narcissus and Other Poems* (London: Henry King, 1873), pp. 4–5.

Figure 1 Cover of Charles Wicksteed's *Our Mother Earth: A Short Statement of the Case of Land Nationalisation* (London: Swan Sonnenschein, 1892).

other, it calls up apocalyptic scenes of desolate wintry barrenness as the mourning Demeter appeals to Zeus to rescue her daughter.

> 'Dear God of heaven, who art wont to make
> The whole earth happy with thy smiling brow,
> And rich in thine embraces, seeing now
> The trees are weeping and the land is bare […].'

(41)

Such poetic visions of destruction depart from the celebratory depictions of lush natural beauty in contemporaneous works such as William Morris's *The Earthly Paradise* (1868–70) or Richard Jefferies's *After London* (1885). Departing from Morris and Jefferies, Carpenter's language instead resonates with the sombre imagery in many reformist tracts of the 1880s, which presented the desultory and untilled stretches of land owned by absentee landlords as evidence of the need for far-reaching reform.

The complementary depictions of Earth as caring parent and as alienated, non-human other are central to Carpenter's literary writings of the 1870s. In an unpublished notebook from the mid-1870s, which contains scraps of poems that would later form part of *Towards Democracy*, Carpenter began to translate these leitmotifs into the medium of Whitmanesque free verse. One of the manuscript poems, 'Signs without Words', revisits the idea (familiar from *Narcissus*) of Earth as a personified abstraction that appears impossibly aloof from the sphere of human concerns: 'all men sleep,' the poem notes, 'But Earth sleeps never: in the silent spaces / Where our thought ends, she breathes new cycles.' Earth inhabits a planetary temporality that constitutively eludes and transcends human 'thought'. And while nature and the elements appear to exist in a kind of pre-established harmony, they are wholly indifferent to the speaker's yearning to enter into poetic communion with them: 'Ocean in her far hollows has turned away; / The air sleeps—sleeps with closed heavy lids—and all men sleep, / Surely the old Earth also. / Surely what all men say is likeliest true: the old Earth sleeps, the Sea sleeps in its hollows.'[12] Carpenter's notebooks demonstrate that the writing of *Towards Democracy* did not take place exclusively during his residence at Millthorpe, but that the composition of the poem's first book was a long and drawn-out process that had its origins in the 1870s. Carpenter's early poetic writings, including the drafts in his personal notebooks, are significant because they contradict the myth that Carpenter's move to Millthorpe coincided with an absolute intellectual and artistic break. These texts outline conflicting views of Earth—as nurturing mother and as alienating presence, as concrete natural environment and as abstract

---

[12] ECC, 'Signs without Words', Notebook from mid-1870s, MSS 3.

concept—that would play a central role in the poetry and social criticism Carpenter composed during the high tide of land reform agitation in the 1880s.

'Signs without Words' looks ahead to the poem sequence 'Earth's Voices', a collection of forty-two short texts first printed in Carpenter's debut collection *Narcissus*. 'Earth's Voices' offers a deep-space view of planet Earth, and the speaker imagines himself as a space traveller listening to the melody of the celestial bodies: 'Earth', it seems to him, is singing 'with a single note / Amid the spheric chant' (89). The speaker sees the light of the Sun travel across the planet's surface where it sustains life until 'Earth's black edge' plunges the globe back into darkest night. The planetary view adopted in 'Earth's Voices' involves a tension that will also be central to book 1 of *Towards Democracy*. This internal friction stems from Carpenter's attempt to distinguish between *Earth* as the entirety of the globe's vast habitable surface (what 'Earth's Voices' calls 'the round / Of Earth') and enclosed *land* as a form of privatized commercial property. The parcelling-up of the Earth, 'Earth's Voices' suggests, leads to unnatural disharmony as the planet's 'single note' fractures into disjunctive sounds and rhythms. Carpenter's planetary metaphors resonate with the language of social tracts that championed the cause of land reform less than a decade later. For land reformers, the planetary perspective possessed such exceptional symbolic potency because it made it possible to imagine Earth as an entire commons unscathed by privatization and the enclosure system—and it also offered an anticipatory image of reformed property relations under which commodified land would once more be restored to the wholeness of collectively owned Earth. The poems in *Narcissus* were written some time before land agitation reached a fever pitch in the 1880s but they begin to register a dangerous imbalance between the self-interested desire to appropriate land for commercial purposes and the finite supply of arable ground. 'Earth's Voices' frequently celebrates the bountifulness of Earth, but it also recognizes that ground is a scarce resource. One of the poems in the sequence discovers that the entire planet has been divided up into 'impassable fixed pale[s]' which create an existential 'want' for land that cannot be satisfied (106). These lines anticipate Carpenter's later attack on land monopolies for creating 'an absolute famine in land': 'The demand, the outcry, for land is great,' he concluded in 1907, 'but the supply is scanty.'[13] And a set of lecture notes from 1895 concludes: 'Many Sm[all] Holdings wanted. More access *necessary*'.[14]

Carpenter's treatment of the relationship between Earth and its inhabitants received a significant new inflection in the early poem 'In the Grass: By a Monad (of Leibniz)'. As Carpenter recalled in his autobiographical *My Days and Dreams*,

---

[13] Carpenter, 'The village and the landlord' [1907], in *Socialism and Agriculture* ed. Edward Carpenter, T. S. Dymond et al. (London: Fifield, 1908), pp. 5–19 (p. 16).
[14] ECC, Manuscript notes for lecture on 'Smallholdings and Allotments' (October 1895), MSS 115; orig. emphasis.

he had read William Michael Rossetti's bowdlerized edition of Walt Whitman's poems—the first volume of Whitman's verse to be published in Britain—shortly after it had come out in 1868, and the title of 'In the Grass' offers a thinly veiled allusion to the title of Whitman's major poetic work *Leaves of Grass*.[15] Contrary to the expectations called up by the poem's title, however, Carpenter's text is locked in an anti-Whitmanian nightmare, as the monad's proximity to the ground fails to bring it into closer communion with the life-giving forces of nature. The title of the poem references Gottfried Wilhelm Leibniz's seventeenth-century theory of monads to foreground the speaker's claustrophobic alienation from the rich natural world that surrounds him:

> Here in the grass they laid me long ago,
>   Far from the tumult and the tears of men,
> Soft in the summer grass, forlorn and low—
>   The face of all the world is changed since then.
> Here, on my back, and scarce beneath the turf,
>   To lie and lie for many a summer day,
> Hearing the faint far ocean-sweeping surf,
>   Seeing the blue midnoon and twilight grey.
> [...]
> Here, void of will, of action unaware,
>   And dwindled to a mere perceptive point,
> Changeless I watch the light divide the air
>   And glitter on each reedy knot and joint.
>
> (147)

'Changeless I watch the changes of the sky', the monad concludes, affirming its complete detachment from Earth's seasonal rhythms. At the same time, the monad's sheer passivity ('they laid me...to lie and lie...void of will') forms a stark contrast with the busy commotion of the world that surrounds it. Compared to the life force that pervades nature, the monad is reduced to an immobile speck ('a mere perceptive point') whose residual perceptual and sensory activity opens up no meaningful rapport with its surroundings. The monad's atomistic self-containment recalls Narcissus's absorption in his mirror image, and like 'Narcissus', Carpenter's poem about the monad can be read as a wistful reflection on the links that ought to tie humans to the ground they inhabit.

'In the Grass' crucially shifts attention from the non-human scale of Earth's planetary rhythms—addressed in pieces such as 'Earth's Voices' and 'Signs without Words'—towards the question of how humans might show greater

---

[15] Carpenter, *My Days and Dreams*, pp. 64–5.

responsibility for and responsiveness to the ground on which they dwell. In doing so, 'In the Grass' takes up observations about the social pathologies of land ownership that had become increasingly prominent in Carpenter's thinking about Earth in the 1870s. For example, in his manuscript notes for an unpublished lecture on 'Materialism', delivered to the Leeds Cooperative Society in November 1874, Carpenter had proposed his own highly idiosyncratic brand of material-ism.[16] This materialism is clearly distinct from its Marxist counterpart, which was being propagated by the Social Democratic Federation and its combative leader Henry Mayers Hyndman from 1881 onwards. Instead of embracing an econo-mistic framework of explanation, Carpenter's lecture notes recommend a new attentiveness to nature's materiality:

> Here is a stone—the commonest object—what do I know about it? It is hard, to me, but to a steamhammer it w^d be clay—I must learn its real nature somehow else. Smooth—others w^d find it rough as the Earth is to us. Brown—to a colour blind green, to a blind no colour. [. . .] In other words these are qualities but they do not tell me of the thing which possesses these qualities & they must not be confused. Self and one's complexion. These are ways in which it affects us, sensations excited in us, but what it is that excited—we do not thus learn. [. . .] We go out into the world: the ground is solid [. . .] the play of life is about us, the green is on the trees but behind it all & close upon us, as close as any of these things, is the matter which underlies them all.
>
> What is it that thus endorses on all sides, upholds us through the ground, presses us through the passive table [. . .]? Who will answer?

The passage returns us to the basic ontological property of the world around us—the sheer fact of its material existence that Carpenter calls 'solidity'—but the essay also indicates that the encounter with the concrete 'earth', 'ground', and 'stones' involves us in an ethically charged dialectical movement: the contact with the ground that supports us prompts new questions about ourselves, and it returns us, finally, to the urgent question of how we can successfully 'know' (and relate to) the Earth. Carpenter concludes his lecture by calling for a fresh attentiveness to the seemingly inert matter that 'endorses on all sides' and that 'upholds' and 'presses us'—this new form of 'knowing', he suggests, will not depend on a sense of scientific and epistemological mastery but on a new and more intimate respon-siveness to humans' natural surroundings.[17]

---

[16] ECC, Manuscript notes for a lecture on 'Materialism' (22 November 1874), MSS 7.

[17] In a related discussion, Daniel Wright has recently explored how Thomas Hardy's novels work to direct our attention to the fact of the world's material existence. Whereas Hardy asks us (in Wright's phrase) 'to attend to the [world's] obdurate but abstract groundwork rather than to the concrete object, to dark matter rather than to visible matter', Carpenter's writings promote a form of ethical attention

Similar questions undergird the reflections on land ownership that came to dominate Carpenter's works of the early 1880s. In an essay entitled 'Private Property' (1886), Carpenter argues that the problem of 'property' is bound up with the question of the owner's 'proper' relationship to his land. The essay opens with an anecdote about a 'gentleman who owned a large property' but who turns out to be ignorant of the natural features of his estate when he is questioned by a visitor. 'In what sense did that gentleman own that land?', Carpenter asks. If '[t]o own means to confess, to recognize, to acknowledge', this landlord—though legally entitled to call the land his own—cannot be said to 'own' the land any more than the self-contained monad of 'In the Grass'.[18] 'Private Property' contrasts the landowner's alienation with the farmers' intimate knowledge of the land:

While the people about him and working on the land are continually thinking (as I have often had occasion to notice) what can be done for the land, how they can best do justice to it—spending affection and thought upon it—and indeed grieving when they see it neglected, when they see it undrained or insufficiently manured, or allowed to run to waste and dishevelment—even though these matters are as the saying is "not their concern," and make no difference to their pockets. While, I say, the common people spend this love and affection on the land, the legal owner, as a rule is thinking concerning it of only one thing—and that is how much money he can get out of it.   (116)

Unlike the fabled *homo economicus* of classical political economy who seeks to maximize the financial gain he can extract from his land, Carpenter advocates an ethos of proprietary care and concern, of custodial 'affection and thought', that is independent of legal entitlements. In proposing a positive and active relationship to the shared ground we inhabit, 'Private Property' continues a line of thinking about land ownership begun in the 'Materialism' lecture and in poems such as 'Narcissus', 'Earth's Voices', and 'In the Grass'. The imagery of these early poems could without much difficulty be repurposed in the context of Carpenter's fledgling concern with more meaningful forms of ownership and with the related question of land nationalization.

(what I call 'care' or 'attentiveness') that is oriented towards concrete objects. See Wright, 'Thomas Hardy's groundwork', *PMLA* 134.5 (2019): 1028–41 (p. 1030). Carpenter's identification of stones as the 'commonest objects' of our attention—and as metonyms of the natural world as such—was almost certainly inspired by his encounter with the remarkable collection of minerals, agates, flints and quartzes which John Ruskin had donated to the city of Sheffield in order to enable the city's silversmiths to contemplate at leisure the beauty of the natural materials with which they worked.

[18] Carpenter, 'Private property' [1886], in Carpenter, *England's Ideal and Other Papers on Social Subjects* (London: Swan Sonnenschein, 1887), pp. 115–38 (p. 115). Carpenter had first proposed 'private property' as a lecture topic to Edward Pease, the secretary of the Fabian Society, in 1885 (Carpenter, Letter to Edward Pease, 1 December 1885, FSLSE, A/6/3–70).

'England for All': Debates about Land Reform in the 1880s

Malcom Chase, the late historian of nineteenth-century land debates, has observed that '[t]he early 1880s marked the high point of land reform agitation in Victorian Britain.'[19] Land reform had a long prehistory to which participants of all political hues contributed, including socialist radicals, free-trade liberals, and Tory landlords. Yet while land agitation had been a prominent feature of British political life since the fifteenth century, it only 'reached a peak in the hundred years after 1730', when a large portion of common land in England became enclosed.[20] The decision to enclose land had played a key role in the eighteenth-century industrial revolution: by distributing land among private owners, enclosures permitted more intense cultivation of land and promised a more consistent supply of food to Britain's growing population. However, the privatization of the commons also generated opposition, notably among the dispossessed poor whose livelihood had for centuries relied on unrestricted access to the soil. As the nineteenth century progressed, critics of private landownership, including the Land Nationalization Society, frequently invoked Britons' natural right of free access to the land. Carpenter's political stance on land reform echoes the popular radicalism that was taken up and amplified by the land nationalization movement from the 1880s onwards.[21] The Land Nationalization Society's popular-radical rhetoric, which presented land as the shared property of all citizens, runs thick in *Towards Democracy*, including the following passage from book 4 (1902):

> To place a nation squarely on its own base, spreading out its people far and wide in honoured usefulness upon the soil,
>
> Building up all uses and capacities of the land into the life of the masses,
>
> So that the riches of the Earth may go first and foremost to those who produce them [...]
>
> But to-day the lands are slimed and fenced over with denials.[22]

---

[19] Malcom Chase, '"Wholesome object lessons": The Chartist Land Plan in retrospect', *The English Historical Review* 118.475 (2003): 59–85 (pp. 72–3).

[20] Alun Howkins, 'From Diggers to dongas: The land in English radicalism, 1649–2000', *History Workshop Journal* 54 (2002): 1–23 (p. 7).

[21] Large quantities of pamphlets from the Land Nationalization Society survive in the Carpenter Archives in Sheffield, and many of these pamphlets were heavily annotated by Carpenter. ECC, Carpenter/Library/2.

[22] Carpenter, *Towards Democracy* (London: Allen & Unwin, 1905), p. 392. The four parts of Carpenter's work appeared in 1883, 1885, 1892, and 1902, respectively. All further references in this chapter will be to the 1905 complete edition. Quotations will be followed by *TD* and the page number. For the composition history of the different parts of *Towards Democracy*, see Sheila Rowbotham, *Edward Carpenter: A Life of Liberty and Love* (London: Verso, 2009), p. 71.

'Earth', here, becomes the conceptual capstone of Carpenter's redistributive vision. Like the popular radicals of previous centuries, Carpenter indicates that '[the] people' are entitled to reclaim the enclosed ('fenced-over') country from the landlords. In the context of the 1880s and 1890s however, this kind of radicalism was often inflected by other political tonalities. First, the language of popular radicalism—with its far-reaching calls for the break-up of land monopolies—was partly co-opted by Whiggish liberals who called for free trade in land and advocated the creation of privately bought and owned smallholdings.[23] This liberal line of argument suggested that the best way to democratize land distribution was by selling (or renting out) small plots to individual farmers and their families. Second, radical calls for the nationalization of land also received a boost from a different set of political demands, namely the agitation of the Irish National Land League. Following the election of Charles Stewart Parnell as its president, the Land League added a nationalist edge to the discussion that had been lacking from many previous attacks on land monopolization in England.[24] Land reform in Ireland possessed particular political urgency because much Irish land was owned by English landlords who spent little or no time on their vast Irish estates. Such absentee landlordism, the Land Leaguers argued, added insult to injury as it consigned Irish farmers to cultivating the land for English owners who had little more than a commercial interest in their property. Land reformers in England— liberals and radicals alike—quickly picked up on the nationalist dimensions of the Irish debate, and they began to tap into the rhetoric of the Irish Land League to build an analogous case for land reform in England. For example, Alfred Russel Wallace's popular primer *Land Nationalisation* (1882) devoted a whole chapter to the Irish situation, and Carpenter's friend Henry Hyndman likewise wrote at length on the topic in *England for All* (1881), the book which Carpenter credited with converting him to political radicalism.[25]

[23] The popular-radical political idiom of land reform is discussed in Malcolm Chase, 'Chartism and the land: "The mighty people's question"', in *Land Question*, eds. Cragoe/Readman, pp. 57–73; see also Rollo D. Arnold, 'The "Revolt of the Field" in Kent, 1872–79', *Past & Present* 64.1 (1974): 71–95. The liberal Anti-Corn Law League's place in the history of the British land reform movement is discussed in Anthony Howe, *Free Trade and Liberal England, 1846–1946* (Oxford: Clarendon Press, 1997), pp. 70–110; and Howe, 'The "Manchester School" and the landlords: The failure of land reform in early Victorian Britain', in *Land Question*, eds. Cragoe/Readman, pp. 74–91.

[24] For a comparative account of the reform movements in England and Ireland, see Philip Bull, 'Irish land and British politics', in *Land Question*, eds. Cragoe/Readman, pp. 126–45. See also Roy Douglas, *Land, People and Politics: A History of the Land Question in the United Kingdom* (London: Allison & Busby, 1976), pp. 32–4.

[25] Wallace, *Land Nationalisation* [1882] (London: Swan Sonnenschein, 1896), pp. 30–51; Hyndman, *England for All* (London: Gilbert & Rivington, 1881), pp. 112–30. Carpenter noted apropos of Hyndman's book that 'the instant I read [...] *England for All*—the mass of floating impressions, sentiments, ideals, etc., in my mind fell into shape—and I had a clear line of social reconstruction before me.' See *My Days and Dreams*, p. 114. The most important theorist of land reform in the period, the American Henry George, also commented extensively on the Irish case. George suggested in several of his publications that the cases of landlordism in England and Ireland were essentially analogous: 'The truth', he noted in 1881, 'is that the Irish land system is simply the general system of civilization.'

Carpenter's literary treatment of land ownership echoes these overlapping rhetorical strategies, and it can sometimes be difficult to disentangle the hybrid amalgamation of reformist idioms present in his writings. By the end of the century, however, many land nationalizers began to emphasize the possibility of allowing individuals to rent (rather than buy) land from the state.[26] This position offered a compromise solution between some of the views outlined above: on the one hand, the creation of smallholding tenancies promised a wide-ranging structural remedy for the monopolization of landed property while also pushing back against (liberal) calls for a free trade in land; on the other, the proposed creation of tenancies attributed a significant managerial role to the state while also giving individuals the opportunity to flourish on their own land and to exercise custodial duties towards it. These arguments seem to have resonated with Carpenter—not least because they managed to combine the call for sweeping institutional reform with a substantive ethical vision that emphasized the emergence of a more intimate and responsible relationship to the land. Carpenter's particular contribution to these discussions, I shall argue, consisted in his poetic attempt to imagine this newly emerging ethos not simply as the result of institutional reform but also as its enabling precondition, as an *entgegenkommende Lebensform* that would foster the popular desire for an anti-monopolistic, redistributive politics.

The conjunction of material and ethical reform that characterized land nationalization debates and that energized Carpenter's thinking on the topic, combines two modalities of late nineteenth-century reformism that are sometimes held to be irreconcilable: on the one hand, the materialism represented by the Fabian Society, with its emphasis on gradual institutional change and slow administrative reform; and on the other, the ethical idealism more commonly associated with the Fellowship of the New Life, of which Carpenter was a key member. Literary and cultural historians have only recently begun to draw attention to the mixed quality of this reformist mode. For example, Ruth Livesey observes that Carpenter's interest in institutional reform was characterized by 'a remarkable disregard of the boundaries [between materialism and idealism] that over a century later seem impassable divides';[27] and the political historian Kevin Manton agrees that reformers such as Carpenter, Wallace, and Sidney Ball 'rejected the dichotomies of their society, such as individual-society,

---

Indeed, even George's compatriots were not spared from the ignominies of this system of ownership, for 'our large American landowners [are] also generally absentees'. See *The Land Question* [1881], in *The Writings of Henry George*, vol. 4 (New York: Doubleday, 1898), pp. 1–109 (pp. 10, 13).

[26] For a good summary of this broad consensus in the 1870s and 1880s, see Douglas, *Land, People and Politics*, pp. 15–122.

[27] Livesey, 'Morris, Carpenter, Wilde, and the political aesthetics of labor', *Victorian Literature and Culture* 32.2 (2004): 601–16 (p. 604). Applying these observations to Carpenter, Livesey finds that 'part of the pleasure of examining Carpenter's works now is the very resistance of his ideas to our neatly bound categories of idealism and materialism' (609).

ends-means, and materialism-ethicalism'.[28] The case of Carpenter is exemplary in this respect as it indicates the facility with which such intellectual connections and political allegiances were forged.

Before we turn to the aesthetic dimensions of Carpenter's reformist vision, we can shed some further light on the political content of these poetic experiments by looking briefly to the foundational work of two central figures of the land nationalization movement—the American economist Henry George and Carpenter's friend Alfred Russel Wallace. In the early 1880s, George, a brilliant speaker, had given a series of lectures in Britain in which he proposed a single tax on all privately owned land. This single tax was intended as a radical redistributive measure and it won George many British supporters.[29] The tax, George argued, would help to erode the monopolization of land, but the money generated in this way could also be used for a series of welfare measures that would ameliorate the condition of the labouring classes. The main work in which George presented his ideas, *Progress and Poverty* (1879), became a textbook for land reformers on both sides of the Atlantic, and it has been described as an important inspiration for the Edwardian welfare reforms I discuss in the next two chapters.[30] In contrast to David Ricardo, who had claimed that labour was the central standard yard by which all economic value must be measured, George pointed out that land was even more fundamental to value production because it provided the necessary basis for labour itself:

I merely wish to correct that impression which leads so many people to talk and write as though rent and land tenures related solely to agriculture and to agricultural communities. Nothing could be more erroneous. Land is necessary to all production, no matter what be its kind or form; land is the standing-place, the workshop, the storehouse of labor; it is to the human being the only means by which he can obtain access to the material universe or utilize its powers. Without land man cannot exist. To whom the ownership of land is given, to him is given the virtual ownership of the men who must live upon it.[31]

Because of its absolute economic importance, land constituted a common good that belonged by right to the everyone. No one, George argued, should be entitled

[28] Manton, 'The fellowship of the new life: English ethical socialism reconsidered', *History of Political Thought* 24.2 (2003): 282–304 (p. 282).

[29] In the 1880s Henry George addressed letters to the Land Nationalization Society which were then read out at the organization's meetings. See e.g. Alfred Russel Wallace's recollections in 'Land Nationalisation Society Conference This Day', *Echo* (16 January 1882): 3. A helpful account of George's influence can be found in Avner Offer's *Property and Politics, 1870–1914: Landownership, Law, Ideology, and Urban Development in England* (Cambridge: Cambridge University Press, 1981), pp. 184–200.

[30] George's influence on Edwardian reformers is discussed in Geoffrey Lee, *The People's Budget: An Edwardian Tragedy* (London: Shepheard-Walwyn, 1996), pp. 32–43.

[31] George, *The Land Question* (1881), p. 27. All further references will be given parenthetically.

to alienate these collective property rights by selling or buying plots of land. George also contended that land was not a form of property like any other because its value tended to increase even if no improvements were made to it. This meant that landowners were becoming richer simply because the country's population kept growing and the country's wealth continued to increase. As Carpenter's friend (and eager Georgite) Wallace explained, 'the whole commercial value of land is the creation of society, increasing just as population and civilization increase.'[32] The class structure of society, George insisted, would not be fundamentally affected by an overly cautious expansion of land ownership because '[e]ven if the number of the owners of soil could thus be increased, the soil [. . .] would still be in the hands of a class, though of a somewhat larger class. And the spring of misery would be untouched' (33). George's arguments found wide dissemination among English land reformers because they could be taken to support the radical redistribution of land envisioned by liberals and socialists alike. Indeed, George himself pointed out that his policy proposals were intended as a broad church for land reformers who otherwise had little in common: 'There are those', he noted, 'who may look on this little book as very radical, in the bad sense they attach to the word. They mistake. This is, in the true sense of the word, a most conservative little book. I do not appeal to prejudice and passion. [. . .] I do not incite to strife; I seek to prevent strife' (97).

In England, George's lectures and essays helped to convert H. G. Wells, George Bernard Shaw, and Keir Hardie (the Scottish union leader and future founder of the Labour Party) to socialism.[33] However, his arguments received their most resounding contemporary endorsement in Wallace's writings. Wallace echoed much of the economic detail of George's analyses, as well as many of his specific reformist proposals, but he also invested them with an ethical pathos that was largely absent from George's more academic prose. For Wallace, land national-ization was not only a matter of redistributing economic wealth or of combatting the entrenched British class system. Instead, by enabling a larger number of individuals to become tenants on state-owned land, land nationalization promised to make the bulk of the population healthier, happier, and more attentive to their environment and well-being: 'We are, therefore, warranted in concluding', Wallace declared, 'that, in order to effect a real and vital improvement in the condition of the great mass of the English nation, not only as regards physical well-being, but also socially, intellectually, and morally, we must radically change our system of land-tenure.'[34] In book 4 of *Towards Democracy* Carpenter expected that the redistribution of land would produce similarly beneficial outcomes:

---

[32] Wallace, 'The "Why" and the "How" of land nationalisation (I)', *Macmillan's Magazine* 287 (September 1883): 357–67 (p. 357).

[33] Gertrude Himmelfarb, *Poverty and Compassion* (New York: Knopf, 1991), p. 319.

[34] Wallace, *Land Nationalisation*, p. 18.

Healthy and well-formed of limb, self-reliant, enterprising, alert, skilled in the use of tools, able to cope with Nature in her moods, and with the Earth for their sustenance, loving and trustful of each other, united and invincible in silent faith. Where is the Statesman who makes it the main item of his programme to produce such a population? Where the Capitalist, where the Landlord? (*TD* 464)

Wallace and Carpenter took an idealized view of rural living and of the relationship of agricultural labourers to their land. While the existing economic dispensation had 'pauperise[d] a large section of the labouring classes' and 'degrade[d] them socially and morally', the nationalization of land would finally restore the 'birthright of every Englishman—the freedom to enjoy and utilise some portion of his native soil [...] in the interest of all'.[35] For the first time in centuries, land nationalization would provide unrestricted 'access to the natural products which are essential to life'.[36] By the same token, the democratization of land ownership would nourish new and shared forms of life by enabling individuals to live in closer communion with nature and with each other. In a serialized article published in *The Contemporary Review* in 1880, Wallace spelled out the implications of these claims by developing a dual model of 'ownership' that programmatically fused his concerns with the materialistic-structural and the idealistic-ethical sides of land nationalization. The two-part essay, entitled 'How to nationalize the land', maintains that '[t]he interest of a landowner in his property is of two kinds, commercial and sentimental, and these together constitute its value to him'.[37] While Wallace admitted that under capitalism commercial value had crowded out the 'sentimental value' of land, he challenged the Georgite view which maintained that the redistribution of economic values was the principal or indeed the only question that was at stake in the political struggle about land. Wallace's essays of the early 1880s attempted to enrich George's conception of land ownership by 'show[ing] that it is possible to give full satisfaction to every just sentiment of ownership of the land' (722)—taking the land away from the current elite of upper-class proprietors, Wallace contended, would simultaneously increase the national net total of its 'sentimental value' because the state would give more individuals the opportunity to live on, tend to, and cultivate the earth.[38]

It was via Wallace that Georgite ideas filtered through to Carpenter. And if the work of George and earlier land reformers can help us understand the larger

[35] Wallace, *Land Nationalisation*, p. 122.   [36] Wallace, *Land Nationalisation (I)*, p. 357.
[37] Wallace, 'How to nationalize the land: A radical solution of the Irish land problem', *The Contemporary Review* 38 (November 1880): 716–36 (p. 719).
[38] Wallace's (and Carpenter's) conceptual distinction between 'true' and 'false' ownership is rooted in a much longer tradition of socialist thought. For example, it recalls Pierre-Joseph Proudhon's differentiation between (commercial) 'property' and (ethically meaningful) 'possession': while '[p]roperty was a legal power, backed up by force and fraud, granted to owners and heirs', Proudhon argued, the possessor knew to be 'responsible for the thing entrusted to him'. See Laura Brace, *The Politics of Property: Labour, Freedom and Belonging* (Edinburgh: Edinburgh University Press, 2004), p. 120.

political stakes of Carpenter's poetic engagement with the idea of collectively owned ground, *Towards Democracy*'s particular vision of an emerging ethos of proprietorial care is best understood in analogy to the notion of sentimental ownership developed by Wallace. Wallace's distinction between two discrete types of land value notably corresponds to Carpenter's differentiation between land and Earth in *Towards Democracy*: while Earth in Carpenter's poetry came to signify habitable ground as a form of the common good, land signalled its primarily commercial status as private property. Accordingly, it was under the label of Earth that Carpenter began to envision a non-instrumental relationship to the land, a mode of Wallacean 'true ownership'.

'True Ownership' and the Commons in *Towards Democracy*

The basic biographical contours of Carpenter's experiments in rural living at Millthorpe Cottage are quite well known. Carpenter's decision to leave Sheffield, where he had been working as a University Extension lecturer, and to buy a rural smallholding on the edge of the Peak District has often been seen as an iconic expression of the simple-lifer movement of the late nineteenth century. Millthorpe Cottage has been celebrated as a homosexual commune which allowed Carpenter and his working-class partner George Merrill to live together at a safe distance from the public eye. As Carpenter recalled in his autobiography *My Days and Dreams*, he had 'long[ed] for a country home' since at least 1879 when 'the absolute necessity for a more open-air life began to make itself felt'.[39] Having spent most of his life in cities—first in his parents' comfortable upper-middle-class home in Brighton and later in Sheffield—rural living seemed to hold out the possibility of a simplified existence unhampered by the moral constraints of respectable society. Carpenter and Merrill's audacious experiment in queer domesticity has occasionally been derided by later socialists—most infamously by George Orwell who ridiculed Carpenter's lived utopia of cross-class brother-hood in order to boost his own revolutionary credentials.[40] In what follows, I am not primarily concerned with the homosocial and homosexual bonds that were formed at Millthorpe, or with the rich genealogy of male homosociality that stands behind them.[41] Instead I want to home in on the reformist thinking that helped to

---

[39]   Carpenter, *My Days and Dreams*, p. 101.

[40]   For Orwell's notoriously homophobic blacklist of socialist 'cranks' ('fruit-juice drinkers, nudists, sandal-wearers, sex-maniacs'—the list goes on), see *The Road to Wigan Pier* (London: Penguin, 2001), p. 161.

[41]   In fact, Carpenter and Merrill did not meet until 1891. The prehistory and afterlives of Carpenterian homosociality have been traced by Seth Koven (who comments on the 'taint of unnatural fraternity' that haunted the all-male environment of the settlement movement) as well as by Janice Ho (who finds echoes of Carpenterian homosociality in E. M. Forster's democratically expanded understanding of social citizen-ship). See Koven, *Slumming: Sexual and Social Politics in Victorian London* (Princeton: Princeton

foster the growth of such counter-hegemonic spaces by insisting on the more equitable distribution of land.[42]

Carpenter's plans to set up house in the country crystallized relatively early, around 1879, when he met the scythe-maker Albert Fearnehough, a tenant who lived in a small cottage on the farm of Carpenter's friend Charles Fox.[43] As Carpenter's biographer Sheila Rowbotham points out, Fox was 'one of the small independent proprietors who had stubbornly survived' the monopolization of land in the nineteenth century while many other 'farms were being rented from large landowners' (62). Fearnehough invited Carpenter to live with him and his wife outside Sheffield, and Carpenter's early reformist ideas were vitally shaped by his first-hand experience of farm life after moving in with the Fearnehoughs in May 1880.[44] Fox's life—and, by association, the life of the Fearnehough family— came to embody Carpenter's vision of a self-sufficient rural existence. Yet, for Carpenter, moving to the countryside was also closely intertwined with the more personal desire to embark on a new kind of writing. As he noted in a letter to Charles Oates, his close friend from student days: 'I am looking out for a small homestead with about 10 acres of land near Sheffield [. . .] where I can embark in some agricultural work—chiefly fruit-growing—with the assistance of two friends who have some experience in that line.' 'Such agricultural work,' he added, would be conducive to his literary labours as it would finally give him the energy to prepare 'some of my prophetic writings [i.e. the pieces that would form the first part of *Towards Democracy*] with a view to publication'.[45]

It is certainly true that Carpenter brought with him an intellectual's construct of rural existence. 'Being in imagination everything the city is not,' Rowbotham observes, 'the countryside appeared as a blank which could then have "Innocence", "Simplicity" and "Escape" projected on it' (64). This does not mean that Carpenter simply opted out of contemporary political discussion altogether. Carpenter's inter- est in the land reform debates of the 1870s indicates that it is necessary to see his aspirational ethical idealism as part of a broader historical arc that also includes technical reformist discussions about the exploitation of rural labour, the unearned

University Press, 2006), p. 239; and Ho, *Nation and Citizenship in the Twentieth-Century British Novel* (Cambridge: Cambridge University Press, 2015), pp. 30–3. Also: Sarah Cole, *Modernism, Male Friendship, and the First World War* (Cambridge: Cambridge University Press, 2003), pp. 21–91.

[42] To put this another way: the state, as it emerges in the land reform debates discussed here, organizes spaces which are the material precondition for acts of (artistic, sexual, social, agricultural) experimentation. The state facilitates individual flourishing rather than acting as its (technocratic) enemy. For an influential anti-state account of land as the basis of subaltern agency and 'inventiveness', see James C. Scott, *Seeing Like a State: How Certain Schemes to Improve the Human Condition Have Failed* (New Haven: Yale University Press, 1998), pp. 342–5.

[43] For Rowbotham's account of this friendship, see *Edward Carpenter*, pp. 62–4. See also Chushichi Tsuzuki, *Edward Carpenter: Prophet of Human Fellowship* (Cambridge: Cambridge University Press, 1980), pp. 39–42.

[44] Carpenter's own account of this episode is featured in *My Days and Dreams*, pp. 99–108.

[45] ECC, Letter to Charles Oates, 27 November 1882, Sheffield Archives, MSS 351–34.

rent of (absentee) landlords, and the status of private and public property. Carpenter effectively took sides in these heated debates when, after coming into an inheritance of £6,000 after the death of his father in April 1882, he decided to buy the seven-acre smallholding in Millthorpe. It might seem that by investing in a smallholding—by converting a patch of 'Earth' into a privately-owned parcel of 'land'—Carpenter went against one of the basic tenets of the land nationalizers whose works he had been studying. Indeed, as we have seen, many land reformers on the left of the political spectrum, including some of the socialist circles in which Carpenter moved, rejected the institution of small-scale proprietorship because it would not transform the underlying class structure of British society: 'the soil', George had cautioned, 'would still be in the hands of a class, though of a somewhat larger class.' By buying a smallholding near Sheffield, Carpenter became a member of this new 'class'—a decision which could seem to subvert the more distant goal of land nationalization: 'three acres and a cow,' William Morris acerbically warned in 1886, 'will not bring about a very great revolution'.[46]

Carpenter reflected on the problematic status of smallholdings in a slightly later text, first published as a Fabian Tract in 1907 under the title 'The village and the landlord'. The creation of 'smallholds', Carpenter explained, did not contribute directly to the ideal of land nationalization, but it provided a kind of halfway house on the road towards more comprehensive reforms. 'The village and the landlord' can be read as a retrospective defence of Carpenter's decision to buy the land near Millthorpe, but the text also voices some deeper reservations about the drawbacks of full land nationalization:

> There are two main directions in which to go in the matter of secure tenure. One is the creation of more small landholds; the other is the throwing of lands into the hands of public authorities, and the creation of permanent tenures under them. Though the latter embodies the best general principle, I do not think that forms a reason for ruling out freeholds *altogether*. In all these matters variety is better than unification. [...] In the same way, with regard to public ownership, if anything like nationalisation of land is effected, I think it should decidedly be on the same principle of variety—creating not only State and municipal ownership, but ownership by country councils, district councils, parish councils, etc.[47]

Like Wallace, Carpenter anticipates that the state will play a key role in the reappropriation and redistribution of land, but he also worries that the total collectivization of land will involve an unacceptable level of governmental

---

[46] Morris, 'Notes on passing events', *The Commonweal* 2.41 (1886), p. 46.

[47] Carpenter, 'The village and the landlord' [1907], in *Socialism and Agriculture*, ed. Edward Carpenter, T. S. Dymond et al. (London: Fifield, 1908), pp. 5–19 (p. 14), orig. emph. Carpenter adhered to this view with remarkable consistency, calling in 1916 for a 'handling of the land so as to afford the most general access to it [...]; a guarded public ownership of land' (*My Days and Dreams*, p. 127).

intervention that ultimately restricts the ability of individuals to pursue their personal idea of the good life. Carpenter seems to want it both ways here, calling for the nationalization of land (and the subsequent redistribution of land by means of temporary tenancies) while also aiming to secure, for future occupants, freedoms that had previously only been available to independent farmers like Fox or to smallholders like Carpenter himself. The tensions that undergird these observations in 'The village and the landlord'—between public and private property; between the common good and individual freedom—also animate *Towards Democracy*, the magnum opus on which Carpenter had embarked while living on the Fearnehough's farm at Bradway. The poem translates these political tensions into the more specifically literary question of how an individual poetic voice can become the basis of a genuinely democratic common style. *Towards Democracy* thus becomes the central testing site for Carpenter's version of the reformist literary mode: responding to the language of late Victorian land debates, the poem seeks to create a portable style that will be capable of acting as a shared poetic ground for future writers and artisans.

Carpenter recalled in his autobiography that the first part of *Towards Democracy* was mostly 'written in about a year [...] by early in 1882', during his first encounter with rural life at Bradway.[48] The first volume of *Towards Democracy* is pervaded by references to land and Earth, and the prevalence of these terms clearly reflects Carpenter's immersion in country life during this period. While the two terms are never simply antonymous in the poem, Carpenter often uses 'land' to refer to ground as a form of fixed private capital, whereas 'Earth' typically signifies a fundamentally non-instrumental relationship between humans and the ground they inhabit. *Towards Democracy* begins with an ecstatic invocation of 'freedom' by a group the text refers to as the 'earth-children' (*TD* 4). The 'earth-children', a motley group consisting of agricultural workers and peasant labourers, engage in communal springtime activities:

The little red stars appear once more on the hazel boughs, shining among the catkins; over waste lands the pewit tumbles and cries as at the first day; men with horses go out on the land—they shout and chide and strive—and return again glad at evening; the old earth breathes deep and rhythmically, night and day, summer and winter, giving and concealing itself.   (*TD* 5)

The passage indicates that humans rely on the cultivation of arable ground for the satisfaction of their basic needs. Instead of stressing the physical exertion that is involved in tilling the land, however, Carpenter foregrounds the bountiful acts of 'giving' by which nature shares its plenty with the earth-children. This

---

[48] Carpenter, *My Days and Dreams*, p. 108.

relationship of reciprocal giving and sustenance—the earth-children enter into closer proximity with the ground by tilling it, and they are in turn rewarded with the fruits of the Earth—recalls ideas Carpenter had articulated in his 1874 'Materialism' essay. Indeed, the idea of reciprocal relations between humans and nature was to form a key element of Carpenter's thinking about sentimental land ownership well beyond the 1880s.[49]

In *Towards Democracy*'s opening pages, the voice of the poem alternates between an ecstatic and intensely lyrical style and a detached register that seems to take its cadences from the impersonal natural rhythms which it describes. The lines about the earth-children look back to Carpenter's poetry of the mid-1870s by reminding us that natural life is characterized by cyclical rhythms—'night and day, summer and winter'—which transcend the linear temporality of human life. Subsequent paragraphs develop the idea of Earth's 'deep and rhythmic' breathing, but they also elevate Earth to the status of a quasi-mythological, anthropomorphized entity (reverentially spelled with a capital 'E' in the text):

> The old Earth breathes deep and rhythmically, night and day, summer and winter; the cuckoo calls across the woodland, and the willow-wren warbles among the great chestnut buds; the labourer eases himself under a hedge [...].
>
> (*TD* 6)

The opening of *Towards Democracy* revisits the profoundly alienating sense of non-human time described in 'Earth's Voices', but it also discovers in everyday life a temporality that corresponds to the cyclical quality of Earth's soft 'breathing': 'The Earth remains and daily life remains, and the scrubbing of doorsteps, and the house and the care of the house remains' (*TD* 5). Having established Earth as the central motif of these opening pages, Carpenter warns that economic self-interest threatens to parcel up Earth's integral wholeness: 'The Earth is for you, and all that is therein—save what anyone else can grab' (*TD* 19). England's soil has been divided up among the landlords, and its magnificence consequently no longer derives from the beauty of the Earth itself but from the artificial 'splendour' of the stately manors that have been erected all across the countryside: the speaker passes '[t]hrough the great magnificent land, through its parks and country palaces and bewildering splendors of the resorts of wealth' (*TD* 22). Carpenter's nightmarish vision of land-grabbing individualism and of the social pathologies that accompany it—a variation on the theme of narcissistic alienation addressed in 'Narcissus' and 'In the Grass'—is countered on the same page by an anticipation

---

[49] Many years later Carpenter highlighted the 'earth-children' passage in his personal copy of *Towards Democracy*, pencilling in a marginal comment to reaffirm that 'I know that to the end'. ECC, Copy of *Towards Democracy* (Unwin, 1892) with handwritten notes by Carpenter, Carpenter/Library/1/105.

of a future when the land will no longer be enclosed, when 'the borders are trampled', and when it will again be possible to wander 'far afield and into the untrodden woods' (*TD* 19).

The redistribution of privately owned land becomes the object of the poem's most powerful prophetic energies. The Earth belongs to 'the People' as a whole, rather than to individual proprietors:

> O know well that it shall be. That the land they dwell on, that the Earth, for whatsoever people is worthy, shall become impossible to be separated from them—even in thought.
>
> Of those who are truly the People, they are jealous of their land; the woods and the fields and the open sea are covered with their love—inseparable from life.
>
> Every hedgerow, every old lumb and coppice, the nature of the soils in every field and part of a field, the suffs, the bedrock, pastures, ploughlands and fallows; [...]
>
> (*TD* 60)

These lines imagine the reopening of the enclosed land in terms that are clearly rooted in the populist rhetoric of contemporaneous debates about land nationalization. Yet to claim that the language of this passage amounts to a retrograde celebration of a mythical Englishness would be to exaggerate the reactionary nature of Carpenter's politically radical ruralism.[50] In Carpenter's poem, the figure of the 'People' serves as a strategic and counterhegemonic construction that looks to earlier moments of popular resistance against socio-economic dispossession such as the fourteenth-century Peasants' Revolt, the English Civil War of the seventeenth century, and the mid-nineteenth-century Chartist revolts. *Towards Democracy*'s appeal to the 'true People' does not signal an ethnonationalist populism but rather refers us back to a concept of 'true' (or 'worthy') ownership that is distinct from the purely legal claims of the landlords. '[T]he common clay knows the tread of its true owner', Carpenter writes in the same section of the poem, before proceeding to address an imaginary interlocutor:

> Do you think that [...] any land will rise into life, will display her surpassing beauty, will pour out her love, to the touch of false owners—to people who finger banknotes, who make traffic, buying and selling her, who own by

---

[50] The careers of certain figures of the land nationalization movement, including Carpenter's friend Wallace, point to a continuity between the reformist concerns of the 1880s and later attempts to enshrine a hypostatized English national identity in institutions such as the National Trust. However, to insist on such local historical continuities is to ignore the entangled debates about land ownership that characterized the period under examination here. For the influence of Wallace's ideas on the National Trust, see Jennifer Jenkins, 'The roots of the National Trust', *National Trust Centenary Issue* (1995): 3–9.

force of title deeds, laws, police—who yet deny her, [...] ashamed to touch her soil with their hands?   (*TD* 59)

Like Wallace, who had discussed land nationalization under the label of sentimental value and interest, Carpenter here repurposes the narrowly legal term 'ownership' to describe the new and shared ways of life that will result from the more democratic distribution of land. The attempt to critique and revise the legal language of commercial proprietorship from within entails a rhetorical manoeuvre that occurs at several key points in his poems and essays from the 1880s: taking a term that occupies a central place in the language of law and bourgeois property relations, Carpenter begins to unearth sedimented meanings that lie concealed in these verbal resources. The passage quoted above specifically re-signifies capitalist ownership in the light of a new kind of non-commercial proprietary ethos. While the landlords (the 'false owners') are indifferent towards the land, Carpenter intimates that 'true' ownership will become manifest in an affective stance that is characterized by care, 'love', and tact (what Carpenter calls 'touch').

The opposition of false (commercial) and true (sentimental) proprietorship structures many of Carpenter's writings from this period, and it also sheds light on his analogous conceptual distinction between land and Earth. In his essay on 'Private Property', Carpenter writes:

We may now pass on to a consideration of what property really means. If legal ownership is a negative thing, is there some reality of which it is, as it were, the shadow—which it has at some time or other vainly tried to represent? [...]

Can we get anything out of the word Property itself? [...] That which is 'proper' to a thing. What are the properties of brimstone — its essential characteristics, qualities, relations to other things? What is the property of chalk as distinguished from cheese? What are the properties of vegetable life, of animal life? What is the essential Property of Man?

This last is the question of questions. Amid all the shows and illusions, is it possible that the reality which we seek is hidden here? What if material property is only a symbol and indication of it? All the scrambling after calculable wealth, all the delusions and illusions, all the bog-floundering and fatuous wisp-catching are not in vain, if they lead us to find an answer to *that*, if they show us at last the wealth which is truly incalculable.[51]

Mapping the different valences of the term 'property', Carpenter uses the same rhetorical move he had introduced to divulge the hidden meanings of 'ownership'.

---

[51]   Carpenter, 'Private property', pp. 119–21.

His revision of the term 'property' resembles a form of etymological recovery work that retrieves the signifying core of a word that has been all but voided of any real meaning through legal overuse. While property—as a source of economic value and as the guarantor of civic rights (including the right to vote)—is an elementary component of bourgeois society, true proprietorial right implies the ethical question of care and propriety, of the owners' 'proper' relationship to the soil. Negative liberty—the language of legal guarantees and entitlements that Carpenter describes a purely 'negative thing'—is here recast as a form of positive freedom, as a shared form of life oriented towards the common good. Carpenter's idiosyncratic etymological procedure is important because it allows him to find shards of a different future order within the limited linguistic and aesthetic resources of the present.[52] Speaking in more strictly political terms, we could say that this mode of thinking is reformist rather than revolutionary: it implies that the future must be imagined not by a daring act of utopian projection but through painstaking engagement with existing social and institutional forms. Instead of rejecting given arrangements out of hand, Carpenter engages in a mode of counter-hegemonic critique that sets the stage for a speculative elaboration of hitherto neglected (artistic, social, political) potentialities.

This method of speculative critique functions as a master trope in Carpenter's literary and non-literary writings of the period. For example, his anti-Darwinian theory of socio-biological evolution—arguably the most misunderstood and most maligned aspect of his thinking—posits the existence of a life force that effects change from within individual organisms instead of relying on evolutionary competition between individuals. In one of his central essays on biological and social development, Carpenter referred to the action whereby new meanings emerge from within the dead husk of the old as a process of 'exfoliation': 'The order seems to be: first, a feeling—a dim want or desire; then the feeling becomes conscious of itself, takes shape in thought [...]. The process appears as a movement from within outwards.'[53] This pattern of thought helps to explain why Carpenter never embraced the medievalism propounded by fellow socialists

---

[52] Carpenter's attempt to recuperate the neglected meanings of words can easily be mistaken for an unreflective infatuation with the reified resources of common speech. This has led some critics to describe Carpenter's 'bland middle style' as too poetically 'straightforward', contrasting it unfavourably with the resplendent 'American *Hochsprache*' of his poetic model Walt Whitman (see Elfenbein, 'Whitman, democracy, and the English clerisy', *Nineteenth-Century Literature* 56.1 [2001]: 76–104 [p. 92]). Carpenter's interest in the verbal resources of English builds on a much longer (socialist) tradition that reflected on the ambiguity of the term 'property' and its cognates. Marx's *The German Ideology*, for example, had pondered the relationship between propertyless (*eigentumslose*) workers and their proper role (*eigentümliche Rolle*) as a new social force. See Marx, *Die Deutsche Ideologie*, in *Marx-Engels Gesamtausgabe*, vol. 3 (Berlin: Dietz, 1978), pp. 9–530 (e.g. pp. 212–13).

[53] Edward Carpenter, 'Exfoliation', in *Civilisation: Its Cause and Cure* (London: Swan Sonnenschein, 1889), pp. 129–47 (p. 133). In the same essay Carpenter describes his own thinking on the topic as 'Lamarckian' because it identifies a pervasive life force (and not Darwinian natural selection) as the root cause of species variation.

such as William Morris: in Carpenter's view medieval society with its ossified division into estates appeared as an outmoded form of social life, a discarded stage whose morphological constraints humanity had outgrown. The attempt to revert to this medieval model of social life signified a reactionary escapism which ignored the essentially progressive nature of social and political life.[54] The model of individual and social morphology which Carpenter developed in the 1880s sheds additional light on his scepticism of revolution in political matters. Carpenter's decision to buy a smallholding, to acquire landed property, involved just the kind of double movement I have been describing: the practice of estab-lishing smallholdings continued to be implicated in the structures of economic exchange which characterized capitalist societies, but it also permitted Carpenter to experiment with the forms of true (post-capitalistic) ownership so eagerly anticipated in book 1 of *Towards Democracy*. To put this another way, while Carpenter agreed that the harmful 'influence of Property' was 'apparent enough' in a society that was as profoundly torn by class divisions as Britain, the private acquisition of land also promised to create an opening for an alternative praxis of living that would otherwise have been impossible to realize.[55]

For a text steeped in the language of social prophecy, *Towards Democracy* remains surprisingly silent on the question of who is going to lead the country towards its post-enclosure future. Several passages in book 1 of Carpenter's poem appear to locate social agency in the dispossessed agricultural and industrial labourers:

> Do you suppose it is all for nothing that the eyes of brothers avoid in the street,
> and none sees what is before him; that the heel is upon the head, and Earth alone

---

[54] The Fabian audience to which Carpenter presented his evolutionist theories in 1898 accused him of an unfounded and essentially passive belief in social betterment, what they regarded as 'naïve Hegelianism'. This accusation derives in part from an essay by the social-liberal thinker D. G. Ritchie who had presented Hegelianism as a more rational (and therefore allegedly more benign) version of Darwinian evolution. See Ritchie, 'Darwin and Hegel', in *Darwin and Hegel, with Other Philosophical Studies* (London: Swan Sonnenschein, 1893), pp. 38–76. Elsewhere, Ritchie echoed Carpenter by asserting that

> we cannot rest in the critical or negative stage of modern individualism. But does that imply a return to the mediaeval type of society? to 'the good old days' of aristocratic and ecclesiastical domination? By no means. It implies an advance to a stage in which all that is most precious in individualism must be retained along with the stability of social conditions which individualism has destroyed.

> See *Darwinism and Politics* (London: Swan Sonnenschein, 1889), pp. 57–8.

The audience's hostile response to Carpenter's theories is recorded in Henry Mead's *T. E. Hulme and the Ideological Politics of Early Modernism* (London: Bloomsbury, 2015), p. 66.

[55] Carpenter, 'Civilisation: Its cause and cure', in *Civilisation*, pp. 1–50 (p. 25). For a more critical assessment, see Ted Underwood's observation that the 'agrarian [...] tradition of republican idealism [...] tended in fact to generate a zone of ideological consensus between the gentry and the upper ranks of the middle class, which could agree at least that property of some kind or another was a precondition for political responsibility'. Underwood, *The Work of the Sun: Literature, Science, and Political Economy, 1760–1860* (London: Palgrave Macmillan, 2005), p. 44.

regards the faces of them that are oppressed—that the stones in the wintry fields are become confidants, and the ground is sown with compressed thought, like seeds? (*TD* 48)

Earth itself sympathizes with the plight of these downtrodden workers, yet the passage hardly reads like a call to revolutionary action. Indeed, even though Carpenter's 'Private Property' essay praised labourers for 'spending affection and thought upon the land', he was in fact doubtful when it came to the ability of the urban and rural working classes to take matters into their own hands and to change their socio-economic situation. The closing section of *My Days and Dreams*, programmatically entitled 'Rural questions', is vexed by the agricultural labourers' 'complete non-interest in reform' and their 'positive indifference to anything not patently visible to the eye'. Recalling conversations with rural labourers during those formative years of the early 1880s, Carpenter remarks: 'The good folk would talk about a particular field and really with amazing detail about its history, its climate, its soil, its suitability for such and such crops, and so forth; but if you broached any phase of the Land Question (however really important to them)—their eyes would soon glaze and their conversation revert to their pigs or potatoes.'[56] These comments crucially complicate Wallace's celebration of sentimental ownership. Carpenter points out that the labourers' 'true ownership' of the land—their intimate knowledge of the Earth and the care which they expend on it—paradoxically blinds them to the more abstract structural and political question of land reform.

While he was writing *Towards Democracy*, Carpenter found himself faced with a difficulty that resulted, on the one hand, from his hesitations about statist centralization, and on the other, from his scepticism regarding the 'People's' ability to develop their own insurrectionary *élan*. In response, Carpenter envisioned a transitional phase in which a new class of smallholders like himself—cosmopolitan and local at the same time[57]—would take over the task of developing a new social consciousness 'from within outwards'. Carpenter was wary of the claim that private property had to be collectivized at all costs—instead he argued that state-organized reform involved a democratization of private ownership that

[56] Carpenter, *My Days and Dreams*, pp. 282–3.

[57] In a recent discussion of the Victorian legal notion of 'occupancy' (i.e. forms of non-permanent proprietorship), Elaine Hadley identifies the local as the scale at which Victorian novels rehearse attitudes of proto-cosmopolitan 'disinterestedness'. Carpenter engages in a broadly analogous manoeuvre: his literary writings systematically privilege the local (as opposed to the nation) as the site where cosmopolitan identities can be forged. See Elaine Hadley, *Living Liberalism: Practical Citizenship in Mid-Victorian Britain* (Chicago: University of Chicago Press, 2010), p. 288. Ernest Belfort Bax, whose journalism I discussed in Chapter 1, echoed these sentiments when he bemoaned the 'illogicality of this administrative halting-place [i.e. the nation] between the local community and the system of nations [in which] the whole system of things is international' ('Revolution of the Nineteenth Century', in *The Ethics of Socialism* (London: Swan Sonnenschein, 1890), pp. 31–56 (p. 40)).

would foster the growth of new forms of life centred around proprietary tact and care. In a related vein, Carpenter's smallholding in Millthorpe was not the isolated counter-cultural enclave of a utopian dreamer, but a site where experiments in living made it possible to imagine, with some degree of experiential concreteness, a future political dispensation in which fully democratized ownership would be the order of the day.[58] Carpenter doubted the revolutionary potential of the oppressed masses, and *Towards Democracy* accordingly presents the voice of the speaker—rather than the inarticulate suffering 'People' itself—as the source of the poem's most prophetic lines. One of these passages imagines the speaker's merging with the solid ground: 'the solid earth alone is left. I am buried (I too that I may rise again) deep underfoot among the clods. [...] This is the solid earth in the midst of which I am buried' (*TD* 17). This proleptic vision of the speaker's burial figures his interment, his merging with the ground, as a necessary prerequisite of spiritual rebirth:

> To descend, first;
>
> To feel downwards and downwards through this wretched maze of shams for the solid ground—to come close to the Earth itself and those that live in direct contact with it. [...]
>
> This—is it not the eternal precept?—is the first thing: to dig downwards. After the young shoot will ascend—and ascending easily part aside the overlying rubbish.   (*TD* 28)

The speaker's immersion in the ground signals Carpenter's release from the anxieties that had haunted his poem 'In the Grass'. In that earlier text, the speaker had found himself 'laid [...] beneath the turf' while remaining affectively detached from the Earth itself. However, in the passage from *Towards Democracy*, the speaker's prophetic voice (rooted in the first-person singular pronoun) also serves to set him apart from the undifferentiated mass of agricultural workers, from the People who are tilling the land. As Carpenter's essay 'Rural questions' indicates, only the speaker—or other individuals like him—will be able to connect the individual experience of rural life to a recognition of the specific

---

[58] Like many other aspects of the Carpenter myth, the popular reading of his works as the manifestation of an individualist utopianism can be traced in part to the *Edward Carpenter, in Appreciation* (1931)—the influential collection that featured contributions by E. M. Forster, Goldsworthy Lowes Dickinson, and other luminaries. One of the contributors to the volume, the housing reformer and engineer Raymond Unwin, who had known Carpenter at Millthorpe, claimed that Carpenter 'was driven into the country to find himself, and to write *Towards Democracy* as the experience of his disentanglement.' See Unwin, 'Edward Carpenter and "Towards democracy"', in *Edward Carpenter, in Appreciation*, ed. Gilbert Beith (London: Allen & Unwin, 1931), pp. 234–43 (p. 234).

structural and systemic deficiencies that make the reparative intervention of the state so urgent and necessary in the first place.

Carpenter's Common Style

One of the problems Carpenter encountered in composing *Towards Democracy* was how an individual poetic voice might come to function as the basis for a genuinely plural, democratic literary style. Carpenter's response to this dilemma drew on the language of the land reformers in order to imagine his own writing as a common ground that could be appropriated and inhabited by all. Early on, *Towards Democracy*'s reference to the Earth's 'deep and rhythmic breathing' introduces a self-reflexive element into the text that pictures the characteristic properties of Whitmanesque free verse—long lines which obey the natural rhythms of the human breath rather than the constraining formal grids of metre and rhyme—as the properties of Earth itself. Carpenter makes these analogies more explicit in an explanatory 'Note' on *Towards Democracy* that was first published in 1894 and later appended to first complete edition (1905) of the poem. While the shorter pieces published in *Narcissus* had tried 'to speak to an intimate personal relation between myself and the reader', Carpenter explained, *Towards Democracy* aimed 'to find an absolutely common ground [...] and to write the book on and from that common ground'. Such a book, he expected, would speak to any of the 'personalities into whose hands it would happen to come'.[59] Carpenter hoped that a democratic style could be realized through non-traditional poetic forms and, more specifically, through his appropriation of Whitman's free verse:

> Against the inevitable drift out of the more classic forms of verse into a looser and freer rhythm I fairly fought, contesting the ground [...] inch by inch during a period of seven years in numerous abortive and mongrel creations—till in 1881 I was finally compelled into the form (if such it can be called) of 'Towards Democracy'.[60]

The metaphorical terrain that is demarcated by Carpenter's references to Earth and land is the most important innovation he brought to Whitman's poetic idiom.[61] But

---

[59] Carpenter, 'A note on "Towards Democracy"' [1894], in *Towards Democracy*, pp. 511–19 (p. 511).

[60] Carpenter, 'A note', p. 518.

[61] Of course, *Leaves of Grass* does offer some precedent for Carpenter's attention to Earth as a metaphor for his own poetic enterprise. Whitman's 'A Song of the Rolling Earth', for example, claims to find 'words, the substantial words [...] in the ground and the sea [...] those are the words / I myself am a word with them', although the same poem insists that 'the truths of the earth' are ultimately 'untransmissible by print'. See 'A Song of the Rolling Earth', in *The Portable Walt Whitman*, ed.

Carpenter's 'Note' also indicates that his theorization of a poetic common ground cannot be separated from his own experiments in rural living. Echoing his remarks in the 1882 letter to Charles Oates, which had presented the activities of writing and agricultural work as inextricably intertwined, some sections of *Towards Democracy* even suggest that the words of Carpenter's poem are rooted in the tilled ground of Millthorpe itself: the poetic 'word', one passage notes, is 'uttered out of the ground from between the clods' (*TD* 16).

The problems which Carpenter encountered in constructing a plural poetic voice stemmed from the persistence in *Towards Democracy* of a narrowly delimited subjectivity centred on the first-person pronoun 'I'. These tensions created a peculiar embarrassment for Carpenter: while his social philosophy emphasized the central importance of individual flourishing, he realized that the frequency with which the (Whitmanesque) first-person pronoun figured in his poetic work made the book 'naturally liable to a charge of egotism'.[62] Carpenter variously reprises the metaphor of burial in order to disperse the speaker's individuality and dispel the threat of lyric narcissism:

> I will be the ground underfoot and the common clay;
>
> The ploughman shall turn me up with his ploughshare among the roots of the twitch in the sweet-smelling furrow;
>
> The potter shall mould me, running his finger along my whirling edge [...];
> The bricklayer shall lay me: he shall tap me into place with the handle of his trowel[.]   (*TD* 73)

The reformist literary mode that finds expression in *Towards Democracy* reflects the lessons about ownership and land nationalization that Carpenter had absorbed in the 1870s and early 1880s: the poem's defining property is that it can be inhabited by everyone and therefore cannot really be said to belong to anyone in particular. In the passage above the speaking voice appears to belong to the text itself, to the 'ground underfoot and the common clay', inviting us to reimagine the poem as an object that can be remoulded and adapted by future writers and artisans. *Towards Democracy* is accordingly best described, following Carpenter, not as a tool of overt reformist propaganda but as a textual terrain open to all.[63] Later

---

Michael Warner (London: Penguin, 2004), pp. 158–64 (pp. 158–9). The earth-minded title of *Leaves of Grass* notwithstanding, Whitman had drawn most of his metaphors from other elements such as water and air—a point I return to at the end of this chapter.

[62] Carpenter, 'Note', p. 515.

[63] Elizabeth Miller offers an alternative account of *Towards Democracy*'s style. Pointing to the relatively narrow class base of Whitman's (and Carpenter's) audience, she emphasizes that although Carpenter's poetry worked towards 'a cogent ethics of radical intersubjectivity', its investment in an experimental elite aesthetic meant that it 'was decidedly not broad', eluding 'immediate comprehension, much less comfortable familiarity'. See Elizabeth Carolyn Miller, *Slow Print: Literary Radicalism and Late Victorian Print Culture* (Stanford: Stanford University Press, 2013), pp. 184–5.

sections of the poem offer numerous variations on this theme. For example, one of the poems in book 2 (first published in 1885) compares the even furrows created by the plough to the long lines of Carpenter's text: 'Ye dark ploughed fields and grassy hills, and gorses where the yoldring warbles—write your myriad parallel gossamers among my lines!' (*TD* 247). And yet another passage imagines Earth and poetic word entering into such osmotic proximity that they become almost indistinguishable: 'Ah! the live Earth trembles beneath the passionate deep shuddering words run along the ground. [. . .] Surely, surely, age after age out of the ground itself arising, from the chinks of the lips of the clods and from between the blades of grass, up with the tall growing wheat surely ascending' (*TD* 13–14).

When Carpenter settled into his new life at Millthorpe in the early 1880s, he found that Whitman's works offered a style that answered to his changing poetic needs. 'Whitman's full-blooded, copious, rank, masculine style', Carpenter confidently declared in the 1894 'Note', 'must always make him one of the world's great originals. [. . .] He has the amplitude of the Earth itself.'[64] These remarks indicate that Whitman's poetry was the common ground Carpenter wished to inhabit, yet they obscure the true extent to which Carpenter's appropriation of the Whitmanesque involved a creative reworking of the American poet's style. The most notable change, Andrew Elfenbein has noted, consisted in Carpenter's decision to 'exchange [Whitman's] line for the paragraph'—an alteration that served to 'slow down the pace' of Whitman's free verse.[65] We could say that by privileging the form of the extended, prose-like paragraph over the individual rhythmic line, Carpenter aimed to make Whitman's poetry itself more 'solid' and more earth-like.[66]

For Carpenter, the principal attraction of Whitman's oeuvre was not the American poet's 'purposeful obscurity', but the fact that *Leaves of Grass* talked about a country where the democratization of property rights seemed already to have taken place.[67] Many reformers, including Wallace, were pointing to the United States as an important historical precedent for land nationalization in Britain. North America provided enough land for everyone, they believed, and the Homestead Acts

---

[64] Carpenter, 'A note', p. 518. For an indication of the British reception of Whitman's 'new, vigorous, and masculine' style, see Ruth Livesey, 'Democracy, culture, and criticism: Henry James revisits America', in *The American Experiment and the Idea of Democracy in British Culture, 1776–1914*, ed. Ella Dzelzainis and Ruth Livesey (New York: Routledge, 2016), pp. 179–96 (p. 184).

[65] Elfenbein, 'Whitman', p. 94. See also Steven Marsden's more comprehensive account of Whitman's influence in '"Hot Little Prophets": Reading, Mysticism, and Walt Whitman's Disciples', PhD thesis, Texas A&M University (2004), pp. 215–365; repository.tamu.edu>, accessed on 12 June 2020.

[66] In his autobiography Carpenter recalled that 'the central [poetic] quality' he had hoped for 'during the period of gestation and suffering that preceded the birth of [*Towards Democracy*]' was formal '*solidity*' (*My Days and Dreams*, p. 192).

[67] Gary Schmidgall, *Containing Multitudes: Walt Whitman and the British Literary Tradition* (New York: Oxford University Press, 2015), p. 314.

of the 1860s and 1870s guaranteed the land's even distribution.[68] Among the poems that seem to have spurred Carpenter's enthusiasm for the United States as a model for land nationalization was Whitman's 'Starting from Paumanok' (1860). In this poem state boundaries are effortlessly transcended by the continent's sprawling topography, by its vast panorama of 'interminable plateaus' and 'pastoral plains':

> Interlink'd, food-yielding lands!
>
> Land of coal and iron! land of gold! land of cotton, sugar, rice!
>
> Land of wheat, beef, pork! land of wool and hemp! land of the apple and the grape!
>
> Land of the pastoral plains, the grass-fields of the world! land of those sweet-air'd interminable plateaus!
>
> Land of the herd, the garden, the healthy house of adobe!
>
> Lands where the north-west Columbia winds, and where the south-west Colorado winds!
>
> Land of the eastern Chesapeake! land of the Delaware!
>
> Land of Ontario, Erie, Huron, Michigan!
>
> Land of the Old Thirteen! Massachusetts land! land of Vermont and Connecticut!
>
> Land of the ocean shores! land of sierras and peaks![69]

'Starting from Paumanok' was the text that had opened Rossetti's 1868 landmark edition of Whitman's poetry, and it set the tone for Carpenter's subsequent reception of the American writer. Several of the early pieces in *Towards Democracy* read as though Carpenter had updated Whitman's poem for the English context:

> England spreads like a map below me. I see the mud-flats of the Wash striped with water at low tide, the embankments grown with mugwort and sea-asters, and Boston Stump and King's Lynn, and the squaresail brigs in the offing.

---

[68] On the US as a model for British land reformers, see Jamie Bronstein, 'The homestead and the garden plot: Cultural pressures on land reform in nineteenth-century Britain and the USA', *The European Legacy* 6.2 (2001): 159–75 (esp. pp. 159–67). Celebratory assessments of the United States were contradicted by a smaller number of sceptical voices. One of these sceptics was Henry George himself, who drew attention to the fact that 'large American landowners'—just like their British counterparts—were 'generally absentees'. See George, *Land Question*, p. 13. The brutal and large-scale disappropriation of land from the continent's native inhabitants is a gaping blind spot in the texts of most reformers.

[69] Whitman, 'Starting from Paumanok', in *Poems by Walt Whitman*, ed. by William Michael Rossetti, pp. 67–88 (p. 82).

Beachy Head stands up beautiful, with white walls and pinnacles, from its slopers of yellow poppy and bugloss; the sea below creeps with a grey fog [...].

I descend the Wye, and pass through the ancient streets of Monmouth and Bristol. I thread the feathery birch-haunted coombs of Somerset.

I ascend the high points of the Cotswolds, and look out over the rich vale of Gloucester to the Malvern hills, and see the old city clustering round its Church, and the broad waters of the severn [sic], and the distant towers of Berkeley Castle.

(*TD* 54)

'I see a great land poised as in a dream,' Carpenter concludes, 'I see a great land waiting for its own people to come and take possession of it' (*TD* 58). Carpenter's poem dissolves the enclosures of contemporary England in favour of an all-encompassing vision of the country's landscape. At the same time, however, the distinctly regionalist emphasis of the above passage, with its references to King's Lynn, Beachy Head, and the Cotswolds, also reflects Carpenter's attempt—in 'The village and the landlord' and elsewhere—to imagine a more cautious form of state-organized land nationalization that will grant decentralized (regional and local) authorities a measure of administrative autonomy.

Carpenter had visited Whitman for several weeks in 1877 and again in 1884. In his recollection of these visits, published in 1906 under the title *Days with Walt Whitman*, Carpenter included a chapter on the 'Poetic Form of *Leaves of Grass*' which does much to elucidate his appropriation of Whitman's style. Carpenter observes that Whitman's 'pil[ing] up' of sentences—this 'strange surging and swelling reiteration' of syntactic units—creates 'the picture of the immense earth'.[70] Whitman's unbinding of established literary styles has the effect of releasing poetry's tightly organized metrical units into a flow of free rhythm, yet in Carpenter's eyes this poetic procedure also performatively renders the vast terrain of the American continent itself.[71] This view received encouragement from Whitman's 'Preface to the First Edition of *Leaves of Grass*', which predated Rossetti's selection of Whitman's poetry by a decade. In his 'Preface', Whitman claimed that the unenclosed land in North America facilitated forms of active citizenship—a shared orientation towards the common good—that most European countries lacked. The undivided land, wrote Whitman, provided the 'common ground' on which Americans could meet as equals.[72] The Preface clearly

[70] Carpenter, 'The poetic form of "Leaves of Grass"', in *Days with Walt Whitman: With Some Notes on his Life and Work* (London: George Allen, 1906), pp. 103–30 (pp. 118–19).

[71] In *Days with Walt Whitman* Carpenter attacked Rossetti's anthology *Poems by Walt Whitman*. Rossetti's decision to turn *Leaves of Grass* into a marketable commodity by cutting it up into a reader's digest of isolated poems, Carpenter insisted, resembled the act of parcelling up the Earth itself. *Leaves of Grass*, Carpenter declared, needed to 'stand whole, unbroken, undivided' (p. 113).

[72] Whitman, 'Preface to the First Edition of Leaves of Grass', in *Poems by Walt Whitman*, pp. 29–64 (p. 48).

left a great impression on Carpenter, and it helps to explain his determined idealization of the United States as an example of the great things that state-organized land nationalization might achieve in England.[73]

In *Towards Democracy* Carpenter sought to create a portable style—a poetic language and literary form that could be easily repurposed and adapted in the heated reformist climate of the 1880s. Disappointingly for Carpenter, however, his attempt turned out to be relatively inconsequential in literary-historical terms as the poem fell on deaf ears with a larger reading public. There is a real sense that Carpenter was, for some years in the 1880s and 1890s, his own most attentive audience: he kept revisiting the text of *Towards Democracy* and continually added new sections while also updating and expanding his older poems. Carpenter tended to the poetic ground of *Towards Democracy* with the kind of devotion and care that he had tried to elicit in others, constantly hoping that his poem would finally turn into the soil where a collective desire for social change might take root.[74] In the 1890s, when it became clear that Carpenter's text had failed to gather a sizable popular readership and when the land reform debates of the previous decades slowly began to fade from public consciousness, the tone of *Towards Democracy* also started to change. In book 2 of the poem—and even more noticeably in books 3 and 4—the language of earth-like 'solidity' that had been so prominent in the first part of the poem gives way to metaphors of the sea and air. The poems which Carpenter wrote during these years likewise place less and less emphasis on the familiar themes of agrarian labour and local rootedness. Instead, these pieces take a keener interest in slow processes of suffusion and permeation that transcend the local: 'And it seemed to me, as I looked', one of the poems in book 2 observes of the life-force's 'aerial spirit', 'that it penetrated all these things, suffusing them' (*TD* 183). As Carpenter left behind the specific political contexts that had energized the first part of *Towards Democracy*, his imagery took on an increasingly ethereal and transcendent aspect: 'I give my body to the sea. [. . .] My soul, if it be so, to peregrinate all creature-kingdoms and every condition of man' (*TD* 190). 'Suddenly I am the Ocean itself,' another poem, entitled 'By the Shore', chimes in: 'I feel beings like myself all around me, I spread myself through and through them, I am merged in a sea of content' (*TD* 193–4). These new metaphors reflect Carpenter's move away from land reform debates,

---

[73] Whitman's paean to the 'undivided' soil of the United States also resonated powerfully with the nationalism that inflected English debates about the state-organized nationalization of land. Carpenter's later additions to *Towards Democracy* make the links between his own writings and Whitman's ecstatic prose even more evident. 'The People' of the United States, Whitman enthused in *Democratic Vistas* (1871), were '[l]ike our huge earth itself' (*Democratic Vistas*, in *Portable Walt Whitman*, pp. 317–83 [p. 332]). Carpenter, who had read *Democratic Vistas*, seized repeatedly on Whitman's idea in book 4 of *Towards Democracy*, referring to 'the land (the Demos)' as 'the foundation-element of human life' (*TD* 390).

[74] Earth remained a potent metaphor in Carpenter's essays on social questions, if not in his poetry. In *My Days and Dreams* he expressed his longing for 'a situation [. . .] which will satisfy the *root* demands, the *rooting* demands,—those that have the power of growth in them' (p. 128; orig. emph.).

but they also poignantly capture his yearning for a broader socialist movement which would no longer be fissured by factional infighting and whose more inclusive 'oceanic character' might finally deliver a broader readership for *Towards Democracy*.[75]

The picture that emerges from books 3 and 4 of *Towards Democracy* is one that will be familiar to readers who regard Carpenter as the prophet of universal love, (male) fellowship, and Eastern religion. To be sure, Carpenter himself did much to propagate this particular view of his intellectual and poetic identity after 1890. Writing to his close friend Kate Salt during his spiritually transformative trip to India and Ceylon in 1890, he remarked that in Hinduism 'the most intimate & esoteric teaching [...] is thoroughly *democratic*. While preserving the belief in Caste as a veil [...], it ultimately lays it aside completely—and such words as Freedom, Equality, Joy become its watchwords. The individual "I" ascends & becomes one with the universal "I", & sharer of the most intense happiness, without at the same time losing its true individuality.'[76]

Carpenter's excited letter anticipates a crucial shift in his poetic outlook, and it accurately chronicles the new religious and intellectual enthusiasms that were to occupy him from 1890 onwards. While Carpenter's hopes are still for a fully '*democratic*' community in which the influence of social classes and 'Castes' is minimized, this egalitarian vision is no longer actualized through a painstaking engagement with the question of institutional reform that had animated Carpenter's writing in the early 1880s, but through a meditative turn away from the world and an immersion in the 'universal' self. Critics sometimes point to Carpenter's interest in Hinduism and Vedanta as the key to his poetic *oeuvre*. However, emphasizing this aspect of Carpenter's later work risks ignoring the specific reformist contexts which informed his early writings, and it also threatens to eclipse the political tensions with which these works engaged. Carpenter himself drew attention to the shift in his poetic and intellectual preoccupations in the 1894 'Note' to *Towards Democracy*. The most recent part (book 3) of *Towards Democracy*, he observed, was more '[t]ender and meditative, less resolute and altogether less massive' than the first book: the new poems 'had the quality of the fluid and yielding air rather than of the solid and uncompromising earth'.[77]

The kind of radical short-circuiting of individuality (the self) and universality (the cosmos) that finds articulation in the 1890 letter made it increasingly difficult for Carpenter to register the urgency of questions that pertained to the intermediary (political) scale of institutional organization and social reform. As this chapter has indicated, it was precisely this middle ground that Carpenter had sought to

---

[75] For Carpenter's idea of an 'oceanic' socialism, see *My Days and Dreams*, p. 126. Sheila Rowbotham's biography offers an excellent discussion of this notion in the context of Carpenter's intellectual development (*Edward Carpenter*, pp. 313–15).

[76] ECC, Letter to Kate Salt, 24 November 1890, MSS 354–11; orig. emph.

[77] Carpenter, 'A note', p. 519.

occupy for much of the 1880s and that informed his aspirational understanding of land redistribution in terms of a new kind of democratic *Sittlichkeit*. While Carpenter's interest in the reformist literary mode began to wane as early as 1890, it was only several years later—after many of the utopian communes established by land reformers in the late 1800s had dissolved—that the ethical dimension of land ownership began to fade from public debate. 'From 1916,' the historian Malcom Chase explains, 'the land question [was] redefined away from issues of ownership [...] towards those of land administration': confronted with the urgent pressures of a wartime economy, 'land reform' came to be treated 'solely as a means towards tackling the problem of land management'.[78] However, as I have suggested, it would be a mistake to underestimate the significant political, cultural, and poetic import which the ethical idiom of land reform possessed around 1900. It is only under conditions like those pertaining today—in the midst of a political climate that tends to reduce the question of land ownership to a managerial issue—that the scandalous large-scale privatization of public lands can pass nearly unnoticed.[79] In Britain these processes were accelerated by the Thatcherite privatization of land associated with the formerly nationalized industries of coal, water, steel, and railways. It is indicative of our contemporary 'discursive disability' that we have so long lacked the political vocabulary to describe these processes and drive home their existential urgency.[80]

---

[78] Chase, 'Wholesome object lessons', p. 84.

[79] See Christophers, *Appropriation of Public Land*; and Anna Minton, *Ground Control: Fear and Happiness in the Twenty-First Century City* (London: Penguin, 2012).

[80] Tony Judt, *Ill Fares the Land* (New York: Penguin, 2010), p. 34. See the Introduction to this book for discussion of Judt.

4

'Kinetic' Reform

H. G. Wells and Redistributive Taxation

H. G. Wells's optimism about the technological and scientific promise of modernity stands in stark contrast to the ruralist inflection of Edward Carpenter's reformist vision. Yet the speculative impulse that energizes Wells's literary writings and social criticism of the Edwardian years resembles the one that spurred Carpenter's association of state-organized land tenures with a new proprietary ethos of tact, care, and concern. As Wells explained in his *Experiment in Autobiography* (1934), his particular involvement in the slow politics of reform was structured around an awareness of the 'incompatibility' of the speed of 'scientific [...] progress with the existing political and social structures'.[1] The question that arose from this observation was whether it was possible for existing socio-political arrangements to be transformed in light of new 'scientific' insights while also avoiding the violent convulsions of a radical revolutionary rupture. Wells's writings, I suggest, imagine the possibility of substantive institutional change by picturing it in terms of a gradual shift in ethical practices of wealth-sharing—in other words, they imagine institutional change in terms of a combined development of 'scientific' insight (notably in the fields of economics and social science) and the historically grown structures of social life (*Sittlichkeit*).

Wells's main intellectual contribution to statist thought is usually seen to reside in his grand vision of a world state. As he noted in his autobiography, his interest in the idea of a world state had started with the publication of *Anticipations* (1901), his influential collection of speculative essays on social and political topics. In *The Outline of History* (1920), Wells explained that the sovereign world state was intended to unify humankind in security and prosperity, ensuring peace between nations by replacing the horrific iniquities of colonial rule with a more democratic global polity. Wells did not see the world state as a homogenizing force. On the contrary, it was designed to enable self-government so that individual states could participate in it on terms which answered to their own needs. The importance of Wells's thinking about the cosmopolitan world state is now well recognized. However, it would be an anachronism to attribute too much significance to the idea in connection with Wells's early work. While Wells first

---

[1] Wells, *Experiment in Autobiography* [1934] (New York: J. B. Lippincott, 1967), p. 556.

British Literature and the Life of Institutions: Speculative States. Benjamin Kohlmann, Oxford University Press.
© Benjamin Kohlmann 2021. DOI: 10.1093/oso/9780198836179.003.0005

introduced the concept of the world state in *Anticipations*, the 'early model' presented there 'amounts to little more than global confederation': it was 'only with the Great War and Wells's recognition that sovereignty over such issues as arms, colonies and raw materials had to be ceded by nation-states if peace was to last,' that he 'reject[ed] the nation-state as the ideal model of governance in the world.'[2] In turning to Wells's Edwardian years, then, this chapter will aim to shed light on an underexplored aspect of his literary thinking about the nation-state and its institutions.[3]

Throughout his career, Wells saw clearly that Britain's economic system was massively leveraged in favour of monopolized capital—an observation which applied equally to old (landed) privilege and new (financial) wealth. Around 1900, however, his thinking about wealth distribution underwent a significant transformation, as his earlier focus on the threats and promises of revolutionary rupture gave way to a growing interest in the potential of institutional reform. Wells's writings of the early 1900s, I suggest here, notably explore the role which new taxation schemes might play in socio-political reconstruction. As the economic historian Martin Daunton has pointed out, in the late Victorian and Edwardian years, taxation came to occupy a central place in the reformist imagination: while taxes had previously been regarded as a neutral means of securing revenue, William Harcourt's 1894 budget and Lloyd George's 1909–10 budget (which acquired the byname 'People's Budget') began to treat fiscal reform as a means to change society by moving taxation in a more progressive, redistributive direction. Taxes, Daunton notes, constituted a 'language of social description' which helped to defuse social conflicts by shifting attention from 'hierarchical' and 'binary perceptions of society' towards less antagonistic models of social integration.[4] These new forms of graduated and progressive taxation entailed a new institutional idiom which relied on more nuanced distinctions between different kinds of incomes, and which furthered a new understanding of how state intervention might contribute to social justice. As the French economist Thomas Piketty reminds us, taxation is 'not a technical matter. It is pre-eminently

---

[2] John S. Partington, 'H. G. Wells and the world state: A liberal cosmopolitan in a totalitarian age', *International Relations* 17.2 (2003): 233–46 (p. 244, fn. 10). Imagining the state at a planetary scale relieved Wells of the need to declare his exclusive commitment to any one of Edwardian Britain's socialist (or radical Liberal) organizations. Wells's relationship to the Fabian Society, for example, was notoriously rocky, a point I return to later.

[3] While the model of active citizenship which Wells developed in the early 1900s would later form the basis for his assertion 'of common purpose and need for collaborative action' in the world state, these later developments—Wells's transition from a reformism centred on the British nation-state to a fully 'cosmopolitan' perspective—will not be the topic of my discussion here. On the geographical expansion of 'collaborative action', see Duncan Bell, 'Founding the world state: H. G. Wells on empire and the English-speaking peoples', *International Studies Quarterly* 62 (2018): 867–79 (p. 869).

[4] Daunton, *Trusting Leviathan: The Politics of Taxation in Britain, 1799–1914* (Cambridge: Cambridge University Press, 2001), p. 386.

a political and philosophical issue, perhaps the most important of all political issues. Without taxes, society has no common destiny.'[5] Piketty draws our attention to the paradox that while taxation is woven more intimately and continuously into citizens' lives than most other aspects of the state, we often treat it as a merely 'technical' affair. But Piketty's account also highlights the fact that taxation debates around 1900 involved a significant aspirational dimension, what Wells in 1906 called that 'very complex, imperfect elusive idea, the Social Idea, [. . .] struggling to exist and realise itself in a world of egotisms, animalisms, and brute matter'.[6] This new institutional language, I argue, is taken up in Wells's social criticism of the period, and it also left its mark on the forms of his fiction.

The view that taxation constitutes a new (quasi-mimetic) language of social description as well as an (aspirational) articulation of society's collective ends is echoed in the distinctive narrative design of Wells's works. As previous critics have observed, Wells's late Victorian and Edwardian writings frequently alternate between social-realist and utopian registers. I explore this uneasy cohabitation of narrative impulses in Wells's work by reading his fiction of the period—including *A Modern Utopia* (1905) and *A New Machiavelli* (1911)—alongside a range of his non-literary writings. Taken together, these texts indicate that Wells's commitment to a mode of slow reformist politics is only imperfectly captured by the terms *realism* and *utopianism*. While the two terms enable us to link the spheres of institutional reform and literary production, they can too easily be taken to imply that Wells's works are governed by an irresolvable tension between quasi-sociological description and the desire for revolutionary change. Contrary to this view, the version of the reformist literary mode that we meet with in Wells's Edwardian works is best described as a mixed mode that figures realism and utopianism as two moments of a single speculative movement: the two narrative impulses, I argue, jointly contribute to the enterprise of translating the period's rhetoric of social division into a reformist idiom that anticipates the growth of 'collective self-consciousness' and a 'collective sense of the state'.[7] In a related vein, taxation (as Wells came to think of it) was a means of practical-minded socio-economic reconstruction that relied on painstaking attention to existing social conditions, as well as an attempt to reimagine society on the basis of a new and collective ethos.

---

[5] Piketty, *Capital in the Twenty-First Century* (Cambridge, MA: Harvard University Press, 2014), p. 493.

[6] Wells, 'The so-called science of sociology', *The Sociological Review* 3.1 (1906): 357–69 (p. 367).

[7] Wells, *New Worlds for Old* (London: Macmillan, 1909) p. 283. In a similar spirit, Wells noted in a memorandum to the Fabian Society from 1906: 'We regard Socialism as essentially a development of constructive ideas and motives, as a great moral and intellectual movement' (FSBL, MS Add. 62992, f.19).

From Revolution to Reform: Class conflict in Wells's Early Novels

Whereas Wells's works from the early 1900s 'tend to privilege styles of [political] change that would be minimally destabilizing', his slightly earlier scientific romances from the 1890s dramatize the explosive threat of class conflict.[8] Wells's first published novel, *The Time Machine* (1895), famously imagines the long-term evolutionary consequences of class division, and the novel's representation of two distinct races—the cultivated Eloi and the troglodytic Morlocks—can without much difficulty be read as allegorizing the social conflicts that beset late Victorian Britain. John S. Partington notes that *The Time Machine*'s bleak predictions are 'simple extrapolations from [Wells's] own time'; and Darko Suvin speculates that the time traveller's contempt for the beastly Morlocks 'flows from [. . .] Wells's own class prejudices and fears of the proletariat.'[9] Such deeply ingrained class loathing makes itself felt in the time traveller's 'disgust' towards the Morlocks' physical appearance: discovering them to be 'filthily cold to the touch', the narrator instinctually 'shrink[s]' from their 'pallid bodies'.[10] The physical threat which the 'carnivorous' Morlocks pose to the middle-class narrator likewise points to the subtext of class struggle that underpins Wells's story.[11] When it is read in this way, the novel manifests the simmering class conflicts that are associated with Britain's 'anti-communist imaginary'—the brief political moment of the 1880s and 1890s when insurrection by Britain's domestic working class seemed imminent in the wake of the Paris Commune of 1871.[12] Wells leaves no doubt that this radical class polarization is socially (and phylogenetically) debilitating: while the Eloi were once 'the favoured aristocracy', they are now 'decayed to a mere beautiful futility'; conversely, the Morlocks' subservient position—they are the Eloi's 'mechanical servants'—means that they have devolved into a purely 'subterranean' underclass.[13]

The Time Machine offers the first, though by no means the only figuration of class conflict in Wells's early scientific romances. As the protagonist of *When the*

---

[8] Douglas Mao, 'The point of it', in *Utopianism, Modernism and Literature in the Twentieth Century*, ed. Alice Reeve-Tucker and Nathan Waddell (London: Palgrave Macmillan, 2013), pp. 19–38 (p. 29). John S. Partington agrees that Wells's Edwardian works call for the 'erosion of class barriers' in the interest of social integration. See John S. Partington, 'H. G. Wells: A political life', in *Utopian Studies*, 19.3 (2008): 517–76 (p. 519).

[9] Partington, '*The Time Machine* and a *Modern Utopia*: The static and kinetic utopias of the early H. G. Wells', *Utopian Studies* 13.1 (2002): 57–68 (p. 58); Darko Suvin, 'Introduction', in *H. G. Wells and Modern Science Fiction*, ed. Darko Suvin and Robert M. Philmus (Lewisburg: Bucknell University Press, 1977), pp. 9–29 (p. 24).

[10] Wells, *The Time Machine*, ed. Marina Warner (London: Penguin, 2005), p. 51.

[11] Wells, *Time Machine*, p. 54.

[12] Matthew Beaumont, *Utopia, Ltd: Ideologies of Social Dreaming in England, 1870–1900* (Leiden: Brill, 2005), p. 47.

[13] Wells, *Time Machine*, p. 58.

Sleeper Wakes (1899) rises from his two-hundred-year-long hibernation, he finds himself in a similarly divided and dystopian world. The regime that has seized power, known as The Council, claims to act in the interest of the workers while in reality amassing capital through the exploitation of cheap proletarian labour. The disenfranchised workers, who live on the subterranean 'underside' of the booming cities, are no longer the 'burly labourers of the old Victorian times': sickly-looking and 'disease[d] with their lips and nostrils a livid white', this subproletariat resembles the Morlocks—and like the Morlocks, it is plotting to rise up in mutiny against the ruling capitalist caste.[14] The narrator fraternizes with the workers and supports their revolution, even though he begins to suspect that their leaders are just as corrupt and deceitful as the governing elite. Indeed, soon after the revolution, it becomes clear that the disenfranchised workers have in their turn been manipulated by a man called Orlog, a Machiavellian mastermind who has planned all along to seize the revolutionary moment in order to crown himself the state's new autocratic leader.

Despite some superficial similarities, *When the Sleeper Wakes* departs from *The Time Machine* by making its concern with contemporary political struggles and economic inequalities more explicit. When the novel's protagonist awakes in the future, he discovers that he has made (quite literally in his sleep) vast amounts of money: he has profited from an economic system that is skewed in favour of a plutocratic elite, as his stocks have kept accruing extravagant 'compound interest'.[15] The topical resonance of Wells's central plot device must have been apparent to the novel's first readers: while annual income from labour had been liable to taxation throughout the Victorian period, capital gains of the kind accumulated by the sleeper were frequently exempt from such legislation.[16] Wells's protagonist discovers that his tremendous wealth has made him the ruler of the world and that the now-dominant capitalist plutocracy has swept away the political institutions of earlier centuries. It turns out that even the proletarian dictatorship represented by Orlog operates within this plutocratic logic: as soon as the old ruling caste is ousted, Orlog replaces it with a new elite that maintains an iron grip on society and that firmly keeps the old working class in its allotted place. As Wells explained in his 'Preface' to the novel's 1921 reissue, he had written *When the Sleeper Wakes* at a time when he believed that there was no escaping the 'nightmare' of the plutocratic state and the class tensions to which it gave rise.[17]

My abbreviated outline of two of Wells's early scientific romances helps to throw into relief the artistic departure that is marked by his 1904 novel *The Food*

---

[14] Wells, *When the Sleeper Wakes* (New York: Modern Library, 2003), pp. 226, 228.
[15] Wells, *When the Sleeper Wakes*, pp. 17, 50.   [16] See Daunton, *Trusting Leviathan*, p. 205.
[17] Wells, *The Sleeper Awakes* (London: Penguin, 2005), p. 7. *The Sleeper Awakes*, first published in 1910, is a revised version of Wells's 1899 novel.

of the Gods and How it Came to Earth (1904), one of Wells's key works of science fiction. *The Food of the Gods* is often read as a continuation of Wells's class war narratives of the 1890s, yet the novel is also deeply embedded in reformist debates about taxation that Wells was engaged with at this stage of his career. *The Food of the Gods* occupies a transitional position in Wells's oeuvre insofar as it can be read as his first extended literary response to ongoing debates about the role of redistributive taxation: 'our whole story is one of dissemination', the novel announces with a view to the slow diffusion and trickle-down spread of the miraculous growth substance Herakleophorbia IV.[18] The novel starts as Herakleophorbia IV—colloquially known to its enthusiasts as 'Boomfood' or 'the Food of the Gods'—is being engineered in a chemical lab. When injected into an organism, the substance triggers extreme growth, leading animals, plants, and humans to 'boom' to five times their ordinary size. While every effort is made to keep Boomfood secret, the substance soon makes its way into the larger population through black-market backchannels and non-official 'centres of distribution' (87). The outsized animals and humans that have consumed the substance soon begin to create problems: while the animals wreak havoc in the countryside, the authorities struggle to supply sufficient food and drink for the growing population of giant humans. The state's failure to build supply chains that provide nourishment for the giant children breeds fears that the giants might revolt, and before long, these developments lead to the emergence of new forms of populist politics. One reactionary politician proposes that the giants be used as a cheap labour force in the country's chalk pits and that they be denied the right to reproduce. Tensions escalate between the humans and the 'Children of the Food', and the novel concludes as the world is poised on the verge of a long and violent conflict over resources.

The Food of the Gods can be read as a Malthusian nightmare about the exponential growth of the lower classes and their unstoppable emergence as a social force. In an essay from 1889, Wells had come out in support of Thomas Malthus's theory that population increase periodically outstrips the supply of food, and his 1904 novel takes a distinctly bleak view of the social effects that are produced by the uncontrolled growth of the working classes.[19] However, to make Malthus's *Essay on the Principle of Population* (1798) into the principal intertext of *The Food of the Gods* is to miss the particular importance which the novel attaches to questions of circulation and distribution rather than to the perceived threat of excessive reproduction or procreation. When Herakleophorbia is first introduced in the novel, it is presented as an enhancement of the human organism; the medication has been designed as an artificial supplement to that

---

[18] Wells, *The Food of the Gods and How It Came to Earth* (Mineola, NY: Dover, 2006), p. 93. Subsequent references are given parenthetically.

[19] See Wells, 'Mr H. G. Wells on socialism', *Science School Journal* 18 (1889): 152–5 (p. 154).

invisible 'necessary substance in the blood' which causes humans to grow but which is also 'used up by growth' (7). Boomfood functions as a corrective to the human organism's perpetual tendency towards physical exhaustion: it is a scientific means of transcending, to a certain extent if not completely, the limitations of human life. Wells's narrator agrees that Boomfood contributes to humankind's 'progress': 'In spite of prejudice, in spite of law and regulation, in spite of all that obstinate conservatism that lies at the base of the formal order of mankind, the Food of the Gods, once it had been set going, pursued its subtle and invincible progress' (93). The cornucopian promise symbolized by Boomfood explodes the political and economic monopolies of the old social elites by creating alternative structures of production and occasioning the emergence of new 'centres of distribution'. The 'bigness' which the novel antici-pates is thus not primarily associated with the middle-class fear of a newly emboldened proletariat, but with the vision of new distributive structures—of a reformed social order—that will be capable of accommodating and matching the enormous potency of Boomfood itself. *The Food of the Gods* recalls Wells's earlier anxieties about social division and unrest, but it also suggests that scientific progress and the necessary democratization of distributive mechan-isms are irreversible:

> Meanwhile, quietly, taking their time [...], the Children of the Food, growing into a world that changed to receive them, gathered strength and stature and knowledge, became individual and purposeful, rose slowly towards the dimen-sions of their destiny. Presently they seemed a natural part of the world, all these stirrings of bigness seemed a natural part of the world [...]. (93–4)

The prophetic tone of these sentences anticipates certain passages in *A Modern Utopia* (published only one year later) rather than looking back to the earlier scientific romances of the 1890s with which the plot of *Food of the Gods* shares some of its narrative raw material. However, unlike *A Modern Utopia*, Wells's 1904 novel ultimately fails to contain fears of class warfare. For example, while the narrator takes the side of the 'Children of the Food', he also echoes with some apprehension the traditionalist *ressentiment* that is voiced by the novel's populist demagogues, who invoke 'the wisdom of our forefathers, the slow growth of venerable institutions, moral and social traditions that fitted our English national characteristics as the skin fits the hand,' as a means of combatting the crisis (129). This conservative resistance to the forces of social, economic, and scientific change—and the concomitant failure to adapt existing 'institutions' in response to new social pressures—eventually culminates in violent conflict. As the novel closes, a war between the Children of the Food and the 'little people' (144)—the physically and intellectually diminutive representatives of the old order—appears unavoidable.

Wells and the Language of Tax Reform

The Food of the Gods, Simon J. James has noted, produces the kind of 'cognitive estrangement' that is typical of Wells's earlier romances by 'draw[ing] attention to the inability of conventional modes of representation, notably history and the newspaper, to represent experiences [of "technological or scientific innovation"] adequately'.[20] As James notes, this estrangement derives in part from Wells's contrapuntal narrative method which relays key events in the narrative only indirectly and thereby brackets readerly immersion in favour of an attention to particular social and scientific questions. Just as central to the novel's political work is Wells's stereoscopic narrative technique which forces readers to keep one eye on a specific contemporary problematic (Edwardian debates about redistributive fiscal mechanisms) and the other on the fantastically dystopian consequences of a failure to perform large-scale structural adjustments in the interest of easing social conflict. In contrast to Wells's earlier romances, the science that brings into focus the novel's central problematic—and that might also hold out the key to its solution—is not evolutionary theory (*The Time Machine*), biomedical vivisection (*The Island of Doctor Moreau*), or optics (*The Invisible Man*), but the emerging field of welfare economics that had begun to emerge towards the end of the nineteenth century.[21]

During the Edwardian years, Wells's earlier apocalyptic interpretation of social history—energized in part by Darwinian and Malthusian theories—began to give way to a belief in the possibility of reform, and Wells increasingly came to see the adaptability of state institutions as the catalyst for a non-coercive process of social integration. This view received a boost from new work in the field of economics—work that seems to have reached Wells through organizations such as the Fabian Society which he had joined for five tumultuous but crucial years in 1903. The new proposals that were being advanced by reformist economists relied on the central distinction between earned and unearned wealth: while money could be rightfully *earned* through labour, *unearned* wealth included property that had not been attained by way of individual effort, for example inheritance, rent, interest, or other forms of gains on existing capital. The American land reformer Henry George, whose works I discussed in the preceding chapter, had contributed centrally to the establishment of this reformist vocabulary in the 1880s.[22] In *Progress and Poverty* (1879), the study that catapulted him to transatlantic fame,

---

[20] James, *Maps of Utopia: H. G. Wells, Modernity, and Utopia* (Oxford: Oxford University Press, 2012), p. 149.

[21] For the disciplinary formation of this field (including discussion of works by Henry Sidgwick, Alfred Marshall, and Arthur Cecil Pigou) and its influence on literary production, see my '"The end of laissez-faire": Literature, economics, and the idea of the Welfare State', in *Late Victorian into Modern*, ed. Laura Marcus et al. (Oxford: Oxford University Press, 2016), pp. 448–62.

[22] See e.g. Roy Douglas, *Land, People and Politics: A History of the Land Question in the United Kingdom* (London: Allison & Busby, 1976), p. 48.

George had argued that the accumulation of landed wealth in the hands of a few owners put an artificial constraint on the ability of the economy to operate 'naturally': such monopolization impeded the circulation of wealth that would (so George hoped) increase the welfare of larger portions of the population. George's economic analyses led him to argue for a number of state-run initiatives, including the introduction of a so-called 'single tax' on land. This single tax, George believed, could be wielded like a magic wand: he was convinced that—since most British land was privately owned—a sufficiently high tax on the rental value of property would generate enough revenue to make most other forms of taxation superfluous, and thus ease the economic burden on the bulk of the population.

Wells credited *Progress and Poverty* with converting him to socialism in the 1880s, and George's book features prominently in his *Love and Mr Lewisham* (1900) where it convinces the novel's protagonist of the necessity of institutional reform.[23] George Bernard Shaw, Wells's fellow Fabian in the early 1900s, also played an important role in popularizing George's reformist ideas. In the landmark volume *Fabian Essays* (1889), Shaw had concluded that, in light of the entrenched antagonism between earned and unearned wealth, it was best for 'the State [to] be trusted with the rent of the country'.[24] Owing in part to the influence of Fabians such as Shaw, George's initial use of the term *rent* to refer to income from landed wealth was significantly expanded during the 1890s and early 1900s, and it came to signify any form of unearned wealth, including income from financial capital or shares.[25] Wells soon picked up on this new range of meanings. In *Anticipations*, his most important early collection of sociological speculations, he emphasized the similarities between landed property and other types of unearned wealth:

> share property is property that can be owned at any distance and that yields its revenue without thought or care on the part of its proprietor; it is, indeed, absolutely irresponsible property, a thing that no old world property ever was. [...] Related in its character of absolute irresponsibility to this shareholding class is a kindred class that has grown with the growth of the great towns, the people who live upon ground rents.[26]

[23] Wells, *Love and Mr Lewisham* (London: Penguin, 2005), p. 53. For George's place in Wells's intellectual biography, see Norman and Jeanne Mackenzie, *The Life of H. G. Wells: Time Traveller* (London: Littlehampton, 1973), p. 41.

[24] Shaw, 'The transition to social democracy', in *Fabian Essays in Socialism* (London: The Fabian Society, 1889), pp. 173–220 (p. 182). Shaw's earliest literary statement of this position was his play *Widowers' Houses* (1892), a scathing exploration of rent-collecting in London. On the central place of rent in early Fabian debates, see also Mark Bevir, *The Making of British Socialism* (Princeton: Princeton University Press, 2011), pp. 145–51. Sidney Webb, whose early views tended to be less collectivist than Shaw's, argued in *Fabian Essays* that the 'differentiation and graduation' of taxes offered a reformist way forward for Britain. See Webb, 'Historic', in *Fabian Essays*, pp. 30–61 (p. 54).

[25] Daunton, *Trusting Leviathan*, p. 296.

[26] Wells, *Anticipations of the Reaction of Mechanical and Scientific Progress upon Human Life and Thought* (Mineola, NY: Dover, 1999), p. 41.

The language of earned and unearned wealth originated in an older distinction between 'industrious' and 'spontaneous' incomes. The latter two terms had played an important role in mid-Victorian taxation debates when Liberal and Tory governments came under pressure to differentiate between income from trade or the professions (that is, 'industrious' incomes), on the one hand, and income from capital or land ('spontaneous' incomes), on the other. When the question of differentiation re-emerged towards the end of the century, it bore a much sharper moral inflection: the language of earned and unearned wealth did not just denote an economic fact, but (as the passage from Wells suggests) it specifically served to condemn the 'absolute irresponsibility' of all unearned forms of wealth. The significant political repercussions of this moralized language soon became evident: whereas George's early arguments about the taxation of landed property had failed to bring about immediate and substantive reforms, the much-publicized interventions of Shaw, Wells, and others helped to turn taxation reform into a key plank of Lloyd George's 1909–10 People's Budget.

The changes in the language of taxation that I have outlined above did not signify minor or merely superficial shifts in the technical idiom of economic analysis. Instead, as Daunton notes, these changes were indicative of deep transformations in political attitudes and in the 'language of social description' itself:

> The divisions between spontaneous and industrious incomes, and between earned and unearned income, were both based on a binary conception of society, yet the implications were somewhat different. The former suggested a need to relieve productive income of taxes in order to foster a dynamic capitalist society based on profit; the latter could be associated with a wider attack on the pursuit of profit as the basis of society and a desire to replace capitalism by socialism.[27]

Daunton's analysis suggests that Edwardian fiscal debates had significant cultural implications, but it also indicates that these changes in the language of taxation reform are best understood as a slow process that involved the gradual metamorphosis of existing fiscal taxonomies rather than their wholesale displacement by a radically new terminology. As Daunton shows, the new language of tax reform gave socialists unprecedented political leverage. Wells, too, was increasingly convinced that Britain's social and political institutions could be transformed in a progressive direction, and that these reformed institutions would be capable of defusing the threat of social confrontation and revolution. Socialists, Wells explained in an essay from 1906, were not 'a little band' of revolutionaries 'in an individualistic or quite unenlightened and hostile world': instead, they were progressive reformers who recognized that the world—notwithstanding its

---

[27] Daunton, *Trusting Leviathan*, p. 386.

current 'inadequate and feeble organization'—was 'teem[ing] with undeveloped possibilities'.[28] Wells's essay mutes the danger of abrupt revolutionary rupture by rearticulating utopianism in the reformist register of slow politics. Change is here imagined not as a total rejection of existing social forms but as the close description and deliberate 'development' of 'possibilities' inherent in the present social order. Given the relative success of new taxation schemes in the period, Wells had reason to be optimistic. More nuanced forms of graduated taxation had been introduced by Harcourt's government in 1894 and these were considerably extended by Lloyd George's in 1909-10: both budgets took important steps towards developing the tax system into 'a means of integration and not conflict' by treating it 'as a tool to change the structure of society' and steering it in a 'more radical, redistributive direction'.[29]

The new proposals for taxation reform were invigorated by arguments that emerged from the burgeoning field of welfare economics. Starting in the 1890s, political economists had begun to offer fresh rationales for the graduation of taxes. Building on the Oxford economist Francis Y. Edgeworth's innovative application of marginal utility theory to fiscal questions, these ground-breaking accounts suggested that an individual's ability to pay taxes differed in relation to their income: instead of advocating that all citizens be taxed the same amount, marginal utility theory suggested that individuals with higher incomes were able to pay higher taxes relative to their income without significantly decreasing their total welfare.[30] The Harcourt budget responded to such arguments by reducing indirect taxation, i.e. taxes on commodities that weighed most heavily on low-income earners, while increasing direct taxation, i.e. taxes on income and capital. Most significantly, perhaps, the budget introduced steeper death duties, thereby reducing the total amount of unearned wealth that could be inherited by any single individual. The Harcourt budget relied on the principle of differentiation by distinguishing between earned and unearned wealth, but it also crucially introduced an element of graduation by increasing the tax percentile in proportion to the total amount of capital bequeathed or inherited.[31] If these details seem overly technical, we need them—here as well as in other chapters—in order to understand how social reformers sought to create openings for material institutional

[28] Wells, 'Faults of the Fabian' [1906], in Samuel Hynes, *The Edwardian Turn of Mind* (Princeton: Princeton University Press, 1968), pp. 390–409 (p. 391).

[29] Martin Daunton, 'Payment and Participation: Welfare and State-Formation in Britain, 1900-1951', *Past and Present* 150 (1996): 169–216 (p. 173); and Daunton, 'Welfare, Taxation and Social Justice: Reflections on Cambridge Economists from Marshall to Keynes', in *No Wealth but Life: Welfare Economics and the Welfare State in Britain, 1880–1945*, eds. Roger E. Backhouse and Tamotsu Nishizawa (Cambridge: Cambridge University Press, 2010), pp. 62–88 (pp. 66, 71-2).

[30] Wells's knowledge of these arguments, and the contribution of marginal utility theory to consumerist discourse in *Tono-Bungay*, is explored in William Kupinse's 'Wasted value: The serial logic of H. G. Wells's *Tono-Bungay*', *NOVEL* 33.1 (1999): 51–72.

[31] See Donald Winch, *Wealth and Life: Essays on the Intellectual History of Political Economy, 1848–1914* (Cambridge: Cambridge University Press, 2009), p. 287.

change. The Harcourt budget specifically helped to set the ground for the heated reformist debates of the early 1900s. Similarly, the Liberal Party's budget of 1909–10 was denounced by some as too socialist, and it owed its populist byname ('People's Budget') in part to the progressive tax it introduced on a wide range of high incomes (not only on inherited wealth).[32] Yet while the People's Budget is still occasionally described as a singularly radical body of legislation, it is more appropriate to see it as the culmination of a historical process through which radical calls for differentiation were consolidated and integrated into the Edwardian political consensus.[33]

The wide-ranging political implications of the 1909–10 budget were not lost on contemporary observers. While Victorian political economists had tended to regard graduated taxation as the confiscation of private property by the state, Edwardian advocates of tax reform argued in the lead-up to the 1909–10 budget that citizenship was earned through active involvement in society and the state. In this context, being a 'tax-payer became almost synonymous' with citizenship and tax-paying increasingly became a 'badge of class status'.[34] If the identification of citizen and taxpayer—and the problematic association of both with the middle-class male breadwinner—seems unduly normativizing to us today, we should also note the gulf that separates the Edwardian view of tax-paying as a badge of active citizenship from more recent (and generally uninspiring) views that present taxation as a mechanical necessity enforced on citizens from above. Most importantly, perhaps, the Edwardian shift in the language of tax reform also codified a new understanding of the common good—and of individual economic entitlement—by defining individual property not in terms of static *wealth* but in terms of dynamic and composite *incomes*: while wealth was generally taken to signify a fixed amount of capital that was embodied in stable values such as land and that could be handed down from generation to generation, thinking about capital in terms of income suggested the essential fluidity of *all* property. I will return to this important point in more detail later in this chapter, when I discuss the work of Wells's friend, the economist Leo Chiozza Money, whose book *Riches and Poverty* (1905) was instrumental in shifting attention away

---

[32] Bruce K. Murray, *The People's Budget 1909/10: Lloyd George and Liberal Politics* (Oxford: Clarendon Press, 1980), pp. 34–5. See also Derek Fraser, *The Evolution of the British Welfare State: A History of Social Policy since the Industrial Revolution*, 4th ed. (London: Palgrave Macmillan, 2009), esp. pp. 186–8.

[33] The historian Philip Harling comments on the significant role which tax debates played in the centralization of the state. See Harling, *The Modern British State: A Historical Introduction* (Cambridge: Polity Press, 2001), p. 126. Lauren Goodlad describes the integration of certain socialist shibboleths into Edwardian legislation as part of a larger attempt to pacify the social realm and erect a 'bulwark' against more radical claims for social reconstruction. See Goodlad, *Victorian Literature and the Victorian State: Character and Governance in a Liberal Society* (Baltimore: Johns Hopkins University Press, 2004), p. 234 *passim*.

[34] James E. Cronin, *The Politics of State Expansion: War, State, and Society in Twentieth-Century Britain* (London: Routledge, 1991), p. 8; Daunton, *Trusting Leviathan*, p. 360.

from static concepts of wealth towards the kinetic nature of flows of income: if capital values such as landed wealth could be expressed in fluid monetary terms, those seemingly 'fixed' values (Money noted) were not in fact different from any other type of income. To think in terms of income, Money suggested, involved a qualitative conceptual leap that made it possible to envision the large-scale redistribution and democratization of all socially created wealth.

Wells's novels and social criticism of the early 1900s are steeped in the morally charged language of fiscal reform I have just described. The report of a Fabian Society Special Committee, which Wells co-drafted in 1906–07, pushed for a unified stance on taxation reform in the hope that it would enable Fabians to take a more active role in parliamentary politics;[35] and the first works of social criticism and speculation which Wells wrote after his scientific romances of the late 1890s—including *Anticipations* and its follow-up volume *Mankind in the Making* (1903)—likewise reflect his reformist optimism. In his first lecture to the Fabian Society from 1904, which was subsequently reprinted as an appendix to *Mankind in the Making*, Wells called for a 'limited socialism'. As Wells presented it, this 'limited socialism' promoted a version of 'intelligent individualism': it would not deny individuals the right to own property, but it would allow the state to reappropriate parts of their income in the form of taxes. This brand of reformist socialism, Wells explained, would look 'not so much to the abolition of property' as such but to the 'abolition of inheritance, and to the intelligent taxation of property for the services of the community'.[36]

In articulating the notion of a limited socialism, Wells was returning to an idea he had previously aired in *Anticipations*. There, he had expressed the hope that 'graduated legacy duties and specially apportioned income taxes' might be able to make inroads into the substantial 'shareholding element' of late Victorian society, which had 'by elaborate manipulation' managed to gather the 'property of the world [...] into a more or less limited number of hands'.[37] These comments indicate that Wells was moving away from the antagonistic class rhetoric of his mentor Shaw, and that, like Carpenter, he came to believe that the radical *élan* of socialism should be redirected into the channels of social reform. As Wells pointed out in his contribution to the essay collection *The Great State* (1912), the reformist mode he envisioned was distinct both from economic libertarianism, with its blind faith in the 'spontaneous and planless activities of people', and from the revolutionary demands of radical anarchists. In fact, Wells claimed, however much economic individualism and anarchism differed in theory, they effectively 'converge[d] in practice upon *laissez-faire*' because both denied the need for concerted and progressive political action. What was required instead, he

---

[35] For the unpublished report, see 'Report of the Special Committee', FSLSE, B/5/2.
[36] Wells, *Mankind in the Making* (London: Chapman and Hall, 1904), p. 400.
[37] Wells, *Anticipations*, pp. 44–5.

contended, were 'those types which believe supremely in systematic purpose,' those human 'Constructors' who would develop the socio-economic system in new directions while avoiding social disruption.[38] Echoing the drift of Edwardian taxation debates, Wells urged that the graduated death duties introduced by Harcourt be 'materially extended' so as to encompass a universal graduated and differentiated income tax.[39] When taxation was construed in this manner, it would cease to be seen as an act of expropriation, as an act of *filching* property for the state'.[40] Instead, the 'new system' of graduated taxes would show up new avenues for effective reform by offering an unprecedentedly fine-grained picture of the actual distribution of incomes: it would be as 'true to the reality of life and to right and justice as we can [be]'.[41] Wells's phrase captures the generative tension that characterized Edwardian debates about taxation, and that integrated the need for accurate social description ('true to the reality of life') with the anticipatory vision of a social sphere accountable to ideals of democratized ownership and participation ('true [. . .] to right and justice').

Wells's vision of state institutions as the embodiment of a lived ethos of sharing—as the equitable distribution of citizens' shares in the common good—found fullest expression in *A Modern Utopia*, the text I turn to in the next section. However, the aspirations which drove Wells's thinking about these issues were also articulated in some of his best-known realist novels of the period. *Kipps* (1905), for example, the novel which Wells had scrambled to finish so that he could commence work on *A Modern Utopia*, offers sustained reflections on the problem of wealth accumulation. The novel centres on Arthur ('Artie') Kipps, who experiences a meteoric rise from humble lower-middle-class beginnings to the higher echelons of London society when he comes into an unexpected inheritance after the death of his grandfather. The property inherited by Artie includes a house as well as an annual sum of £1,200. The unpublished first draft of the novel—entitled *The Wealth of Mr Waddy* and written in the late 1890s following Harcourt's introduction of higher death duties—had focussed on Artie's grandfather, an egomaniacal rich man whose larger-than-life presence recalls the financier Augustus Melmotte of Anthony Trollope's *The Way We*

---

[38] Wells, 'The past and the Great State', in H. G. Wells et al. (eds.), *The Great State: Essays in Construction* (London: Harper, 1912), pp. 1–46 (pp. 22–3).

[39] Wells, *Mankind*, p. 285. Wells's place at the heart of these political debates and his friendship with key political players—well beyond the comparatively narrow remit of the Fabian Society—has been reconstructed in a series of important essays by the historian of economic thought Richard Toye. See Toye, 'H. G. Wells and Winston Churchill: A reassessment', *H. G. Wells: Interdisciplinary Essays*, ed. Steven McLean (Cambridge: Cambridge Scholars, 2008), pp. 147–61; 'H.G. Wells and the New Liberalism', *Twentieth-Century British History* 20.2 (2008): 156–85; and '"The great educator of unlikely people": H. G. Wells and the origins of the welfare state', in *No Wealth but Life*, ed. Backhouse/Nishizawa, pp. 161–88.

[40] Wells, 'The past and the Great State', p. 27; orig. emph.   [41] Wells, *Mankind*, p. 285.

Live Now (1875).[42] By contrast, the published version of the novel abandons the satirical stock figure of the greedy rich man in order to focus its attention on the effects which Artie's unexpected legacy has on his subsequent life. The novel modulates the logic of the Victorian inheritance plot by charting the social and moral effects of Artie's inheritance rather than presenting this inheritance as the plot's final and happy denouement. Instead of magically resolving the various complications of the novel's plot, inheritance itself *is* the moral problem which *Kipps* sets out to address.

By inheriting his grandfather's money, Artie becomes a rentier, that *bête noir* of turn-of-the-century socialists.[43] He eagerly embraces the opportunity of social rise and becomes engaged to the beautiful but opportunistic Helen Walshingham, who uses Artie to establish her own family in London's high-society. Artie is saved from marrying the scheming Helen when he reconnects with his former childhood friend Sid. Sid informs Artie that he (Artie) is not entitled to his wealth, because he has not properly 'earned' it: "'I'm a Socialist, you see," said Sid, "I don't 'old with Wealth. What *is* Wealth? Labour robbed out of the poor. At most it's only yours in trust.'"[44] Artie is subsequently introduced to Sid's socialist mentor Masterman—modelled on the New Liberal politician C. F. G. Masterman—, who explains to Artie the reasons for the socialists' principled rejection of amassed wealth.[45] Money is no longer 'what it ought to be, the token given for service', as the growth of global speculative commerce obfuscates money's status as a medium of social relations (228).[46] Unlike the radical socialist neophyte Sid, however, Masterman does not believe that it will be necessary to do away with money as such; instead he thinks that incomes can once again become meaningful indicators of social relations if they are (re)distributed more democratically.

As Wells indicated in *Anticipations* and *The Making of Mankind*, the two works of speculative sociology he completed while working on *Kipps*, a fairer distribution of money was possible by way of new forms of taxation. It is interesting in this context that under the ambitious new tax regime imagined in Wells's two essay collections, Artie's own inheritance would be subject to higher graduated taxation.

---

[42] See Wells, *The Wealth of Mr Waddy*, ed. Harris Wilson (Carbondale: Southern Illinois University Press, 1969).

[43] The extension of the term *rent* to signify not just returns on landed property but any kind of unearned income had gained currency with the posthumous publication of Mill's 'Chapters on Socialism', and it was seized on eagerly by Sidney and Beatrice Webb. The term also entered the academic discourse of economics: as Alfred Marshall observed in a famous aside in *Principles of Economics* (1890), landed rent was in reality only 'the leading species of a large genus' which prominently included inherited wealth. See Marshall, *Principles of Economics*, 8th ed. (London: Macmillan, 1920), p. 412.

[44] Wells, *Kipps* (London: Penguin 2005), p. 180; orig. emph. Further references will be given in the text.

[45] Masterman was a member of the Liberal Party's left wing and one of the masterminds behind the 1909–10 People's Budget and the 1911 National Insurance Act.

[46] Fittingly, Artie's money is later gambled away by Helen's brother, who is a financial speculator, leaving Artie free to marry his childhood sweetheart Ann.

His new wealth falls squarely into the two central fiscal rubrics outlined in *The Making of Mankind*: on the one hand, duties on inheritance, and on the other, 'the intelligent taxation' of higher incomes 'for the services of the community'. *Kipps* even specifies the annual sum that will be available to Artie: '"This is Kipps," [Masterman] said, "The chap I told you of. With twelve 'undred a year"' (227). The sum of £1,200 corresponds to the amount that was being mooted in taxation debates as the sum above which incomes should be taxed at equal rates regardless of whether they were earned or unearned.[47] As Artie leaves Masterman's house, he looks at the world around him afresh—with the eyes, as it were, of a tax collector:

> His soul looked out upon life in general as a very small nestling might peep out of its nest. What an extraordinary thing life was to be sure, and what a remarkable variety of people there were in it.
>
> He lit a cigarette, and speculated upon that receding group of three, and blew smoke and watched them. They seemed to do it all right. Probably they all had incomes of very much over twelve hundred a year.   (237)

The narrator's specific attention to incomes mimics and gently ironizes Artie's parvenu obsession with wealth, but it also echoes the attention that was brought to income scales in the context of contemporary debates about taxation. The novel's attention to individual incomes notwithstanding, the most important overall narrative effect of Wells's new belief in the socially integrative potential of tax reform is the book's side-lining of the threat of class conflict. While Masterman, the novel's hardened senior radical, attacks 'those rich beasts above' who 'claw and clutch' for money (227), Wells does not show much interest in spelling out the material effects of the class struggles to which Masterman's combative rhetoric alludes. Indeed, the prolonged revisions to which Wells subjected *The Wealth of Mr Waddy* can quite easily be seen to contribute to one combined effect: by reducing the role of Kipps's Melmottian grandfather Mr Waddy, as well as the space allotted to his socialist mentor Masterman, the final version of *Kipps* minimizes the sense of class antagonism that had dominated Wells's earlier fictions of the 1890s.[48]

[47] This point was made by Wells's friend, the economist Leo Chiozza Money, and others. Money's influential book *Riches and Poverty* (1905) eventually settled on the slightly lower amount of £1,000. See Money, *Riches and Poverty*, 4th ed. (London: Methuen, 1908), pp. 301–2. Wells, too, mooted the amount in his pamphlet *The Misery of Boots* (1907), first published as an article in *Independent Review* in December 1905. Written at the height of the Edwardian debates about taxation, Wells' text mocks wealthy reformers who do not tire of criticizing capitalists but who are reluctant to 'pay income tax on twelve hundred a year'. See *The Misery of Boots* (London: Fabian Society, 1905), p. 32.

[48] For an account of Wells's second thoughts regarding Masterman's place in the narrative, see Harris Wilson, 'The death of Masterman: A repressed episode in H. G. Wells's *Kipps*', *PMLA* 86.1 (1971): 63–9.

If debates about tax reform exert an influence on the themes and narrative structure of *Kipps*, Wells's novel *Tono-Bungay* (1909) speaks more specifically to Wells's growing frustration with the apparent intellectualism and political ineffi-cacy of the Fabian Society, which Wells had left a year before the novel was published. *Tono-Bungay* revolves around a central character, the narrator George Ponderevo, who is convinced by his enterprising uncle Edward to sell a quack medicine called Tono-Bungay. Unlike the uncannily effective Herakleophorbia IV, Tono-Bungay is a hoax product whose sales keep increasing solely thanks to Edward's expert advertising of the product. George is eventually disgusted by the entire swindle and decides to leave his uncle's company. However, he soon recognizes that Tono-Bungay is itself only a symptom of the more pervasive social ills that affect capitalist societies: 'This irrational muddle of a community in which we live gave him that [money], paid him at that rate for sitting in a room and telling it lies. For he created nothing, he invented nothing, he economized nothing.'[49] In Wells's eyes, advertisers—like bankers and financiers—are middle-men who 'vociferate for the ten-millionth time some flatulent falsehood about a pill' and get 'pa[id] at nuisance rates'.[50] They are the quintessential capitalists because instead of engaging in productive labour they 'haggle [themselves] wealthy' (69) by maximizing their clients' financial profit.

Tono-Bungay does not simply echo the reformist optimism of *Anticipations* and *Mankind in the Making*. Rather, the novel complements the economic analyses of those works by providing what I have called (in Chapter 1) a sympto-mology of market-mediated forms of social life—a literary diagnosis of the psychological and emotional toll of capitalism. *Tono-Bungay* points out that the pursuit of voracious economic self-interest erodes individuals' ability to see themselves as part of a larger social community. George discovers this while talking to his friend Bob Ewart:

> [Bob] made me feel very clearly, what I had not felt at all before, the general adventurousness of life, particularly of life at the stage we had reached, and also the absence of definite objects, of *any concerted purpose* in the lives that were going on all round us [. . .] He brought out, sharply cut and certain, the immense effect of purposelessness in London that I was already indistinctly feeling.
>
> (111–12; my emphasis)

George's subsequent encounters with Bob further illustrate that the ineffectual intellectualism that Wells associated with the Fabian Society will not be sufficient to endow national politics with new 'concerted purpose'. The Fabians' main

---

[49] Wells, *Tono-Bungay* (London: Penguin, 2005), p. 220. Subsequent references are given paren-thetically.
[50] Wells, *Anticipations*, p. 92 fn.

shortcoming, George notes in his recollection of one Fabian meeting, is that they become excessively involved in 'the most inconclusive discussions you can imagine' (115). These remarks reflect the experiences that had led Wells to leave the Fabian Society in 1908. Wells had felt increasingly at odds with what he came to regard as the central tenet of Fabianism, namely the defeatist conviction that the 'capitalism system' constitutes 'one social immensity [. . .] gigantic and invincible' (115). Fatally for his politics, Bob fails to imagine how effective political change might be possible: renouncing revolution as a matter of political principle leads him directly into a resigned acceptance of capitalism's apparent 'invincib[ility]'.

Whereas current scholars tend to describe the Fabian Society as an important motor for political reform in Britain around 1900, Wells's portrayal of the Fabians indicates that they are unable to move beyond the frozen binary of political quietism and revolutionary negation. Fabians like Bob, Wells suggests, take an unduly limited view of the nature of institutional reform and they do not pay sufficient attention to its ethical dimension: for all their noisy condemnations of the amassing of wealth in the hands of the few, they fail to explain how reformers can elicit a new 'concerted purpose'—a shared *entgegenkommende Lebensform*— that will make it possible to think about state-centred reform as more than just a mechanical institutional fix. Wells's works indicate that in the years leading up to the 1909–10 People's Budget, he came to see tax reform—and the new democratic ethos of sharing that he associated with it—as key to the speculative conjunction of economic, political, and ethical reform.

Towards the Tax State in *A Modern Utopia*

The slow transformations associated with institutional reform—as opposed to the disruptive shocks of class conflict or social revolution—became the object of the most intense political energies in Wells's writings of the early 1900s. In his pamphlet *The Discovery of the Future* (1902), for example, Wells programmatically distinguishes between what he dubs 'legal' and 'legislative' types of mind. The former, he points out, is essentially 'submissive': it 'must constantly refer to the law made, the right established, the precedent set, and consistently ignore or condemn the thing that is only seeking to establish itself'; by contrast the latter is the 'legislative, creative, organizing, or masterful type, because it is perpetually attacking and altering the established order of things'.[51] Wells is careful not to set up a false dichotomy, and he adds that even the 'legislative mind' has to build on the social and legal forms of the present in order to formulate its vision of the future. Legislative political styles, Wells explains, 'see the present' as a set of tools

---

[51] Wells, *The Discovery of the Future* (London: Fisher Unwin, 1902), p. 7.

that need to be developed, as 'material for the future, for the thing that is destined to be'.[52] The process of legislation ('law-making') that Wells has in mind here does not point us to the revolutionary 'originality of a law that [has] to invent itself in the absence of any precursor' or that is created through a radically generative act of 'performative self-fashioning'.[53] Wells's future-directed legislative utopianism entails the aspirational repurposing of the resources of the present, rather than a projection of radical revolutionary alterity.

Wells's advocacy of legislative practices responds to the reforms that were being proposed or implemented during the Edwardian years. The slow movement of institutional reform that Wells describes in *The Discovery of the Future* notably resembles the logic of 'creative representation' that Daunton identifies as being central to the period's taxation debates: fiscal policy 'did not simply represent' the existing social order, but also involved 'debates over the form that society should take'.[54] The economic language of graduation, which entailed the detailed description of different income brackets, became a way of *representing* society as it was, but it also entailed a *creative* (or 'legislative') element that imagined the piecemeal emergence of new institutional arrangements. Because the fiscal system could be used to 'alter the structure of society', debates about taxation touched on substantive questions about the nature of the common good and the possibility of shared political participation. 'Fiscal policy defined as well as expressed identities,' Daunton writes, stressing the innovative or legislative aspect of institutional reform: 'Should taxation remove money for the government and leave the social structure unchanged; or should it remove money in order to change the social structure?'[55]

In *The Discovery of the Future* Wells maintains that the legislative remaking of the state's redistributive structure will be at the heart of society's '*kinetic* reorganization'.[56] Wells's choice of adjective here links his 1902 essay to *A Modern Utopia* which famously begins by opposing 'kinetic' and 'static' forms of utopianism:

The Utopia of a modern dreamer must needs differ in one fundamental aspect from the Nowheres and Utopias men planned before Darwin quickened the thought of the world. Those were all perfect and static States, a balance of happiness won for ever against the forces of unrest and disorder that inhere in things. One beheld a healthy and simple generation enjoying the fruits of the earth in an atmosphere of virtue and happiness, to be followed by other virtuous,

---

[52] Wells, *Discovery*, p. 7.

[53] I borrow this description of the spontaneous and revolutionary production of new legal forms from Rebecca Comay's *Mourning Sickness: Hegel and the French Revolution* (Stanford: Stanford University Press, 2011), p. 44.

[54] Daunton, *Trusting Leviathan*, p. 137.   [55] Daunton, *Trusting Leviathan*, pp. 52, 137–8.

[56] Wells, *Discovery*, p. 59; orig. emph.

happy, and entirely similar generations, until the Gods grew weary. Change and development were dammed back by invincible dams for ever. But the Modern Utopia must be not static but kinetic, must shape not as a permanent state but as a hopeful stage, leading to a long ascent of stages. Nowadays we do not resist and overcome the great stream of things, but rather float upon it.[57]

Wells evokes Darwin's evolutionist theory to describe the temporal and mobile character of modern utopias. The sentences which follow rearticulate these Darwinian echoes in a more active register; they uncouple the concept of change from the slow time of biological development and frame it more firmly in the language of reformist discourse:

> For one ordered arrangement of citizens rejoicing in an equality of happiness safe and assured to them and their children for ever, we have to plan a flexible common compromise, in which a perpetually novel succession of individualities may converge most effectually upon a comprehensive onward development.   (11)

The combination of evolutionist and reformist language in the opening pages of *A Modern Utopia* makes Wells sound less like Darwin and more like Eduard Bernstein, the German social-democratic Marxist theorist who advocated a Fabian-style 'evolutionary socialism'. In the late 1890s Bernstein had attacked the orthodox Marxist position, which insisted on the historical necessity of revolution, by calling for a cross-class approach and a broad alliance between socialists and other progressives. Bernstein submitted that contrary to what Marx had predicted, the proletariat's living conditions were improving and not growing more desperate—a gradual transition to socialism would therefore be preferable to the revolutionary route. Like Wells (or the Fabians Sidney and Beatrice Webb), Bernstein advocated a mode of legislative change that worked through the limited social and political resources of the present: 'I am not concerned with what will happen in the more distant future', Bernstein noted in *Evolutionary Socialism* (1899), 'but with what can and ought to happen in the present, for the present and the nearest future.'[58] Wells's utopia is likewise not located in a distant future, as had been the case with prominent predecessors such as Edward Bellamy's *Looking Backward, 2000–1887* (1888) or William Morris's *News from Nowhere* (1890). *A Modern Utopia* is set in a remote galaxy '[o]ut beyond Sirius' (15), yet the narrator,

---

[57] Wells, *A Modern Utopia* (London: Penguin, 2005), p. 11. Further references are given parenthetically in the text.

[58] Bernstein, *Evolutionary Socialism: A Criticism and Affirmation* (New York: Schocken, 1961), p. 163. In an important article, Ruth Levitas identifies this reformist impulse—with its characteristic blend of mimetic description and aspirational transformation—as a forgotten form of 'utopian sociology' around 1900. See Levitas, 'Back to the future: Wells, sociology, utopia and method', *The Sociological Review* 58.4 (2010): 530–47.

who inadvertently enters utopia by way of a rift in the space continuum in the Swiss Alps, crucially presents this utopia as inhabiting the same moment in time as Edwardian Britain. Indeed, Wells's utopian planet is in several ways an exact replica of the actually-existing world—a point which the novel drives home brilliantly by claiming that each human being in contemporary Britain has a utopian *doppelgänger*, and that the Earth's biology and geography are perfectly identical to the utopian planet's.

Wells's utopian world functions not as a narrative projection of radical onto-logical difference but as the actualization of as yet 'undeveloped possibilities', which characterize the narrator's (and the readers') own present. This impression is intensified by the novel's discursive and thematically arranged chapters, which offer systematic coverage of topics such as 'Utopian Economics', 'Race in Utopia', and 'Women in a Modern Utopia'. This formal organization trips up the text's narrative momentum and it underscores the critical and exploratory function of Wells's socio-economic utopia vis-à-vis the book's Edwardian present. Wells's text gives a reformist inflection to utopia—a genre which, some critics insist, is at heart a revolutionary (rather than merely evolutionary or progressive) literary form: 'Utopian form', as Fredric Jameson has influentially noted, 'is itself a representa-tional meditation on radical difference, radical otherness. [...] In order adequately to represent such changes, the modification of reality must be absolute and totalizing: and this impulsion of the Utopian text is at one with a revolution-ary and systemic concept of change rather than a reformist one.'[59] Wells's novel usefully complicates this understanding of utopia's revolutionary ontology. The mode of world-making we encounter in *A Modern Utopia* is not simply identical with the radically prophetic visions of Morris's or Bellamy's texts. Instead, as G. R. Stirling Taylor pointed out in *The Great State* (the collection of essays that Wells co-edited), Wells's utopian society relies on a systematic and deliberate 'development' of the elements of 'social organization [...] which make up the world to-day'. Well's utopia is the product of conscious 'social reform' rather than untrammelled dreaming.[60]

Wells carefully highlights the similarities that exist between the utopian society depicted in *A Modern Utopia* and the world which the narrator and his botanist-

---

[59] Jameson, *Archaeologies of the Future: The Desire Called Utopia and Other Science Fictions* (London: Verso, 2005), pp. xii, 39.

[60] See G. R. Stirling Taylor, 'The Present Development of the Great State', in Wells et al. (eds.), *The Great State*, pp. 272–99 (p. 276). By the same token, Wells refrains from presenting his utopia as a fixed blueprint for progressive reform. For example, he insists that the social world depicted in *A Modern Utopia* will still be subject to the 'limitations of human possibility' (12) and the de-territorialized forces of global capital. Wells's utopia is also not immune to the imperfections that beset political institutions. The novel's hesitations about utopian world-making are mirrored in the text's unstable narrative voice which repeatedly deflates the grand style of socio-political prophecy by offering anecdotal information about the amorous complications of the narrator's botanist-companion. On the instabilities of the narrative voice in *A Modern Utopia*, see Patrick Parrinder's *Shadows of the Future: H. G. Wells, Science Fiction and Prophecy* (Liverpool: Liverpool University Press, 1995), pp. 96–7.

friend have temporarily left behind. For example, as Roger Fry remarked in his contribution to *The Great State*, Wells's utopia retains 'a vast superstructure of private trading' instead of doing away with the idea of private property as such.[61] Wells's emphasis on the state's role in facilitating (economic) circulation looks back to the topical preoccupations of *The Food of the Gods*, while his qualified defence of the institution of private property instantiates the kind of non-revolutionary reformist thinking that also found expression in *Mankind in the Making* and the People's Budget. Similar to Carpenter, who had sought to re-signify the capitalist notion of 'ownership' in his essays and poetry of the 1880s and 1890s, Wells does not advocate the abolition of property as such, but rather aims to democratize private wealth by rearticulating it in terms of redistributable income flows. Wells's defence of private property here contrasts with the primitive communism that is championed in other works of the utopian tradition, ranging from Thomas More's *Utopia* (1516) to Morris's *News from Nowhere*.[62] As Wells's narrator observes during his early explorations in utopia, property (including money) is 'a good thing in life, [...] and I do not see how one can imagine anything at all worthy of being called civilization without it'. Moreover, while property grants individuals a minimum of autonomy, Wells also recognizes that it functions as a token of the individual's constitutive dependency on others: '[i]t is therefore the reconciliation of human interdependence with liberty' (55). Finally, because the actions of buying and selling tie humans together, the acquisition of property is not in itself objectionable—always provided that its scope is limited so as to minimize economic exploitation. Indeed, Wells came to believe that economic exchange conceived in these terms could function as the motor of a fully global civilization.[63]

Echoing Wells's attempt in *The Discovery of the Future* to arbitrate between the 'legal' and 'legislating' types of mind, *A Modern Utopia* mandates a slow form of structural change that rearticulates property as a fluid entity. Pushing beyond the class-bound rhetoric of ('static') wealth, *A Modern Utopia* begins to reimagine property in terms of the ('kinetic') circulation and (re)distribution of taxable graduated incomes. As Wells's narrator points out, the precise extent of what ought (or ought not) to count as private property cannot be determined in advance, because it 'is a quantitative question, be it remembered, and not to be dismissed by any statement of principle. Our Utopians will meet it, I presume, by detailed regulations, very probably varying locally with local conditions' (35). The

---

[61] Fry, 'The artist in the Great State', in *The Great State*, ed. Wells et al., pp. 249–72 (p. 271).

[62] On 'primitive communism' in the utopian narrative tradition, see e.g. Jameson, *Archaeologies of the Future*, pp. 28–30. And also: Anna Vaninskaya, *William Morris and the Idea of Community: Romance, History, and Propaganda* (Edinburgh: Edinburgh University Press, 2010), pp. 82–3.

[63] Wells's hope that globalization would contribute the growth of a cosmopolitan ethos is indebted to the brand of free-trade utopianism that the historian Frank Trentmann has called the Edwarwdian period's central 'prophetic' creed. See Trentmann, 'The strange death of free trade: The erosion of "Liberal Consensus" in Great Britain, c. 1903–1932', in *Citizenship and Community*, ed. Eugenio Biagini (Cambridge: Cambridge University Press, 1996), pp. 219–50 (p. 224).

'conditions' which determine—or 'quanti[fy]'—the precise domain of 'private' and 'public' property will involve a sliding scale of taxes:

> [Private property] might be made a privilege to be paid for in proportion to the area occupied, and the tax on these licences of privacy might increase as the square of the area affected. A maximum fraction of private enclosure for each urban and suburban square mile could be fixed. A distinction could be drawn between an absolutely private garden and a garden private and closed only for a day or a couple of days a week, and at other times open to the well-behaved public. Who, in a really civilised community, would grudge that measure of invasion? Walls could be taxed by height and length, and the enclosure of really natural beauties, of rapids, cascades, gorges, viewpoints, and so forth made impossible. So a reasonable compromise between the vital and conflicting claims of the freedom of movement and the freedom of seclusion might be attained. [...]   (35)

To the extent that *A Modern Utopia* envisions the resocialization of wealth through the levying of taxes, it is possible to see in the text 'an exposition of the ideas of the welfare state'.[64] The vision of an internally differentiated and 'kinetic' social whole pervades many of Wells's works of the early 1900s, including the three books that have been described as his Edwardian trilogy: *Anticipations*, *Mankind in the Making*, and *A Modern Utopia*.[65] The above passage specifically suggests that, by the time Wells composed his trilogy, he had begun to modify George's arguments for a single tax on unearned landed wealth by advocating a more broadly and discriminately applied graduated tax that would be calculated individually on the basis of income proportionality. But the passage I have just cited also indicates that Wells was aware of concerns, voiced by opponents of income tax graduation across the political spectrum, that the state's attempts to determine individual incomes might turn out to be too intrusive—that they would entail a much greater 'measure of invasion' into people's privacy than indirect taxes that were being levied on specific commodities. Many feared that the introduction of new forms of graduated and progressive taxation—of the type advocated by Money and Wells—would put Britain on a slippery slope towards authoritarianism.

Taxes and Taxonomies in *A Modern Utopia*: Wells and Leo Chiozza Money

A Modern Utopia outlines a series of governmental and welfarist mechanisms, including healthcare, sanitation, state-supported child-care, and a more humane

---

[64] Parrinder, *Shadows of the Future*, p. 102.
[65] For the thematic cohesiveness of this 'trilogy', see Nathan Waddell, *Modernist Nowheres: Politics and Utopia in Early Modernist Writing, 1900–1920* (London: Palgrave Macmillan, 2012), p. 41.

penal system. And yet, there is a real sense in which taxation is foundational to these other provisions because it generates much of the revenue that will be necessary to fund them. As I have already indicated, Wells's thinking about taxation was centrally influenced by the work of the economist Leo Chiozza Money. Money's books were widely read by reformers and, as a Liberal MP, Money was among Lloyd George's key economic advisers on the 1909–10 budget. Money was also one of the most prominent contributors to the 1912 volume *The Great State*, which Wells co-edited, but Wells's acquaintance with Money's ideas went back at least to 1905. The friendship between the two men had been initiated by Wells, who wrote to Money on 6 December 1905 to say that he had 'just been reading your *Riches and Poverty* with great appreciation', and went on to add that he 'would be very glad to make your acquaintance'.[66] Wells's discussion of private and public property in *A Modern Utopia*—the book he had just completed— shared much conceptual ground with *Riches and Poverty*, Money's bestselling work on income distribution and taxation that had been published just a few months earlier. Over the course of the next few years Money and Wells met up frequently, visiting each other's homes in London and Kent on numerous occasions. Wells quoted approvingly from *Riches and Poverty* in his 1907 pamphlet *The Misery of Boots*; and in 1906, when the Fabian Society sought to launch a book series that would print key works by contemporary socialists, Wells proposed a new edition of Money's *Riches and Poverty* alongside his own *A Modern Utopia*.[67] In a slightly later letter, dated 26 April 1910, Wells reasserted 'my very great admiration of you': 'When I admire you', Wells wrote, 'I feel like a coal hammer admiring a clock—or a mincing machine. While I slap off lumps you chop up, arrange, fret away.'[68] The emphatic terms in which Wells expressed his personal appreciation are remarkable even when they are placed in the larger context of Wells's voluminous correspondence of the time. Wells's remarks in the 1910 letter, written just three days before the passing of the People's Budget on 29 April, are particularly illuminating because they indicate that Wells had come to regard Money as the superior workman ('While I slap off lumps you chop up, arrange, fret away')—as one of the creative Constructors hailed in *A Modern Utopia*. Money, we might say, had become Wells's *miglior fabbro*.

It is hard to overestimate the influence which Money's writings of the early 1900s had on Wells's version of the reformist literary mode as well as on Edwardian reformist debates more generally. Never a person to lack self-

[66] Wells, Letter to L. C. Money, 6 December 1905, LCMA, Add. 9259/iv/6, Folder IV.

[67] Wells's proposal was recorded by Edward Pease, the first historian of the Fabian Society and its long-time secretary. See Pease, *The History of the Fabian Society* (London: Fifield, 1916), p. 169.

[68] Wells, Letter to L. C. Money, 26 April 1910, LCMA, Add. 9259/iv/6, Folder IV. Money eagerly repaid such compliments. In one of his letters to Wells, dated 1 January 1908, he confessed that 'I am eternally grateful to you for the work you are doing'. Another, dated 5 March 1908, reiterates that 'socialism will eternally be your debtor for the great work you are doing'. See HGWP, Series 3, Box 25, M-409.

confidence, Money noted in his unpublished autobiography that *Riches and Poverty* had 'proved to be germinal. It bred books, pamphlets, lectures, debates, political speeches, acts of parliament. [...] It made budgets of a new type. [...] It was a factor of importance in the building of the Labour Party. I remember attending a Fabian lecture in London [...] in which Sidney Webb asked his audience the rhetorical question: "What is the cause of Labour unrest?" and answered it in two words: "Chiozza Money." '[69] *Riches and Poverty* had started out from the observation that by far the largest portion of the United Kingdom's national income was being enjoyed by a mere tenth of the population. This analysis of the lopsided distribution of capital and incomes, Money recalled in his autobiography, 'had, of course, a direct bearing upon taxation, and its publication exercised a decisive influence at the Treasury': 'in view of the astonishing monopolization of the bulk of capital by a few, a fresh graduation was called for. [...] It was right and proper to use differential taxation to raise a fund for social regeneration.'[70] Money's writings made a significant impact on the high tide of Edwardian taxation debates, and they also left a mark on contemporary works of fiction. Richard Whiteing's popular social problem novel *Ring in the New* (1906), for example, featured a protagonist who authors reformist articles (including one item conspicuously titled 'Riches, Comfort, and Poverty') and whose ideas for tax reform are very clearly modelled on Money's.[71]

While *Riches and Poverty* was published too late to have a direct influence on Wells's novel, the intellectual links between *A Modern Utopia* and Money's writings of the early 1900s are clear enough.[72] Most importantly, and of particular relevance to Wells's version of the reformist literary mode, Money advocated new fiscal taxonomies that were built around the concept of *income* rather than *wealth*. As Money explained in his contribution to *The Great State*, measuring per capita 'material wealth'—notably financial increments on fixed capital assets such as land, houses, or machines—was not enough: we would be 'struck not with the greatness, but with the paucity of the figure. It amounts to just over £23 [per annum] per head of the population.'[73] In order better to describe and remedy the 'ill-distribution' of Britain's 'riches', Money proposed a fundamental reorientation of economic discourse towards the concept of 'total national income':

[69] Money, Unpublished Autobiography [dated 1939], LCMA, Add. 9259/iv/6, Folder I (p. 370).

[70] Money, Unpublished Autobiography, pp. 384–5, 370–1. 'This part of my taxation program', Money continued, 'was in the main accomplished within a few years by the Lloyd George budget of 1909.'

[71] Whiteing, *Ring in the New* (London: Hutchinson, 1906), p. 115. The name of Whiteing's protagonist, 'George Leonard', echoes Money's Christian name, Leo George.

[72] Money's book also touched on other topical issues dear to Wells, including the question of gender equality (an issue addressed in Wells's novel *Ann Veronica* from 1909) and of state support for mothers (a question that resonated with Wells's own call for an 'Endowment of Motherhood'). See Money, *Riches and Poverty*, pp. 8–9, 165–6.

[73] Money, 'Work in the Great State', in *The Great State*, ed. Wells et al., pp. 68–119 (p. 89).

The income of the United Kingdom, defined as the aggregate of all the wages, salaries, and profits of the individuals who compose the nation, is about twice as great as the one thousand million pounds arrived at above [in Money's calculation of "material wealth"]. The national income measures not material increment alone, but all the services, good, bad, and indifferent, useful and useless, beneficent and maleficent, which are built up upon the basis of the material income. The national income measures not merely the wage of a useful boiler-maker, but the salary of a useless clerk, or the fee paid to a lawyer for making a woman, much more moral than himself, confess her failings in the witness-box.[74]

Money argued that his recalibration of the reformist vocabulary would offer a more comprehensive view of society as an economic totality, and that it would also go to show that, contrary to what previous estimates had suggested, 'we are a people with a magnificent [total national] income.'[75] The new taxonomy proposed in *Riches and Poverty*, Money argued, would reveal that 'the chief ramifications of the social problem'—i.e. working-class unrest at one end of the social spectrum and spendthrift luxury at the other—'are but varying effects springing from one cause, the Error of Distribution.' New ways of taxing individual incomes would make it possible to re-socialize excessive personal incomes and to 'employ' them 'for national ends'.[76] Harcourt's 'famous Budget of 1894' received warm praise from Money because it had 'successfully carried into effect [...] heavy and graduated Death Duties':

> It is amusing now to recall the stout resistance which was offered to the reform. The increased Death Duties have come to be one of the chief mainstays of the Budget and the murmurings against them have completely died away. I now urge that [...] the time has come to take Sir William Harcourt's work a little further.[77]

Echoing Wells's comment on the 'creative construction' performed by 'legislating' minds, Money argues that innovative death duties and taxation of incomes will provide the 'Golden Key' to a fairer redistribution of incomes and to a future in which fewer individuals will suffer want.[78]

---

[74] Money, 'Work in the Great State', pp. 89–90.   [75] Money, *Riches and Poverty*, p. 156.
[76] Money, *Riches and Poverty*, p. 155.
[77] Money, *Riches and Poverty*, p. 306. On Harcourt, see also *Riches and Poverty*, p. 44.
[78] Money, *Riches and Poverty*, pp. 155–6. The work of the socialist economist J. A. Hobson reprises Money's arguments about the sum total of taxable incomes. Invoking Money's work on taxation reform, Hobson noted in 1906: 'The application [...] of our social theory of taxation involves careful scientific experimentation, with the object of finding out what proportion of the different sorts and grades of income can be taken without encroaching on living wages and living profits.' However, Hobson concluded, 'no one acquainted with the structure of modern industrial society [...] can doubt the existence of a taxable fund of socially-created income ample to meet the expenditure involved in the measures of social reform.' See Hobson, 'The taxation of monopolies', *Independent Review* 9 (1906), 20–33 (p. 33).

Adopting the language of *A Modern Utopia*, we could say that Money's proposals signalled a shift from an essentially 'static' view of material wealth towards a more 'kinetic' understanding of the nation's total national income. In doing so, *Riches and Poverty* hinted that property itself was a more fluid concept than had hitherto been recognized. Income, Money's statistics suggested, should not be considered merely as a single payment made in return for a particular service or commodity. Rather, from the point of view of the economic system as a whole, national income as such was in permanent flux, undergoing only transient materializations into salaries, expenses, or welfare provisions. Private property, conceived in terms of kinetic flows of income, was constantly being reabsorbed into public circulation. The very idea of what counted as private property was thus a matter of legislative convention and compromise. As Wells observed in *The Misery of Boots*—the 1907 pamphlet that had concluded by praising Money's *Poverty and Riches*—genuine fiscal reform had the power to 'change our conventional admission of what is or is not property'.[79]

Poverty and Riches pits Money's understanding of property as an unstable and fluid entity against some of the foundational philosophical tenets of nineteenth-century liberal political economy. In a closely related vein, Wells's view that 'property is a plastic and fluctuating convention' (62) serves as a critique of the everyday conception that *homo economicus* is entitled to the ownership of whatever he manages to acquire by legal means. *A Modern Utopia* roundly dismisses the idea that the economic realm consists of a 'practically unlimited number of avaricious adult units, incapable of any other subordinate groupings than business partnerships' (62). Instead, Wells's book projects a complex field of redistributive mechanisms, legal entitlements, and tax exemptions. 'Modern Utopian statesmanship' will look to 'secure to a man' a certain minimum amount of 'legitimate property', i.e. 'all those things that become, as it were, by possession, extensions and expressions of his personality; his clothing, [...] the tools of his employment, his books, the objects of art he may have bought or made' (67). These 'intimate' things will be 'free even from taxation' (67) since they are understood to belong to individuals in more than a purely economic sense: they form part of the person either because they meet the most basic of human needs (e.g. clothing) or because they embody non-material values and are expressive of the owner's personality (e.g. artworks and books). Wells proceeds to list items that should be 'taxed lightly' (68) because they are immediately useful to their owners, including 'household furniture', or '[a] horse, perhaps, in certain districts, or a bicycle, or any such mechanical conveyance personally used' (67). But Wells's kinetic utopian state

---

[79] Wells, *Misery of Boots*, p. 33. As I have been suggesting, similar ideas were being proposed by progressive New Liberals. The political theorist L. T. Hobhouse, for example, echoed such thinking when he argued that '[w]e must not assume any of the rights of property as axiomatic.' See Hobhouse, *Liberalism and other Writings* (Cambridge: Cambridge University Press, 1994), p. 48.

also mandates the large-scale social reappropriation of certain other forms of property:

> What he did not choose to gather and assimilate to himself, or assign for the special education of his children, the State will share in the lion's proportion with heir and legatee. This applies, for example, to the property that a man creates and acquires in business enterprises, which are presumably undertaken for gain, and as a means of living rather than for themselves.   (68)

Wells's extended discussion of property rights anticipates a revised understanding of the concept of social sharing and of property itself. Several contemporary reviews pointed out that the text's patient unfolding of taxation schemes was key to its reformist vision. Wells, one critic noted in *The Spectator*, 'shows Utopia proceeding—by increased limitation and taxation, by extension and multiplication of State rights, by frequent revision of endowments, and other very prosaic and humdrum methods—to rob property, not of all its pleasures, but of most of its terrors'.[80] In *A Modern Utopia*, private property is not a naturally given entity which precedes taxation—rather, it is a convention whose economic and political function is open to 'legislative' critique and revision. As Wells commented in 1906, any form of income was 'a purely provisional and law-made thing' and, as such, it was amenable to progressive reforms that sought to repair the economic structure of British social life.[81]

Two recent legal theorists, Thomas Nagel and Liam Murphy, have worked to reactivate the aspirational dimension of tax reform by stressing that the fiscal practice of income taxation necessarily implies a fluid notion of property. Emphasizing the state's arbitrating role in defining the boundaries between private and public property, Nagel and Murphy argue against what they dub 'everyday libertarianism', i.e. the 'robust and compelling fantasy that we earn our income and the government takes it away from us'.[82] Private property, they contend against the welfare state's libertarian critics, does not possess an absolutely autonomous existence and validity, nor is it a natural right: 'The tax system [...] is not an incursion on a distribution of property holdings that is already presumptively legitimate. Rather, it is among the conditions that *create* a set of property holdings, whose legitimacy can be assessed only by evaluating the justice of the whole system, taxes included.'[83] Murphy and Nagel aim to defamiliarize culturally hegemonic assumptions about personal property and individual desert ('everyday

---

[80] Warren, Unsigned review in the *Spectator* (21 October 1905), in *H. G. Wells: The Critical Heritage*, ed. Patrick Parrinder (London: Routledge, 2002), pp. 117–21 (p. 120).

[81] Wells, 'Faults of the Fabian', p. 399.

[82] Murphy and Nagel, *The Myth of Ownership: Taxes and Justice* (Oxford: Oxford University Press, 2002), p. 176.

[83] Murphy/Nagel, *Myth of Ownership*, pp. 36–7; orig. emph.

libertarianism', in their phrase), but they also emphasize the positive role which taxation can play in furthering an alternative understanding of national income as a socially produced and collectively shared good. In their telling—as in Wells's and Money's account—the state's redistributive mechanisms are not simply bureau-cratic 'instrument[s]' which protect property rights that have been acquired by virtue of participation in the free market.[84] One of the ends of state action is to push back against the deeply ingrained cultural prejudices of everyday libertarianism and to resist (what Thomas Piketty calls) the 'patrimonial', dynastic capitalism that was prevalent in the late nineteenth century and that is again resurgent today. 'If one wants to get beyond [the] logic of endless accumulation,' Piketty writes, 'one needs to equip oneself with the intellectual and institutional means to transcend the idea of private property.' Taxation provides one such 'institutional means' insofar as it embodies the idea of 'true social ownership of capital'.[85]

In *A Modern Utopia*, the speculative movement that associates structural reform with the emergence of a new democratic ethos is captured by Wells's central generic innovation: the presentation of a utopian world that resembles the narrator's Edwardian present in most of its external (topographical and biological) features.[86] When the traveller and his botanist-friend first enter utopia through the space-rift in the Swiss Alps, there are initially no visual clues to inform them that they have in fact entered an alternative world: 'We should scarcely note the change. Not a cloud would have gone from the sky. It might be the remote town below would take a different air. [...] Yet I have an idea that in some obscure manner we should come to feel at once a difference in things.' (17) This opening account contrasts programmatically with canonical utopian works—from More's *Utopia* to Bellamy's *Looking Backward*—that rely on visually manifest differences between utopia and our own world as a way of allegorizing utopia's radically distinct ontological status. What is most remarkable in the Wellsian text, then, is precisely the sheer *un*remarkability of its initial shift into the utopian genre. The apparent identity of our world and utopia serves to highlight the importance of 'different habits, different traditions, different knowledge, different ideas' (22): what marks out this alternative world as utopian, Wells suggests, is subtly woven into the texture of social custom and the fabric of *Sittlichkeit*. Wells's narrative procedure—an apparent duplication of reality that eventually gives way to an intensified recognition of altered structures of social organization and to a changed ethos—corresponds to the structural dynamic of Edwardian reformism

---

[84] Murphy/Nagel, *Myth of Ownership*, p. 41.

[85] Piketty, *Capital and Ideology* (Cambridge, MA: Belknap, 2020), pp. 129–30, 285.

[86] Other features of the text could be discussed in this context as well. For example, the name given to the narrator of the text—'The Owner of the Voice'—suggests that the Voice is only a temporary and fluctuating possession that can at any point break free of its owner. This is precisely what happens towards the end of *A Modern Utopia* when the expository voice no longer belongs to the narrator but to his Utopian *doppelgänger*. See Parrinder, 'Utopia and meta-utopia in H. G. Wells', *Utopian Studies* 1 (1987): 79–97 (pp. 86–7).

itself, which tends to value discreet modes of socio-economic change over the spectacular ruptures associated with revolutionary action, and which emphasizes the social (*sittlich*) dimensions of institutional reform. Echoing the institutional logic of creative representation discussed above, the beginning of *A Modern Utopia* dramatizes the gradual emergence of the utopian impulse from within a prior mimetic one. In so doing, Wells's text gestures towards a hybrid generic mixture—what we could call aspirational realism—that serves to convey a sense of the 'undeveloped possibilities' inherent in the established order of things. This realism is not characterized by a politically quietist 'ontological commitment to the status quo' but by a reformist impulse that works through the forms of the present in order to go beyond them.[87]

The internal logic of institutional reform supplies the formal pattern that makes it possible Wells to project a fictional social world. However, Edwardian debates about taxation (including the work of Money) also resonate with another key aspect of Wells's kinetic utopia, its emphasis on the absolute 'uniqueness' of each individual. In an early aside to the reader, Wells's narrator comments that '[i]n the reiterated use of "Unique", [...] in the insistence upon individuality and the individual difference as the significance of life, you will feel the texture' of the kinetic utopia (20). In Wells's Edwardian trilogy this emphasis on the cultivation of individual ends is intended to pre-empt the slippage from large-scale economic socialization to social homogenization. As Wells explains, utopian 'humanity' manifests the apparent paradox of individual lives lived in common— 'as a multitude of unique individuals in a mass' (182)—with the support of an interventionist state. Wells's argument, Simon James observes, is directed against the laissez-faireist assumption that 'the movement from homogeneity to heterogeneity requir[es] less and less state intervention'.[88] Like the writers discussed in previous chapters, Wells points out that the state provides the social infrastructure that makes it possible for singular ('unique') identities to flourish in the first place. 'The State is for Individualities', Wells insists in his chapter on 'Utopian Economics': 'The State is for Individuals, the law is for freedoms, the world is for experiment, experience, and change: these are the fundamental beliefs upon which a modern Utopia must go' (66). As I noted in the Introduction, works

---

[87] Jameson, *Antinomies of Realism* (London: Verso, 2015), p. 145. Linda R. Anderson similarly notes that Wells sought to modify the realist novel because it 'operated within a framework of social fixity'. See Anderson, 'Self and society in H. G. Wells's *Tono-Bungay*', *Modern Fiction Studies* 26.2 (1980): 199–212 (p. 201). Needless to say, my discussion of this instance of generic mixing does not exhaust the text's persistent and unruly blending of forms and styles. As Sarah Cole reminds us in her important recent study of Wells, *A Modern Utopia* is a text 'that constantly tests its own condition of being: if it is a utopia, it is one whose novelistic qualities continually threaten the status as utopia; if it is a novel, it is one whose storyline is drowned out by its utopian imperative to discourse in detail about the envisioned world. These contrasts and tensions rule the novel from its opening pages.' See Cole, *Inventing Tomorrow: H. G. Wells and the Twentieth Century* (New York: Columbia University Press, 2019), p. 70.

[88] James, *Maps of Utopia*, p. 132.

written in the reformist literary mode sometimes draw our attention to subject positions that are excluded from these works' democratically expanded conception of social citizenship. And yet, of all the writers discussed in this book, Wells is the one whose writings are most often associated with the potentially coercive aspects of turn-of-the-century statism. For critics who are sceptical of Wells's particular version of statism, the Samurai—the ruling caste of Wells's utopian state—embody the essence of his unacceptably hierarchical authoritarianism.[89] The emphasis on uniqueness in *A Modern Utopia* is intended to guard against such authoritarian excesses, and we should not simply dismiss Wells's attempts—in his reform-minded Edwardian trilogy, if not in his prophetic post-war writings—to ensure that his version of the reformist literary mode remains hospitable to the emergence of counter-hegemonic critique and non-normative identities.

In the context of the present discussion, I want to focus on a more local discursive affinity that connects Wells's attention to 'uniqueness'—along with his qualified defence of private property—to the changing language of social description that characterized Edwardian debates about tax reform. As Money observed in *Riches and Poverty*, tax reformers required significantly more fine-grained fiscal taxonomies that would allow them to describe the composition of individual incomes as well as the relation between different kinds of income. By articulating individual tax obligations in terms of relative incomes, these highly specific modern taxonomies departed from the old practice of local rate-collecting, which had relied on antiquated data and differed widely from county to county.[90] *Riches and Poverty* is thick with tables and graphs that seek to graduate wages according to a series of nuanced tax brackets (Figure 2). One table breaks down a hypothetical 'composite income' according to different taxonomic 'schedules' (Figure 3), with Schedule A reflecting rents from real estate and houses, Schedule C specifying profits from government stock and dividends, Schedule D listing gains from trade and commerce, and so on. While the method of determining taxes in relation to a complex aggregate of categories was not itself new, earlier 'schedules' had been hamstrung by a lack of descriptive accuracy.[91] According to Money, the loose and baggy classifications used by nineteenth-century tax reformers, including George's proposals for a 'single tax', had failed to keep step with an economic reality in which income structures were in incessant flux. By contrast, Money insisted that more detailed fiscal monitoring by the government would yield a much more precise survey of individual incomes.

---

[89] Equally well known is Wells's propagation of untenable views about race and eugenics as well as *Modern Utopia*'s rejection of universal suffrage and its endorsement of state-organized surveillance. It is also worth pointing out that even some of the welfarist measures for which Wells is often celebrated (such as the 'Endowment of Motherhood') first emerged in the late nineteenth century among eugenicist fears about the future of the 'race'.

[90] Harling, *Modern British State*, p. 124.   [91] Daunton, *Trusting Leviathan*, p. 185.

WAGES IN 1886. THE BOARD OF TRADE SUMMARY OF RATES OF WAGES (NOT ACTUAL EARNINGS) DERIVED FROM THE DETAILED EXAMINATION OF 38 SELECTED INDUSTRIAL OCCUPATIONS

	Men. Per Cent.	Women. Per Cent.	Boys. Per Cent.	Girls. Per Cent.
Half Timers . .	—	—	11.9	27.2
Under 10s. per week	0.1	26.0	49.7	62.5
10s. to 15s. per week	2.4	50.0	32.5	8.9
15s. to 20s. „	21.5	18.5	5.8	1.4
20s. to 25s. „	33.6	5.4	0.1	—
25s. to 30s. „	24.2	0.1	—	—
30s. to 35s. „	11.6	—	—	—
35s. to 40s. „	4.2	—	—	—
Above 40s. „	2.4	—	—	—
Total . .	100.0	100.0	100.0	100.0
	s. d.	s. d.	s. d.	s. d.
Average Rate of wages . .	24 9	12 11	9 2	6 5

Figure 2 Table, 'Wages in 1886', from Leo Chiozza Money, *Riches and Poverty*, 4th ed. (London: Methuen, 1908), p. 20.

The numerous categories laid out in *Riches and Poverty* were accordingly intended as a combinatory heuristic rather than a fixed grid that could be applied indiscriminately—they would make it possible to calculate with an unprecedented level of granularity how much tax money individual citizens owed the government. The potential of these new 'assessments', Money noted with obvious satisfaction, would be 'enormous'.[92]

Money's insistence on taxonomic specificity and his insights into the provisional nature of classifications resonate with Wells's pointed reflections on uniqueness. When *A Modern Utopia* was first published, Wells added as an appendix a paper which he had given to the Oxford Philosophical Society in 1903. Entitled 'Scepticism of the Instrument', the essay demonstrates that Wells's concern with uniqueness was rooted in a principled opposition to the reified

---

[92] Money, *Riches and Poverty*, p. 29.

HYPOTHETICAL COMPOSITE INCOME

Schedule.			Amount.
A.	Profits from the Ownership of Lands, Houses, etc.		£500
B.	„	from the Occupation of Lands . .	200
C.	„	from Government Securities . . .	200
D.	„	as an Author	100
D.	„	as a Solicitor (Partner in a firm the total profits of which are £5,000) .	2,500
D.	„	from Investments in a Public Company (Total profits of the Company £55,000)	500
D.	„	Investments in Municipal Stock . .	100
D.	„	from Investments in Foreign Bonds (payable by coupons cashed in the United Kingdom)	100
D.	„	Salary as a Land Agent . . .	500
E.	„	Salary as a Borough Auditor . .	300
			£5,000

Figure 3 Table, 'Hypothetical Composite Income', from Money, *Riches and Poverty*, p. 32.

abstractions of classificatory systems. 'My opening doubt,' Wells writes, 'is essentially a doubt of *the objective reality of classification* [...] There is no property of any species, even the properties that constitute the specific definition, that is not a matter of more or less' (254; orig. emph.). Wells's comment is couched in the language of evolutionary theory, yet there is a clear affinity between Money's discussion of taxation—of the gradual 'more or less' that Money sought to capture in the tables and graphs which filled *Riches and Poverty*—and Wells's related exploration of taxonomies as fluid and 'provisional classifications'.[93]

Tax reform carried an aspirational charge in the Edwardian period because it tendered a solution to 'the problem of combining progress with social stability'—a problem, as Wells admitted in *A Modern Utopia*, whose solution 'had never been accomplished in Utopia before' (182). Wells also shared the belief that reformed institutions could encourage 'public-spirited conduct' in a way that states had not

[93] For a helpful discussion of Wells's interest in questions of (evolutionary, philosophical, metaphysical and scientific) taxonomies, see Harvey N. Quamen, 'Unnatural interbreeding: H. G. Wells's *A Modern Utopia* as species and genre', *Victorian Literature and Culture* 33.1 (2005): 67–84 (esp. pp. 69–72).

previously managed to do.[94] This was so, Wells reasoned, because the institutions of the reformed state were no longer alien bureaucratic impositions but had become integral to the way citizens were living their lives. In *Anticipations*, the book which Money confessed to reading 'with a good deal of agreement and immense interest', Wells used the term 'New Republic' to describe the lived praxis he associated with the realization of institutional reform.[95] State-centred institutional reform, Wells argued, would mark 'the opening phase of a period of ethical reconstruction, a reconstruction of which the New Republic will possess the matured result.'[96] Wells decided to drop the phrase 'New Republic' from *A Modern Utopia*, yet many of the contributors to Wells's edited volume *The Great State* were quick to seize on the term to describe the *Lebensformen*—the new ethos of collective sharing—that Wells had associated with the reformed state. The legal scholar E. S. P. Haynes, for example, compared the citizen of the future to a new kind of 'Athenian': 'The essential point,' Haynes insisted, 'is for every citizen to regard justice and legislation as part of his own work, and the whole apparatus of the State as his possession, instead of as alien things imposed on him by such persons as cabinet ministers and judges.'[97] The New Republic's institutions would be the material manifestation of a new kind of active citizenship—as such, they would no longer be external to the sphere of the social, 'alien things imposed on [it]' or a mere set of administrative mechanisms positioned outside it. Wells's speculative understanding of reform made it possible to imagine the state as a 'common idea [. . .] of which this Modern Utopia is merely the material form' (91).

Reform and Resignation: *The New Machiavelli*

In the early 1900s, Wells believed that socialists 'should remain outside the constraints of party organisations' so as not to antagonize members of the middle class who might look favourably on the sweeping social reforms proposed by the oppositional Liberal Party. Taking up positions outside established parties, Wells maintained, would enable socialists to 'work out their positions on all aspects of life, argue their case, and convert the public'.[98] Wells held this view during the years he spent in the conventicles of the Fabian Society (1903-8), and it corresponds broadly to the Fabians' professed policy of permeation, that is, the belief that socialist ideas ought to be given the widest possible circulation rather than

---

[94]   C. J. Bond, 'Health and Healing in the Great State', in *The Great State*, pp. 142–80 (p. 173).

[95]   Money, Letter to H. G. Wells, 1 May 1906, HGWP, Series 3, Box 25, M-409.

[96]   Wells, *Anticipations*, p. 161. For T. H. Green's idealization of classical (Athenian) democracy, see my discussion in Chapter 2.

[97]   Haynes, 'Law and the Great State', in Wells (ed.), *The Great State*, pp. 181–95 (p. 187).

[98]   Partington, 'Wells: A Political Life', p. 530.

remain confined to any one party. As I have suggested, this valorization of slow politics is echoed in the opening pages of *A Modern Utopia* which experimentally suspend the formal protocols of utopia that privilege forms of abrupt, comprehensive, and partisan change. In the years after the publication of Wells's book, however, the political landscape of Britain—and the place of socialism within it— began to change in ways that necessitated adjustments in political strategy and (Wells thought) artistic outlook. In 1905 the Conservative government under Arthur Balfour lost its majority and the Liberal Henry Campbell-Bannerman became prime minister. The Liberal Party would retain power in the following general elections and continue to form minority and majority governments until 1915, with H. H. Asquith acting as prime minister from 1908. However, the true rising force of these years was the Labour Party, and it was only through the support of the twenty-nine newly created Labour MPs that the appointment of Campbell-Bannerman as prime minister became possible. Labour was opening up positions to the left of the Liberals, and many reformers, including Wells, were beginning to gravitate towards this new political space.

If the year 1905 signified the beginning of the end of the Liberal Party, it proved a windfall for socialists. '[I]t was recognised,' former Fabian secretary Edward Pease recalled in his account of the Society's history, 'that Socialism was no longer the creed of a few fanatics, but a political force supported, actively or passively, by the great organizations of Labour throughout the country, able to fight, and sometimes to beat both the older parties. A new era in politics had begun.'[99] Wells soon sided with the new Lib-Lab government and argued vociferously against the fielding of socialist candidates elsewhere in the country lest they might divert votes away from Labour.[100] As Wells became increasingly embroiled in the parliamentary politics of the period, the forms of his fiction began to change as well. In his novel *The New Machiavelli*, Wells notably abandoned the speculative reformist mode of *A Modern Utopia* and focussed more narrowly on the inevitable pressures and compromises of parliamentary politics. As he noted in 1912, shortly after *The New Machiavelli* had been published, the 'modern novel [. . .] is the only medium through which we can discuss the great majority of the problems which are being raised in such bristling multitude by our contemporary social development, [including] the immense cluster of difficulties that arises out of the increasing complexity of our state'.[101] Wells accords the novel pride of place as the literary form most suited to the reformist moment around

---

[99] See Pease, *History of the Fabian Society*, p. 167. For Wells's relationship to Labour and its leader Keir Hardie, see Mackenzie/Mackenzie, *Time Traveller*, pp. 203–7.

[100] See Partington, 'Wells: A Political Life', pp. 533–4; Toye, 'H.G. Wells and the New Liberalism'; and Wells, 'An open letter to an elector in NW Manchester, 21 April 1908', in *The Correspondence of H. G. Wells*, ed. David C. Smith (London: Pickering & Chatto, 1998), vol. 2, pp. 214–17. Wells himself ran as a Labour candidate for London University in two general elections in the early 1920s.

[101] Wells, 'The contemporary novel', in Wells, *An Englishman Looks at the World* (London: Cassell, 1914), pp. 148–69 (p. 163).

1900 (a position T. H. Green, Mary Augusta Ward, or E. M. Forster could easily have agreed with). However, Wells's remark also indicates that *The New Machiavelli* is a far cry from the reformist optimism of his Edwardian trilogy, and I want to suggest that the novel is best read a complex record of what Wells came to regard as the Achilles' heel of slow politics—the possibility that parliamentary politics might dissipate any real reformist momentum. The Lib-Lab triumph in the 1905 election created an atmosphere in which the 'legislative' reorganization of society, its creative reconstruction, increasingly seemed within reach, and the early portions of *The New Machiavelli* reflect the reformist excitement of these years. Yet when the novel is considered in its entirety, Wells's account of the political career of Richard Remington—from youthful socialism and Liberal reformism to Conservative elitism—resembles the arc of a pessimistic political *Bildungsroman* that proceeds from idealism to adult pragmatism.

The novel, which is narrated retrospectively by Remington's older self, begins by relating Remington's youthful desire to work towards a complete recasting of Britain's economic and political system. At this point in his career, Remington sympathizes with socialism and is happy to remain outside the conventicles of the existing parties. However, following his marriage to a rich heiress, he opportunistically chooses to enter parliament on a Liberal ticket, and when he recognizes that the ruling Conservative Party offers him even greater chances to satisfy his Machiavellian political ambition, Remington switches allegiance again. Remington eventually gets his comeuppance when his love affair with a young student, Isabel Rivers, becomes public: his political career is abruptly cut short and in a last reversal Remington decides to leave his wife and friends in order to emigrate to Italy, where he writes the account of his life that makes up Wells's novel.

In the book's opening pages, Remington's aspirations resemble those of the Samurai, the administrators and guardians of the public order described in *A Modern Utopia*. The older Remington, who narrates the story, duly identifies these ambitions with a distinctly utopian 'vision of the strengthened and perfected state'.[102] As Wells points out, the true 'protagonist in this story' will be Remington's evolving political 'vision': 'The state-making dream is a very old dream indeed in the world's history', the old Remington muses, but it has 'play [ed] too small a part in novels' (10–11). Remington's reflections recall the opening paragraphs of *A Modern Utopia*, but *The New Machiavelli* immediately deflates such utopian expectations by pointing out that 'too abstract a dream of statesmanship' is bound to collapse when it is confronted with the necessary compromises of parliamentary politics (10). The title of Wells's novel accordingly invokes 'Machiavellianism' not just as a ready shorthand for ruthless political opportunism but as a name for the broader problem of translating political aspirations into

---

[102] Wells, *The New Machiavelli* (London: Penguin, 2005), p. 11. Further references are given parenthetically in the text.

reality. As Remington himself recognizes, modern politics is 'in a condition of affairs infinitely more complex' than the one described by Machiavelli, because 'power itself [...] has become more multitudinous, because it has dispersed itself and specialized' (12–13).

The necessity of effecting trade-offs between reformist aspiration and the pressures of *Realpolitik* reappear at all stages of Remington's *Bildung*. His early political convictions are inherited from his socialist father, who advocates a gradual and piecemeal approach to institutional reform—and the opening chapters of the novel show the compatibility of such reformist gradualism with the 'Hegelian' view of the state that is passed on to Remington by his college tutor Codger (92). In what appears to be a nod to the character of Henry Grey in Ward's *Robert Elsmere*, Codger's Hegelian idealism initially appeals to the young Remington because it allows him to see the state as a construct whose institutions embody a shared social ethos.[103] Remington's test case for this understanding of institutions is a new set of proposals for taxation reform: 'Local rates,' Remington notes apropos of the closing decades of the nineteenth century, 'became a common topic, a fact of accumulating importance' (37). Wells seems to have in mind the Fabian tracts of the 1880s, including important early contributions by Shaw, which had called for the institution of central municipal boards that would collect local rates and distribute the money where it was most needed. The money levied in this way, Shaw and other Fabians argued, would contribute to the common good by supporting public works and the construction of water and gas infrastructure. In stark contrast to this hopeful Fabian assessment of municipal governing bodies, the older Remington draws attention the grave shortcomings of this system: far from implementing a rational and scientific mode of governance, Remington points out, local boards tend to become mired in local conflicts, nepotism, and partisanship, thus exerting a 'corrupt and devastating rule' (23) over the urban populations they are intended to serve. Looking back to his youthful socialism and sympathetic view of Fabian schemes, the old Remington is struck by his naiveté: he admits that the purely 'intellectual convictions' he had acquired under Codger's academic tutelage were bound to founder once they became exposed to the reality of democratic 'social life as a multitudinous confusion out of hand' (92–3).

The young Remington's reformist hopes are briefly rekindled in 1894 by William Harcourt's government, 'whose Death Duties had seemed at first like a socialist dawn' (97). The death duties, though by no means a comprehensive realization of the socialists' utopian dreams of extensive fiscal redistribution, seem to mark the beginning of a shift away from the predominantly antagonistic class rhetoric of the 1880s. Recalling Wells's own enthusiasm for taxation reform in the 1890s and early 1900s, Remington specifically excoriates the Fabians for believing

---

[103] *The New Machiavelli* also cites Mary Ward ('Mrs Humphry Ward') as an influence on Remington's early thinking (97; 167).

in classes as fixed social categories. Such categorial 'types', Remington submits, exist only in the minds of dogmatic socialists:

> If [the Fabians] had the universe in hand I know they would take down all the trees and put up stamped tin green shades and sunlight accumulators. Altiora [Beatrice Webb] thought trees hopelessly irregular and sea cliffs a great mistake. [...] Though it was an Hegelian mess of which I had partaken at Codger's table by way of a philosophical training, my sympathies have always been Pragmatist. I belong almost by nature to that school of Pragmatism that, following the medieval Nominalists, bases itself upon a denial of the reality of classes, and of the validity of general laws.   (173–4)

Like 'The Scepticism of the Instrument' (the essay which Wells had appended to the first edition of A Modern Utopia), The New Machiavelli repeatedly mocks this language of classes and classifications as a crude form of political thinking. When Remington visits the room of a fellow undergraduate, he notices a socialist propaganda poster that sports the stereotypical image of a worker: to Remington's friend 'the figure upon his wall of a huge-muscled, black-haired toiler swaggering sledge-hammer in hand across a revolutionary barricade, seemed the quintessence of what he had to expound' (98). The larger-than-life figure of the worker, Remington contemptuously notes, embodies a naïve and 'melodramatic' (99) view of class relations. In an echo of 'The Scepticism of the Instrument', it is only when Remington revises his belief in classificatory systems in light of a modern awareness of 'uniqueness' that he learns to see social reality as a field of mobile and changeable (kinetic) social relations rather than as the clash of (static) social types. Remington's development here clearly parallels Wells's and Money's shift from a Marxisant focus on class conflict towards the vision of a socio-economic system that is susceptible to immanent transformation by way of fine-grained fiscal taxonomies.

Remington derides the apparent crudeness of the Webbs' classist thinking, partly because, at this point in his political Bildung, he is still convinced that institutions must be understood as embodiments of what A Modern Utopia had called a 'common idea'. The importance of a lived ethos of responsibilities and obligations that is materialized in institutions finds expression in the discussions that Remington has with his friend Willersley during a walking holiday in Switzerland. Remington notes admiringly that his friend

> has lived for social service and to do vast masses of useful, undistinguished, fertilising work. Think of the days of arid administrative plodding and of contention still more arid and unrewarded, that he must have spent! [...] He does it without any fee or reward except his personal self-satisfaction in doing this work, and he does it without any hope of future joys and punishments.
>
> (113–14)

The setting in the Swiss Alps recalls the precise moment at which *A Modern Utopia* had pivoted into a speculative reformist mode that combined the novel's utopian impulse with a mimetic, patiently descriptive one. In an apparent nod to Wells's 1905 book, *The New Machiavelli* briefly modulates into a utopian register:

> We planned half in earnest and half Utopianising, a League of Social Service. [...] We talked of the splendid world of men that might grow out of such unpaid and ill-paid work as we were setting our faces to do. We spoke of the intricate difficulties, the monstrous passive resistances, the hostilities to such a development as we conceived our work subserved, and we spoke with that underlying confidence in the invincibility of the causes we adopted that is natural to young and scarcely tried men.   (114–15)

In contrast to *A Modern Utopia*, these utopian passages in *The New Machiavelli* are explicitly flagged for our attention. The fact that they are interspersed into a predominantly realist, biographical narrative creates zones of local generic ambiguity that signal the coexistence in Wells's text of two divergent languages—one legal and the other legislative, as it were: 'We could not tell from minute to minute', Remington notes, 'whether we were planning for a world of solid reality, or telling ourselves fairy tales about this prospect of life' (117). Remington's dismissive comment about 'fairy tales', written retrospectively from the position of his later conservative politics, indicates how far he has come from the idealist and aspirational ('legislative') reformism of his youth.

The young Remington eventually decides to enter parliamentary politics—a decision that marks the key moment in his realpolitikal *Bildung*. After being voted into parliament on the Liberal ticket in 1905—'follow[ing] the return of Mr Campbell-Bannerman to power'—Remington's first political battles take him straight to the frontlines of contemporary politics. In his speeches Remington pits his ambitious vision of fiscal redistribution against the Conservatives' defence of old wealth. However, his speeches receive a lukewarm reception, even among his own party peers:

> I spoke [...] of the splendid projects and possibilities of life and order that lay before the world, of all that a resolute and constructive effort might do at the present time. "We are building a state," I said, "secure and splendid, we are in the dawn of the great age of mankind." Sometimes that would get a solitary "'Ear, 'ear!" (209)

The fact that Remington gives this impassioned reformist speech in 1905—the year in which *A Modern Utopia* was published—invites us to read his idealism as a coded representation of Wells's own reformist ambitions at the time. In contrast to Wells's Edwardian trilogy, however, *The New Machiavelli* shows that such utopianism becomes stymied by tactical political trade-offs. Parliamentary politics, Remington concludes when his speeches fall on deaf ears among his own party, is 'a kind of dogfight'. As he becomes wise to parliamentary tactics, Remington falls in line with his party's conservative wing and begins to parrot its defence of the absolute sanctity of private wealth.[104] When he eventually defects from the ranks of the party, he does so over the People's Budget, whose overall redistributive thrust is now much too radical for his taste:

> I made my breach with the party on the Budget.
>
> In many ways I was disposed to regard the 1909 Budget as a fine piece of statecraft. Its production was certainly a very unexpected display of vigour on the Liberal side. But, on the whole, this movement towards collectivist organisation on the part of the Liberals rather strengthened than weakened my resolve to cross the floor of the house. [...] I did object most strenuously to the idea of [...] attempting to produce beneficial social results through the pressure of taxation upon the land-owning class. [...] The drift of the government proposals was all in the direction of sweating the landowner to get immediate values from his property, and such a course of action was bound to give us an irritated and vindictive land-owning class, the class upon which we had hitherto relied—not unjustifiably—for certain broad, patriotic services.   (308)

The passage subverts any direct biographical analogy between Remington and Wells: whereas Wells was in sympathy with the proposals of the Liberal Party's radical wing, Remington is terrified that taxes on landed property will turn this formerly stable source of wealth into just another form of fungible, kinetic income.[105] Such economic reforms, Remington now believes, will lead to the demise of the old national elites and their reliable stewardship of the country's cultural, social, and political affairs.

Remington is now ready to undergo the last of his political metamorphoses. As a way of furthering his career, he decides to change party affiliation again, aligning himself with the Conservative Party which (he believes) embodies 'established responsibility' and 'established propertied interest' (257). While Remington's growing disappointment with parliamentary politics mirrors Wells's own disillusionment with the Liberal Party as the principal agent of institutional change, Wells presents Remington's volte face as a purely opportunistic political move that

---

[104] Remington also starts to look more kindly on Joseph Chamberlain's proposals for Tariff Reform. Tariff Reform was in some respects taxation reform's jingoistic and aggressively protectionist sibling: intended to boost trading relations within the British Empire through a system of protectionist taxes, it appealed to nationalist and imperialist sentiments that Wells himself tended to regard with much scepticism. Like Remington, Chamberlain had over the course of his career traversed the political spectrum, moving from radical Liberalism to Conservative imperialism.

[105] Toye, 'Wells and the New Liberalism', p. 171.

paradoxically leads him to see England's old, landed elites as the embodiment of the nation's future. Remington retreats into a politically regressive anti-utopia in which old wealth is so venerated—and where traditional ways of life are so passionately embraced—that the need for progressive reform never even seems to arise.[106] This nostalgic vision bears more than a passing resemblance to the conservative anti-capitalism of contemporaneous Christian polemicists such as Hilaire Belloc, whose *The Servile State* (1912) lamented the passing of the organic forms of communal life he associated with the Catholic middle ages. Similar to Belloc's thinking, Remington's defence of time-honoured traditions imagines a social world in which existing forms of life are so tightly integrated with established institutions that there don't seem to be any openings for future-directed critique.[107]

For a few decades around 1900 the cause of institutional reform seemed to be endowed with an almost utopian aura, and Wells's works—including the loose trilogy consisting of *Anticipations, Mankind in the Making*, and *A Modern Utopia*—reflect and amplify this reformist excitement. However, Wells's speculative association of new and socially integrative institutions with a new redistributive ethos of sharing remained fragile. For one, following his departure from the Fabian Society in 1908, it seems to have been unclear to Wells which political organization would offer the right institutional home for his reformist ambitions: if the Edwardian trilogy had begun to formulate a maximalist (planetary) answer to this question, *The New Machiavelli* offers us a claustrophobic vision of parliamentary infighting. But Wells's reformist vision was also threatened by spasmodic returns of the class conflicts he had depicted in his early scientific romances. One particularly dramatic instance of national unrest occurred in 1911, around the time of the publication of *The New Machiavelli*, when the recently established Transport Workers' Federation decided to support a sailors' strike at the Port of London. The event soon escalated into a national strike during which the nation's main ports and railway networks ground to a standstill. Wells commented on the volatile domestic situation in an essay published in May 1912:

---

[106] This conservative anti-utopia, which celebrates the old landed elites, has its ideological counterpart in the politically progressive 'Constructors' hailed in Wells's Edwardian trilogy. Remington himself discovers in his new Toryism elements of the static utopias of 'Plato or [...] More' (279) that Wells had derided in *A Modern Utopia*.

[107] We should not underestimate the potential critical dimension of this medievalism—a fact prominently illustrated by the recent work of Giorgio Agamben, who finds in Christian (Franciscan) monasticism the model of a non-alienated praxis of living that 'call[s] into question' the very assumption of 'norms as separate from life' (Agamben, *The Highest Poverty: Monastic Rules and Form-of-Life* [Stanford: Stanford University Press, 2013], p. 60). What Wells would object to in Belloc (and also, one can assume, in Agamben) is the fundamentally anti-progressivist thrust of their medievalism—a principled political objection that echoes Carpenter's opposition to the medievalism of William Morris (see Chapter 3).

Our country is, I think, in a dangerous state of social disturbance. The discontent of the labouring mass of the community is deep and increasing. It may be that we are in the opening phase of a real and irreparable class war.

Since the Coronation [of George V in 1910] we have moved very rapidly from an assurance of extreme social stability towards the recognition of a spreading disorganisation.[108]

Wells's article betrays a disillusionment with the reparative potential of institutional reform that closely mirrors the various political disappointments recorded in *The New Machiavelli*. Yet even after the seemingly halcyon days of the Edwardian decade had ended, Wells did not completely abandon his belief in the integrative potential of social reform at a national level. In 1923, for example, following the cataclysm of World War I, Wells once more turned to taxation as a non-disruptive means of social reconstruction. A 'more general diffusion of spending power' might be achieved, Wells reasoned, by raising new levies on capital: such taxes could be 'applied mainly to the relief of the taxation of the ordinary man, and so it will release money for ordinary spending'.[109] Wells crucially no longer couches the role of the state vis-à-vis the economy in moral terms (of fairness, equality, or equal opportunity). Instead, his comments echo what became the new orthodoxy regarding the role of the state in the years after 1918. This new economic orthodoxy was variously articulated in the interwar decades by J. A. Hobson, John Maynard Keyes, and others. It responded to the dire conditions of post-war economic austerity and to the remoter threat of social revolution that emanated from the revolutionary events of 1917 by framing the role of the nation-state in narrowly economistic language, stressing the state's function in stimulating consumer demand (what Wells refers to as 'spending power') rather than its responsibility to promote social justice. It was partly in opposition to this more restricted economic understanding of the nation-state that Wells's post-war writings began to develop the programmatic vision of the world state familiar to most critics today. In the imaginative space that was opened up by the idea of a planetary state, Wells was at liberty to reactivate key elements of his Edwardian thinking that had been temporarily eclipsed by the environment of post-war economic austerity—including the aspirational understanding of the state in terms of an ethos of active citizenship and a shared orientation towards the common good.

---

[108] Wells, 'The Labour Unrest', in Wells, *An Englishman Looks at the World*, pp. 43–94 (p. 43).
[109] Wells, 'To the Electors of the London University General Election, November 1923', in *Correspondence of H. G. Wells*, vol. 3, pp. 159–62.

5

Welfare State Romance

E. M. Forster and Unemployment Insurance

E. M. Forster's works have long been celebrated for espousing an ethos of fellowship that gives due weight to individual liberty while also recognizing the importance of human solidarity and sociability. According to this popular reading, Forster's novels embody a form of democratic egalitarianism that leaves enough room for individuality—what Wells had called 'uniqueness'—to flourish. 'Two people pulling each other into salvation,' Forster explained in 1930, 'is the only theme I find worthwhile.'[1] Forster's fiction offers many variations on the theme of solidarity which extends across the divides of age, class, and race—from the homoerotic cross-class attraction described in *Maurice* (1913–14) to the comradeship that connects Cyril Fielding and Dr Aziz in *The Passage to India* (1924). The codification of this particular reading of Forster's work is inextricably connected to the disciplinary history of literary studies: it was in the context of the 1940s and 1950s that the celebration of a distinctly 'Forsterian' ethos made it possible for critics to turn him into the patron saint of a revisionist literary historiography that sought to keep open a space for artistic production outside the ideological Cold War binary of (consumerist) individualism and collectivist homogeneity.[2] Recent scholarship has highlighted the stark limitations of this critical account by drawing attention to the conjunctural and situational preconditions—ranging from the exclusive (and almost exclusively male) circles of pre-1914 Cambridge to the vaster subtexts of British imperialism—that made it possible for Forsterian fellowship to double as the model for a democratic polity in the first place.[3] And yet, these recent critical interventions notwithstanding, the overall picture of Forster's ethical commitments has remained remarkably intact.

Readings which emphasize Forster's special artistic advocacy of fellowship tend to bracket questions of political rationality and structural reform by suggesting that Forster showed comparatively little interest in systemic questions of

---

[1] Forster, *Commonplace Book*, ed. Philip Gardner (Stanford: Stanford University Press, 1985), p. 64.

[2] See, most notably, Lionel Trilling's wartime celebration of Forster (*E. M. Forster* [New York: New Directions, 1943]), which became the nucleus for Trilling's later exploration of the 'liberal imagination'.

[3] See, e.g., Lois Cucullu, 'Shepherds in the parlor: Forster's Apostles, pagans, and native sons', *NOVEL* 32.1 (1998): 19–50; Jesse Matz, 'Masculinity amalgamated: Colonialism, homosexuality, and Forster's Kipling', *Journal of Modern Literature* 30.3 (2007): 31–52; and Janice Ho, *Nation and Citizenship in the Twentieth-Century Novel* (Cambridge: Cambridge University Press, 2015), pp. 25–58.

British Literature and the Life of Institutions: Speculative States. Benjamin Kohlmann, Oxford University Press.
© Benjamin Kohlmann 2021. DOI: 10.1093/oso/9780198836179.003.0006

socio-economic organization.[4] Such questions—much like the institutional structures of the state itself—will by necessity appear external to the vital spontaneity of personal connections. In an influential account of Forster's scepticism vis-à-vis institutional reform, Michael Levenson has observed that in the early 1900s Forster's preference was very clearly for the 'negative freedom' defended by nineteenth-century liberals rather than for the 'positive freedom' Levenson associates with the 'collectivist' projects of the New Liberalism. Forster, argues Levenson, 'sees crumbling around him that "new liberalism" [. . .] with its plans for continued legislative reform on a large scale. And when Forster holds on to his individualism, he places himself in effect at an earlier stage of liberal ideology when the emphasis had fallen upon the removal of constraints': '[F]aced with these alternatives, he unhesitatingly chooses private before public, friend before country.'[5]

Forster himself did much to encourage this particular reading of his novels when he famously described himself as belonging to the 'fag-end of liberalism',[6] and there has consequently been a tendency to underestimate the extent to which Forster's early artistic preoccupation with personal ties was mediated by an attention to questions of institutional reform. As Lauren Goodlad reminds us, however, Forster's remark about his 'fag-end' liberalism was made late in life (in 1946), and it must be understood as an articulation of Forster's 'growing unease with the bureaucracy of the [post-1945] welfare state' rather than as an oblique comment on the reformist debates of the Edwardian years.[7] The present chapter addresses this particular nexus by suggesting that Forster's Edwardian novels offer complex engagements with the period's reformist literary mode. Instead of rejecting state-centred institutional reform, I argue, these texts imagine new state institutions as integral infrastructural supports for individual flourishing and as intimately woven into the fabric of social life itself.

The works that Forster wrote around 1910 specifically engage with the heated public debates that surrounded the passing of the National Insurance Act in 1911. The National Insurance Act included provisions for ill health and unemployment

---

[4] The phrase 'universal brotherhood' recurs with some frequency in Forster's writings of the early 1900s. Forster's 'Locked Diary' offers a detailed chronicle of his appropriation of Whitman's and Carpenter's ethos of brotherhood; see *The Journals and Diaries of E. M. Forster*, ed. Philip Gardner, vol. 2: *The Locked Diary* (London: Pickering and Chatto, 2011). It is only in the intimate and sheltered 'democracy of the caffè', Forster noted in *Where Angels Fear to Tread* (1905), that 'the brotherhood of man' can become 'a reality'. Forster, *Where Angels Fear to Tread* (London: Arnold, 1975), p. 36.

[5] Levenson, *Modernism and the Fate of Individuality: Character and Novelistic Form from Conrad to Woolf* (Cambridge: Cambridge University Press, 1991), pp. 87–8.

[6] Forster, 'The challenge of our time', in *Two Cheers for Democracy* (New York: Harcourt, 1951), pp. 54–8 (p. 56).

[7] 'At the launch of his literary career,' Goodlad adds, 'Forster had supported the political innovations of contemporaries such as G. M. Trevelyan and [the radical New Liberal] C. F. G. Masterman.' Goodlad, *The Victorian Geopolitical Aesthetic: Realism, Sovereignty, and Transnational Experience* (New York: Oxford University Press, 2015), p. 208.

in several trades, and it was widely perceived, across the political spectrum, as a step in the direction of more comprehensive forms of welfare provision. This chapter reads *Howards End* (1910) alongside some of Forster's other literary and non-literary works from the period, including the novel fragment *Arctic Summer* on which Forster began to work shortly after completing *Howards End* and which he soon abandoned for reasons I will explore later. Forster's writing during these years is informed by reflections on what *Howards End* calls 'preparedness'—that is, by the attempt to set up institutional safeguards that will protect vulnerable members of society against the systemic risk of unemployment. As Michael Szalay has pointed out, we should not treat questions of national insurance as a narrowly technical or merely actuarial matter: social insurance is an 'answer not simply to unemployment and other economic exigencies, but far more broadly, to the displacing conditions of modern life in a rapidly evolving capitalist society'.[8] *Howards End*, which understands human suffering in these more expansive terms, is the closest Forster came to writing a welfare state novel. While the topical question of unemployment insurance and the broader concern over the extension of statal mandates are rarely thematized explicitly in Forster's novels, we do not need to read Forster's work against the grain in order to make visible the impress of these debates. Instead, my reading indicates that central generic parameters of Forster's work—what we could call the strain of welfare state romance in Forster's later Edwardian writings—echo the speculative and aspirational dimensions of the reformist literary mode.

Dystopia, Reform, and the Welfare State

Critics who choose to discuss Forster's engagement with the state and its (executive, judicial, and legislative) institutions usually remark that he was wary of the mechanisms of coercion and supervision that he associated with centralized government. One commentator has noted that Forster's fictional and non-fictional writings seek to dispel any belief 'in the discrete reality of the state': Forster regards the nation-state not 'as an entity in itself with [...] interests to be protected, but simply as a sum total of individual citizens.'[9] Such claims seem to be borne out by 'The Machine Stops', the short story which Forster composed around the time he began to work on *Howards End*. First published in 1909, and later collected in Forster's 1928 short story volume *The Eternal Moment*, 'The Machine

---

[8] Szalay's study concerns the literary history of the American welfare state in the 1930s and 1940s, but central aspects of his discussion also apply to the historical contexts explored here. See his *New Deal Modernism: American Literature and the Invention of the Welfare State* (Durham, NC: Duke University Press, 2000), p. 8.

[9] Frederick Crews, *E. M. Forster: The Perils of Humanism* (Princeton: Princeton University Press, 1962), p. 22.

Stops' has become known for being Forster's main contribution to the genre of dystopian fiction. There has been much disagreement about the precise targets of Forster's satire, with critics pointing to fields as diverse as communication technology, biomedicine, and organization theory.[10] Like many other twentieth-century dystopias, however, 'The Machine Stops' also addresses itself to a theme that is foundational to many of these more specific targets—the idea of the strong state.

Set in a remote future, in the aftermath of a catastrophe that has made the surface of the earth unfit for human habitation, Forster depicts human society as atomized and dispersed, with individuals living in isolation from one another in underground cells. The 'machine'—'humm[ing] eternally' and operated by a sinister 'Central Committee' who use it for purposes of supervision and thought control—has been identified as a prescient statement on the twentieth century's totalitarian regimes.[11] In this context, the decision of the central character, Kuno, to escape from his cell in order to visit the surface of the Earth, indicates the defiant assertion of an irrepressible self, a liberating escape from the tightly regulated constraints of technological modernity. 'The Machine Stops' suggests that Kuno's breakout from this latter-day Platonic cave is the result of his unquenchable desire for real human contact ('I want to see you not through the machine', Kuno tells his mother; (173)), and his escape is intended to remind us that any form of technological progress will need to be responsive to human needs. 'Man is the measure', Kuno affirms: 'That was my first lesson. Man's feet are the measure for distance, his hands are the measure for ownership, his body is the measure for all that is lovable and desirable and strong'. (197) The text entertains the possibility that technology might be restored to human proportions and that it can in principle function as a device by which humans comprehend and relate to the world. However, Kuno's reassertion of his humanity—and his attempts to 'reintroduce the personal element' (223) to counteract the atomization effected by this fully technicized society—are promptly censored by the Central Committee. Kuno is threatened with 'Homelessness', that is, with banishment from the underground hive. Forster's apparent critique of totalitarian institutions, as well as his attention to the atomizing consequences of hypermediated environments, seem to offer such a prescient anticipation of the authoritarian nightmare depicted in George Orwell's *Nineteen Eighty-Four* (1948) that the story's resonances with its own more immediate historical contexts have often gone unnoticed.

---

[10] See Gorman Beauchamp, 'Technology in the dystopian novel', *Modern Fiction Studies* 32.1 (1986): 53–63; Mark Decker, 'Politicized dystopia and biomedical imaginaries: The case of "The Machine Stops"', in *New Boundaries in Political Science Fiction*, ed. Donald M. Hassler and Clyde Wilcox (Columbia: University of South Carolina Press, 2008), pp. 53–63; and Paul March-Russell, '"Imagine, if you can": Love, time, and the impossibility of utopia in E. M. Forster's "The Machine Stops"', *Critical Survey* 17.1 (2005): 56–72.

[11] Forster, 'The Machine Stops', in *The Celestial Omnibus & The Eternal Moment* (New York: Harcourt Brace, 1998), pp. 171–231 (p. 180). Further page numbers are given in the main text.

This includes Forster's keen interest in the question whether the expansion of social welfare policies mooted during the Edwardian years would act as an institutional scaffold that supported individual and collective welfare, or whether this new social legislation would constrain the space available for individual expression.

Kuno's mother, Vashti, reveres the machine as a life-sustaining and life-enhancing mechanism. There is 'one book', we are told, which she keeps always 'by her side, on the little reading-desk' in her cell: 'This was the Book of the Machine. In it were instructions against every possible contingency. If she was hot or cold or dyspeptic or at a loss for a word, she went to the book, and it told her which button to press. The Central Committee published it.' (179) During the Edwardian years, public discussion about the implementation of national insurance and the introduction of unemployment benefits often presented these new provisions as so many types of institutional 'machinery'. For example, William Beveridge—Forster's friend and arguably the most prominent proponent of welfare reform in twentieth-century Britain—called for 'the extension of the whole or part of this machinery [of state-organized insurance]', adding the proviso that certain 'details of administration and machinery must be left to be filled in by practice'.[12] Similar references to 'The Machinery of the [National Insurance] Act', along with calls for new kinds of 'Administrative Machinery', can be found across many of the book-length interventions by Orme Clarke, A. S. Pringle, and other prominent participants in the debate about national insurance.[13] Forster echoes this language in his 1909 story, presenting the 'machine' as a grotesque combination of air conditioner, radiator, and mandatory health-service. At the same time, 'The Machine Stops' interweaves this new reformist language with a line of critique which runs through several of Forster's works from the period and which suggests that the attempt to make life immune to 'every possible contingency' is typical of a middle-class mindset fearful of risk and the unforeseen. 'Our life today', Forster complained in an essay on 'The Poems of Kipling' (1908), 'is so sheltered, so safe, [...] so guarded on all sides from all that may injure the body or disturb the soul.'[14] *Howards End* similarly takes aim at the idea of 'preparedness': '[w]ith infinite effort we nerve ourselves for a crisis that never comes', Forster writes: 'the most unsuccessful [life] is not that of the man who is taken unprepared, but of him who has prepared and is never taken. On a tragedy of that kind our national morality is duly silent. It assumes that preparation against danger is

---

[12] See Beveridge, *Unemployment: A Problem of Industry*, 2nd ed. (London: Longmans, 1910), pp. 164, 193, *passim*.

[13] Orme Clarke, *The National Insurance Act 1911* (London: Butterworth, 1912), esp. pp. lxxxiii-xc; Pringle, *The National Insurance Act, 1911: Explained, Annotated, and Indexed* (Edinburgh: W. Green, 1912), esp. pp. 12–23.

[14] Forster, 'The poems of Kipling', in *The Creator as Critic and Other Writings* ed. Jeffrey M. Heath (Toronto: Dundurn Press, 2008), pp. 26–40 (p. 27).

in itself a good.'[15] *Howards End* and the essay on Kipling—along with a series of similar observations littered across Forster's writing of the period—offer pointed comments on the institutionalization of social welfare in the early 1900s, and I will return to them in more detail later in this chapter. At this point in my discussion, I invoke these remarks only briefly in order to indicate Forster's concern that institutional safeguards which protect human life against external forces can become a hindrance to individual flourishing when they are wrongly regarded as 'in [themselves] a good'. It is when 'preparedness' calcifies into a mental habit that fetishizes the sheltered life (as in the case of Vashti) that we become alienated from life itself, including the benign kinds of risk—ranging from the thrill of aesthetic pleasure to the serendipity of human encounters—that Forster thought we should welcome into our lives.

The satirical thrust of 'The Machine Stops' extends to what Forster regarded as the potentially self-perpetuating quality of reformist activity. The idea that existing institutional structures keep being adjusted and reconfigured—to the point where such technocratic improvements become an entirely self-serving exercise— is ironized in Forster's story, where a so-called 'Mending Machine' is tasked with fixing bugs that affect the machine's central apparatus. For example, when certain defects in the main machine's 'sleeping apparatus' become too inconvenient ('the beds, when summoned by their tired owners, failed to appear' (223)),

> [t]he Committee responsible for the failure was assailed by complainants, whom it referred, as usual, to the Committee of the Mending Apparatus, who in its turn assured them that their complaints would be forwarded to the Central Committee. But the discontent grew, for mankind was not yet sufficiently adaptable to do without sleeping. [...] But the Committee of the Mending Apparatus now came forward, and allayed the panic with well-chosen words. It confessed that the Mending Apparatus was itself in need of repair. The effect of this frank confession was admirable. (223–4)

As second- and third-order troubleshooting apparatuses, the Mending Machine and the machines that fix the Mending Machine describe the kind of uncoupling of technological rationality from human concerns that Forster feared most. The main machine has long ceased to serve its original function of sustaining human life, yet paradoxically this seems to make it more and more indispensable and unassailable: against Vashti's 'talk' that 'a god made the Machine', Kuno objects— to no avail—that '[m]en made it, do not forget that. Great men, but men. The Machine is much, but it is not everything' (173–4).

---

[15] Forster, *Howards End*, ed. Paul B. Armstrong (New York: Norton, 1998), p. 79.

In the early 1900s multiple socio-historical vectors converged to create a context in which the introduction of state-mandated contributory insurance could be advanced as a viable political option. Following the experience of mass unemployment during the so-called Long Depression of 1873–96, the National Insurance Act of 1911 undertook to systematize the more local forms of insurance provision that had previously been offered by trade unions and mutual societies. At the same time, building on the flurry of urban exploration literature of the 1880s and 1890s, new books—prominently among them the collection *From the Abyss* (1902) by Forster's friend C. F. G. Masterman—were drawing attention to the terrifying scenes of East End unemployment that made such new insurance schemes necessary. Lloyd George admitted that he had been especially impressed by the 'superb scheme' of centralized insurance he learned about during a visit to Germany in 1908: several decades later, Beveridge could still recall Lloyd George's budget speech of April 1909, in which Lloyd George had called for Britain to put itself 'in this field on a level with Germany' and adding that 'we should not emulate [Germany] only in armaments'.[16] Lloyd George's comment creates a link between the German warfare and (proto-)welfare states, and it is not difficult to detect in 'The Machine Stops' a suspicion of this troubling convergence between two languages of institutional reform—one emphasizing the ethical imperatives of cross-class responsibility and care, and the other calling for forms of military technocratic efficiency. These languages were joined emblematically in Bismarckian Germany—never more so than in the Wilhelmine years leading up to World War I—and it did not require Richard Haldane's enthusiastic Prussophilia to remind Edwardian political commentators of this link.[17] 'The Machine Stops' presents the growth of institutional structures as a rigid imposition on (and negation of) the organic spontaneity of human life, and the various rules to which the citizens of Forster's dystopian society are expected to conform double as a parody of Prussian-style law and order policies.

Many of Forster's literary engagements with state-centred reform tended to be satirical. Even so, it seems that as debates about the necessity of national insurance gathered political momentum around 1910, Forster felt the need to revise his default approach to the topic by developing formal resources that made it possible for him to think through arguments in favour of welfarist reform. Central to this artistic project, I suggest, was Forster's attempt to imagine the centralized provision of care not as a set of administrative machine-like procedures or bureaucratic mechanisms, but as the embodiment of a new and collective ethos of mutual responsibility. *Howards End* is the text in which Forster begins to experiment with a speculative reformist idiom that pictures emerging institutional structures in terms of the new *Lebensformen* which they will nourish.

[16] Beveridge, *Power and Influence* (London: Hodder and Stoughton, 1953), p. 80.
[17] See Chapter 1 for discussion of Haldane's Prussophilia and his calls for a 'Hegelian Army'.

Blaming the System: *Howards End* and the 'Abyss of Unemployment'

If Lloyd George's appeals to Bismarckian Prussia and Haldane's philosophically amped-up militarism were unappealing to Forster, other routes were available that made it possible for him to enter into Edwardian conversations about national insurance. One entrée into these debates was provided by the work of Goldsworthy Lowes Dickinson, Forster's close friend and former mentor at King's College, Cambridge. Dickinson exerted a great intellectual influence on Forster, through his philosophical writings as well as through his personal example as a (homosexual) member of the Bloomsbury Group. Dickinson's early works had leaned on an idiosyncratic reading of (Neo-)Platonic philosophy in order to advocate tolerance in face of a plurality of individual ethical ends. By contrast, Dickinson's books of the early 1900s began to articulate a more substantive understanding of the common good that was irreducible to the mere sum total of individual wills or desires. This line of argument, which Dickinson presented in several publications, including *The Meaning of Good* (1901), went significantly beyond the Paterian hedonism he had previously embraced. Cast in the form of a Platonic dialogue, the central section of *The Meaning of Good* offers some discussion of the idea of 'A General Good':

> "You assert, then, that everyone's Good is distinct from everyone else's, and that there is no common Good; but that each one's pursuit of his own Good is essential to the realization of the Good of all the rest."
>
> "Yes," [Parry] said; "roughly, that is the kind of thing I believe."
>
> "Well, but," I continued, "on that system there is at least one thing which we shall have to call a common Good."
>
> "And what is that?"
>
> "Society itself! For society is the condition indispensable to all alike for the realization of any individual Good; and a common condition of Good is, I suppose, in a sense, a common Good."[18]

This passage mediates individuality and society by showing that the realization of individual desires never takes place outside the sphere of the social. Dickinson here goes beyond a mere proclamation of universal brotherhood which (on Dickinson's account) would entail an impossible and quasi-mystical union of individual interests; but he also critiques the radical version of negative freedom proposed by '[m]en like Bentham', whose philosophy entitled individuals to

---

[18] Dickinson, *The Meaning of Good: A Dialogue*, 3rd ed. (London: Brimley, 1906), p. 28.

'sharpen [their] wits and fill [their] pocket[s]' (23). In contrast to these extreme positions, Dickinson presents society itself as the 'common Good'—as a kind of necessary background condition that enables citizens to pursue their own ends.

It seems that Dickinson's new philosophical interest in the idea of the common good was sparked in part by the work of the British Hegelians, notably by the writings of John M. E. McTaggart, whose books Dickinson had been studying.[19] Hedonism is unthinkable without negative freedom, yet the 'society' which Dickinson identifies as the 'indispensable condition' of human self-realization is not simply reducible to the economic individualism Hegel had presented as the defining feature of *bürgerliche Gesellschaft*.[20] Indeed, Dickinson shows a greater interest in the state as the third and culminating aspect Hegelian *Sittlichkeit*: he goes on to suggest, for example, that the institutional formation of the state can be understood as a mode of social life in its own right—although his arguments here invoke Aristotle's theorization of the ethos of the city-state rather than Hegel's speculative arguments in the *Philosophy of Right* (53–4). As Dickinson clarifies elsewhere in *The Meaning of Good*, and as the passage cited above suggests, his attempts to link individual and collective by way of a capacious notion of the 'social' do not propagate an organicist belief in the (quasi-natural) congruence of individual and collective values. Instead, he is anxious to make room for an elaboration of the institutional forms of the 'State [. . .] as a thing apart, towards the maintenance of which conscious efforts may be directed' (119).

Dickinson's thinking is relevant to the present discussion because it sheds light on one of the intellectual sources for Forster's literary engagement with the 'common Good' and with the state as a shared form of life. Reframing Forster's Edwardian writings in this way also helps to direct attention away from competing philosophical models of the 'good' that have dominated critical accounts of Bloomsbury modernism, including most prominently G. E. Moore's insistence on the radical indefinability of the 'good'.[21] In contrast to Moore's thinking, Dickinson's notion of the 'common Good'—including his argument that 'conscious efforts' must be expended in the reform of the state—implies that the

---

[19] In his intellectual biography of J. M. E. McTaggart, Dickinson recalls attending McTaggart's Cambridge lectures on Hegel in the 1890s, and also professes an interest in Hegel's idealism. McTaggart, who was Dickinson's senior by three years, became his close friend. See Dickinson's biography *J. McT. E. McTaggart* (Cambridge: Cambridge University Press, 1931), pp. 53–4, 84–5. McTaggart's *Studies in Hegelian Cosmology* (1901) opened with a Preface that declared its author's 'indebtedness' to Dickinson and thanked him for commenting on the manuscript of the book.

[20] As Hegel had pointed out, the economic orientation of *bürgerliche Gesellschaft* tended to produce a disenfranchised and exploited 'rabble' (*Pöbel*) that was effectively barred from full participation in society: the *Pöbel*, Dickinson might say, is excluded from the common good. See Hegel, *Grundlinien der Philosophie des Rechts* (Frankfurt/Main: Suhrkamp, 1986), pp. 389–90 (§ 244).

[21] For Michael Levenson's important account of Moore's influence on early modernism, see his *A Genealogy of Modernism: A Study of English Literary Doctrine, 1908–1922* (Cambridge: Cambridge University Press, 1984), pp. 92–4. For a more specific treatment of Moore's influence on Forster, see David Sidorsky, 'The uses of the philosophy of G. E. Moore in the works of E. M. Forster', *New Literary History* 38.2 (2007): 245–71.

(infra)structural conditions which enable the realization of individual goods can be described with some degree of specificity. It was in this spirit that reformers around 1900 were proposing a series of adjustments to the structure of the state that included the guarding against financial monopolies, the question of land ownership, the introduction of new types of graduated and progressive taxation, and the implementation of unemployment insurance. Dickinson's text helped to direct Forster's attention towards the value of structural reform while also highlighting that it was possible to think about state institutions as intimately bound up with the sphere of the social.

Forms of private insurance, including different types of fire, property, and life insurance, had been well-established features of British life throughout the nineteenth century. Britain dominated the international insurance trade until World War I, and its domestic market for insurance was the world's largest.[22] By contrast, many unemployment schemes in Britain were being operated as trusts by mutual societies and trade unions.[23] Numerous scholars, including François Ewald, Pierre Rosanvallon, and Anthony Giddens have pointed out that these trusts formed some of the nuclei from which the institutions of the British welfare state were able to grow.[24] The national unemployment insurance that was passed by British parliament in 1911 was limited to trades in which unemployment occurred in cyclical (seasonal) fashion, yet these nationalized insurance models also marked the beginning of a systematic expansion of older mutual-aid schemes to larger risk collectives. Forster's exploration of 'preparedness' in *Howards End* centres on the lower-middle-class character of Leonard Bast, and Leonard's occupation—he works as an insurance clerk at the fictional 'Porphyrion Fire Insurance Company' in London—provides a textual clue that Forster was in fact entering the debate about insurance and unemployment benefits. Fire insurance had been at the forefront of the British insurance business since the seventeenth century, and by the nineteenth century it had come to be closely associated with the growing risks of industrial modernity.[25] Edwardian advocates of unemployment benefits frequently pointed to the success story of fire insurance as a possible template for nationalized health and unemployment insurance. As one contributor to the *Westminster Review* remarked in 1909: 'Labour is much more liable to

---

[22] Robin Pearson, *Insuring the Industrial Revolution: Fire Insurance in Great Britain* (Aldershot: Ashgate, 2004), p. 365.

[23] See, for example, Robert L. Carter and Peter Falush, *The British Insurance Industry since 1900: The Era of Transformation* (London: Palgrave Macmillan, 2009), p. 9; and Derek Fraser, *The Evolution of the British Welfare State: A History of Social Policy since the Industrial Revolution*, 4th ed. (London: Palgrave Macmillan, 2009), esp. pp. 129–31.

[24] See François Ewald, *L'État providence* (Paris: Grasset, 1986); Pierre Rosanvallon, *The New Social Question: Rethinking the Welfare State* (Princeton: Princeton University Press, 2000); and Anthony Giddens, 'Risk and responsibility', *The Modern Law Review* 62.1 (1999): 1–10.

[25] Paul Fyfe, 'Accidents of a novel trade: Industrial catastrophe, fire insurance, and *Mary Barton*', *Nineteenth-Century Literature* 65.3 (2010): 315–47 (p. 320).

unemployment than property is to fire.'[26] The same article went on to explain that unemployment was in most cases the outcome of systemic forces which lay outside the control of individuals: 'the unemployed are not a fixed and regular quantity—not an army always composed of the same units. […] The unemployed of today may be the employed of to-morrow, and the employed of to-day may be the unemployed of to-morrow.'[27] The article echoes a common early twentieth-century argument in favour of national insurance by indicating that the existence of an unemployed reserve army of labour is one of capitalism's constitutive flaws—a social burden that needs to be distributed equally on the shoulders of all citizens rather than weighing only on the unemployed themselves. Jason Puskar notes that late nineteenth- and early twentieth-century debates about insurance 'help[ed] produce complex conversations about culpability and causation' and that these conversations in turn entered the period's literary discourses.[28] In analogous fashion, *Howards End* turns to the case of Leonard Bast—who loses his job as an insurance clerk and finds himself hard up and unemployed, destroyed by forces partly outside his control—in order to engage questions of systemic risk as well as debates about the distribution of ethical and economic responsibility in structurally complex capitalist societies.

One of the main plotlines of *Howards End* concerns the attempt of the bohemian upper-middle-class Schlegel sisters, Helen and Margaret, to make the downtrodden Leonard the object of their charity. Leonard's acquaintance with the Schlegel sisters begins with a chance encounter. Having briefly met the sisters at a Beethoven concert, Leonard accompanies Margaret back to Wickham Place, the Schlegels' London home, in order to retrieve his umbrella, which Helen has accidently taken home with her. While Leonard is soon forgotten by the Schlegel sisters, he continues to reminisce about this meeting. However, it is only two years later that Leonard musters the courage to return to Wickham Place and explain to the Schlegels his desperate desire to escape the material pressures of lower-middle-class life. His stumbling confessions—he hopes to live a Schlegelian life surrounded by high culture and art—are received with a mixture of amusement and fascination by the two sisters and their brother Tibby. Helen and Margaret soon decide to engage in a social experiment that will alter the course of Leonard's life forever. Acting on a vaguely felt responsibility towards the 'poor' (94), Helen and Margaret consider how they might help to improve Leonard's lot. Even though the sisters' plan to help Leonard through various personal

---

[26] Thomas Good, 'Unemployment, insurance, and labour exchanges', *Westminster Review* (May 1909): 544–51 (p. 546). In the late Victorian period, fire insurance companies had in fact begun to expand their activities considerably, with several companies entering the market for personal accident insurance. See, e.g., Carter/Falush, *British Insurance Industry*, pp. 6–8, and Fraser, *Evolution*, pp. 199–201.

[27] Good, 'Unemployment, insurance, and labour exchanges', p. 545.

[28] Puskar, 'William Dean Howells and the insurance of the real', *American Literary History* 18.1 (2006): 29–58 (p. 46).

interventions owes much to Victorian-style charity, Forster's depiction of these interactions is better understood, I want to argue, as a critical contribution to Edwardian welfare debates which recognized that 'charity based on personal relation [had] los[t] its power to reconcile' different social classes.[29] To put this another way: instead of affirming an outdated model of personalized philanthropy, the presence of Leonard Bast in Forster's novel raises broader questions about the social allocation of economic vulnerability and about the promise of publicly funded mechanisms of institutionalized care.

The question of how society should look after its most vulnerable members is rehearsed most directly in Chapter 15 of Forster's novel. Helen and Margaret attend a dinner party which has been organized by a number of female friends and which doubles as an informal political discussion club. The issue to be debated that evening is how the poorer members of society, those who might at any moment plunge into the 'abyss of unemployment' (36), ought to be supported. The 'case' of Leonard Bast, as everyone soon begins to refer to it, becomes the central touchstone in this debate. For the sake of inciting argument, the discussants are divided into two groups—advocates of 'property', who deny outright the desirability of any kind of charitable action, and 'philanthropists', who lobby for personal and localized interventions benefitting the poor. The champions of propertied interest defend the socio-economic status quo by insisting that '[m]oney was the fruit of self-denial, and the second generation had a right to profit by the self-denial of the first. What right had "Mr. Bast" to profit?' (92). By contrast, the philanthropists insist that wealth brings with it certain responsibilities towards society's disadvantaged members. They argue that

> [s]omething must be done for 'Mr. Bast'; his conditions must be improved without impairing his independence; he must have a free library, or free tennis-courts; [...] he must be assigned a Twin Star, some member of the leisured classes who would watch over him ceaselessly (groans from Helen); he must be given food but no clothes, clothes but no food, a third-return ticket to Venice, without either food or clothes when he arrived there. In short, he might be given anything and everything so long as it was not the money itself.   (92)

The debate between the defenders of the socio-economic status quo and the advocates of personalized charity rehearses deliberative procedures that recent scholars such as Amanda Anderson have described as the hallmark feature of the literary aesthetic of progressive liberalism. By prompting individuals to inhabit viewpoints that differ from their own, such debate encourages an openness to argumentative critique that temporarily denaturalizes the discussants' own social

---

[29] See Siegel, *Charity and Condescension: Victorian Literature and the Dilemmas of Philanthropy* (Athens: Ohio University Press, 2012), p. 33.

position and that 'promote[s] an understanding of reflective distance as an achieved and lived practice.'[30]

Chapter 15 of *Howards End* can be read in terms of the liberal aesthetic described by Anderson and others. Yet, while these scenes open up a dialogic space for the self-reflexive critique of hegemonic social roles, Forster also takes particular care to stress the social homogeneity of this group of discussants. For example, the confident gesture of social categorization that reduces Leonard to a typical 'case' indexes an aloof class perspective that is used to treating the precariously employed (and the unemployed) as an undifferentiated and otherwise featureless group. The question which Chapter 15 poses for us with particular urgency, therefore, is how it might be possible for a socially progressive politics to emerge from within this seemingly self-enclosed social space. Forster gestures towards this possibility, not by celebrating debate as an end in itself, but by expressing the unspoken (hegemonic) terms and socio-economic preconditions on which such debate is premised. Helen and Margaret both point out angrily that the choice between 'property' and 'philanthropy' constitutes a false and reductive dichotomy. Margaret is the first to vent her opposition to upper-middle-class philanthropy: personalized philanthropy, she insists, is complicit with the socio-economic status quo because it reinforces historically entrenched social hierarchies. Rejecting the claim that philanthropy must involve the distribution of particular goods ('food but no clothes, clothes but no food, a third-return ticket to Venice'), she advocates giving money to the economically deprived members of society. Only forms of care that are organized on the principle of monetary aid will succeed in treating beneficiaries as individuals who are capable of choosing their own ends:

> Give them a chance. Give them money. Don't dole them out poetry-books and railway-tickets like babies. Give them the wherewithal to buy these things. When your Socialism comes it may be different, and we may think in terms of commodities instead of cash. Till it comes give people cash, for it is the warp of civilisation, whatever the woof may be. The imagination ought to play upon money and realise it vividly, for it's the—the second most important thing in the world. It is so slurred over and hushed up, there is so little clear thinking—oh, political economy, of course, but so few of us think clearly about our own private incomes, and admit that independent thoughts are in nine cases out of ten the result of independent means. Money: give Mr. Bast money, and don't bother about his ideals. He'll pick up those for himself.   (93)

---

[30] Anderson, *The Way We Argue Now: A Study in the Cultures of Theory* (Princeton: Princeton University Press, 2006), p. 2.

Instead of cultivating Leonard's tastes by providing him with goods that signify a socially dominant high culture (a 'library', 'tennis courts', 'food', 'clothes', a 'ticket to Venice'), Margaret submits, the best way to support Leonard is by granting him economic security.[31] Margaret presents 'Socialism' as the aspirational endpoint of the debate about social care: it is only when capitalism has been overcome, she suggests, that material goods will cease to be purveyors of a class-bound culture. In the present, however, reformist compromises with the culture of capitalism continue to be necessary. Margaret's proposals respond to this recognition by outlining a model of social care that recognizes the significance of money as the 'warp' of human life. Providing money to those in need is an anti-revolutionary gesture because it serves to perpetuate the existence of the money form, but on Margaret's account giving out money also crucially makes it possible to conceptualize the uncoupling of the means of leading a good life (the economic 'warp') from a particular set of normative ends (the hegemonic understanding of what constitutes the good life in the first place). The other discussants are quick to observe that Margaret's comments fail to conform to either of the two positions— 'property' and 'philanthropy'—under discussion. 'I cannot have you speaking out of your rôle', she is admonished by the lady of the house who presides over the discussion (92–3). And, sure enough, Margaret's plans for monetary relief are soon rejected by a resounding majority.

Margaret's proposals, which turn out to be too radical and sweeping for the other members of the discussion club, can be read as elaborating on new proposals for a basic income that were entering public conversation around 1910. The notion of universal basic income (UBI) has received much fresh attention in recent years (following the financial crash of 2008), yet the historical roots of the idea extend much farther back, and they include early twentieth-century debates about a 'state bonus scheme'. The founders of the State Bonus League— an organization established in 1918, following the large-scale suffering and austerity of World War I—frequently referenced the reformist debates of the pre-war years as the starting point of their movement. As the League's leader, Bertram Pickard noted in a programmatic treatise (*A Reasonable Revolution: Being a Discussion of the State Bonus Scheme—A Proposal for a National Minimum Income*, 1919), inspiration for the state bonus scheme had come from the Liberal Party's espousal of the idea of a 'national minimum wage' in 1909, as well as from feminist calls for more adequate remuneration of female domestic labour.[32] The introduction of a national minimum income, Pickard argued, was intended to act much like a 'gigantic insurance scheme': it promised a 'solution' to

---

[31] Of course, Margaret's argument isn't quite as generously non-normative as my comments up to this point have suggested. Margaret does not finally endorse a genuine plurality of ends: Leonard, she anticipates, will ultimately come around to the cultured ideals held by the Schlegels themselves.

[32] Pickard, *A Reasonable Revolution: Being a Discussion of the State Bonus Scheme—A Proposal for a National Minimum Income* (London: Allen & Unwin, 1919), p. 51.

the twinned social problems of unemployment and mass immiseration that was at once 'comprehensive' and 'simple'.[33] Funded by siphoning off a certain amount of money from the country's GDP, national minimum income would combine the beneficial effects of the Edwardian insurance reforms ('Health Insurance, Old Age Pensions, Poor Law, Unemployment Insurance, Other Pensions, Income Tax Abatements') into a single powerful instrument.[34] Margaret's proposals echo these ideas but they also set the stage for the novel's broader reflections on the desirability of new types of institutionalized relief, including the introduction of new forms of collectivized insurance against the risk of unemployment.

As Helen and Margaret walk home after the dinner party, they happen to meet a friend (and Margaret's future husband), the businessman Henry Wilcox. While Margaret is telling Henry about her plans to support Leonard Bast, she casually mentions that Leonard is a clerk at the 'Porphyrion Fire Insurance Company'. Henry interrupts her with an 'Olympian laugh': 'My dear Miss Schlegel, I will not rush in where your sex has been unable to tread. I will not add another plan to the numerous excellent ones that have been already suggested. My only contribution is this: let your young friend clear out of the Porphyrion Fire Insurance Company with all possible speed' (97–8). The Porphyrion, Henry explains, 'will smash' because it lacks reinsurance (98). The sisters are worried that their newly acquired protégé might lose his employment, and after some soul-searching, they decide to pass on Henry's advice to Leonard. Leonard, who is eager to please his benefactresses, wastes no time and quits his job—a decision that sets him on a steep downward trajectory. After taking on a new position at a bank at a significantly reduced salary, Leonard is among the first to be laid off when the bank runs into financial difficulties. As a result of Henry's advice—obtained second-hand from an informant inside the insurance market and relayed to Leonard by the Schlegel sisters—Leonard's life spirals out of control and he plunges into the abyss of unemployment.

Shortly after Leonard has left the Porphyrion, it becomes clear that Henry's predictions about the company's economic dire straits were quite simply wrong: the firm manages to avoid collapse, and it soon recovers from its temporary financial difficulties. When Henry is confronted by the Schlegel sisters, he seems entirely indifferent to Leonard's fate. 'I am grieved for your clerk,' he tells Helen: 'But it is all in the day's work. It's part of the battle of life' (137). Helen rebuffs Henry, pointing out that he, too, bears some responsibility for Leonard's fate.

---

[33] Pickard, *A Reasonable Revolution*, pp. 19, 22. Pickard is here quoting from, and elaborating on, Evelyn Mabel and Dennis Milner's 1918 pamphlet *Scheme for a State Bonus* (1918).

[34] Pickard, *A Reasonable Revolution*, p. 23. The authors of the best recent philosophical defence of basic income note that the state bonus, as envisioned by Pickard, was pitched 'at 20 percent of GDP per capita' and 'would be funded by contributions from everyone with any income at all'. Philippe van Parijs and Yannick Vanderborght, *Basic Income: A Radical Proposal for a Free Society and a Sane Economy* (Cambridge, MA: Harvard University Press, 2017), p. 79.

Henry roundly rejects this idea: 'A clerk who clears out of any concern, good or bad, without securing a berth somewhere else first, is a fool, and I've no pity for him' (136). If anyone or anything is to blame, he notes, it is the economic fluctuations of the capitalist system. Taking the offensive, Henry admonishes Helen:

> "A word of advice. Don't take up that sentimental attitude over the poor. See that she doesn't, Margaret. The poor are poor, and one's sorry for them, but there it is. As civilisation moves forward, the shoe is bound to pinch in places, and it's absurd to pretend that any one is responsible personally. Neither you, nor I, nor my informant, nor the man who informed him, nor the directors of the Porphyrion, are to blame for this clerk's loss of salary. It's just the shoe pinching—no one can help it; and it might easily have been worse."
>
> [...] Helen quivered with indignation.
>
> [...] "By all means subscribe to charities—subscribe to them largely—but don't get carried away by absurd schemes of Social Reform." (138)

Henry's comments are levelled at Helen's 'sentimental attitude', but they also take aim more broadly at the undirected do-goodery that Henry associates with turn-of-the-century socialism. Henry's language—notably his disclaimer that 'the shoe' of the capitalist system is bound to 'pinch'—recalls Wells's pamphlet *The Misery of Boots* (1907), which had noted that for the socialist, '[t]he thought of the multitudes so much worse off than him in this matter of foot-wear gives no sort of satisfaction. Their boots pinch *him* vicariously.'[35] Henry, who considers himself so safe from existential risk that the suffering of others becomes a matter of sublime indifference to him, is constitutionally unable to feel the current of vicarious pain that connects those who suffer and those who would help.[36] Yet, if Henry's whole being—his self-help ethic and his indifference towards those who are economically vulnerable—has been shaped by a system of monopolized capitalist accumulation, much the same could be said of Helen's 'sentimental' (and, as we discover later in the novel, erotically charged) attraction to Leonard. Like Henry, Helen sees the capitalist system as a tightly integrated and unchangeable totality—her belief in the redemptive power of intensely personal

---

[35] *The Misery of Boots* (London: Fabian Society, 1905), p. 18; orig. emph.

[36] In 1910, Goldsworthy Lowes Dickinson had written a play, *Business*, which critiqued economic individualism in identical terms, by highlighting the psychological deformations bred by capitalism. The play's protagonist, modelled on John D. Rockefeller, consistently refuses to take responsibility for the economic distress of others by pointing to the 'vastness' and 'complexity' of the economic system. GLD, 'Business,' GLD/4/2. On Forster's familiarity with the play, see E. M. Forster, *Goldsworthy Lowes Dickinson* [1934] (New York: Harcourt Brace, 1962), pp. 133–4; see also Dickinson, *The Autobiography of Goldsworthy Lowes Dickinson and Other Unpublished Writings* (London: Duckworth, 1973), pp. 173–4.

relationships, Forster hints, is as unlikely to bring about large-scale change as Henry's complacent defence of the status quo.

Henry's speech reminds us that blaming the system can be a convenient way of dispelling personal responsibility, but his comments also take on broader significance in the context of Edwardian debates about unemployment insurance. Henry claims that it simply does not make sense to talk about individual culpability in complex economic systems. 'Oh come, come!', he protests when Helen complains that he is downplaying his role in Leonard's tragedy, 'you're not to blame. No one's to blame.' Helen, who has been insisting that Leonard now 'has less, owing to us', is dumbfounded by Henry's reply: 'Is no one to blame for anything?', she objects (137). The question of (economic) responsibility resonates throughout *Howards End*. Pondering the impenetrable vastness and opacity of the capitalist economy, Leonard is overcome by a sense of profound disorientation. Leonard, we are told in language that recalls 'The Machine Stops', 'understood his own corner of the machine, but nothing beyond it' (101). Lacking knowledge of the system of which he is only a small part, he succumbs to economic fatalism: 'in the end they [people like Leonard] fall over the edge. It's no good. It's the whole world pulling. There will always be rich and poor' (163). Leonard's resigned conclusion echoes Henry's own self-serving remarks about the 'shoe pinching': 'if wealth was divided up equally,' Henry had explained to Margaret, 'in a few years there would be rich and poor again just the same' (113). While these passages present us with a claustrophobic vision of inevitable socio-economic segregation, Forster crucially empties this vision of the revolutionary implications I discussed with a view to Wells's early scientific romances. As Margaret's proposals in Chapter 15 indicate, *Howards End* instead begins to reframe class relations by presenting responsibility as a fundamentally distributed property of socio-economic systems that does not attach to any particular person or social class. This revised understanding of responsibility is also mirrored in Forster's epigraph to the novel (*'Only connect...'*): while the epigraph is usually taken to indicate Forster's nostalgic longing for an organicist community, it also acts as a spur to reformist thought that marks the starting point for the book's engagement with new arguments for economic redistribution.[37]

Forster's account of the rapid downward trajectory of Leonard's life resonates with the broader systemic questions that were raised by Edwardian debates about unemployment insurance and welfare reform. As William Beveridge argued in his influential book *Unemployment: A Problem of Industry* (1909), the National

---

[37] There is some biographical evidence of Forster's interest in the debates about (economic) responsibility that culminated in the People's Budget. Writing to his friend, the socialist sympathiser Malcolm Darling in December 1909, Forster expressed dismay at the House of Lord's decision to overturn Lloyd George's budget, which had proposed a number of new redistributive measures. See Letter to Malcolm Darling, 10 December 1909, in *Selected Letters of E. M. Forster—Volume 1: 1879–1920*, ed. Mary Largo (London: Arena, 1985), p. 99.

Insurance Act rested on the premise that there was bound to be an 'irreducible minimum of unemployment' in capitalist societies.[38] It was a mistake to attribute joblessness to a lack of personal probity on the part of those who happened to be out of work, but it was equally short-sighted to blame unemployment exclusively on employers. Instead, Beveridge noted, unemployment was a structural property of liberal economies. The journalist G. W. Bailey, writing in the *Westminster Review* in 1908, explained that

> in the present industrial system Capital is undoubtedly supreme, only curbing its claims under strong pressure on the part of the State or the organised masses of the workers. It is not so much the individual capitalist's fault no doubt. If he does not get the utmost possible amount of work from his employees for the lowest possible wage, less scrupulous, or more capable, rivals will speedily ruin him. [. . .] It is not primarily then the fault of the individual capitalist that wages are low, or that hours are long: It is the system [. . .] which has robbed the individual of his right to work.[39]

The 'jangle of causes and effects' (233) that makes up the capitalist system dislocates our common-sense intuition that social agency and moral responsibility are rooted in decisions made by autonomous individuals. The kind of systemic perspective advocated by Bailey can easily look like a quietist affirmation of the status quo, and his article indeed comes close to parroting Henry's self-serving refusal of personal responsibility. However, Bailey does not simply endorse economic laissez-faireism or neglect the particular psychological pathologies that it produces. Instead, his imaginative attempt to adopt the point of view of the system as a whole produces a totalizing view of the economy that can in turn create an opening for future state regulation, for 'strong pressure on the part of the State'. As Bruce Robbins explains,

> if system makes blaming difficult, [. . .] it is no less true that without system, blaming [. . .] is not really possible. In order to blame well, one has to know that this is not just any random suffering, the result of nature or accident or perhaps even the fault of the sufferer. [. . .] The paradox is this: you can't blame without system, which teaches you what must and what can be changed, what is and isn't merely the work of nature, human or otherwise. But you also can't blame with it, for system fatally weakens the link between individual sufferer and individual perpetrator.[40]

---

[38] Beveridge, *Unemployment*, pp. 68–77.

[39] George Bailey, 'The right to work', *Westminster Review* (December 1908): 618–28 (p. 619).

[40] Robbins, 'Blaming the system', in *Immanuel Wallerstein and the Problem of the World: System, Scale, Culture*, eds. David Palumbo-Liu, Bruce Robbins, and Nirvana Tanoukhi (Durham, NC: Duke University Press, 2011), pp. 41–63 (pp. 58–9).

Bailey's article and Forster's novel try to blame *with* the system in the sense that they refuse to endorse a full (revolutionary) overhaul of existing socio-economic arrangements. Instead, both texts echo reformist arguments that sought to grasp the economy as a complex whole and that aimed at devising institutional solutions for the inequities which this system produced. In the periodical press and in numerous book publications, social reformers argued for the redistribution of the nation's socially generated total national income by offering detailed statistical accounts that documented who were the most vulnerable and disadvantaged members of the British economic system. Instead of placing the blame for unemployment squarely at the feet of the system's richest profiteers, these texts recall Beveridge's work by presenting unemployment as a systemic problem that necessitates system-scale remedies. What was required, the advocates of unemployment insurance insisted, was an abstract understanding of the economic system as a whole that would dispel once and for all the myopic focus on individual suffering they associated with Victorian-style charity.

The Case for Social Welfare: William Beveridge and Unemployment Insurance

Howards End is generally more sympathetic to the promises of institutional reform than has been recognized, and Forster seems to have understood that only substantive institutional transformations, including the collectivization of the risk of unemployment, would make it possible to protect individuals from the destructive forces of the market. As we shall see, *Howards End* develops a speculative mode that uses categories of genre to figure the beneficial effects of these reforms not just in the abstract but, more congenial to Forster's liberal ethos, in terms of the lived experience of solidary individuals. Beveridge's work was a particularly influential catalyst for Forster's sympathetic engagement with—and aesthetic response to—the idea of national unemployment insurance, and we should therefore give some attention to Beveridge's *Unemployment* before returning to *Howards End*. At first sight, Beveridge's *Unemployment*, a study that relies heavily on statistical evidence, might seem an unpromising intertext for *Howards End*. However, Forster's now-infamous narratorial comment—'We are not concerned with the very poor. They are unthinkable, and only to be approached by the statistician or the poet' (36)—vastly underplays the impact which Beveridge's statistically corroborated arguments in favour of state-organized welfare had on Forster. Critics have found ample evidence of the influence of the 'poet' Edward Carpenter in Forster's novel (notably the Carpenterian belief in universal brotherhood), and we should expect to find similar traces of the progressive ideas propounded by the 'statistician' Beveridge.

Beveridge and Forster had been friends in preparatory school, and they continued to correspond and meet regularly in the early 1900s.[41] Beveridge is probably best remembered today as the author of the 1942 government report (popularly known as the Beveridge Report) that helped inspire the post-war establishment of the National Health Service. However, Beveridge's advocacy of social reform had started much earlier, in the years leading up to the National Insurance Act of 1911. One of the tasks Beveridge had set himself in *Unemployment* was to identify 'the problem of the underlying causes of cyclical fluctuation in trade and employment' (viii). As he notes in his introduction to the book, cyclical unemployment had long been known to be a feature of the agricultural sector (where labour was dependent on the changing seasons), but labour statisticians were now beginning to recognize that this type of unemployment also extended to numerous other trades, including construction, shipbuilding, and engineering (all of which would be covered by the unemployment schemes introduced as part of the National Insurance Act). Beveridge acknowledges the significance of seasonal factors, but he is also quick to stress that in industrialized societies this type of unemployment is chronically exacerbated by the fact that the supply of (unskilled) labour is bound to outstrip the marketplace demand for such labour.[42] To acknowledge the systemic nature of unemployment thus 'enables the risk of unemployment in all its forms to be appreciated as a normal incident of industry'—as a 'risk that is very hard to appreciate and still harder to provide against' (226). Beveridge's book pays attention to a cluster of factors that can trigger surges in unemployment, ranging from seasonal changes in the weather to necessary job training and transitioning periods. There was bound to be an 'irreducible minimum of unemployment' (68) in industrial societies, and Beveridge's multicausal model indicated that it was difficult to predict which trades and professions were going to be hit hardest by the next wave of unemployment.

Given the deep structural roots of unemployment, full employment under capitalism was an unrealizable pipe dream, and as Beveridge argued, it fell to reformers to find alternative institutional remedies. Beveridge admits that such fixes can only ever be palliative: 'To a very large extent therefore it must suffice to aim at preventing; not unemployment itself, but the distress which it now involves' (220). In the concluding chapter of his book ('Principles for future policy'),

---

[41] The Beveridge Papers at the London School of Economics contain a number of letters which testify to the renewed friendship between Forster and Beveridge between 1906 and 1911. Beveridge wrote to Forster on several occasions to congratulate him on the publication of his most recent works, and Forster in turn kept Beveridge abreast of his ongoing literary projects while also occasionally recording details of their meetings in his journals.

[42] Beveridge would agree with Marx that structural unemployment—the existence of an unemployed surplus population—is a constitutive feature of capitalist societies as such. For Marx's most influential explication of the concept, see *Capital*, vol. 1 (London: Penguin, 1976), pp. 781–94 (Vol. 1, ch. 25).

Beveridge finally presents his proposals for one such measure—a nation-wide, publicly funded unemployment insurance scheme. 'The principle of insurance', Beveridge concludes, 'affords the most satisfactory, because the most flexible, method of making general provision for unemployment' (228). Due to the systemic factors which contribute to the rise in unemployment figures, Beveridge and many progressive politicians insisted that national insurance ought not to be limited to a few trades. Pointing to an 'invaluable report' published by the Imperial Statistical Department in 1906, Beveridge concludes that there are 'no insuperable difficulties of a technical character to the formation of an insurance system'—indeed, the 'problems' involved in extending this nationalized system beyond a few select trades were 'ascertainable and not very wide' (228-9).

Literary scholars usually associate the Schlegel family's German background with their idealist and thoroughly *bürgerlich* belief in the spiritually redeeming force of classical music and high culture. However, the proximity of Forster's novel to Edwardian debates about national insurance also suggests an alternative reading. Margaret's proposal to give money to Leonard echoes the German schemes for unemployment insurance that many contemporary observers, including Beveridge and Lloyd George, were citing as a possible model for Britain. There was 'ample warrant in foreign example for giving State encouragement to [the] extension' of insurance to other trades, Beveridge concluded: 'There would, according to the [...] German report already quoted, be no impossibility in the State's applying the principle of insurance to the risk of unemployment quite generally and comprehensively' (230).[43] In a related vein the rhetorical gesture that turns Leonard's story into a 'case' in Chapter 15 is not only, as I claimed earlier, the result of upper-middle-class condescension—it also opens up the possibility that individual cases of unemployment can be articulated with analogous cases across different industries.

Following Lloyd George's much-publicized trip to Germany in 1909 as an observer of the German insurance scheme, it became common political wisdom (Beveridge observed) that '[i]nsurance is needed to provide for the maintenance of the reserves while standing idle and of the displaced men while waiting for re-absorption. [...] The provision required is one adaptable to an immense variety of individual cases' (229). Reformist proposals of this sort were intended in part to ensure the continued operation of the capitalist system: it would be in the interest of all tax-paying citizens, one commentator explained, to provide relief to the unemployed because 'the problem before us is not how to *abolish* the unemployed,

---

[43] An anonymous review of Beveridge's *Unemployment* found that 'Germany nowadays is held up as a model to all good social reformers, and our civil servants are always being hurried over there to look around.' See 'Out of Work Theories', *Saturday Review of Politics, Literature, Science, and Art* (6 November 1909): 570-1 (p. 571). For a related assessment, see also Sir Alfred Mond, 'German working-class insurance', *The English Review* (June 1911): 486-506.

but how to *keep them efficient, respectable, and within call*.[44] Far from ushering in a bright new age of collectivist socialism, unemployment insurance was designed to shore up national production: it would maintain the reserve army of labour in good working order while the latter was awaiting its temporary reintegration into the job market. At the same time, however, the reformist proposals championed by Beveridge and others were animated by a genuine desire to mitigate economic pressure on the most precariously positioned members of society.[45] Not least, these proposals involved a significant element of economic redistribution. Since the introduction of unemployment insurance would serve the good of all members of society, many Edwardian reformers argued, expenses for state-organized welfare should be transferred to the general taxpayer through a rising income tax.[46] This taxation model had already been tested successfully in the case of the Old Age Pensions (introduced in 1908), and it continued to be the Liberal government's favoured means of increasing domestic revenue.[47] As I indicated in my discussion of Wells in the previous chapter, it became possible to think about the taxation of income not as the confiscation of the fruits of individual effort but as the social reabsorption of a common product. When it came to unemployment insurance, one observer remarked in 1907, there was a fundamental 'identity of interest' between all members of British society.[48] And another commentator pointed out that unemployment 'probably costs the State more in the long run than any other disease of the social body; and it is quite beyond the individual's power to avoid.'[49] The conjunction between debates about unemployment insurance and higher taxation captures the growing recognition of the systemic and distributed nature of socio-economic responsibility,

[44] Good, 'Unemployment, Insurance, and Labour Exchanges', p. 544; orig. emph.

[45] *Unemployment* also did not feature the nefariously eugenicist arguments that had marred Beveridge's earliest work on the topic. In 1906, Beveridge had asserted that 'those men who through general defects are unable to fill such a "whole" place in industry, are to be recognised as "unemployable". They must become the acknowledged dependents of the state, removed from free industry and maintained adequately in public institutions, but with the complete and permanent loss of all citizen rights.' Beveridge, 'The problem of the unemployed', *The Sociological Review* 3.1 (1906): 323–41 (p. 327).

[46] See Martin Daunton, *Trusting Leviathan: The Politics of Taxation in Britain, 1799–1914* (Cambridge: Cambridge University Press, 2001), p. 299.

[47] The *Independent Review*, the influential Liberal periodical that had been cofounded by Forster's Cambridge mentor Dickinson in 1903, and to which Forster contributed on a regular basis, strongly advocated the use of a more finely graduated income tax in order to increase the revenue available for expanded welfarist measures. See, for example, Leo Chiozza Money's 'Mr. Asquith's opportunity: Towards a just income tax', *Independent Review* 12 (1907): pp. 260–8. As Forster observed in his biography of Dickinson, the *Independent Review* advocated 'a constructive policy at home. It was not so much a Liberal review as an appeal to Liberalism from the Left to be its better self'. See Forster, *Goldsworthy Lowes Dickinson*, p. 115.

[48] Thomas Good, 'Some aspects of the labour problem', *Westminster Review* (March 1907): 278–88 (p. 280).

[49] Bailey, 'The Right to Work', p. 618.

but it also marks the moment when 'only connect' became the progressive mantra of Edwardian reformers.[50]

Howards End and the 'Tragedy of Preparedness'

Forster's novel evinces an understanding of risk that resonates closely with the writings of Edwardian social reformers, and it also works towards a formal articulation of the foundational questions—about responsibility, structural unemployment, and the nature of state-organized care—that were being raised by the proponents of institutional reform. In Howards End, the question of risk is addressed most explicitly by Margaret following the death of her friend Mrs Wilcox. In a passage I referenced towards the beginning of this chapter, Margaret looks back to her siblings' series of chance encounters with the Wilcoxes:

> Looking back on the past six months, Margaret realized the chaotic nature of our daily life, and its difference from the orderly sequence that has been fabricated by historians. Actual life is full of false clues and sign-posts that lead nowhere. With infinite effort we nerve ourselves for a crisis that never comes. The most successful career must show a waste of strength that might have removed mountains, and the most unsuccessful is not that of the man who is taken unprepared, but of him who has prepared and is never taken. On a tragedy of that kind our national morality is duly silent. It assumes that preparation against danger is in itself a good, and that men, like nations, are the better for staggering through life fully armed. The tragedy of preparedness has scarcely been handled, save by the Greeks. Life is indeed dangerous, but not in the way morality would have us believe. It is indeed unmanageable, but the essence of it is not a battle. It is unmanageable because it is a romance, and its essence is romantic beauty. Margaret hoped that for the future she would be less cautious, not more cautious, than she had been in the past.   (79)

Risk and the unforeseen are here presented as something we should welcome into our lives. Far from posing an existential threat, risk can add a sense of excitement without which our lives would be drab and, it seems to Margaret, not worth living. For Margaret, life is electric with a sense of the 'dangerous' and the

---

[50] Many progressive thinkers across the liberal and socialist camps began to support the idea that 'the state had a role in setting right the shortcomings of an economic system which had produced poverty on such a scale as would put self-improvement beyond the capacity of the individual'. Geoffrey Finlayson, Citizen, State, and Social Welfare in Britain, 1830–1990 (Oxford: Clarendon Press, 1994), p. 161. To be sure, the proposals that were mooted in the lead-up to the National Insurance Act frequently ran ahead of what turned out to be pragmatically possible. Thus, when the Act was finally passed, it involved only relatively small payments from a centralized state-run fund, with most revenue being raised through contributions by employers and employees.

'unmanageable', yet it is not (for the Schlegels in any case) a 'battle' in which the stakes are life or death. The ideas on which Margaret touches here radiate out into the novel, connecting this passage to the rest of the book. For example, the passage looks back to an earlier scene in which Margaret contradicts her overcautious aunt's plan to pre-empt a second tryst between Helen and Henry's son Charles: 'there's no need for plans,' she rebukes her aunt, because 'those who prepare for all the emergencies of life beforehand may equip themselves at the expense of joy' (43). Margaret's declared desire to embrace the 'joy[ful]' 'emergencies of life' performs an aestheticization of contingency that makes risk seem less threatening by presenting it under the sign of 'romance'.[51] This aestheticization is fully contingent on the siblings' financial independence, and as the novel reminds us, the Schlegels' ability to welcome risk as a source of excitement—their ability to enjoy the 'unmanageability' of life—is possible only because they are (economically) protected against many forms of existential risk. The 'economic' is the central term that pegs together the 'politico-economical-aesthetic atmosphere that reigned at the Schlegels'' (43) by creating a protected space in which the siblings' preoccupation with art and the inner life as well as their interest in the politics of reform can safely unfold. 'Romance' is the name which Howards End gives to this constellation of terms ('politico-economical-aesthetic') when they are fused into a unified Lebensform or etherealized into an all-pervading 'atmosphere'.

Importantly, however, Forster's novel initiates a movement of defamiliarization and critique that confronts the Schlegels' economically secure life of romance with Leonard's exposure to the threat of tragedy. Over the course of the novel, Forster allows the two terms—romance and tragedy—to enter into a series of different combinations that serve to reveal their dialectical relationship. In the passage cited above, for example, the meaning of the term 'tragedy' is already coloured by Margaret's intense desire for a life of romance and excitement: the 'tragedy of preparedness' referred to in the text names a form of life that deliberately insulates itself against the jolting sensation of the new and unexpected. As Margaret views it, the 'tragedy of preparedness' is not the result of a personal lack of courage, but a fully collective failure of the 'national morality' which insists that 'preparation against danger is in itself a good'.

The tragedy of preparedness is a recurring theme in Forster's Edwardian writings. However, many of these scattered allusions to the tragedy of preparedness only come into focus once we view them through the lens of Howards End's more sustained treatment of this theme in the months leading up to the National Insurance Act. While 'The Machine Stops' took a dystopian view of 'the Book of

---

[51] The understanding of romance here and elsewhere in Forster's Edwardian writings owes much to R. A. Scott-James's 1908 book Modernism and Romance, which had called on writers to 'bring out the marvellous and unexpected'—'the eternal thrill'—from 'the midst of the familiar'. Scott-James, Modernism and Romance (London: John Lane, 1908), pp. 9, 218. Scott-James would go on to review Howards End in the Daily News on 7 November 1910.

the Machine' with its 'instructions against every possible contingency', other texts indicate that for Forster the question of how life can be opened up to danger and the unforeseen was in part an aesthetic one: 'our life today is so sheltered, so safe,' Forster had noted in his essay on Kipling's poetry, 'we are so protected by asphalt pavements, creosoted palings, and policemen, so guarded on all sides from all that may injure the body or disturb the soul, that in literature we are apt to rush to the other extreme, and worship vitality unrestrainedly.'[52] The desire for romance is here cast as a specifically aesthetic reaction against the contemporary preoccupation with security and (national) insurance. In Forster's account, the spheres of literature and art offer compensatory fantasies which resemble the ones Margaret imagines from the security and upper-middle-class comfort of her London home.

Most contemporary readers will struggle to identify the tragedy of preparedness as a form of tragedy at all, and for good reason. Indeed, *Howards End* itself reminds us of the limitations of Margaret's understanding of romance as well as of the inadequacy of her idealizing ('Greek') view of tragedy. The novel repeatedly draws our attention to the nineteenth-century family resemblance between capitalism and romance—and to the interdependence of the Wilcoxes' capitalist imperialism and the Schlegels' liberal aestheticism—by linking Margaret's longing for a life of risk to her attraction to Henry, whom she will eventually marry. The same character traits that make Henry indifferent to Leonard's fate—his seemingly limitless self-confidence and his larger-than-life entrepreneurial ambition— also make him an exemplary and resourceful businessman. Henry resembles the charismatic heroes of the 'romance of free trade', a Victorian literary genre that glorified *homo economicus* as a resolutely independent figure keen to take risks in the single-minded pursuit of wealth.[53] Had Forster decided to organize *Howards End* around Henry, the novel would likely resemble one of the 'Romances about Capital' that Forster described in a diary entry about Joseph Conrad's *Nostromo* (1904).[54]

---

[52] Forster, 'The Poems of Kipling', p. 27.

[53] This genre has been described by Ayşe Celikkol in *Romances of Free Trade: British Literature, Laissez-Faire, and the Global Nineteenth Century* (Oxford: Oxford University Press, 2011). D. H. Lawrence complained in a letter to Forster that the latter had very nearly committed the 'deadly mistake of glorifying those *business* people in *Howards End*'. Lawrence had a point: Forster's support of free enterprise in the early 1900s is well documented, and as Perry Meisel notes, the discourse of *Howards End* is permeated by a topical vocabulary of economic speculation and exchange. For Lawrence's letter to E. M. Forster, from 20 September 1922, see Warren Roberts et al. (eds.), *The Letters of D. H. Lawrence*, vol. 4: *1921–24* (Cambridge: Cambridge University Press, 1987), p. 391; orig. emph. For the economistic language of *Howard End*, see Meisel, *The Myth of the Modern: A Study in British Literature and Criticism after 1850* (New Haven: Yale University Press, 1987), pp. 173–82. In later life Forster came to feel reservations about '[t]he doctrine of *laisser-faire*' because 'it has led to the capitalist jungle'. See 'The challenge of our time', in *Two Cheers for Democracy* (London: Arnold, 1972), pp. 55–60 (p. 57).

[54] Philip Gardner (ed.), *The Journals and Diaries of E.M. Forster*, 3 vols (London: Pickering and Chatto, 2011), I, 165.

Margaret's engagement to Henry suggests that her desire for romance finds vicarious fulfilment through her connection with the sphere of commerce. Yet while parts of the novel underscore the link between capitalism and romance, the rest of Forster's book—notably the story of Leonard's fall into unemployment— asks us to treat this link with considerable scepticism. The form of life which the novel designates by the term *romance*—the joyful openness to risk and the unforeseen—remains inaccessible to Leonard, whose existence teeters precariously on the brink of unemployment. Leonard's life, Forster writes, 'was a grey life, and to brighten it he had ruled off a few corners for Romance. [...] He did not want Romance to collide with the Porphyrion, still less with [his wife] Jacky. [The Schlegels] to him were denizens of Romance, who must keep to the corner he had assigned them, pictures that must not walk out of their frames' (89). As Forster's narrator suggests, Margaret's aestheticizing conception of tragedy—with its archaic ('Greek') insistence on the aristocratic singularity and nobility of suffering—fails to give a satisfactory account of the threat of structural mass unemployment experienced by Leonard and diagnosed by Edwardian reformers. Leonard's peculiar situation, which permanently lingers in the 'grey' limbo of not-quite-tragedy and not-quite-romance, can be productively understood in terms of what Lauren Berlant has called 'the waning of genre': genres, Berlant writes, describe the stability of particular forms of life (they 'provide an affective expectation of the experience of watching something unfold'), and their 'waning' occurs when 'conventions of relating fantasy to ordinary life and depictions of the good life appear to mark archaic expectations about having and building a life.'[55] The unattainability of Leonard's desire for the sunlit uplands of Schlegelian romance likewise catapults him into a drawn-out and eventless present: 'Where there is no money and no inclination to violence tragedy cannot be generated. He could not leave his wife, and he did not want to hit her. Petulance and squalor were enough' (90). Leonard's existence, in which 'tragedy cannot be generated' and romance remains permanently unattainable, gives rise to experiences of formlessness of the kind Berlant describes.

For Margaret, preparedness signifies the elimination of enjoyment as such rather than the reformist promise of a life less exposed to existential risk.[56] It is only later, after Leonard has fallen into the abyss of unemployment, that the novel begins to glimpse a distinctively modern mode of tragedy. This form of tragedy is not named as such in the novel, but its outlines swim into focus as the insufficiency of the other categories proposed in the text—'romance' and the 'tragedy of preparedness'—becomes apparent. For example, Margaret's idealizing view of

---

[55] Berlant, *Cruel Optimism* (Durham, NC: Duke University Press, 2011), p. 6.

[56] The unattainability of total security—the illusory idea that insurance can 'make us carefree' and offer 'the calm enjoyment of resting on 'solid' ground'—is discussed in John T. Hamilton's *Security: Politics, Humanity, and the Philology of Care* (Princeton: Princeton University Press, 2013), pp. 185 *passim*.

life—'[it] is indeed dangerous [...] but the essence of it is not a *battle*'—is implicitly rejected later in the novel when Henry callously remarks that Leonard's fall into unemployment is simply part of 'the *battle* of life' (137). While Henry's remark tries to disguise the (historically specific) conditions of the capitalist marketplace by passing them off as a quasi-universal feature of human life, the phrase 'battle of life' manages to capture the constant exposure to existential risk that is experienced by those living on the brink of unemployment. Such experiences of risk participate in conditions of 'crisis ordinariness'— Berlant's term for social regimes under which life feels permanently truncated, 'more like desperate doggy paddling than like a magnificent swim out to the horizon.'[57] In contrast to the permanent anti-climax of crisis ordinariness, however, Forster keeps open the possibility of mobilizing the term 'tragedy' as a political category that highlights the precarity suffered by Leonard and others like him: departing from Margaret's romanticized view of risk and tragedy, *Howards End* shows us that Leonard's real tragedy is not one of preparedness but of being economically *un*prepared.

Howards End, Amanda Anderson notes, 'keep[s] in play the intractable energies of liberal critique' through the 'force of character-character argument'—a point that is illustrated by the debate about philanthropy in Chapter 15.[58] As I have suggested, however, Forster's novel invites not only the critical examination of individual opinions (about charity, say, or about laissez-faireism), but of entire forms of life, including Margaret's vision of a *Lebensform* that happily coincides with the aesthetic properties of romance. *Howards End* performs this critique by drawing attention to the material preconditions that make Margaret's aspirational vision possible in the first place. The Schlegels and Wilcoxes 'stand upon money as upon islands', Margaret reflects: 'It is so firm beneath our feet that we forget its very existence. It's only when we see someone near us tottering that we realize all that an independent income means. [...] I begin to think that the very soul of the world is economic, and that the lowest abyss is not the absence of love, but the absence of coin' (46). As Forster reminds us through a series of scenes that are interspersed into the main plot of the novel, the provision of insurance is a key part of these safeguards. When Henry's son Charles runs over a dog with his car, he is unfazed because the family's 'insurance company sees to that' (154). In a similar scene, following another road accident caused by one of the Wilcoxes, Mrs Wilcox announces that 'as we've insured against third party risks, it won't so much matter' (65). The relative narrative insignificance of these short scenes is precisely what makes them meaningful—it reminds us that the securities provided by insurance are woven into our day-to-day lives at such a deep level that they become inseparable from the way we conduct our everyday lives. In the case of the

[57] Berlant, *Cruel Optimism*, p. 117.
[58] Anderson, *Bleak Liberalism* (Chicago: University of Chicago Press, 2016), p. 95.

Wilcoxes, private insurance is shown to exacerbate family habits of romantic recklessness and risk-taking (not to mention dangerous driving!). Even so, these local reflections on 'preparedness' create openings that facilitate the novel's sustained dialogue with topical Edwardian debates about national insurance. The sentence that deplores modern Britain's 'tragedy of preparedness' was only included by Forster at proof stage, and it seems intended to sharpen the contrast between the Schlegels' (and Wilcoxes') veneration of romance, on the one hand, and Leonard's existential exposure to risk, on the other.[59] Unlike the tragedy of preparedness, which suggests that the insured life will lack in excitement, the tragedy of unpreparedness shows that life cannot be fully enjoyed *unless* it is cushioned against the worst kinds of socio-economic risk.

It is significant that much like tragedy, the category of romance, too, is subjected to a process of conceptual transformation and revision in Forster's text. In contrast to what the published version of the novel suggests about the class-bound nature of romance and its unattainability to Leonard, the closing chapters of *Howards End*'s manuscript version begin to imagine the possibility of a romance-like ending for Leonard. This glimpse of Leonard's transposition into the realm of romance is all the more tantalizing for its brevity and counterfactual nature: 'Could he have died with his arms round Helen, his end would have seemed beautiful. But life refuses to end. It goes on after the curtain should fall.'[60] These sentences (from the manuscript version of Chapter 41) invoke the 'beauty' that Margaret had previously described as the 'essence' of romance, as we fleetingly catch sight of Leonard sharing in the romance-like life of the Schlegels: 'What had Leonard accomplished? Romance—fragments of beauty and adventure that spring from nothing and result in nothing, and must remain fragments until the last judgment'.[61] The attempt to imagine the possibility of a romance-like ending for Leonard ultimately breaks down when he succumbs to a heart-attack after being assaulted by Charles Wilcox. While there is little in the narrative (either in the manuscript or in the published version) that could have prevented Leonard's death, we can observe an important difference between the two endings. While the published version tries to make up for Leonard's death by offering Forster's readers the vision of a socially homogeneous and pastorally unified English *Gemeinschaft*, the manuscript version briefly entertains the possibility of a more egalitarian expansion of romance beyond the narrow social class represented by the Schlegels and Wilcoxes. In doing so, the manuscript version echoes the hopes of Edwardian advocates of national insurance who argued that new institutions of care would enable a similar expansion of economic security to larger swathes of the

---

[59] Forster, *The Manuscripts of* Howards End (London: Arnold, 1973), p. 103.

[60] Forster, *Manuscripts of* Howards End, p. 322.

[61] A later version of the manuscript passage replaces 'adventure' for 'joy', thus linking Leonard's brief move into the sphere of romance even more strongly with Margaret's decision to espouse risk. See Forster, *Manuscripts of* Howards End, p. 324.

population. Forster gives us a speculative view of new institutions of care in terms of a democratically extended form of life ('romance') whose relative economic safety means that it can afford to open itself to 'fragments of beauty and joy'. This aspirational mobilization of the genre of romance, I suggest in what follows, calls for an interpretive hermeneutic that does not aim at demystifying particular generic choices by pointing to their latent political content but that restores to these very generic choices their immanent political force.

Racing the Sun: *Arctic Summer* and State Romance

In *Howards End*, the concepts of tragedy and romance undergo a process of recalibration and revision that is energized by the pressure of Leonard's existential drama. As I have indicated, this process can be described as reformist insofar as it builds towards a double recognition of the tragedy of *un*preparedness and the democratization of access to the self-determined life of 'romance'. In concluding this chapter, I want to develop the cue that is provided by the novel's manuscript ending. Whereas *Howards End* is mainly engaged in a critique of the genre categories it invokes, other texts by Forster begin to foreground the speculative charge that characterized the Edwardian reformist literary mode, and in so doing they point us towards the vision of new forms of life in which tragedy has been permanently attenuated into a new kind of collectively shared condition of romance. As 'The Machine Stops' indicates, Forster was deeply sceptical of reformist proposals that presented state intervention as the panacea for all social ills. While the novel fragment *Arctic Summer* echoes this scepticism by satirizing the hyperbolic ambitions of a government official, it also marks Forster's most sustained attempt to enter imaginatively into the reformist literary mode. *Howards End* is thus best understood as a transitional text, written at a time when the (vaguely Whitmanian or Carpenterian) ethos of friendship and brotherhood came under increasing pressure due to range of systemic social issues, including the problem of unemployment.

Forster's thinking about the speculative reformist mode comes into focus in a draft essay on which he was working between 1905 and 1907. First delivered in 1905 as a talk to the Cambridge branch of the Fabian Society under the title 'Happy versus Sad Endings', the paper slowly evolved into a longer address, entitled 'Pessimism in Literature', which Forster gave at the Working Men's College in London in 1907.[62] Both versions of the paper begin by diagnosing the

---

[62] For the original version, see *The Creator as Critic*, pp. 23–6; for the revised and expanded version, see Forster, *Albergo Empedocle and Other Writings* (New York: Liveright, 1971), pp. 129–45. References here are to the 1905 version rather than the later text with which Forster was dissatisfied (*Creator as Critic*, p. 324). Page numbers will be given in the text.

'pessimism' that Forster finds to be pervasive in 'modern literature' as new writers 'each year find it more and more difficult to be cheerful with sincerity' (23). At the root of this pessimism, Forster claims, lies the modern (post-religious) recognition of the impermanence of all things, a worldview which the talk dubs 'tragedy'. Much like Wells (who had built on Charles Darwin's evolutionary theory to explain the idea of 'kineticism'), Forster turns to evolutionary biology for the clearest expression of the idea of absolute impermanence: contemporary 'serious writers', he submits, agree with Darwin's melancholy insight that 'everything is in perpetual change' (25). According to Forster, naturalism is the artistic movement that responds most faithfully to this vision of endless and unmitigated transformation. Contrary to what the 'pessimistic' novels of naturalists such as George Gissing might suggest, however, 'a tragedy need not necessarily end in a catastrophe—in other words a "sad" book need not have a "sad" ending' (24). The catastrophist strain in most naturalist novels, Forster claims, too hastily absolutizes tragedy by presenting it as the last word on life as such. Building on his roughshod survey of contemporary intellectual trends, Forster's paper offers two related propositions regarding the future of the novel:

I. Modern books ought—on the whole—to end unhappily, because (a) the idea of evolution [and] (b) the habit of detecting discomfort have entered too deeply into the modern mind for the artist to neglect them.
II. Unhappy books need not imply unhappy life, because art and life have different aims. The one aims at what is permanent, even if it is sad. The other aims at what is cheerful and gracious, even if it is transitory. (26)

While 'tragedy' occupies a necessary (and indeed 'permanent') place in modern literature, in our own finite and 'transitory' lives most of us aspire to happiness, however fleeting it may turn out to be. Forster's talk concludes with a third proposition that tries to resolve this apparent contradiction between art and life: 'to these two assertions I should like to add a third: that if the world succeeds in producing a literature that is sincerely cheerful, that literature will be the greatest that the world has ever known' (26). In contrast to *Howards End* (which directs our attention to Leonard's tragedy of unpreparedness), Forster's 1905 lecture ends by envisioning a future in which art will have ceased to be the medium of tragedy ('unhappiness'). The idea of a 'sincerely cheerful' literature—much like Forster's brief reconfiguration of romance in the unpublished version of *Howards End*—models the contours of a speculative reformist mode that anticipates a future in which fewer members of society will be exposed to the tragic consequences of risk. 'Happy versus Sad Endings', we could say, offers us the optimistic vision of a literature that will be the artistic image of the democratization of romance.[63]

Arctic Summer, the new novel project on which Forster embarked shortly after publishing *Howards End*, engages more explicitly with romance as the medium of a 'sincerely cheerful' future literature and its bearings on the sphere of welfarist politics. In November 1911, soon after the publication of *Howards End*, Forster wrote a letter to his friend Rupert Brooke which made reference to his work on the book. The letter states Forster's hope 'to put all I can remember of your paper into a novel [. . .]. You have not to mind. "It will never get written unless." '[64] Brooke had delivered the paper in question to the Cambridge branch of the Fabian Society in December 1910, and Forster had been in the audience. Brooke's lecture reflects on the desirability of centrally organized state sponsorship of the arts, and it specifically proposes the further graduation of income tax in order to fund state support for artists. Brooke is careful to distinguish his own attention to institutional reform from what he describes as Carpenter's and Whitman's politics of universal fellowship ('Brotherhood', Brooke declares, 'will not be heard of in this paper.').[65] The development of new state structures, Brooke observes, promises to contribute to the 'great liberty and security and independence [of] each man' (1), and these benefits should extend to artists as well. 'We have forsworn Revolution for a jog-trot along Social Reform,' Brooke notes, 'and there is plenty of time to take things with us on the way—Art above all' (8). Brooke's proposal to offer 'security' to artists by redistributing federal funds makes explicit reference to Edwardian debates about redistributive taxation as well as to public conversations about national insurance around 1910: state-organized support programmes for artists, Brooke maintains, 'should go on concurrently with taxation', so that they will 'be a financially minor, but actually important part of the annual Budget' (17).

Forster's interest in Brooke's lecture likely stemmed from the fact that the talk spoke immediately to the concerns that had animated *Howards End*. Like Forster, Brooke exposes the economic foundations that make possible the *Lebensform* which *Howards End* had described as romance—a materially secure life whose defining features are its openness to aesthetic pleasure and its embrace of the thrill of the new. 'The people who produce art', Brooke explains, 'are, if you look into it, nearly always dependent on unearned income' (2). In ways Forster would have appreciated, Brooke subjects his own social position to trenchant critique: 'Upper-

---

[63] Jock Macleod offers a related discussion of the 'language of optimism' that undergirded Edwardian arguments for extended welfare provisions as well as the period's progressivist 'reformist liberalism'. See Macleod, *Literature, Journalism, and the Vocabularies of Liberalism: Politics and Letters, 1886–1916* (London: Palgrave Macmillan, 2013), p. 179.

[64] Forster, Letter to Rupert Brooke 24 November 1911, in *Selected Letters*, p. 126.

[65] Rupert Brooke, *Democracy and the Arts* (London: Rupert Hart-Davis, 1946), p. 3. Brooke's lecture was only printed in 1946 because its topic clearly spoke very directly to post-war attempts—by John Maynard Keynes and others—to galvanize support for state sponsorship of the arts. Further references will be given parenthetically.

class young people who live on money they don't earn and dabble with painting or writing (I am one) are always, and so finely, a little too *temperamentvoll* to be interested in "politics". It's much easier and much splendider to assume that social organization or disorganization has no effect on people' (29). Because 'romance' is dependent on social organization, it will only become more generally available once the nation's economic resources are distributed in more egalitarian fashion. Fiscal redistribution—what Brooke calls 'collective control'—will help 'to diminish and extinguish the number of those dependent on unearned income' while also democratizing access to economic safeguards (2).

Like *Howards End*, Brooke's lecture calls not for the abolishment of romance but for its democratization—a line of thought Forster took up again in *Arctic Summer*. Forster had begun to work on this new book in 1911, but in the spring of 1912, after a first burst of creative activity, the novel petered out. Drafts of a few chapters of *Arctic Summer* survive, and they tell the story of an English civil servant, Martin Whitby, whose frustration with the limitations of his own administrative position leads him on to dream of bright new age of government.[66] The novel opens with a near-fatal accident at the train station in Basle. As Martin makes a dash for the train in order to secure seats for his family, he slips and is only just saved from falling under the moving train thanks to the lightning reactions of another young Englishman, Clesant March. Following this heroic intervention, Clesant is described as having 'the look and gesture of a warrior. He impressed Martin very much, and half an hour later he set out down the corridor to find him and to thank him'.[67] Clesant, who responds with cool indifference to Martin's profuse expressions of gratitude, seems to have stepped straight out of one of the medieval chivalric romances that Forster invokes as a point of comparison elsewhere in the text. Over the course of the remaining chapters of *Arctic Summer*, as the Marches and Clesants get to know each other, the contrast between Clesant and Martin intensifies further—for example, the aristocratic Clesant is increasingly irritated by Martin's modern convictions and progressive political ideals as well as by the Whitbys' bemused dismissal of the importance of aristocratic pedigrees. As Forster noted in a letter to Forrest Reid shortly after aborting work on *Arctic Summer*, the intellectual, political, and psychological contrast between Martin and Clesant proved to be the major stumbling block to his progress on the novel: 'I had got my antithesis all right, the antithesis between the civilised man, who hopes for an Arctic summer [a 'period when all is light'], and the heroic man who rides into the sea. But I had not settled what was going to

---

[66] As Stanford Rosenbaum points out in his invaluable account of Forster's work on the novel, 'the manuscripts of *Arctic Summer* are complicated' and the order in which individual chapter were written is difficult to reconstruct. In what follows, I focus on elements of the plot that are identical across most of Forster's draft versions. See Rosenbaum, *The Early Literary History of the Bloomsbury Group*, vol. 3: *Georgian Bloomsbury, 1910–1914* (London: Palgrave-Macmillan, 2003), p. 69.

[67] Forster, *Arctic Summer and other Fiction* (London: Arnold, 1980), pp. 120–1.

happen, and that is why the novel remains a fragment.'[68] Forster's comment suggests a rigid antagonism between Clesant's embodiment of a heroic life modelled on aristocratic romance and Martin's unadventurously meticulous reformist progressivism. Contrary to *Howards End*, however, where Henry's entrepreneurial derring-do is squarely matched by Helen's 'sentimental' socialism, Forster's sympathies in *Arctic Summer* lie quite clearly with one of the two central characters: while Martin's stolid earnestness is unlikely to win him many admirers, Clesant's neurotic obsession with social status is profoundly disturbing from the start, and it comes to a head when Clesant discovers that his brother has been rusticated from Cambridge after getting into trouble with prostitutes. Clesant, who is livid at the news, attacks his brother: 'Oh, you swine—you lout with a gentleman's face—get away from us to your own sort and do it again. Go to hell [...] I curse you.' This brutal rejection by his status-obsessed family drives Clesant's brother to commit suicide. The structuring opposition between Clesant and Martin implies not only a contrast between two different temperaments but between two wholly distinct views of British society: while Clesant looks back nostalgically to an imaginary age of aristocratic valour and romance, Martin anticipates a future that will be more democratic and egalitarian (though also, Forster implies, more reliant on bureaucratic organization).

Its truncated textual state notwithstanding, it is clear that *Arctic Summer* begins to imagine a new (and more modern) type of romance-like heroism through the unlikely figure of Martin Whitby himself. This new kind of romance differs signally from the version of romance Forster associated with the capitalist Henry Wilcox and the aristocrat Clesant March. As Martin informs his friend Lady Borlase, he dreams of a new great age for the state:

> my new era is to have no dawn. It is to be a kind of Arctic Summer, in which there will be time to get something really great done. [...] Dawn implies twilight, and we have decided to abolish them both. Several societies exist for the purpose, to none of which you have as yet subscribed.[69]

The startling luminosity of this arctic summer, which seems to banish ambiguity and contingency altogether, captures Martin's absurdly grandiose expectations for the future accomplishments of the interventionist state. Martin's hopes, we are told, are partly the result of living too protected a life: 'In the Army or at sea he would have been unmasked long ago,' the narrator concludes, 'but he had slipped from one shelter to another, from home to Cambridge, from Cambridge to a government office' (158). This sheltered upbringing has led Martin to see total protection against risk as the ultimate reformist aspiration. Indeed, his

---

[68] Forster, *Arctic Summer*, p. 162.   [69] Forster, *Arctic Summer*, p. 125.

anticipation of an eternal day of government comes closer to portraying the state as a 'heroic actor' than any other text I have discussed in this book, with the possible exception of Wells's *New Machiavelli*, in which the young reformist zealot Remington holds forth about 'the splendid projects and possibilities of life and order that lay before the world, about all that a resolute and constructive effort might do at the present time. We are building a state [...] secure and splendid, we are in the dawn of the great age of mankind.'[70] *Arctic Summer*'s reprise of this reformist enthusiasm draws directly on Brooke's talk to the Fabian Society in Cambridge: institutional reform, Brooke had declared, involves 'taking our fate into our own hands, controlling the future, shaping Life to our will.'[71] Martin Whitby, Remington, and Brooke are not content to depict the state as an infrastructural support that can be imagined in terms of the new forms of life it helps to enable. Instead, they present it as a secular godhead that transcends the sphere of the social altogether. This radiant vision is at odds with the less monolithic (and less authoritarian) understanding of the state that I have been describing in this book. What we are shown in *Arctic Summer* is not the democratic expansion of romance which Forster had begun to envision in *Howards End* but something closer to Northrop Frye's understanding of romance as a transcendent eternal summer in which all 'ordinary laws' seem 'suspended'.[72]

Arctic Summer is clearly not a straightforward celebration of Brooke's ideas. Instead, the text usefully reminds us that Forster's default view of state institutions tended to be satirical or outright dystopian. *Arctic Summer* could accordingly be described as Forster's attempt to parody the speculative reformist mode— provided we recognize that Forster's text involves a committed effort to enter into the progressive idiom of reform in an attempt to understand it. *Arctic Summer* acknowledges the aspirational force of the speculative reformist mode even as it dials it up to an extreme degree. In so doing, the text echoes the constitutive ambivalences of literary writing about reform that Wells described in 1912: 'It is not only caricature and satire I demand. We must have not only the fullest treatment of the temptations, vanities, abuses, and absurdities of office, but all its dreams, its sense of constructive order, its consolations, its sense of service, and its nobler satisfactions.'[73]

When it is read alongside *Howards End*, *Arctic Summer* indicates Forster's considerable and sustained interest in debates about institutional reform around 1900. Whitby's hopes for a brilliant new age of government give us a version of the

---

[70] I discuss Zarena Aslami's concept of the state as a 'heroic actor' in the Introduction. See Aslami, *The Dream Life of Citizens: Late Victorian Novels and the Fantasy of the State* (New York: Fordham University Press, 2012), esp. pp. 5–8. For Wells: *The New Machiavelli* (London: Penguin, 2005), p. 209.

[71] Brooke, *Democracy and the Arts*, p. 3.

[72] Frye, *The Anatomy of Criticism: Four Essays* (Princeton: Princeton University Press, 1971), p. 33, and on the perennial 'summer' of romance: pp. 186–206.

[73] Wells, 'The Contemporary Novel' [1912], in Wells, *An Englishman Looks at the World* (London: Cassell, 1914), pp. 148–69 (p. 165).

reformist's Wellsian 'sense of constructive order', but they also echo Forster's own call for a new 'sincerely cheerful' literature in 'Happy versus Sad Endings'. In contrast to 'The Machine Stops', which had presented institutions as alien technological impositions on human life, *Arctic Summer* is Forster's most strenuous attempt to develop a style that is attuned to the aspirational reconfiguration of romance he had anticipated in his 1905 talk to the Fabians. Forster's growing frustration with *Arctic Summer* indicates that this experiment led him into an artistic impasse, possibly because it forced him to inhabit a viewpoint which— with the notable exception of *Howards End*—he had previously preferred to treat in a satirical or dystopian vein.[74] And yet, Forster's general scepticism towards the extension of statal mandates notwithstanding, it seems that he looked more generously on the question of interventionist reform for a few important years around 1910. Forster's literary engagement with reformist debates might even offer a clue regarding his 'silent' years as a novelist, which lasted until the publication of *A Passage to India* in 1924. The process that helped Forster overcome his writer's block only began in 1914 when he joined his friend Goldsworthy Lowes Dickinson on a trip to India. Abandoning the crowded playing field of domestic politics for the less familiar terrain of colonial politics enabled Forster to engage afresh with the ethos of friendship and brotherhood that had come under such intense strain in the heated political climate of the early 1900s.

---

[74] Forster's continued hesitations vis-à-vis state-centred reform also led him to view critically the expansion of the welfare state institutions in Britain after 1945. In a 1944 entry in his commonplace book, Forster quoted from a letter sent by Edward Carpenter to Roger Fry in the early 1900s: 'I always feel more and more how hard it is for the rich man (or those born in that state of life) to enter into the kingdom. It is so very easy to drift, instead'. In a spirit that recalls the most sceptical passages from his Edwardian works, Forster added: 'Today for the rich man supply "the properly insured man"' (*Commonplace Book*, p. 163).

Coda

Reformist Legacies

I now believe, though I have not always believed,
that the condition for the success of the long revolution
in any real terms is decisively a short revolution.

Raymond Williams, *Politics and Letters* (1979)

Proponents of the welfare state often look back with considerable nostalgia to the years after 1945, when the so-called post-war consensus in Britain created a political climate that favoured a generous welfare state, nationalization, higher taxes on capital, and strong trade unions. The post-war period is sometimes described as the historical culmination of progressivist Labourite policies, but it has become increasingly clear—thanks to recent work by Thomas Piketty, David Edgerton, Martin Daunton, and others—just how anomalous the convergence of social stability, economic growth, and more egalitarian wealth distribution in this period actually was.[1] 'The appearance of consensus,' Daunton observes, 'might well arise from the constraints of economic and political circumstances rather than from any ideological convergence.'[2] Historians who describe the decades after 1910 as a steady onward march of Labourite Reason typically point to the years after 1945 as the moment when the social-reformist projects of the preceding decades finally came to fruition. These projects include several of the causes touched on in this book: for example, in 1947 Clement Attlee's Labour government introduced a development tax that was designed (as the chancellor Hugh Dalton promised) to put an end to certain forms of land speculation and financial landownership;[3] this new land tax was in turn part of a much larger project of

---

[1] See Piketty, *Capital in the Twenty-First Century* (Cambridge, MA: Harvard University Press, 2014); Edgerton, *The Rise and Fall of the British Nation: A Twentieth-Century History* (London: Penguin, 2018). Edgerton offers a revisionist account of the rise of the British welfare state after 1945 which describes it as the continuation of interwar Tory 'nationalist productionist' thinking (xxx).

[2] Daunton, *Just Taxes: The Politics of Taxation in Britain, 1914–1979* (Cambridge: Cambridge University Press, 2009), p. 17.

[3] Labour's post-war Town and Country Planning Act fell short of the type of full land nationalization I discussed in Chapter 3. Moreover, as Brett Christophers notes, 'the national interest would not remain thus privileged for long': when the Conservatives returned to power in 1951 they dismantled the so-called betterment levy. See Christophers, *The New Enclosures* (London: Verso, 2018), pp. 110–11. For a broader account of the afterlives of the language of 'rent' (and rentierism), see Christophers, *Rentier Capitalism: Who Owns the Economy, and Who Pays for It?* (London: Verso, 2020).

British Literature and the Life of Institutions: Speculative States. Benjamin Kohlmann, Oxford University Press.
© Benjamin Kohlmann 2021. DOI: 10.1093/oso/9780198836179.003.0007

fiscal reconstruction that involved significant increases in progressive taxation on the rich;[4] and finally, these new taxation schemes also helped to fund what was arguably the most iconic institutional innovation of the post-war years, the introduction of National Insurance and the creation of the National Health Service (a development that drew much of its momentum from William Beveridge's influential 1942 government report).[5]

Much like the reformist moments I have focussed on in this book, the story of Britain's post-war consensus can be told either as a story of progressivism's cumulative successes or as a sobering tale of political failure—that is, either as the historical triumph of certain demands for redistribution and restructuring, or as the co-optation of radical social energies into a newly solidified political status quo. This key ambivalence—Does reform signal a success of deliberative reason or a failure of radical political will?—is fundamental to the ways we talk about reform. It is possible to detect similar ambiguities in the reformist episodes discussed in preceding chapters, extending all the way back to the establishment of East End settlements in the 1880s. As I suggested in Chapter 2, for instance, Gissing's and Ward's novels present the settlements as sites of educational indoctrination while also indicating that these institutions are capable of opening up spaces for necessary dissent and counter-hegemonic critique. These constitutive ambivalences of the reformist impulse were succinctly captured by the prominent sociologist and social philosopher Helen Lynd, whose 1945 study *England in the 1880s: Toward a Social Basis of Freedom* tried to make sense of the reformist moment of the post-war years by glancing back to the decades around 1900. Taking her cue from a wartime pronouncement by Winston Churchill, Lynd notes:

> If we regard it as a genuine sign of desirable social change that the leader of the Conservative Party and the Coalition Government reiterates the desire [...] that 'No one who can take advantage of higher education should be denied this chance,' and places himself and his colleagues as 'strong partisans of national compulsory insurance for all classes, for all purposes, from the cradle to the grave—then we may view the [eighteen-]eighties as the beginning of a strong people's movement which is gradually bringing England nearer to the building of a better world for men. But, if we regard such a statement as only an ill-fitting mask for further absorption by the ruling class of labor and the aims of the people, a thin disguise for attempts of the government to 'simplify and mollify political divergence', to side-step specific pledges to any 'particular

---

[4] Chapter 4 has offered a partial prehistory of these debates. For the continuation of these debates after World War II, see Kenneth Scheve and David Stasavage, *Taxing the Rich: A History of Fiscal Fairness in the United States and Europe* (Princeton: Princeton University Press, 2016), pp. 185–6.

[5] See Chapter 5 for discussion of Beveridge's early work on unemployment and some of the literary resonances of the Edwardian debate about national insurance.

scheme' except those which insure 'a widespread healthy and vigorous private enterprise'—then we may be inclined to agree with [the guild socialist G. D. H.] Cole and [the socialist and Labour politician Harold] Laski that the significance of the 'eighties was the 'bourgeoisification' of labor and the abortion of a genuine working-class movement.[6]

Lynd discovers surprising similarities between the 1880s and the mid-1940s. This is true in particular of the movement towards an ethos of 'positive freedom' which Lynd identifies as the 1880s' most significant politico-intellectual legacy. In her account, the late Victorian attention to forms of positive freedom—in the 'neo-Hegelian' works of T. H. Green and elsewhere—involved a shift away from the 'tendency to state problems negatively in terms of not seeking what men want but of avoiding what they fear: freedom *from* want, from poverty, from anxiety, from ignorance.'[7] While these goals—freedom from want, poverty, anxiety, ignorance—were all important 'aims of the welfare State' in the 1940s, Lynd argues, political and social theorists around 1900 had gone beyond such purely negative formulations by describing the state as the material embodiment of a set of shared social aims. Lynd hopes that by paying attention to these earlier debates, post-World War II reconstruction will be able to avoid the ideological reduction of the state to an assemblage of institutional and legal safeguards. The reductive view of the state as an ensemble of governmental mechanisms, Lynd warns, makes the state vulnerable to colonization by the forces of the market, turning it into little more than a 'vigorous private enterprise'.

Lynd's analysis is extremely perceptive, although by emphasizing the commonalities between the decades around 1900 and the socio-cultural reconstruction after World War II, she also runs the risk of papering over some significant differences between these two conjunctures. Most importantly perhaps, periods of post-war reconstruction can build on a collective sense of urgency by seizing on opportunities for reform at a time when the extreme socio-economic strain of war has created institutional openings for progressive change. The reformist literary mode around 1900 did not emerge in response to experiences of wartime austerity, thus prompting writers to imagine the growth of welfarist structures as a slow and piecemeal transition towards new institutional regimes. 'Early twentieth-century democratic reformers', the political theorist David Runciman explains, 'were able to take advantage of the enormous slack in the system. There was room to grow the franchise, to grow the debt, to grow the power of national government, to grow the tax base, to grow the party system, to grow the labour movement, to

---

[6] Lynd, *England in the 1880s: Toward a Social Basis of Freedom* (London: Transaction, 1985), p. 412.
[7] Lynd, *England in the 1880s*, p. 427; orig. emph. For the influence of Green's 'neo-Hegelian' thinking, see *England in the 1880s*, pp. 8, 176–8, and *passim*.

grow the public's sense of trust in the state. There was room to grow democracy.'[8] *British Literature and the Life of Institutions* has focussed on moments of educational, land, fiscal, and unemployment reform to suggest that literature became an important site for engagements with this democratizing state. Literature, I have argued, came to be invested with a speculative force that was registered quite explicitly across a wide range of literary works—from Harold Emerson's inept hankering after a 'new poetic form' that will appeal 'to *all* people, to *all* ranks' (in George Gissing's *Thyrza*) to Edward Carpenter's attempt to turn his writing into a poetic common ground; and from Mary Ward's Greenian vision of an ideal 'truth' that is fully actualized in the literary work itself, to H. G. Wells's aspirational realism that shows us how the utopian impulse gradually emerges from within a prior mimetic one.

In concluding, I want to continue this line of inquiry by turning briefly to a set of debates—typically associated with the establishment of the Arts Council of Great Britain in 1946, though in truth extending back at least to the early 1900s—that touched on the nature (and socio-economic preconditions) of literary writing itself. Paying attention to conversations about state sponsorship of the arts, I want to suggest, requires us to take seriously attempts by modernist writers to harness artistic experimentation to the larger project of democratic institutional reform. These attempts exhibit reformism's constitutive ambivalence: on the one hand, they seek to imagine the possibility of a democratic aesthetic; on the other, they are vulnerable to critique because they suppress the disruptive potential of revolution in favour of an aesthetic vision of social integration and political consensus.

My discussion of E. M. Forster's novel fragment *Arctic Summer* in the preceding chapter made reference to Rupert Brooke's *Democracy and the Arts*—a text that called for centralized support of the arts. First delivered as a talk at the Cambridge branch of the Fabian Society in 1910, Brooke's text indicates that debates about centralized state sponsorship of the arts were a feature of reformist conversations during the Edwardian years. Brooke's text was only published with some delay in 1946, thanks in large part to Geoffrey Keynes, the brother of the economist John Maynard Keynes who would shortly be named the Arts Council's founding Chairman. As Geoffrey Keynes noted in his Preface to Brooke's text, the manuscript was overdue for publication, having 'for nearly twenty-five years lain more or less unregarded in my library': 'Now, in 1946, the subject of the paper has suddenly become topical, more topical than when it was written, with the dawning of the Socialist State in England of which Brooke was one of the Minor Prophets.'[9] The possibility of providing state subsidies for the arts had occupied many writers of the 1910s and 1920s, and there is a real sense that this reformist idea is one of British modernism's recurring concerns. This is true in particular of the members

---

[8] Runciman, *How Democracy Ends* (London: Profile, 2018), p. 71.

[9] Brooke, *Democracy and the Arts* (London: Hart-Davis, 1946), p. viii.

of the Bloomsbury circle, whose explorations of the question of artistic autonomy were from the beginning premised on the recognition that creative production depended on economic support.[10] For example, the postimpressionist painter (and Bloomsburyite) Roger Fry echoed Brooke's sentiments in his contribution to *The Great State* (the 1912 essay collection, co-edited by Wells, that I touched on in Chapter 4). Fry's essay, 'The Artist in the Great State', acknowledges that artistic creation requires a measure of economic freedom, but it also insists that such freedom must be reimagined for a post-capitalist world: 'It is the argument of commercialism, as it once was of aristocracy,' Fry writes, 'that the accumulation of surplus wealth in a few hands enables this spiritual life [of art and culture] to maintain its existence, that no really valuable or useless work (for from this point of view only useless work has value) could exist in the community without such accumulations of wealth.'[11] Art that is dependent on monopolized wealth, Fry notes, is likely to find itself degraded to the 'false value' of a status symbol, a signifier of 'ostentation' (257). It is therefore the task of the state to create spaces for the free exercise of creativity that do not simply reproduce the scandalous inequalities of capitalist society: this aim, Fry concludes, can be realized only through 'a greater distribution of wealth' (257) and through 'a considerable levelling of social conditions' (269) that also extends to the methodical provision of state subsidies to artists. On Fry's account, the labour of the artist embodies the contradictions of capitalist society, but it also captures the tensions that will characterize the reformed state of the future: 'the modern artist puts the question of any socialistic—or, indeed, of any completely ordered—state in its acutest form' (259). On the one hand, Fry observes, art that is funded by the state will evince an orientation towards the common good that is generally lacking in art created under capitalism. On the other, 'public art' that is created under the auspices of an interventionist state runs the risk of unadventurous conformism: as Fry points out, the idea that 'public art' is bound to be 'crassly mediocre and inexpressive is so firmly rooted that it seems to have almost the prestige of constitutional precedent' (259). The forms and content of art must not be prescribed by a quasi-authoritarian 'great state': the artist 'demands as an essential to the proper use of his powers a freedom from restraint such as no other workman expects. He must work when he feels inclined; he cannot work to order' (259). Fry's reflections on the 'artist in the great state' double as a meditation on the nature of citizenship—and as such, they resonate with the reformist imaginary I have

---

[10]   Andrew Goldstone, in an important recent discussion of aesthetic autonomy, argues that 'relative autonomy is not a transhistorical feature of literary art but a specific modernist practice, integral to the development of new institutions for literature in the first half of the twentieth century'. Goldstone, *Fictions of Autonomy: Modernism from Wilde to de Man* (New York: Oxford University Press, 2013), p. 186.

[11]   Fry, 'The artist in the great state', in H. G. Wells et al. (eds.) *The Great State: Essays in Construction*, (London: Harper, 1912), pp. 249–72 (p. 252). Further references are given parenthetically.

described in this book. Art, on Fry's account, forms part of a richly realized social sphere that depends on the infrastructural support of state institutions but is not coercively forced under their logic: 'The Great State aims at human freedom; essentially, it is an organisation for leisure out of which art grows' (271). Fry's comment recalls Forster's understanding of 'romance' as a democratically extended *Lebensform* whose relative economic safety grants sufficient 'leisure' to pursue 'fragments of beauty and joy'.[12]

Fry's and Brooke's essays anticipate a large-scale introduction of state sponsorship of the arts that would not be realized until 1946 under the chairmanship of John Maynard Keynes (himself a former member of the Bloomsbury set). Yet, while Brooke and Fry look ahead to the state's 'considerable levelling of social conditions', we have to turn elsewhere for a fully articulated modernist aesthetic that was designed to convey this egalitarian social vision. Virginia Woolf's writings, for example, have been celebrated—by critics such as Gillian Beer, Maria DiBattista, and Jane Marcus—for providing readers with the aesthetic image of an inclusive communality. Woolf's novels, we could say, embody a modernist version of the reformist literary mode—a distinctive alternative to the self-consciously revolutionary mode of avant-garde artistic production I described in Chapter 1.[13] Scholars have tended to home in on Woolf's searing critique of male-dominated institutions—parliament, universities, the medical establishment, the army—, but her interwar writings also give us glimpses of a range of progressive reformist proposals. These engagements include Woolf's visit to the Cooperative Guild movement in the early 1910s (an encounter Woolf recalled with some ambivalence in her 1931 Preface to the collection *Life as We Have Known It*) as well as her famous observation from 1929 that 'a woman must have money and a room of her own if she is to write fiction'.[14]

Woolf's programmatic demand in *A Room of One's Own* looks back in part to Brooke's and Fry's calls for state subsidies, yet her most forward-looking statements on the emerging structures of the welfare state can be found in her essays of the late 1930s and early 1940s. Woolf's book-length essay *Three Guineas* (1938), for example, echoes the language of fiscal redistribution that I identified in Chapter 4, and it describes taxation as creating a web of new social relations and ethical responsibilities ('the income tax which supplies [the] salaries' of government officials and public servants, Woolf notes, 'now stands at about five shillings in the pound. We have all, therefore, an interest in asking how that money is

---

[12] Forster, *The Manuscripts of* Howards End (London: Arnold, 1973), p. 324.
[13] Beer, *Virginia Woolf: The Common Ground* (Edinburgh University Press, 1996); Maria DiBattistta, *Imagining Virginia Woolf: An Experiment in Critical Biography* (Princeton: Princeton University Press, 2009), pp. 78–82; Jane Marcus, 'Thinking back through our mothers,' in: Marcus (ed.), *New Feminist Essays on Virginia Woolf* (Lincoln: University of Nebraska Press, 1981), pp. 1–30.
[14] Woolf, *A Room of One's Own* (London: Penguin, 2004), p. 4.

spent, and upon whom').[15] This interest in institutional structures is given an aspirational reformist direction in 'The Leaning Tower,' the essay that grew out of a lecture Woolf gave to the Workers' Education Association in 1940. Anticipating the emergence of the post-war welfare state (rather than looking back to the fiscal debates around 1900), Woolf argues that new redistributive mechanisms—notably a steeper income tax—will help to create a more egalitarian society by financing new welfarist structures. As Janice Ho observes, Woolf's proposals in 'The Leaning Tower' capture the welfare state's 'promise that the nation would be radically restructured to bring forth a more just and democratic society'—this includes Woolf's understanding of the income tax as a tool 'directed toward funding public institutions universally accessible to all citizens in order to equal-ize, at least to some extent, the structures of class'.[16] Woolf's vision of a 'classless society' seems surprisingly radical, and John Lehmann—the poet, editor, and managing director of the Hogarth Press—even thought it proved that Woolf 'was a socialist' and that 'no one could doubt her sympathy with the struggles of working-class people'.[17] 'There will be no more upper classes; middle classes; lower classes,' Woolf writes: 'All classes will be merged in one class'.[18] What Woolf anticipates here is not so much a classless society as a society in which everyone will have been integrated into the same class. Even so, her remarks are important because they can be read as a prescient anticipation of the post-war welfare state which prominent leftist intellectuals of the 1950s such as Richard Hoggart and Stuart Hall heralded as the embodiment of a new 'sense of classless-ness'. Moreover, her comments also help us to reframe Woolf's own modernist aesthetic as an extension of the speculative reformist mode into the interwar years.[19] As Ho argues, for example, *Mrs Dalloway*'s experimental aesthetic is in dialogue with the welfarist reforms initiated by Lloyd George: the novel 'portrays an emergent social citizenship—a set of imaginative affiliations between strangers from different social backgrounds—that is specifically made possible through the nascent but already-expanding infrastructures of the welfare state.'[20] Woolf's fiction, this suggests, figures the welfare state's emerging institutions in terms of the new social relations and democratized forms of life ('affiliations between strangers from different social backgrounds') which they will enable. Readings

---

[15] Woolf, *Three Guineas* (New York. Harcourt Brace, 1966), p. 46.

[16] Ho, *Nation and Citizenship in the Twentieth-Century British Novel* (Cambridge: Cambridge University Press, 2015), p. 59.

[17] Woolf, 'The leaning tower,' in: *The Moment and Other Essays* (New York: Harcourt Brace, 1948), pp. 128–54 (p. 146); Lehmann, 'A Postscript', *Folios of New Writing* (Spring 1941): 42–6 (p. 44).

[18] Woolf, 'The leaning tower', p. 150.

[19] Hall, 'A sense of classlessness', *Universities and Left Review* 5 (1958): 26–32; and Hoggart, 'Speaking to each other', in: *Conviction*, ed. Norman MacKenzie (London: MacGibbon and Kee, 1958): pp. 121–38. Hogggart's and Hall's comments also resonate with Raymond Williams's 'emphatic commitment to a consensualist evolutionism' in the 1950s and early 1960s. See Williams, *Politics and Letters: Interviews with New Left Review* (London: Verso, 2015), p. 409.

[20] Ho, *Nation and Citizenship*, p. 59.

that seek to stress the reformist thrust of Woolf's writing can point to the moments of interclassism that are made possible by the shifting and blending perspectives of free indirect discourse—a technique that includes Woolf's inter-weaving of multiple narrative voices as well as her use of connecting devices (e.g. *Mrs Dalloway*'s skywriting airplane) to engineer changes in perspective.[21] A text such as *Mrs Dalloway* shows that, social differences notwithstanding, individuals are connected in manifold ways, through shared habits and thoughts as well as through linked perceptions of the world around them.

As I have argued elsewhere, Woolf's reformist aesthetic came under criticism from writers affiliated with the revolutionary communist movement of the later interwar years.[22] These writers—most notably proletarian authors of the 1930s such as John Sommerfield and James Barke—repurposed modernist styles to create the impression of an emerging social collectivity. Adapting the peripatetic narrative voice of *Mrs Dalloway* and *The Waves*, they set out to reveal continuities and divisions among London's richest and poorest citizens. But these proletarian modernists also crucially registered the constraints which Woolf's literary idiom imposed on their communist vision. Whereas Woolf had presented the creation of social collectives as the result of spontaneous energy and communally experienced rhythms, communists such as Sommerfield and Barke were convinced that the social revolution must be the outcome of conscious collective action on the part of a radicalized proletariat. Accordingly, these writers often confront Woolfian (and Joycean) techniques of multivocality with a monologic authorial voice that is intended to capture the certitudes of communist doctrine.

The artistic process of critique that characterized proletarian adaptations of Woolf's aesthetic comes most clearly to the fore in a 1941 issue of Lehmann's literary magazine *Folios of New Writing* that featured several left-wing responses to Woolf's 'Leaning Tower' essay. The responses to Woolf's essay include pieces by the working-class author and coal miner B. L. Coombes ('Below the Tower'), the communist writer Edward Upward ('The Falling Tower'), and the poet Louis MacNeice ('The Tower That Once'). These articles work to expose the class bias of Woolf's reformist understanding of democratic classlessness. For example, Coombes's contribution grants that Woolf's modernist novels offer useful mater-ial for proletarian writers because her texts develop a broadly democratic aesthetic that entails gestures towards a 'classless future'.[23] However, like Sommerfield and Barke, Coombes points out that this aesthetic invariably comes up against the

---

[21] For an excellent general discussion of 'free indirect style' as 'a project to democratize point of view, a project whose endpoint is the abandonment of perspective altogether', see Timothy Bewes, 'Free Indirect', *Political Concepts: A Critical Lexicon*, www.politicalconcepts.org, last accessed 20 June 2020.

[22] The comments in the next few paragraphs draw on my 'Proletarian modernism: Film, literature, theory', *PMLA* 134.5 (2019): 1056–75.

[23] Coombes, 'Below the tower', in: *Folios of New Writing* (Spring 1941): 30–6 (p. 30).

material limits of Woolf's class position. While many revolutionary writers of the 1930s had been eager to learn from the modernists, Coombes submits, Woolf herself had failed to pay any serious attention to the work of the decade's proletarian writers. As a result, her writing was hamstrung by an inability to incorporate the (hitherto artistically marginalized) experiences of the working classes into her fiction. And even if Woolf had wanted to acquire first-hand knowledge about proletarian life, the constraints of her social position would have barred her from doing so:

> Now, I am sure that if Virginia Woolf should visit this mining area in which I live, she would be taken into the parlour—if the family was fortunate to have one—and the behaviour of the adults as well as the play of the children would be restrained to the soberness of a Sunday afternoon; but if I went to that same house I would be invited into the kitchen where the play of the children or the discussion of problems concerning work and living would continue without any pause.[24]

Coombes confronts Woolf's artistic outlook—which sidelines the particularity of working class experience as well as the possibility of a proletarian revolution—with the material conditions of proletarian life in the present.[25] Woolf's style, Coombes suggests, enabled communist writers to experiment with the novelistic representation of classlessness, yet the reformist cast of her novels also pre-empted the more radical implications of their revolutionary communism. To put this another way: if Woolf's artistic interest in 'classlessness' looks forward to the redistributive democracy of the post-war consensus, Coombes reminds us that her novels—much like the emerging institutional structures of the welfare state itself—are insufficiently attuned to non-hegemonic voices and, as such, must be subjected to radical critique.

The question of classlessness that was raised so urgently by proletarian writers and revolutionaries of the 1930s and early 1940s was never merely a matter of aesthetics, nor did it simply disappear after the war. There were those like Cyril Connolly—the influential editor of the literary magazine *Horizon* (1940–49)—who propagated the idea that once the war was over, interwar modernism would once more re-emerge and reign supreme.[26] Writing in the wake of Labour's 1945 General Election victory, Connolly linked his vision of a resurgent modernism to hopes for a more egalitarian reconstruction of Britain's institutions: 'The Election

---

[24] Coombes, 'Below the tower', p. 31.

[25] The other essays in the *New Writing* issue echo Coombes's concerns. For example, MacNeice's essay acknowledges Woolf's aesthetic attempt to represent 'a classless society' but proceeds to contrast it with current socio-economic conditions that leave individuals 'crippled, evasive, divided'. See MacNeice, 'The tower that once', in: *Folios of New Writing* (Spring 1941): 37–41 (p. 37).

[26] Connolly, 'Comment', *Horizon*, 1 (January 1940), p. 70.

result', he wrote in a *Horizon* editorial in September 1945, 'is a blow struck against the religion of money. It has given us a Government of reasonable people, people like ourselves who are "we", not "they", and who are unlikely to be overcome by power.'[27] In this new historical context, modernism would re-establish itself—much as Woolf herself had hoped in 1940—as the aesthetic of a reformed democratic polity.

The Arts Council of Great Britain was to be the central motor for this modernist revival, and the early institutional history of the Arts Council can help us understand why Connolly and other intellectuals came to see modernism as the ideal art for Britain's reformist moment after 1945. Members of the Bloomsbury Group had advocated state sponsorship of the arts from the 1910s onwards, and Keynes's chairmanship of the Council further consolidated the Council's image as the institutional arm of high modernism.[28] The Arts Council's funding was initially limited to music and the arts, and a systematic extension of the Council's activities to literature did not take place until the 1960s. Even so, some of Keynes's pronouncements on the Arts Council and its wartime precursor CEMA (the Council for the Encouragement of Music and the Arts) recall ideas that will be familiar to readers of the Bloomsburyites Brooke and Fry: the artist, Keynes had pointed out as early as 1936, 'needs economic security and enough income, and then to be left to himself, at the same time the servant of the public and his own master'.[29] While it would be possible to extend the literary-historical arc of *British Literature and the Life of Institutions* to the 1940s and 1950s, this more expansive narrative would need to explain how mid-century reformism succeeded in quietly pushing radical voices such as Sommerfield's, Barke's, and Coombes's to the period's political and artistic sidelines. Indeed, as Ben Harker has shown, it was only much later—following important work by critics such as Francis Mulhern and Alan Sinfield—that the left began to 'see the Arts Council as an expression of the cultural logic of post-war [...] social democracy or welfare capitalism, a medium through which an "interwar liberal minority culture" [centred around the Bloomsbury circle and Leavis's *Scrutiny*] "would be diffused through an ever-widening audience" without any fundamental questioning of "what counted as cultural value or the proper forms of cultural participation"'.[30]

---

[27] Cyril Connolly, 'Comment', *Horizon*, 69 (September 1945), pp. 148–55 (p. 149).

[28] See Anna Upchurch, 'John Maynard Keynes, the Bloomsbury Group and the origins of the Arts Council Movement', *International Journal of Cultural Policy* 10.2 (2004): 203–17. Upchurch's article also points to Quentin Bell's *Civilization* (1926) as one of the Arts Council's ur-texts.

[29] Keynes, 'Art and the state', in: *The Collected Writings of John Maynard Keynes*, vol. 28: *Social, Political and Literary Writings*, ed. Donald Moggridge (Cambridge: Cambridge University Press, 2013), pp. 341–9 (p. 344).

[30] Harker, *The Chronology of Revolution: Communism, Culture, and Civil Society in Twentieth-Century Britain* (Toronto: University of Toronto Press, 2021), p. 67 (Harker is here quoting from Francis Mulhern's *Culture/Metaculture*). Harker's fascinating account demonstrates that post-war

And yet, if Connolly had hoped that the Arts Council would inspire a resurgence of interwar modernism, he was mistaken. It is certainly true that under the changed historical conditions of the consensus-oriented post-war state modernism was no longer exposed to the kinds of revolutionary challenges that had been directed at it by the proletarian writers of the 1930s. However, the form of modernist artistic production that survived into the post-1945 period and that received funding from the Arts Council was no longer the mandarin 'High Modernism' (or 'interwar liberal minority culture') which critics sometimes associate with the 1920s—instead, the new art that emerged during the reformist moment of the late 1940s and 1950s responded in complex ways to Keynes's conviction that the state-funded artist would no longer be only 'his own master' but also 'the servant of the public'. Recent work in modernist studies has begun to reconstruct the contours of the 'public modernism' and 'public culture' that crystallized from 1945 onwards.[31] Much of this new scholarship—notably by musicologists and historians of mid-century art—explores the reconstitution of modernism as a more broadly democratic art that took place under the aegis of the Arts Council. For example, musical composers such as Benjamin Britten programmatically abandoned the artistic prestige of interwar modernism (associated with names such as Alban Berg, Béla Bartók, and Arnold Schoenberg) in favour of a more capacious aesthetic that was hospitable to a broader range of popular, low-, and middle-brow styles. The aesthetic that resulted from this strategic hybridization of modernism's formal repertoires was one of 'compromise and synthesis'—an art that was self-consciously consensualist and reformist rather than revolutionary.[32] The 'modern artist', as Fry had remarked in 1912, 'puts the

communist cultural leaders shared much ground with Leavis's Scrutineers and consequently found themselves in agreement with the mission of the Arts Council: 'the party', Harker concludes, 'now attached its central strategy for advance to the structures of a British state' that it had previously recognized as 'deeply enmeshed with a history of imperialism' (p. 81). In a related account, Dave Beech has cautioned that we need to beware 'of identifying the Arts Council, or public subsidy generally, with one version of the political economy of the welfare state': we need 'to remain alert to the tensions and contradictions entailed in combining rival regimes of conservative, liberal and social democratic state intervention.' Beech, *Art and Value: Art's Economic Exceptionalism in Classical, Neoclassical and Marxist Economics* (Leiden: Brill, 2015), p. 130.

[31] For the idea of 'public modernism', see Marina MacKay, *Modernism and World War II* (Cambridge: Cambridge University Press, 2010), pp. 1–21 (here: p. 21). The concept of 'public culture' is discussed by Asha Rogers, who glosses the term as the seemingly paradoxical 'commitment of post-war social democracies to increasing autonomization through state action', see Rogers, *State Sponsored Literature: Britain and Cultural Diversity after 1945* (Oxford: Oxford University Press, 2020), p. 10.

[32] See Chowrimootoo, *Middlebrow Modernism: Britten's Operas and the Great Divide* (Oakland: University of California Press, 2018), pp. 1–29. 'Rather than taking the aesthetic ambivalence [of Britten's operas]—their uneasy position between high and low, modernism and mass culture—as a problem to be resolved,' Chowrimootoo writes, 'I use it to explain their broad appeal' (3). For a discussion of these ideas in relation to the Arts Council's policy-making, see Nathaniel G. Lew, *Tonic to the Nation: Making English Music in the Festival of Britain* (London: Routledge, 2016). As Fred M. Leventhal notes of CEMA, the dehierarchization of artistic production was also carried out at a practical level as 'ordinary people' were being invited to 'experience art as practitioners, not as consumers'. See Leventhal, '"The best for the most": CEMA and state sponsorship of the arts in wartime, 1939–1945', *Twentieth-Century British History* 1.3 (1990): 289–317 (p. 295).

question of any socialistic [...] state in its acutest form'—and this observation also holds for the reformist aesthetic of the years after 1945 when the process of cultural reconstruction meant that artistic creation itself, notably the aesthetic forms of a reconstituted and newly 'public' modernism, came to embody the equalization of class structures and the promises of democratic citizenship.

The debates which surrounded the issue of state sponsorship of the arts between 1910 and 1950 touch on several of the constitutive features of the reformist literary mode that I have described in this book: the democratization of opportunities for individual flourishing; the lingering risk of statal authoritarianism; and the speculative elaboration—in the medium of art—of a shared orientation towards the common good (what Green had called 'active citizenship' and what Keynes described as the artist's intertwined roles of public servant and autonomous creator). It is indicative of the importance of the post-war consensus in Britain's cultural imaginary that the years after 1945 have continued to serve as a central reference point for two widely diverging narratives of the country's social and political development. These narratives mirror the constitutive ambiguities of the reformist impulse I noted at the beginning of this Coda: according to the first account, the post-war years appear as a highpoint of democratization and welfarist expansion, unequalled either before or since; according to the opposing account, 1945 marks the precise historical moment when more radical political energies were silenced by being subordinated to a nominal political 'consensus'.

The disjunction between these two narratives is neatly captured by the post-war work of Raymond Williams. In the Introduction, I presented Williams as a thinker whose early critical works—especially the two studies *Culture and Society* (1958) and *The Long Revolution* (1961)—adopted argumentative procedures that can be identified as broadly reformist. Williams himself admitted in one of the late interviews collected in *Politics and Letters* (1979) that in the 1950s and early 1960s,

> I wasn't sure what kind of state could emerge from the development of electoral democracy. I was saying that I didn't know. Classical social democracy believed that the capitalist state could be progressively dismantled, the capitalist economy converted by degrees into a socialist order. Classical communism held the opposite position, that socialism will always be resisted by the capitalist state which will have to be overthrown by whatever force is necessary to do so. In *Culture and Society* I was really saying that I saw the strength of both positions.[33]

Williams's acknowledgment of these two political options is admirably even-handed, but he also points out that in the immediate post-war years it was the social democratic (reformist, or 'long-revolutionary') position—a position which

---

[33] Williams, *Politics and Letters*, pp. 408–9.

Williams explicitly associates with the turn-of-the-century gradualism of Beatrice and Sidney Webb—that had seemed to win the day. It was only sometime later, from the mid-1960s onwards, that Williams revised this view. His essays from this later period tend to argue that the myth of the post-war consensus had served to mask the consolidation of state power and of the capitalist status quo after 1945. Profoundly disillusioned with the Labour Party's conservative policies under Prime Minister Harold Wilson (1964–70), Williams began to cast doubt on the socialist hope that a restructuring of Britain's economy would be possible under the dominant political system of electoral democracy. By the same token, he also grew increasingly sceptical of the institutions of the post-war welfare state, including the Arts Council, which he now derided as a tool for the imposition of cultural hegemony: 'The true social process of such bodies as the Arts Council is one of administered consensus by cooption.'[34] The Arts Council's central function, Williams insisted in a late essay from 1979, was to impose 'the cultural interests of an older upper-middle and middle-class' on the rest of the nation—a process that effectively eclipsed the revolutionary energies of the 1930s (including the dissident literary tradition of proletarian modernism) by stymying the 'development of socially as well as formally experimental art.'[35]

Williams's comparatively hopeful view of social democracy in the 1950s and early 1960s contrasts sharply with the principled anti-statism of his later works. However, Williams's later comments on the Arts Council offer a view of the post-war welfare state that is arguably too bleak and that greatly underplays the ferment of artistic production that had characterized the two decades after 1945. Williams's retrospective remarks about the reformist moment of the mid-1940s might in fact matter most for what they reveal about the particular historical situation of the left in the 1970s and 1980s—a period when the promise of social-liberal institutional reform seemed dramatically diminished as a consequence of neoliberalization and the razing of working-class communities under Margaret Thatcher. It was under these new historical circumstances, which so hauntingly and depressingly resemble our own, that revolution once more seemed the political option most worth pursuing.

---

[34] Williams, 'The Arts Council' [1979], in: *Resources of Hope* (London: Verso, 1989), pp. 41–55 (p. 44).

[35] Williams, 'The Arts Council', p. 47.

Bibliography

Agamben, Giorgio, *The Highest Poverty: Monastic Rules and Form-of-Life* (Stanford: Stanford University Press, 2013)

Albel, Emily K., 'Toynbee Hall, 1884–1914', *Social Service Review* 53.4 (1979): 606–32

Althusser, Louis, 'On content in the thought of G.W.F. Hegel', *The Spectre of Hegel: Early Writings* (London: Verso, 2014), pp. 17–172

Anderson, Amanda, *Bleak Liberalism* (Chicago: University of Chicago, 2016)

Anderson, Amanda, *The Way We Argue Now: A Study in the Cultures of Theory* (Princeton: Princeton University Press, 2006)

Anderson, Linda R., 'Self and society in H. G. Wells's *Tono-Bungay*', *Modern Fiction Studies* 26.2 (1980): 199–212

Anderson, Perry, *The Antinomies of Antonio Gramsci* (London: Verso, 2017)

Anderson, Perry, 'Components of the national culture', *New Left Review* I.50 (1968): 3–58

Anderson, Perry, 'Modernity and revolution', *New Left Review* I.144 (1984): 96–113

Anker, Elizabeth S., and Rita Felski, 'Introduction', in E. S. Anker and R. Felski (eds.), *Critique and Postcritique* (Durham, NC: Duke University Press, 2017), pp. 1–28

Anon., 'A June song', in *To-Day: A Monthly Gathering of Bold Thoughts* 2 (June 1883), p. 98

Arch, Robert, *E. B. Bax: Thinker and Pioneer* (London: Hyndman, 1927)

Armstrong, Isobel, *Novel Politics: Democratic Imaginations in Nineteenth-Century Fiction* (Oxford: Oxford University Press, 2016)

Armstrong, Isobel, *The Radical Aesthetic* (Oxford: Blackwell, 2000)

Arnold, Rollo D., 'The "Revolt of the Field" in Kent, 1872–79', *Past & Present* 64.1 (1974): 71–95

Aslami, Zarena, *The Dream Life of Citizens: Late Victorian Novels and the Fantasy of the State* (New York: Fordham University Press, 2012)

Avineri, Shlomo, *Hegel's Theory of the Modern State* (Cambridge: Cambridge University Press, 1972)

Backhouse, Roger, and Tamotsu Nishizawa, 'Introduction: Towards a reinterpretation of welfare economics', in Backhouse/Nishizawa (eds.), *No Wealth but Life: Welfare Economics and the Welfare State in Britain, 1880–1945* (Cambridge: Cambridge University Press, 2010), pp. 1–24

Bailey, George, 'The right to work', *Westminster Review* (December 1908): 618–28

Ball, Sidney, 'Moral Aspects of Socialism' [= Fabian Tract No.72] (London: Fabian Society, 1896)

Balibar, Étienne, *Citizenship* (Cambridge: Polity, 2015)

Balibar, Étienne, *Equaliberty: Political Essays* (Durham, NC: Duke University Press, 2014)

Barnett, Anthony, 'Raymond Williams and Marxism: A rejoinder to Terry Eagleton', *New Left Review* I/99 (1976): 47–64

Barnett, Samuel, 'University settlements', in *Practicable Socialism* (London: Longmans, 1888), pp. 165–74

Bax, Ernest B., *A Short History of the Paris Commune* (London: Twentieth Century Press, 1894)

Bax, Ernest B., 'Conscience and commerce', in Bax, *The Religion of Socialism*, pp. 83–92

Bax, Ernest B., 'Criminal law under socialism', in Bax, *The Ethics of Socialism*, pp. 56–75

Bax, Ernest B., *Handbook to the History of Philosophy* (London: George Bell, 1886)

Bax, Ernest B., 'Karl Marx' (=Leaders of Modern Thought 23), *Modern Thought* 3.12 (1881): 349–54

Bax, Ernest B., 'Men versus classes', in Bax, *The Ethics of Socialism*, pp. 99–106

Bax, Ernest B., 'Revolution of the nineteenth century', in Bax, *The Ethics of Socialism*, pp. 31–56

Bax, Ernest B., *Reminiscences and Reflections of a Mid- and Late Victorian* (London: G. Allen & Unwin, 1918)

Bax, Ernest B., 'The curse of civilisation', in Bax, *The Ethics of Socialism*, pp. 106–120

Bax, Ernest B., *The Ethics of Socialism* (London: Swan Sonnenschein, 1890)

Bax, Ernest B., *The Real, the Rational, and the Alogical: Being Suggestions for a Philosophical Reconstruction* (London: Grant Richards, 1920)

Bax, Ernest B., *The Religion of Socialism: Being Essays in Modern Socialist Criticism* (London: Swan Sonnenschein, 1890)

Bax, Ernest B., 'Universal history from a socialist standpoint', in Bax, *The Religion of Socialism*, pp. 1–38

Bax, Ernest B., and Victor Dave, and William Morris, *A Short Account of the Commune of Paris of 1871* (London: Socialist League Office, 1886)

Beauchamp, Gorman, 'Technology in the Dystopian Novel', *Modern Fiction Studies* 32.1 (1986): 53–63

Beaumont, Matthew, *Adventures in Realism* (Oxford: Blackwell, 2007)

Beaumont, Matthew, *Utopia, Ltd.: Ideologies of Social Dreaming in England, 1870–1900* (Leiden: Brill, 2005)

Beech, Dave, *Art and Value: Art's Economic Exceptionalism in Classical, Neoclassical and Marxist Economics* (Leiden: Brill, 2015)

Beer, Gillian, *Virginia Woolf: The Common Ground* (Edinburgh: Edinburgh University Press, 1996)

Behrent, Michael C., Daniel Zamora (eds.), *Foucault and Neoliberalism* (Cambridge: Polity, 2015)

Bell, Duncan, 'Founding the world state: H. G. Wells on Empire and the English-Speaking peoples', *International Studies Quarterly* 62 (2018): 867–79

Benhabib, Seyla, *Situating the Self: Gender, Community, and Postmodernism in Contemporary Ethics* (New York: Routledge, 1992)

Berlant, Lauren, *Cruel Optimism* (Durham, NC: Duke University Press, 2011)

Bernstein, Eduard, *Evolutionary Socialism: A Criticism and an Affirmation* (New York: Schocken, 1961)

Besant, Walter, *All Sorts and Conditions of Men* (Brighton: Victorian Secrets, 2012)

Best, Stephen, and Sharon Marcus, 'Surface reading: An introduction', *Representations* 108.1 (2009): 1–21

Beveridge, William, *Power and Influence* (London: Hodder and Stoughton, 1953)

Beveridge, William, 'The problem of the unemployed', *The Sociological Review* 3.1 (1906): 323–41

Beveridge, William, *Unemployment: A Problem of Industry*, 2nd ed. (London: Longmans, 1910)

Bevir, Mark, *The Making of British Socialism* (Princeton: Princeton University Press, 2011)

Bewes, Timothy, 'Free Indirect', *Political Concepts: A Critical Lexicon*, www.polit icalconcepts.org (2017), last accessed 28 July 2020

Blanton, C. D., *Epic Negation: The Dialectical Poetics of Late Modernism* (New York: Oxford University Press, 2015)

Bobbio, Norberto, 'Is there a Marxist doctrine of the state', in Bobbio, *Which Socialism? Marxism, Socialism, and Democracy*, pp. 47–64

Bobbio, Norberto, *Liberalism and Democracy* (London: Verso, 2005)

Bond, C. J., 'Health and healing in the great state', in Wells, *The Great State: Essays in Construction*), pp. 142–80

Bosanquet, Bernard, 'The duties of citizenship', in Bosanquet (ed.), *Aspects of the Social Problem* (London: Macmillan, 1895), pp. 1–27

Bosanquet, Bernard, 'Review of *The New State* by M. P. Folle', *Mind* 28 (1919): 370

Bosanquet, Bernard, *The Philosophical Theory of the State* (London: Macmillan, 1899)

Bourdieu, Pierre, *On the State: Lectures at the Collège de France, 1989–1992* (Cambridge: Polity, 2014)

Brace, Laura, *The Politics of Property: Labour, Freedom and Belonging* (Edinburgh: Edinburgh University Press, 2004)

Bradley, F. H., *Appearance and Reality* (London: Swan Sonnenschein, 1893)

Bradley, F. H., *Appearance and Reality: A Metaphysical Essay*, 2nd ed. (London: George Allen, 1897)

Bradley, F. H., *Ethical Studies*, 2nd ed. (Oxford: Clarendon Press, 1927)

Briggs, Asa, and Anne Macartney, *Toynbee Hall: The First Hundred Years* (London: Routledge, 1984)

Brink, David, *Perfectionism and the Common Good: Themes in the Philosophy of T. H. Green* (Oxford: Clarendon Press, 2007)

Brooke, Rupert, *Democracy and the Arts* (London: Rupert Hart-Davis, 1946)

Bronstein, Jamie, 'The homestead and the garden plot: Cultural pressures on land reform in nineteenth-century Britain and the USA', *The European Legacy* 6.2 (2001): 159–75

Brown, Wendy, *Undoing the Demos: Neoliberalism's Stealth Revolution* (Cambridge, MA: MIT Press, 2015)

Bull, Philip, 'Irish land and British politics', in Cragoe/Readman, *Land Question*, pp. 126–45

Butler, Judith, *Frames of War: When Is Life Grievable?* (London: Verso, 2016)

Butler, Judith, *Subjects of Desire: Hegelian Reflections in Twentieth-Century France* (New York: Columbia University Press, 1987)

Cachin, Marie-Françoise, '"Non-governmental society": Edward Carpenter's position in the British socialist movement', in *Edward Carpenter and Late Victorian Radicalism*, ed. Tony Brown (London: Frank Cass, 1990), pp. 58–73

Carpenter, Edward, 'A note on "Towards Democracy"', in Carpenter, *Towards Democracy*, pp. 511–19

Carpenter, Edward, 'Civilisation: Its cause and cure', in Carpenter, *Civilisation: Its Cause and Cure*, pp. 1–50

Carpenter, Edward, *Civilisation: Its Cause and Cure* (London: Swan Sonnenschein, 1889)

Carpenter, Edward, *Days with Walt Whitman: With Some Notes on his Life and Work* (London: George Allen, 1906)

Carpenter, Edward, *England's Ideal and Other Papers on Social Subjects* (London: Swan Sonnenschein, 1887)

Carpenter, Edward, 'Exfoliation', in Carpenter, *Civilisation: Its Cause and Cure*, pp. 129–47

Carpenter, Edward, *My Days and Dreams, Being Autobiographical Notes* (London: Allen & Unwin, 1921)

Carpenter, Edward, *Narcissus and Other Poems* (London: Henry King, 1873)

Carpenter, Edward, 'Private property', in Carpenter, *England's Ideal and Other Papers on Social Subjects*, pp. 115–38

Carpenter, Edward, 'The village and the landlord', in *Socialism and Agriculture*, ed. Edward Carpenter, T. S. Dymond et al. (London: Fifield, 1908), pp. 5–19

Carpenter, Edward, 'The poetic form of "Leaves of Grass"', in Carpenter, *Days with Walt Whitman: With Some Notes on his Life and Work*, pp. 103–30

Carpenter, Edward, *Towards Democracy* (London: Allen & Unwin, 1905)

Carter, Robert L. and Peter Falush, *The British Insurance Industry since 1900: The Era of Transformation* (London: Palgrave Macmillan, 2009)

Celikkol, Ayşe, *Romances of Free Trade: British Literature, Laissez-Faire, and the Global Nineteenth Century* (Oxford: Oxford University Press, 2011)

Celikates, Robert, *Critique as Social Practice: Critical Theory and Social Self-Understanding* (London: Rowman & Littlefield, 2018)

Chambers, Samuel A., *The Lessons of Rancière* (Oxford: Oxford University Press, 2012)

Chase, Malcom, 'Chartism and the land: "The Mighty People's Question"', in Cragoe/Readman, *Land Question*, pp. 57–73

Chase, Malcom, '"Wholesome object lessons": The Chartist Land Plan in retrospect', *The English Historical Review* 118.475 (2003): 59–85

Chowrimootoo, Christopher, *Middlebrow Modernism: Britten's Operas and the Great Divide* (Oakland: University of California Press, 2018)

Christophers, Brett, *Rentier Capitalism: Who Owns the Economy, and Who Pays for It?* (London: Verso, 2020)

Christophers, Brett, *The New Enclosure: The Appropriation of Public Land in Neoliberal Britain* (London: Verso, 2018)

Ciccariello-Maher, George, *Decolonizing Dialectics* (Durham, NC: Duke University Press, 2017)

Clarke, Orme, *The National Insurance Act 1911* (London: Butterworth, 1912)

Coit, Emily, 'Mary Augusta Ward's "Perfect Economist" and the logic of anti-suffragism', *ELH* 82.4 (2015): 1213–38

Cole, Andrew, *The Birth of Theory* (Chicago: University of Chicago Press, 2014)

Collard, David, 'Alfred Russel Wallace and the political economists', *History of Political Economy* 41.4 (2009): 605–44

Collini, Stefan, 'Hobhouse, Bosanquet, and the state: Philosophical idealism and political argument in England, 1880–1918', *Past & Present* 72 (1976): 86–111

Collini, Stefan, *Liberalism and Sociology: L. T. Hobhouse and Political Argument in England, 1880–1914* (Cambridge: Cambridge University Press, 1979)

Collini, Stefan, 'Sociology and idealism in Britain, 1880–1920', *Archives européennes de sociologie* 19 (1978): 3–50

Conary, Jennifer, "'Things of the heart and mind': Gender and philanthropy in George Gissing's *Thyrza*', *Victorians Institute Journal* 39 (2011): 293–315

Connolly, Cyril, 'Comment', *Horizon* 1 (January 1940): 70

Connolly, Cyril, 'Comment', *Horizon* 69 (September 1945): 148–55

Cook, Daniel, 'Utopia from the rooftops: H. G. Wells, modernism and the panorama-city', in *Utopian Spaces of Modernism: British Literature and Culture, 1885–1945*, ed. Rosalyn Gregory and Benjamin Kohlmann (London: Palgrave Macmillan, 2012), pp. 105–20

Coombes, B. L. 'Below the tower', in *Folios of New Writing* (Spring 1941): 30–6

Coustillas, Pierre, *The Heroic Life of George Gissing*, 3 vols. (London: Pickering & Chatto, 2011–12)

Cragoe, Matthew, and Paul Readman, 'Introduction', in Cragoe/Readman, *The Land Question in Britain, 1750–1950*, pp. 1–18

Cragoe, Matthew, and Paul Readman (eds.), *The Land Question in Britain, 1750–1950* (London: Palgrave Macmillan, 2010)

Crewes, Frederick, *E. M. Forster: The Perils of Humanism* (Princeton: Princeton University Press, 1962)

Croce, Benedetto, *La storia ridotta sotto il concetto generale dell'arte* (Milan: Adelphi, 2017)

Croce, Benedetto, *What Is Living and What Is Dead of the Philosophy of Hegel* (London: Macmillan, 1915)

Cronin, James E., *The Politics of State Expansion: War, State, and Society in Twentieth-Century Britain* (London: Routledge, 1991)

Cucullu, Lois, 'Shepherds in the parlor: Forster's Apostles, pagans, and native sons', *NOVEL* 32.1 (1998): 19–50

Daunton, Martin, *Just Taxes: The Politics of Taxation in Britain, 1914–1979* (Cambridge: Cambridge University Press, 2009)

Daunton, Martin, 'Payment and participation: Welfare and state-formation in Britain, 1900–1951', *Past and Present* 150 (1996): 169–216

Daunton, Martin, *Trusting Leviathan: The Politics of Taxation in Britain, 1799–1914* (Cambridge: Cambridge University Press, 2001)

Daunton, Martin, 'Welfare, taxation and social justice: Reflections on Cambridge economists from Marshall to Keynes', in Roger E. Backhouse and Tamotsu Nishizawa (eds.), *No Wealth but Life: Welfare Economics and the Welfare State in Britain, 1880–1945* (Cambridge: Cambridge University Press, 2010), pp. 62–88

Dean, Mitchell, and Kaspar Villadsen, *State Phobia and Civil Society: The Political Legacy of Michel Foucault* (Stanford: Stanford University Press, 2016)

Decker, Mark, 'Politicized dystopia and biomedical imaginaries: The case of "The Machine Stops"', in *New Boundaries in Political Science Fiction*, ed. Donald M. Hassler and Clyde Wilcox (Columbia: University of South Carolina Press, 2008), pp. 53–63

den Otter, Sarah, *British Idealism and Social Explanation* (Oxford: Clarendon Press, 1996)

DiBattistta, Maria, *Imagining Virginia Woolf: An Experiment in Critical Biography* (Princeton: Princeton University Press, 2009)

Dicey, A.V., *Lectures on the Relation between Law and Public Opinion during the Nineteenth Century* (London: Macmillan, 1905)

Dickinson, Goldsworthy Lowes, *The Autobiography of Goldsworthy Lowes Dickinson and Other Unpublished Writings* (London: Duckworth, 1973)

Dickinson, Goldsworthy Lowes, *J. McT. E. McTaggart* (Cambridge: Cambridge University Press, 1931)

Dickinson, Goldsworthy Lowes, *The Meaning of Good: A Dialogue*, 3rd ed. (London: Brimley, 1906)

Dixon, Thomas, *The Invention of Altruism: Making Moral Meanings in Victorian Britain* (Oxford: Oxford University Press, 2008)

Douglas, Roy, *Land, People and Politics: A History of the Land Question in the United Kingdom* (London: Allison & Busby, 1976)

During, Simon, *Against Democracy: Literary Experience in the Era of Emancipations* (New York: Fordham University Press, 2012)

Durkheim, Émile, 'The determination of moral facts', in *Sociology and Philosophy* (New York: The Free Press, 1974), pp. 35–62

Durkheim, Émile *The Rules of Sociological Method* (New York: The Free Press, 1982)

Eagleton, Terry, 'Criticism and politics: Raymond Williams', *New Left Review* I/95 (1976): 2–23

Edgerton, David, *The Rise and Fall of the British Nation: A Twentieth-Century History* (London: Penguin, 2018)

Elfenbein, Andrew, 'Whitman, democracy, and the English Clerisy', *Nineteenth-Century Literature* 56.1 (2001): 76–104

Ewald, François, *L'État providence* (Paris: Grasset, 1986)

Fawcett, Henry, *State Socialism and the Nationalisation of Land* (London: Macmillan, 1883)

Felski, Rita, 'Latour and literary studies', *PMLA* 130 (2015): 737–42

Felski, Rita, *The Limits of Critique* (Chicago: University of Chicago Press, 2015)

Feminist Interpretations of G. W. F. Hegel, ed. Patricia Jagentowicz Mills (University Park: Pennsylvania State University Press, 1996)

Fessenbecker, Patrick, 'Autonomy, divinity, and the common good: Selflessness as a source of freedom in Thomas Hill Green and Mary Augusta Ward', in *Women Philosophers on Autonomy; Historical and Contemporary Perspectives*, ed. Sandrine Berges and Alberto L. Siani (London: Routledge, 2018), pp. 149–63

Finlayson, Geoffrey, *Citizen, State, and Social Welfare in Britain, 1830–1990* (Oxford: Clarendon Press, 1994)

Forster, E. M., *Arctic Summer and other Fiction* (London: Arnold, 1980)

Forster, E. M., 'A Great History (II)', in Forster, *The Prince's Tale and Other Uncollected Writings*, pp. 58–63

Forster, E. M., *Commonplace Book*, ed. Philip Gardner (Stanford: Stanford University Press, 1985)

Forster, E. M., *Goldsworthy Lowes Dickinson* (New York: Harcourt Brace, 1962)

Forster, E. M., *Howards End*, ed. Paul B. Armstrong (New York: Norton, 1998)

Forster, E. M., 'Pessimism in literature', in *Albergo Empedocle and Other Writings* (New York: Liveright, 1971), pp. 129–45

Forster, E. M., *Selected Letters*, ed. Mary Largo, 2 vols (London: Arena, 1985)

Forster, E. M., *The Celestial Omnibus & The Eternal Moment* (New York: Harcourt Brace, 1998)

Forster, E. M., 'The challenge of our time', in Forster, *Two Cheers for Democracy* (London: Arnold, 1972), pp. 55–60

Forster, E. M., *The Journals and Diaries of E. M. Forster*, ed. Philip Gardner, vol. 2: *The Locked Diary* (London: Pickering and Chatto, 2011)

Forster, E. M., 'The Machine Stops', in Forster, *The Celestial Omnibus & The Eternal Moment*, pp. 171–231

Forster, E. M., *The Manuscripts of* Howards End (London: Arnold, 1973)

Forster, E. M., 'The poems of Kipling', *The Creator as Critic and Other Writings*, ed. Jeffrey M. Heath (Toronto: Dundurn Press, 2008), pp. 26–40

Forster, E. M., *The Prince's Tale and Other Uncollected Writings*, ed. P. N. Furbank (London: Deutsch, 1998)

Forster, E. M., *Two Cheers for Democracy* (New York: Harcourt, 1951)

Forster, E. M., *Where Angels Fear to Tread* (London: Arnold, 1975)

Foucault, Michel, *The Birth of Biopolitics: Lectures at the Collège de France, 1978–1979* (New York: Picador, 2008)

Fraser, Derek, *The Evolution of the British Welfare State: A History of Social Policy since the Industrial Revolution*, 4th ed. (London: Palgrave Macmillan, 2009)

Freeden, Michael, *The New Liberalism: An Ideology of Social Reform* (Oxford: Clarendon Press, 1978)

Fry, Roger, 'The artist in the Great State', in Wells (ed.), *The Great State*, pp. 249–72

Frye, Northrop, *The Anatomy of Criticism: Four Essays* (Princeton: Princeton University Press, 1971)

Fyfe, Paul, 'Accidents of a novel trade: Industrial catastrophe, fire insurance, and *Mary Barton*', *Nineteenth-Century Literature* 65.3 (2010): 315–47

Gardner, Philip (ed.), *The Journals and Diaries of E. M. Forster*, 3 vols (London: Pickering and Chatto, 2011)

George, Henry, 'The land question', in George, *The Writings of Henry George*, vol. 4 (New York: Doubleday, 1898), pp. 1–109

Giddens, Anthony, 'Risk and responsibility', *The Modern Law Review* 62.1 (1999): 1–10

Gissing, George, *Collected Letters of George Gissing*, ed. Paul F. Mattheisen et al. (Athens: Ohio University Press, 1991)

Gissing, George, *Commonplace Book* (New York: New York Public Library, 1962)

Gissing, George, *Demos*, ed. Debbie Harrison (Brighton: Victorian Secrets, 2011)

Gissing, George, *London and the Life of Literature in Late Victorian England: The Diary of George Gissing*, ed. Pierre Coustillas (Brighton: Harvester Press, 1978)

Gissing, George, 'The hope of pessimism', in *Essays and Fiction*, ed. Pierre Coustillas (Baltimore: Johns Hopkins University Press, 1970), pp. 76–97

Gissing, George, *Thyrza*, ed. Pierre Coustillas (Brighton: Victorian Secrets, 2013)

Gissing, George, *Workers in the Dawn*, ed. Debbie Harrison (Brighton: Victorian Secrets, 2010)

Gladstone, William Ewart, Review of *Robert Elsmere*, *The Nineteenth Century* (May 1888): 766–88

Goldstone, Andrew, *Fictions of Autonomy: Modernism from Wilde to de Man* (New York: Oxford University Press, 2013)

Good, Thomas, 'Some Aspects of the Labour Problem', *Westminster Review* (March 1907): 278–88

Good, Thomas, 'Unemployment, Insurance, and Labour Exchanges', *Westminster Review* (May 1909): 544–551

Goodlad, Lauren M. E., 'Liberalism and literature', in *The Oxford Handbook of Victorian Literary Culture*, ed. Juliet John (Oxford: Oxford University Press, 2016), pp. 103–23

Goodlad, Lauren M. E., *The Victorian Geopolitical Aesthetic: Realism, Sovereignty, and Transnational Experience* (New York: Oxford University Press, 2015)

Goodlad, Lauren M. E., *Victorian Literature and the Victorian State: Character and Governance in a Liberal Society* (Baltimore: The Johns Hopkins University Press, 2003)

Gramsci, Antonio, *Selected Prison Notebooks*, ed. Quentin Hoare and Geoffrey Nowell-Smith (London: Lawrence and Wishart, 1971)

Green, Thomas Hill, 'An estimate of the value and influence of works of fiction in modern times', in *Works of Thomas Hill Green*, vol. 3: *Miscellanies and Memoir* (London: Longmans, 1906), pp. 20–45

Green, Thomas Hill, *Lectures on the Principles of Political Obligation and Other Writings*, ed. Paul Harris and John Morrow (Cambridge: Cambridge University Press, 1986)

Green, Thomas Hill, 'Lecture on liberal legislation and freedom of contract', in Green, *Lectures on the Principles of Political Obligation and Other Writings*, pp. 194–213

Green, Thomas Hill, 'Lectures on the principles of political obligation', in Green, *Lectures on the Principles of Political Obligation and Other Writings*, pp. 13–194

Green, Thomas Hill, 'On the different senses of "Freedom" as applied to will and to the moral progress of man', in Green, *Lectures on the Principles of Political Obligation and Other Writings*, pp. 228–250

Green, Thomas Hill, *Prolegomena to Ethics* (Oxford: Clarendon Press, 2004)

Green, Thomas Hill, *'The Witness of God' and 'Faith': Two Lay Sermons*, ed. Arnold Toynbee (London: Longmans, 1886)

Gray, Ann, et al. (eds.), *CCCS Selected Working Papers*, vol. 1 (Abingdon: Routledge, 2007)

Grylls, David, *The Paradox of Gissing* (London: Routledge, 1986)

Gutzke, David, 'Britain's "Social Housekeepers"', in ed. Gutzke, *Britain and Transnational Progressivism* (London: Palgrave Macmillan, 2008), pp. 149–83

Habermas, Jürgen, *Between Facts and Norms: Contributions to a Discourse Theory of Law and Democracy* (Cambridge, MA: The MIT Press, 1996)

Habermas, Jürgen, 'Moralität und Sittlichkeit: Treffen Hegels Einwände gegen Kant auch auf die Diskursethik zu?', *Revue internationale de philosophie* 42 (1988): 320–40

Habermas, Jürgen, 'On Hegel's political writings', in *Theory and Practice* (Boston: Beacon Press, 1974), pp. 170–195

Hadley, Elaine, *Living Liberalism: Practical Citizenship in Mid-Victorian Britain* (Chicago: University of Chicago Press, 2010)

Hall, Stuart, 'A sense of classlessness', *Universities and Left Review* 5 (1958): 26–32

Hall, Stuart, 'Marx's notes on method: A "Reading" of the "1857 Introduction"', in Ann Gray et al. (eds.), *CCCS Selected Working Papers*, vol. 1, pp. 83–111

Hall, Stuart, 'The hinterland of science: Ideology and the "Sociology of Knowledge"', in Ann Gray et al. (eds.), *CCCS Selected Working Papers*, vol. 1, pp. 127–47

Haldane, R. B., *The Reign of Relativity* (London: Macmillan, 1921)

Hamilton, John T., *Security: Politics, Humanity, and the Philology of Care* (Princeton: Princeton University Press, 2013)

Harker, Ben, *The Chronology of Revolution: Communism, Culture, and Civil Society Twentieth-Century Britain* (Toronto: University of Toronto Press, 2021)

Harris, José, *Private Lives, Public Spirit: A Social History of Britain, 1870–1914* (Oxford: Oxford University Press, 1993)

Harris, José, *Unemployment and Politics: A Study in English Social Policy, 1886–1914* (Oxford: Clarendon Press, 1972)

Harling, Philip, *The Modern British State: A Historical Introduction* (Cambridge: Polity Press, 2001)

Harsh, Constance D., 'George Gissing's *Thyrza*: Romantic love and ideological co-conspiracy,' *Gissing Journal* 30.1 (1994): 1–12

Harsh, Constance D., 'Gissing's *The Unclassed* and the perils of naturalism', *ELH* 59.4 (1992): 911–938

Haynes, E. S. P., 'Law and the Great State', in Wells (ed.), *The Great State*, pp. 181–95

Hegel, G. W. F., *Elements of the Philosophy of Right*, ed. Allen Wood (Cambridge: Cambridge University Press, 2003)

Hegel, G. W. F., *Grundlinien der Philosophie des Rechts* (Frankfurt/Main: Suhrkamp, 1986)

Hegel, G. W. F., *Hegel's Political Writings*, ed. Z. A. Pelczynski (Oxford: Clarendon Press, 1964)

Hegel, G. W. F., *Phenomenology of Spirit* (New York: Oxford University Press, 1976)

Hegel, G. W. F., *System der Sittlichkeit* (Hamburg: Meiner, 2002)

Hegel, G. W. F., *The Encyclopaedia of the Philosophical Sciences*, ed. E. Behler (New York: Continuum, 1990)

Hegel, G. W. F., 'The English Reform Bill', in Hegel, *Hegel's Political Writings*, pp. 295–330

Himmelfarb, Gertrude, *Poverty and Compassion* (New York: Knopf, 1991)

Ho, Janice, *Nation and Citizenship in the Twentieth-Century Novel* (Cambridge: Cambridge University Press, 2015)

Hobhouse, Leonard Trelawny, *Liberalism and other Writings* (Cambridge: Cambridge University Press, 1994)

Hobhouse, Leonard Trelawny, *The Metaphysical Theory of the State: A Criticism* (London: George Allen, 1918)

Hobson, J. A., 'The taxation of monopolies', *Independent Review* 9 (1906), 20–33

Hoggart, Richard, 'Speaking to Each Other', in *Conviction*, ed. Norman MacKenzie (London: MacGibbon and Kee, 1958): pp. 121–38

Honig, Bonnie, *Public Things: Democracy in Disrepair* (New York: Fordham University Press, 2017)

Honneth, Axel, *Freedom's Right: The Social Foundations of Democratic Life* (London: Polity, 2014)

Honneth, Axel, *The Pathologies of Individual Freedom: Hegel's Social Theory* (Princeton: Princeton University Press, 2010)

Howe, Anthony, *Free Trade and Liberal England, 1846–1946* (Oxford: Clarendon Press, 1997)

Howe, Anthony, 'The "Manchester School" and the Landlords: The failure of land reform in early Victorian Britain', in *Land Question*, eds. Cragoe/Readman pp. 74–91

Howkins, Alun, 'From Diggers to dongas: The land in English radicalism, 1649–2000', *History Workshop Journal* 54 (2002): 1–23

Hulme, T. E., 'Searchers after reality', *The New Age* 5.13 (1909): 265–6

Hulme, T. E., *Speculations: Essays on Humanism and the Philosophy of Art* (London: Routledge & Kegan, 1936)

Hutchings, Kimberley, *Hegel and Feminist Philosophy* (Cambridge: Polity, 2002)

Hyndman, Henry, *England for All* (London: Messrs. Gilbert & Rivington, 1880)

Hynes, Samuel, *The Edwardian Turn of Mind* (Princeton: Princeton University Press, 1968)

Jacobitti, Edmund E., 'Hegemony before Gramsci: The Case of Benedetto Croce', *The Journal of Modern History* 52.1 (1980): 66–84

Jaeggi, Rahel, *Critique of Forms of Life* (Boston, MA: Harvard University Press, 2018)

Jaeggi, Rahel, *Kritik von Lebensformen* (Frankfurt: Suhrkamp, 2014)

Jameson, Fredric, 'A Note on Literary Realism in Conclusion', in Beaumont, *Adventures in Realism*, pp. 261–70

Jameson, Fredric, *Antinomies of Realism* (London: Verso, 2015)

Jameson, Fredric, *Archaeologies of the Future: The Desire Called Utopia and Other Science Fictions* (London: Verso, 2005)

Jameson, Fredric, 'Authentic *Ressentiment*: The "Experimental" novels of Gissing', *Nineteenth-Century Fiction* 31.2 (1976): 127–149 (p. 147)

Jameson, Fredric, 'Marxist criticism and Hegel', *PMLA* 131.2 (2016): 430–8

Jameson, Fredric, 'Persistencies of the Dialectic', in *Valences of the Dialectic* (London: Verso, 2009), pp. 279–90

Jameson, Fredric, *The Hegel Variations* (London, Verso, 2010)

Jameson, Fredric, *The Political Unconscious: Narrative as a Socially Symbolic Act* (Ithaca, NY: Cornell University Press, 1981)

Jarvis, Simon, 'What is speculative thinking?', *Revue internationale de la philosophie* 227 (2004): 69–83

Jenkins, Jennifer, 'The roots of the National Trust', *National Trust Centenary Issue* (1995): 3–9

Jones, Henry, 'Working faith of the social reformer', in *Working Faith of the Social Reformer* (London: Macmillan, 1910), pp. 1–114

Jowett, Benjamin, *The Dialogues of Plato*, 5 vols (Oxford: Clarendon Press, 1875)

Judt, Tony, *Ill Fares the Land* (New York: Penguin, 2010)

Keating, P. J., *The Working Classes in Victorian Fiction* (London: Routledge, 1971)

Keynes, John Maynard, 'Art and the state', in *The Collected Writings of John Maynard Keynes*, vol. 28: *Social, Political and Literary Writings*, ed. Donald Moggridge (Cambridge: Cambridge University Press, 2013), pp. 341–9

Kohlmann, Benjamin, 'Proletarian modernism: Film, literature, theory', *PMLA* 134.5 (2019): 1056–75

Kohlmann, Benjamin, '"The End of Laissez-Faire": Literature, economics, and the idea of the welfare state', in *Late Victorian into Modern*, ed. Laura Marcus et al. (Oxford: Oxford University Press, 2016), pp. 448–62

Kohlmann, Benjamin, 'The Victorian crisis of laissez-faire: George Eliot, political economy, and the common good', *History of Political Economy* 48.4 (2016): 681–704

Kojève, Alexandre, *Introduction to the Reading of Hegel* (Ithaca: Cornell University Press, 1969)

Kornbluh, Anna, *The Order of Forms: Realism, Formalism, and Social Space* (Chicago: University of Chicago Press, 2019)

Kornbluh, Anna, 'The state of contradiction', *Continental Thought & Theory* 2.4 (2019): 62–70

Korsch, Karl, *Marxism and Philosophy* (London: Verso, 2012)

Kouvelakis, Stathis, 'Lenin as reader of Hegel: Hypotheses for a reading of Lenin's notebooks on Hegel's *The Science of Logic*', in *Lenin Reloaded: Toward a Politics of Truth*, ed. Sebastian Budgen, Stathis Kouvelakis, and Slavoj Žižek (Durham, NC: Duke University Press, 2007), pp. 164–94

Koven, Seth, *Slumming: Sexual and Social Politics in Victorian London* (Princeton: Princeton University Press, 2006)

Laclau, Ernesto, and Chantal Mouffe, *Hegemony and Socialist Strategy* (London: Verso, 1985)

Langland, Elizabeth, 'Gesturing toward an open space: Gender, form, and language in E. M. Forster's *Howards End*', in *Out of Bounds: Male Writers and Gender(ed) Criticism*, ed. Laura Claridge and E. Langland (Amherst: University of Massachusetts Press, 1990), pp. 252–67

Lawrence, D. H., *The Letters of D. H. Lawrence*, ed. Warren Roberts et al., vol. 4: *1921–24* (Cambridge: Cambridge University Press, 1987)

Lee, F. S., 'Ball, Sidney', *Oxford Dictionary of National Biography*, www.oxforddnb.com

Lee, Geoffrey, *The People's Budget: An Edwardian Tragedy* (London: Shepheard-Walwyn, 1996)

Lehmann, John, 'A Postscript', *Folios of New Writing* (Spring 1941): 42–6

Lesjak, Carolyn, 'Reading dialectically', *Criticism* 55.2 (2013): 233–77

Levenson, Michael, *A Genealogy of Modernism: A Study of English Literary Doctrine, 1908–1922* (Cambridge: Cambridge University Press, 1984)

Levenson, Michael, *Modernism and the Fate of Individuality: Character and Novelistic Form from Conrad to Woolf* (Cambridge: Cambridge University Press, 1991)

Leventhal, Fred M., '"The Best for the Most": CEMA and state sponsorship of the arts in wartime, 1939–1945', *Twentieth-Century British History* 1.3 (1990): 289–317

Levine, Caroline, *Forms: Whole, Rhythm, Hierarchy, Network* (Princeton: Princeton University Press, 2015)

Levy, Oscar, 'A reply to Lord Haldane's lecture on German literature', *The New Age* (Supplement) 9.23 (1911): 1–7

Lew, Nathaniel G., *Tonic to the Nation: Making English Music in the Festival of Britain* (London: Routledge, 2016)

Linehan, Thomas, *Modernism and British Socialism* (London: Palgrave Macmillan, 2012)

Livesey, Ruth, 'Democracy, culture, and criticism: Henry James revisits America', in *The American Experiment and the Idea of Democracy in British Culture, 1776–1924*, ed. Ella Dzelzainis and R. Livesey (New York: Routledge, 2016), pp. 179–96

Livesey, Ruth, 'Morris, Carpenter, Wilde, and the political aesthetics of labor', in *Victorian Literature and Culture* 32.2 (2004): 601–16

Lloyd, David, and Paul Thomas, *Culture and the State* (New York: Routledge, 1998)

Losurdo, Domenico, *Hegel and the Freedom of Moderns* (Durham, NC: Duke University Press, 2004)

Love, Heather, 'Close but not Deep: Literary Ethics and the Descriptive Turn', *New Literary History* 41 (2010): 371–91

Lukács, Georg, *Eigenart des Ästhetischen* (Neuwied: Luchterhand, 1963)

Lukács, Georg, *History and Class Consciousness* (Boston: The MIT Press, 1972)

Lukács, Georg, *Tactics and Ethics, 1919–1929* (London: Verso, 2014)

Lukács, Georg, 'What is orthodox Marxism?', in Lukács, *Tactics and Ethics, 1919–1929*, pp. 19–27

Lukács, Georg, *Zur Ontologie des Sozialen Seins* (Neuwied: Luchterhand, 1984)

Lynd, Helen, *England in the 1880s: Toward a Social Basis of Freedom* (London: Transaction, 1985)

Mabel, Evelyn, and Dennis Milner, *Scheme for a State Bonus* (Priestgate: North of England Newspaper Co., 1918)

MacKay, Marina, *Modernism and World War II* (Cambridge: Cambridge University Press, 2010)

Mackenzie, Norman, and Jeanne Mackenzie, *The Life of H. G. Wells: Time Traveller* (London: Littlehampton, 1973)

Macleod, Jock, *Literature, Journalism, and the Vocabularies of Liberalism: Politics and Letters, 1886–1916* (London: Palgrave Macmillan, 2013)

MacNeice, Louis, 'The tower that once', in *Folios of New Writing* (Spring 1941): 37–41

Malachuk, Daniel S., *Perfection, the State, and Victorian Liberalism* (London: Palgrave, 2005)

Maltz, Diana, 'Blatherwicks and busybodies: Gissing on the culture of philanthropic slumming', in *George Gissing: Voices of the Unclassed*, ed. Martin Ryle and Jenny Bourne Taylor (London: Routledge, 2017), pp. 15–28

Mander, W. J., *British Idealism: A History* (Oxford: Oxford University Press, 2011)

Mander, W. J., *Idealist Ethics* (Oxford: Oxford University Press, 2016)

Manton, Kevin, 'The fellowship of the new life: English ethical socialism reconsidered', *History of Political Thought* 24.2 (2003): 282–304

Mao, Douglas, 'The point of it', in *Utopianism, Modernism and Literature in the Twentieth Century*, ed. Alice Reeve-Tucker and Nathan Waddell (London: Palgrave Macmillan, 2013), pp. 19–38

Marcuse, Herbert, *Reason and Revolution: Hegel and the Rise of Social Theory* (London: Routledge, 1942)

March-Russell, Paul, '"Imagine, if you can": Love, time, and the impossibility of utopia in E. M. Forster's "The Machine Stops"', *Critical Survey* 17.1 (2005): 56–72

Marcus, Jane, 'Thinking back through our mothers,' in Marcus (ed.), *New Feminist Essays on Virginia Woolf* (Lincoln: University of Nebraska Press, 1981), pp. 1–30

Marsden, Steven, '"Hot Little Prophets": Reading, mysticism, and Walt Whitman's disciples', unpubl. PhD thesis, Texas A&M University (2004), pp. 215–365; repository. tamu.edu

Marshall, Alfred, *Principles of Economics*, 8th ed. (London: Macmillan, 1920)

Marx, John, 'Literature and Governmentality', *Literature Compass* 8.1 (2011): 66–79

Marx, Karl, *Capital*, vol. 1 (London: Penguin, 1992)

Marx, Karl, *Critique of Hegel's 'Philosophy of Right'*, ed. Joseph O'Malley (Cambridge: Cambridge University Press, 1977)

Marx, Karl, *Die Deutsche Ideologie*, in *Marx-Engels Gesamtausgabe*, vol. 3 (Berlin: Dietz, 1978), pp. 9–530

Marx, Karl, *Economic and Philosophic Manuscripts of 1844*, ed. by Dirk J. Struik, (London: Lawrence and Wishart, 1970)

Marx, Karl, *Grundrisse: Foundations of the Critique of Political Economy* (London: Penguin, 1993)

Marx, Karl, *Selected Writings*, ed. Lawrence Hugh Simon (Indianapolis: Hackett, 1994)

Marx, Karl, *The Civil War in France*, in Marx, *The First International and After*, ed. David Fernbach (London: Verso, 2010), pp. 187–268

Marx, Karl, *Zur Judenfrage (On the Jewish Question)*, in Marx, *Selected Writings* (Indianapolis: Hackett, 1994), pp. 1–26

Matz, Jesse, 'Masculinity amalgamated: Colonialism, homosexuality, and Forster's Kipling', *Journal of Modern Literature* 30.3 (2007): 31–52

McCracken, Scott, 'The commune in exile: Urban insurrection and the production of international space', in *Nineteenth-Century Radical Traditions*, ed. Joseph Bristow and Josephine McDonagh (London: Palgrave-Macmillan, 2016) pp. 113–36

McGowan, Todd, *Emancipation After Hegel: Achieving a Contradictory Revolution* (New York: Columbia University Press, 2019)

McLean, Steven, '"The Fertilising Conflict of Individualities": H. G. Wells's *A Modern Utopia*, John Stuart Mill's *On Liberty*, and the Victorian tradition of liberalism', in *Papers on Language and Literature* 43.2 (2007): 166–89

McTaggart, J. M. E. *Studies in Hegelian Cosmology* (Cambridge: Cambridge University Press, 1901)

Mead, Henry, *T. E. Hulme and the Ideological Politics of Early Modernism* (London: Bloomsbury, 2015)

Medalie, David, *E. M. Forster's Modernism* (London: Palgrave-Macmillan, 2002)

Meisel, Perry, *The Myth of the Modern: A Study in British Literature and Criticism after 1850* (New Haven: Yale University Press, 1987)

Meneses, Juan, *Resisting Dialogue: Modern Fiction and the Future of Dissent* (Minneapolis: University of Minnesota Press, 2019)

Mill, John Stuart, *On Liberty*, in Mill, *On Liberty and Other Essays* (Oxford: Oxford University Press, 1998), pp. 1–128

Mill, John Stuart, *Principles of Political Economy* (New York: D. Appleton & Company, 1884)

Mill, John Stuart, *The Later Letters of John Stuart Mill, 1849–1873*, ed. Francis Mineka and Dwight Lindley (Toronto: University of Toronto Press, 1972)

Miller, Andrew H., *The Burdens of Perfection: On Ethics and Reading in Nineteenth-Century British Literature* (Ithaca: Cornell University Press, 2008)

Miller, Elizabeth Carolyn, *Slow Print: Literary Radicalism and Late Victorian Print Culture* (Stanford: Stanford University Press, 2013)

Mond, Sir Alfred, 'German working-class insurance', *The English Review* (June 1911): 486–506

Mond, Sir Alfred, 'Out of work theories', *Saturday Review of Politics, Literature, Science, and Art* (6 November 1909): 570–71

Money, Leo Chiozza, 'Mr. Asquith's opportunity: Towards a just income tax', *Independent Review* 12 (1907): 260–8

Money, Leo Chiozza, *Riches and Poverty*, 4th ed. (London: Methuen, 1908)

Money, Leo Chiozza, *The Misery of Boots* (Boston: Ball Publishing, 1908)

Money, Leo Chiozza, 'Work in the Great State', in Wells (ed,), *The Great State*, pp. 68–119

Morris, William, 'Notes on passing events', *The Commonweal* 2.41 (1886): 46

Mouffe, Chantal, *For a Left Populism* (London: Verso, 2018)

Muirhead, John, 'How Hegel came to England', *Mind* 36 (1927): 423–47

Muirhead, John *The Service of the State: Four Lectures on the Political Teaching of T. H. Green* (London: John Murray, 1908)

Murphy, Liam, and Thomas Nagel, *The Myth of Ownership: Taxes and Justice* (Oxford: Oxford University Press, 2002)

Murray, Bruce K., *The People's Budget 1909/10: Lloyd George and Liberal Politics* (Oxford: Clarendon Press, 1980)

Neuhouser, Frederick, *Foundations of Hegel's Social Theory: Actualizing Freedom* (Cambridge, MA: Harvard University Press, 2000)

North, Joseph, *Literary Criticism: A Concise Political History* (Cambridge, MA: Harvard University Press, 2017)

Offer, Avner, *Property and Politics, 1870–1914: Landownership, Law, Ideology, and Urban Development in England* (Cambridge: Cambridge University Press, 1981)

Parrinder, Patrick, *Shadows of the Future: H. G. Wells, Science Fiction and Prophecy* (Liverpool: Liverpool University Press, 1995)

Parsons, Gerald, 'A question of meaning. Religion and working-class life', in *Religion in Victorian Britain*, vol. 2: *Controversies*, ed. Gerald Parsons (Manchester: Manchester University Press, 1988), pp. 63–87

Partington, John S., 'H. G. Wells: A Political Life', in *Utopian Studies*, 19.3 (2008): 517–76

Partington, John S., '*The Time Machine* and *A Modern Utopia*: The static and kinetic utopias of the early H. G. Wells', *Utopian Studies* 13.1 (2002): 57–68

Pearson, Robin, *Insuring the Industrial Revolution: Fire Insurance in Great Britain* (Aldershot: Ashgate, 2004)

Pease, Edward R., *The History of the Fabian Society* (New York: Dutton, 1916)

Peterson, William S., 'Gladstone's review of *Robert Elsmere*', *Review of English Studies* 21 (1970): 442–61

Peterson, William S., *Victorian Heretic: Mrs Humphry Ward's* Robert Elsmere (Leicester: Leicester University Press, 1976)

Pickard, Bertram, *A Reasonable Revolution: Being a Discussion of the State Bonus Scheme— A Proposal for a National Minimum Income* (London: Allen & Unwin, 1919)

Piketty, Thomas, *Capital and Ideology* (Cambridge, MA: Harvard University Press, 2020)

Piketty, Thomas, *Capital in the Twenty-First Century* (Cambridge, MA: Harvard University Press, 2014)

Poole, Diana, *Negativity and Politics: Dionysus and Dialectics from Kant to Nietzsche* (New York: Routledge, 2000)

Popper, Karl, *The Open Society and Its Enemies* (London: Routledge & Kegan Paul, 1945)

Pringle, A. S., *The National Insurance Act, 1911: Explained, Annotated, and Indexed* (Edinburgh: W. Green, 1912)

Puskar, Jason, 'William Dean Howells and the insurance of the real', *American Literary History* 18.1 (2006): 29–58

Quamen, Harvey N., 'Unnatural interbreeding: H. G. Wells's *A Modern Utopia* as species and genre', *Victorian Literature and Culture* 33.1 (2005): 67–84

Rae, J., 'The socialism of Karl Marx and the Young Hegelians', *The Contemporary Review* (October 1881): 585–607

Rancière, Jacques, *The Ignorant Schoolmaster: Five Lessons in Intellectual Emancipation* (Stanford: Stanford University Press, 1991)

Rancière, Jacques, *On the Shores of Politics* (London: Verso, 1991)

Rancière, Jacques, *The Lost Thread: The Democracy of Modern Fiction* (London: Bloomsbury, 2017)

Rancière, Jacques, 'The red of *La Chinoise*: Godard's politics', in Rancière, *Film Fables* (Oxford: Berg, 2006), pp. 143–55

Reason, Will, 'Settlements and education', in *University and Social Settlements*, ed. Reason (London: Methuen, 1898), pp. 45–62

Ritchie, D. G., *Darwin and Hegel, with Other Philosophical Studies* (London: Swan Sonnenschein, 1893)

Ritchie, D. G., *The Principles of State Interference* (London: Swan Sonnenschein, 1891)

Ritchie, D. G., 'Locke's theory of property', in Ritchie, *Darwin and Hegel, with Other Philosophical Studies*, pp. 178–95

Robbins, Bruce, 'Blaming the System', in *Immanuel Wallerstein and the Problem of the World: System, Scale, Culture*, ed. David Palumbo-Liu, Bruce Robbins, and Nirvana Tanoukhi (Durham, NC: Duke University Press, 2011), pp. 41–63

Robbins, Bruce, *Upward Mobility and the Common Good: Toward a Literary History of the Welfare State* (Princeton: Princeton University Press, 2007)

Rogan, Tim, *The Moral Economists: R. H. Tawney, Karl Polanyi, E.P. Thompson, and the Critique of Capitalism* (Princeton: Princeton University Press, 2018)

Rogers, Asha, *State Sponsored Literature: Britain and Cultural Diversity after 1945* (Oxford: Oxford University Press, 2020)

Rosanvallon, Pierre, *The New Social Question: Rethinking the Welfare State* (Princeton: Princeton University Press, 2000)

Rosanvallon, Pierre, *The Society of Equals* (Cambridge, MA: Harvard University Press, 2013)

Rose, Gillian, *Hegel Contra Sociology* (London: Verso, 2009)

Rosenbaum, Stanford, *The Early Literary History of the Bloomsbury Group*, vol. 3: *Georgian Bloomsbury, 1910–1914* (London: Palgrave-Macmillan, 2003)

Rosenzweig, Franz, *Hegel und der Staat* (Frankfurt: Suhrkamp, 2010)

Rowbotham, Sheila, *Edward Carpenter: A Life of Liberty and Love* (London: Verso, 2009)

Ruda, Frank, *Hegel's Rabble: An Investigation into Hegel's Philosophy of Right* (London: Bloomsbury, 2013)

Runciman, David, *How Democracy Ends* (London: Profile, 2018)

Scheve, Kenneth, and David Stasavage, *Taxing the Rich: A History of Fiscal Fairness in the United States and Europe* (Princeton: Princeton University Press, 2016)

Schmidgall, Gary, *Containing Multitudes: Walt Whitman and the British Literary Tradition* (New York: Oxford University Press, 2015)

Schoenbach, Lisi, *Pragmatic Modernism* (New York: Oxford University Press, 2011)

Schopenhauer, Arthur, *Parerga and Paralipomena: Volume 1*, ed. Sabine Roehr and Christopher Janaway (Cambridge: Cambridge University Press, 2014)

Schopenhauer, Arthur, *World as Will and Idea*, trans. Robert Haldane and John Kemp (London: Kegan Paul, 1883–6)

Scotland, Nigel, *Squires in the Slums: Settlements and Missions in Late-Victorian London* (London: I. B. Tauris, 2007)

Scott-James, J.A., *Modernism and Romance* (London: John Lane, 1908)

Sedgwick, Eve Kosofsky, *Touching Feeling: Affect, Pedagogy, Performativity* (Durham: Duke University Press, 2002)

Shaw, George Bernard (ed.), *Fabian Essays in Socialism* (London: The Fabian Society, 1889)

Shaw, George Bernard, 'The Transition to Social Democracy', in Shaw (ed.), *Fabian Essays in Socialism*, pp. 173–220

Sichel, Edith, 'Two philanthropic novelists', in George Gissing, *The Critical Heritage*, ed. Pierre Coustillas (London: Routledge, 1972), pp. 114–26

Sidorsky, David, 'The uses of the philosophy of G. E. Moore in the works of E. M. Forster', *New Literary History* 38.2 (2007): 245–71

Sidgwick, Henry, *The Methods of Ethics* (Indianapolis: Hackett, 1981)

Siegel, Daniel, *Charity and Condescension: Victorian literature and the Dilemmas of Philanthropy* (Athens: Ohio University Press, 2012)

Simhony, Avital, 'Beyond negative and positive freedom: T. H. Green's view of freedom', *Political Theory* 21.1 (1993): 28–54

Simhony, Avital, and D. Weinstein, ed., *The New Liberalism: Reconciling Liberty and Community* (Cambridge: Cambridge University Press, 2001)

Simhony, Avital, 'The political thought of the British idealists', in *The Oxford Handbook of British Philosophy in the Nineteenth Century*, ed. W. J. Mander (Oxford: Oxford University Press, 2014), p. 440–61

Skinner, Quentin, 'A third concept of liberty', *Proceedings of the British Academy* 117 (2002): 237–68

Small, Helen, 'George Eliot and the cosmopolitan cynic', *Victorian Studies* 55.1 (2012): 85–105

Sorel, Georges, *Reflections on Violence* (London: Allen & Unwin, 1915)

Stirling Taylor, G. R., 'The present development of the Great State', in Wells (ed.), *The Great State*, pp. 272–99

Sutherland, John, *Mrs Humphry Ward: Eminent Victorian, Pre-eminent Edwardian* (Oxford: Clarendon Press, 1990)

Suvin, Darko, 'Introduction', in *H. G. Wells and Modern Science Fiction*, ed. Darko Suvin and Robert M. Philmus (Lewisburg: Bucknell University Press, 1977), pp. 9–29

Szalay, Michael, *New Deal Modernism: American Literature and the Invention of the Welfare State* (Durham, NC: Duke University Press, 2000)

Taunton, Matthew, 'Cottage economy or collective farm? English socialism and agriculture between Merrie England and the five-year plan', *Critical Quarterly* 53.3 (2011): 1–23

Taylor, Charles, *Hegel and Modern Society* (Cambridge: Cambridge University Press, 2015)

Tellmann, Ute, 'Foucault and the invisible economy', *Foucault Studies* 6 (2009): 5–24

Terada, Rei, 'Hegel's racism for radicals', *Radical Philosophy* 2.05 (2019): 11–25

Theunissen, Michael, *Die Verwirklichung der Vernunft: Zur Theorie-Praxis-Diskussion im Anschluss an Hegel* (Tübingen: Mohr/Siebeck, 1970)

Thomas, David, *The Gramscian Moment: Philosophy, Hegemony, and Marxism* (Leiden: Brill, 2009)

Toye, Richard, 'H. G. Wells and the new liberalism', *Twentieth-Century British History* 20.2 (2008): 156–185

Toye, Richard, 'H. G. Wells and Winston Churchill: A reassessment', *H. G. Wells: Interdisciplinary Essays*, ed. Steven McLean (Cambridge: Cambridge Scholars, 2008), pp. 147–61

Toye, Richard, ' "The great educator of unlikely people": H. G. Wells and the origins of the welfare state', in *No Wealth but Life*, ed. Backhouse/Nishizawa, pp. 161–88

Tratner, Michael, *Deficits and Desires: Economics and Sexuality in Early Twentieth-Century Literature* (Stanford: Stanford University Press, 2001)

Trentmann, Frank, *Free-Trade Nation: Consumption, Civil Society, and Commerce in Modern Britain* (Oxford: Oxford University Press, 2008)

Trentmann, Frank, 'The strange death of free trade: The erosion of "Liberal Consensus" in Great Britain, c. 1903–1932', in *Citizenship and Community*, ed. Eugenio Biagini (Cambridge: Cambridge University Press, 1996), pp. 219–50

Trilling, Lionel, *E. M. Forster* (New York: New Directions, 1943)

Tsuzuki, Chushichi, *Edward Carpenter: Prophet of Human Fellowship* (Cambridge: Cambridge University Press, 1980)

Tyler, Colin, *Common Good Politics: British Idealism and Social Justice in the Contemporary World* (London: Palgrave-Macmillan, 2017)

Tyler, Colin, 'Contesting the Common Good: T.H. Green and Contemporary Republicanism', in *T.H. Green: Ethics, Metaphysics and Political Philosophy*, ed. Maria Dimova-Cookson and W. J. Mander (Oxford: Clarendon Press, 2006), pp. 262–91

Tyler, Colin, *The Liberal Socialism of Thomas Hill Green*, 2 vols (Exeter: Imprint, 2010/2012)

Tyler, Colin, *The Metaphysics of Self-Realisation and Freedom* (Exeter: Imprint, 2010)

Underwood, Ted, *The Work of the Sun: Literature, Science, and Political Economy, 1760–1860* (London: Palgrave Macmillan, 2005)

Unwin, Raymond, 'Edward Carpenter and "Towards Democracy"', in *Edward Carpenter, in Appreciation*, ed. Gilbert Beith (London: Allen & Unwin, 1931), pp. 234–43

Upchurch, Anna, 'John Maynard Keynes, the Bloomsbury Group and the origins of the Arts Council Movement', *International Journal of Cultural Policy* 10.2 (2004): 203–17

Van Parijs, Philippe, and Yannick Vanderborght, *Basic Income: A Radical Proposal for a Free Society and a Sane Economy* (Cambridge, MA: Harvard University Press, 2017)

Vance, Norman, *Bible and Novel: Narrative Authority and the Death of God* (Oxford: Oxford University Press, 2013)

Vaninskaya, Anna, *William Morris and the Idea of Community: Romance, History and Propaganda, 1880–1914* (Edinburgh University Press, 2010)

Waddell, Nathan, *Modernist Nowheres: Politics and Utopia in Early Modernist Writing, 1900–1920* (London: Palgrave Macmillan, 2012)

Wallace, Alfred Russel, 'How to nationalize the land: A radical solution of the Irish land problem', *The Contemporary Review* 38 (November 1880): 716–36

Wallace, Alfred Russel, *Land Nationalisation* (London: Swan Sonnenschein, 1896)

Wallace, Alfred Russel, 'Land Nationalisation Society Conference This Day', *Echo* (16 January 1882): 3

Wallace, William, *Lectures and Essays on Natural Theology and Ethics* (Oxford: Clarendon Press, 1898)

Wallace, William, 'Relations of Fichte and Hegel to Socialism', in Wallace, *Lectures and Essay on Natural Theology and Ethics*, pp. 427–47

Wallace, Alfred Russel, 'The "Why" and the "How" of land nationalisation (I)', in *Macmillan's Magazine* 287 (September 1883): 357–67

Ward, Mary Augusta [Mrs Humphry Ward], *Robert Elsmere*, ed. Miriam Elizabeth Burstein (Brighton: Victorian Secrets, 2013)

Webb, Sidney, 'Historic', in Shaw (ed.), *Fabian Essays in Socialism*, pp. 30–61

Wells, H. G., *A Modern Utopia* (London: Penguin, 2005)

Wells, H. G., *An Englishman Looks at the World* (London: Cassell, 1914)

Wells, H. G., 'An open letter to an Elector in NW Manchester, 21 April 1908', in *The Correspondence of H. G. Wells*, ed. David C. Smith (London: Pickering & Chatto, 1998), vol. 2, pp. 214–17

Wells, H. G., *Anticipations of the Reaction of Mechanical and Scientific Progress upon Human Life and Thought* (Mineola, NY: Dover, 1999)

Wells, H. G., *Experiment in Autobiography* (New York: J. B. Lippincott, 1967)

Wells, H. G., 'Faults of the Fabian', in Hynes, *The Edwardian Turn of Mind*, pp. 390–409

Wells, H. G., *Kipps*, ed. David Lodge (London: Penguin 2005)

Wells, H. G., *Love and Mr Lewisham*, ed. Gillian Beer (London: Penguin, 2005)

Wells, H. G., *Mankind in the Making* (London: Chapman and Hall, 1904)

Wells, H. G., 'Mr H. G. Wells on socialism', *Science School Journal* 18 (1889): 152–155

Wells, H. G., *New Worlds for Old* (London: Macmillan, 1909)

Wells, H. G., 'The Contemporary Novel', in Wells, *An Englishman Looks at the World*, pp. 148–69

Wells, H. G., *The Discovery of the Future* (London: Fisher Unwin, 1902)

Wells, H. G., *The Food of the Gods and How It Came to Earth* (Mineola, NY: Dover, 2006)

Wells, H. G., 'The Labour Unrest', in Wells, *An Englishman Looks at the World*, pp. 43–94

Wells, H. G., 'The Past and the Great State', in Wells, *The Great State*, pp. 1–46

Wells, H. G., *The New Machiavelli*, ed. Michael Foot (London: Penguin, 2005)

Wells, H. G., *The Sleeper Awakes*, ed. Patrick Parrinder (London: Penguin, 2005)

Wells, H. G., *The Time Machine*, ed. Marina Warner (London: Penguin, 2005)

Wells, H. G., *Tono-Bungay*, ed. Edward Mendelson (London: Penguin, 2005)

Wells, H. G., *The Misery of Boots* (London: The Fabian Society, 1907)

Wells, H. G., *The Outline of History* (London: Cassell and Company, 1920)

Wells, H. G., 'The so-called science of sociology', *The Sociological Review* 3.1 (1906): 357–69

Wells, H. G., *The Wealth of Mr Waddy*, ed. Harris Wilson (Carbondale: Southern Illinois University Press, 1969)

Wells, H. G., 'To the electors of the London University General Election, November 1923', in *Correspondence of H. G. Wells*, vol. 3, pp. 159–62

Wells, H. G., *When the Sleeper Wakes*, ed. Orson Scott Card (New York: Modern Library, 2003)

Wells, H. G. (ed.), *The Great State: Essays in Construction* (London: Harper, 1912)

Wempe, Ben, *T. H. Green's Theory of Positive Freedom: From Metaphysics to Political Theory* (Exeter: Imprint Academic, 2004)

Whiteing, Richard, *Ring in the New* (London: Hutchinson, 1906)

Whitman, Walt, *Poems by Walt Whitman*, ed. by William Michael Rossetti (London: John Camden Hotten, 1868)

Whitman, Walt 'A Song of the Rolling Earth', in *The Portable Walt Whitman*, ed. Michael Warner (London: Penguin, 2004), pp. 158–64

Whitman, Walt 'Preface to the first edition of Leaves of Grass', in Whitman, *Poems by Walt Whitman*, pp. 29–64

Whitman, Walt 'Starting from Paumanok', in Whitman, *Poems by Walt Whitman*, pp. 67–88

Wilde, Oscar, *De Profundis and Other Writings* (London: Penguin, 1986)

Wilde, Oscar, *Oscar Wilde's Oxford Notebooks: A Portrait of a Mind in the Making*, ed. Philip E. Smith and Michael S. Helfand (Oxford: Oxford University Press, 1989)

Williams, Raymond, *Culture and Materialism: Selected Essays* (London: Verso, 2005)

Williams, Raymond, 'The Arts Council', in *Resources of Hope* (London: Verso, 1989), pp. 41–55

Williams, Raymond, *The Long Revolution* (London: Chatto & Windus, 1961)

Williams, Raymond, 'Literature and sociology: In memory of Lucien Goldmann', *New Left Review* I/67 (1971): 3–18

Williams, Raymond, *Marxism and Literature* (Oxford: Oxford University Press, 1977)

Williams, Raymond, *Politics and Letters: Interviews with New Left Review* (London: Verso, 2015)

Williams, Raymond, 'The Bloomsbury Fraction', in Williams, *Culture and Materialism: Selected Essays*, pp. 148–70

Wilson, Harris, 'The death of Masterman: A repressed episode in H. G. Wells's *Kipps*', *PMLA* 86.1 (1971): 63–9

Winch, Donald, *Wealth and Life: Essays on the Intellectual History of Political Economy in Britain, 1848–1914* (Cambridge: Cambridge University Press, 2009)

Wood, Ellen Meiksins, *Democracy Against Capitalism: Renewing Historical Materialism* (Cambridge: Cambridge University Press, 1995)

Woolf, Virginia, 'The Leaning Tower,' in *The Moment and Other Essays* (New York: Harcourt Brace, 1948), pp. 128–54

Woolf, Virginia, *A Room of One's Own* (London: Penguin, 2004)

Woolf, Virginia, *Three Guineas* (New York. Harcourt Brace, 1966)

Index